Foreword

This reference book has been compiled from all the manuals in the series of publications "Bosch Technical Instruction" which deal with the topics of "Automotive electrics and electronics". The book's contents are intended to do justice to the interests of a wide range of readers and to satisfy their thirst for knowledge.

Within the last few years, the explosive developments in the field of automotive electrics and electronics have led to far-reaching and radical changes in the SI engine's equipment and in the management of its operation.

Modern engine components can comply with a wide range of different demands, and their combined actions result in:
- reduction of fuel consumption,
- minimisation of pollutant emissions,
- increase of driving comfort,
- improvement of running refinement, and
- optimization of the trouble-free service life of all the engine's parts and assemblies.

This reference book provides comprehensive information on state-of-the-art technical developments of the electrical and electronic engine systems, their design and construction, their status of technical innovation, and the fundamental effects they are having upon conventional SI-engine operation.

Readers who are interested in automotive technology are provided with a detailed, easily understandable description of the SI engine's most important components.

Summary

KW-760-443

Combustion in the spark-ignition engine

The spark-ignition or Otto-cycle engine

Principles

The spark-ignition or Otto-cycle[1]) engine is a combustion engine with externally supplied ignition which converts the energy contained in the fuel into kinetic energy.

The spark-ignition engine employs a mixture-formation apparatus located outside the combustion chamber to form an air-fuel mixture (based on gasoline or a gas). As the piston descends, the mixture is drawn into the combustion chamber, where it is then compressed as the piston moves upward. An external ignition source, triggered at specific intervals, uses a spark plug to initiate combustion in the mixture. The heat released in the combustion process raises the pressure within the cylinder, and the piston pushes down against the crankshaft, providing the actual work energy (power). After each combustion stroke the spent gases are expelled from the cylinder and a fresh air-fuel mixture is drawn in. In automotive engines this exchange of gases is generally regulated according to the four-stroke principle, with two crankshaft revolutions being required for each complete cycle.

The four-stroke principle

The four-stroke spark-ignition engine employs gas-exchange valves to control the gas flow. These valves open and close the cylinder's intake and exhaust tracts:

1st stroke: Induction
2nd stroke: Compression and ignition
3rd stroke: Combustion and work
4th stroke: Exhaust.

Induction stroke
Intake valve: open,
Exhaust valve: closed,
Piston travel: downward,
Combustion: none.

The piston's downward motion increases the cylinder's effective volume and pulls in fresh air-fuel mixture through the open intake valve.

Compression stroke
Intake valve: closed,
Exhaust valve: closed,
Piston travel: upward,
Combustion: initial ignition phase.

Fig. 1: Design concept of the reciprocating piston engine
TDC Top Dead Center, BDC Bottom Dead Center, V_h Stroke volume, V_C Compression volume, s Piston stroke.

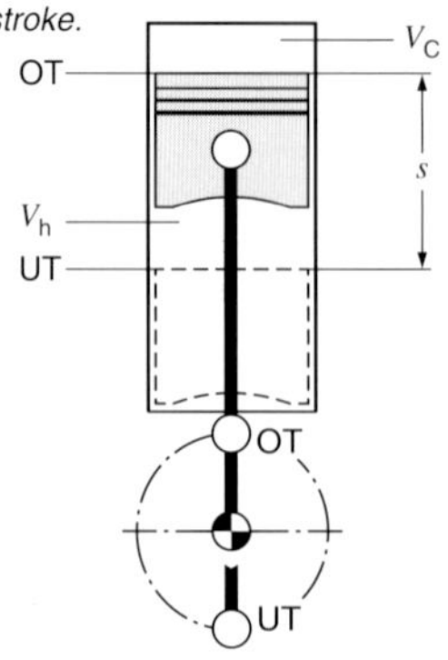

---

[1]) After Nikolaus August Otto (1832 – 1891), who unveiled the first four-stroke gas-compression engine at the Paris World Exhibition in 1878.

AUTOMOTIVE ELECTRIC/ELECTRONIC SYSTEMS

UHI
Millennium
Institute

Please return/renew this item by the last date shown

Tillibh/ath-chlaraidh seo ron cheann-latha mu dheireadh

Imprint

Published by:
© Robert Bosch GmbH, 1995
Postfach 30 02 20
D-70442 Stuttgart.
Automotive Equipment Business Sector,
Department for Technical Information (KH/VDT).

Editor-in-Chief:
Dipl.-Ing. (FH) Ulrich Adler.

Editors:
Dipl.-Ing. (FH) Horst Bauer,
Dipl.-Ing. (FH) Anton Beer,
Ing. (grad.) Arne Cypra.

Layout:
Dipl.-Ing. (FH) Ulrich Adler,
Günter Berger, Joachim Kaiser.

Translation:
Peter Girling.

Technical Graphics:
Bauer & Partner, Stuttgart.

Photographs:
Degussa, Mercedes-Benz (P. 24),
Opel (P. 25),
Volkswagen (P. 341).

Printed in Germany. Imprimé en Allemagne.
2nd Edition: June 1994.
Editorial closing: 31.03.1994.

VDI-Verlag GmbH
Verlag des Vereins Deutscher Ingenieure
Graf-Recke-Str. 85
D-40239 Düsseldorf, Germany
ISBN 3-18-419121-4

(2.0 N)

Die Deutsche Bibliothek – CIP-Einheitsaufnahme

Automotive electric, electronic systems / Bosch.
[Publ. by: Bosch, Automotive Equipment Business Sector,
Department for Technical Information (KH/VDT). Ed.-in-chief: Ulrich Adler.
Ed.: H. Bauer ... Authors: H. Schwarz ... Transl.: Peter Girling].
– 2. Aufl. – Düsseldorf: VDI-Verl., 1995
Dt. Ausg. u. d. T.: Autoelektrik, Autoelektronik am Ottomotor
ISBN 3-18-419121-4 (VDI-Verl.) brosch.
ISBN 1-56091-596-X (SAE, Soc. of Automotive Engineers) brosch.
NE: Adler, Ulrich [Hrsg.]; Robert Bosch GmbH <Stuttgart> /
Unternehmensbereich Kraftfahrzeugausrüstung /
Abteilung Technische Information

Authors

**Spark-ignition engine, engine-design and
operating conditions, fuels for SI engines**
Dr.rer.nat. H. Schwarz, Dr.rer.nat. B. Blaich.

**Exhaust-gas treatment, testing exhaust and
evaporative emissions**
Dipl.-Ing. (FH) D. Günther, Dipl.-Ing. G. Felger,
Dr.-Ing. W. Grözinger, Dipl.-Ing. (FH) W. Dieter.

**Mixture formation, air and fuel supply,
fuel-injection systems**
Dipl.-Ing. (FH) U. Steinbrenner, Dipl.-Ing. G. Felger,
Ing. (grad.) L. Seebald, Dr.rer.nat. W. Huber,
Dr.-Ing. W. Richter, Dipl.-Ing. M. Lembke,
Dipl.-Ing. H. G. Gerngroß, Dipl.-Ing. A. Kratt.
Dr.-Ing. O. Parr, Filterwerk Mann und Hummel,
Ludwigsburg; Dipl.-Ing. A. Förster, Aktiengesell-
schaft Kühnle, Kopp und Kausch, Frankenthal;
Dr.-Ing. H. Hiereth, Mercedes-Benz AG, Stuttgart.

Ignition, spark plugs
Dipl.-Ing. H. Decker, Dr.rer.nat. A. Niegel.

Motronic engine management
Dipl.-Ing. (FH) U. Steinbrenner, Dipl.-Ing. E. Wild,
Dipl.-Ing. (FH) H. Barho, Dr.-Ing. K. Böttcher,
Dipl.-Ing. (FH) V. Gandert, Dipl.-Ing. W. Gollin,
Dipl.-Ing. W. Häming, Dipl.-Ing. (FH) K. Joos,
Dipl.-Ing. (FH) M. Mezger, Ing. (grad.) B. Peter,
Dipl.-Ing. M. Lembke.

Vehicle electrical system
Dipl.-Ing. (FH) F. Meyer.

**Symbols and circuit diagrams,
calculation of conductor sizes**
Dipl.-Ing. (FH) H. Bauer.

**Electromagnetic compatibility (EMC)
and interference suppression**
Dr.-Ing. H. Neu.

Starter batteries, battery chargers
Dr.-Ing. G. Richter, Ing. (grad.) T. Meyer-Staufenbiel.

Alternators
Dr.-Ing. K. G. Bürger.

Starting systems
Dr.-Ing. K. Bolenz.

Unless otherwise stated, the above are all
employees of Robert Bosch GmbH, Stuttgart.

As the piston travels upward, it reduces the cylinder's effective volume and compresses the air-fuel mixture. Just before the piston reaches top dead center (TDC), the spark plug ignites the compressed air-fuel mixture to initiate combustion.

The compression ratio is calculated with the stroke volume V_h and compression volume V_C:

$$\varepsilon = (V_h + V_C)/V_C.$$

Compression ratios ε range between 7 and 13 to one, depending upon engine design. Increasing the compression ratio in a combustion engine enhances its thermal efficiency and provides more effective use of the fuel. For instance, raising the compression ratio from $6:1$ to $8:1$ produces a 12% improvement in thermal efficiency. The latitude for such increases is restricted by the knock (or preignition) limit. Knock refers to uncontrolled mixture combustion characterized by a radical increase in pressure. Combustion knock leads to engine damage. Appropriate fuels and combustion-chamber configurations can be employed to shift the knock limit toward higher compression ratios.

Power stroke
Intake valve: closed,
Exhaust valve: closed,
Piston travel: upward,
Combustion: combustion completed.

When the spark at the spark plug ignites the air-fuel mixture, the gas mixture combusts and the temperature increases. The pressure level in the cylinder also increases, pushing the piston downward. The force from the moving piston is transferred through the connecting rod and to the crankshaft in the form of work; this is the actual source of the engine's power.

Output rises as a function of increased engine speed and higher torque $(P = M \cdot \omega)$.

A transmission incorporating various conversion ratios is required to adapt the combustion engine's power and torque curves to the demands of actual vehicular operation.

Exhaust stroke
Intake valve: closed,
Exhaust valve: open,
Piston travel: upward,
Combustion: none.

As the piston travels upward, it pushes the spent gases (exhaust gases) out through the open exhaust valve. The cycle is then repeated. The periods when the valves are open overlap by a certain degree; this improves the gas-flow and oscillation patterns for enhanced cylinder filling and scavenging.

Fig. 2: Operating cycle of the four-stroke spark-ignition engine

Stroke 1: Induction   Stroke 2: Compression   Stroke 3: Combustion   Stroke 4: Exhaust

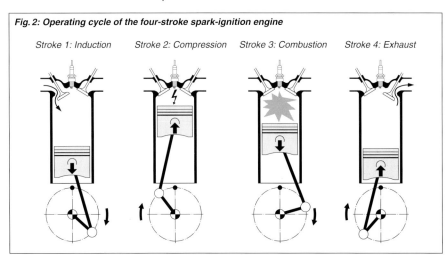

Engine design

The pollutant emission of an engine is influenced by many of its design details. Of course, in addition to pollutant emissions, other engine characteristics must be considered, such as fuel consumption, power output, torque, knocking and smooth running etc. For this reason, every engine development represents a compromise among a number of contradictory requirements.

Compression ratio

The compression ratio is decisive for the thermal efficiency of the engine. However, two factors stand in the way of a general introduction of high compression ratios: the increased tendency to knock and the high pollutant emissions. A high compression ratio increases the temperature level in the combustion chamber. This leads in turn to increased pre-reaction of the fuel, which can cause the self-ignition of parts of the air-fuel mixture before they are reached by the normal flame front. This increased tendency to knock increases the octane number required by the engine. Suitable combustion-chamber design can inhibit this tendency somewhat.

In addition, the higher temperature level in the combustion chamber which is associated with higher compression ratios causes an increase in the NO_x emissions, since a higher combustion-chamber temperature moves the reaction equilibrium more in the direction of the NO_x concentration, and in particular due to the fact that the speed of reaction of NO_x formation is increased. This fact, together with the lower octane number of unleaded fuel, has led to engine designs for countries with stringent emission regulations, such as the USA and Japan, that have lower compression ratios than do comparable European designs. For this reason, the fuel consumption of these designs is correspondingly higher.

In the case of catalytic-converter equipped vehicles designed to satisfy future European emissions requirements, an attempt is being made to avoid this increase in consumption due to lower compression ratios by means of design changes in the intake manifold and combustion chamber, and through complex forms of engine management.

Combustion-chamber shape

The shape of the combustion chamber has a considerable influence on the emission of unburnt hydrocarbons. Since the emission of unburned hydrocarbons originates from crevices and layers next to the cylinder walls, combustion chambers with complicated shapes and large surface areas cause high HC emissions. For this reason, compact combustion chambers with small surface areas are more favorable. With their intensive charge turbulence, they reduce the octane requirement by means of rapid combustion. Together with the high compression ratios thus made possible, such a design facilitates the realization of a lean-burn concept. This results in lower exhaust emissions along with good efficiency, since a defined charge turbulence at the spark plug is important to ensure reliable ignition of the air-fuel mixture. With less turbulence, the conditions (mixture condition, residual exhaust-gas content) at the spark plug at the moment of ignition vary from working cycle to working cycle due to random local factors. This causes fluctuations in the flame-front propagation times, resulting in variations in the combustion process from cycle to cycle. Turbulence in the combustion chamber considerably reduces these cyclical fluctuations.

The position of the spark plug in the combustion chamber is likewise very important for pollutant emissions and for fuel consumption. When the spark plug is positioned centrally in the cylinder this provides short flame travel. The result is rapid and relatively complete conversion, and thereby lower emissions of unburned hydrocarbons (Fig. 1). Ignition with two spark plugs in the combustion chamber (so-called dual ignition) provides a further shortening of flame travel and, as a result, positive effects on pollutant emissions and fuel consumption. In addition, due to the short flame travel, a compact combustion chamber with central plug positioning or with dual ignition reduces the engine's octane requirement. This advantage can be exploited by increasing the compression ratio and, as a result, the engine's efficiency.

Four-valve engines with two intake and two exhaust valves per cylinder are particularly favorable in this respect (Fig. 2). The four-valve design permits compact combustion chambers with central spark plug position and, thus, short flame travel. Charge-cycle characteristics are also improved.

Valve timing

The charge cycle, i.e. the exchange of burned gas in the cylinder for fresh mixture, occurs through the alternate opening and closing of the intake and exhaust valves. The valve timing, which defines the opening and closing of these valves, and the valve lift curve, which is determined by the cam profile, affect the charge-cycle process. The fresh charge quantity which is drawn into the cylinder determines the torque and power of the engine. The residual gas, i.e. the quantity of burned mixture remaining in the cylinder and not exhausted during the time the exhaust valve is open, influences ignition and combustion. This quantity is important for efficiency and for the emissions of unburned hydrocarbons and oxides of nitrogen. During the valve-overlap phase, i.e. when the intake and exhaust valves are simultaneously open, depending on pressure conditions, fresh

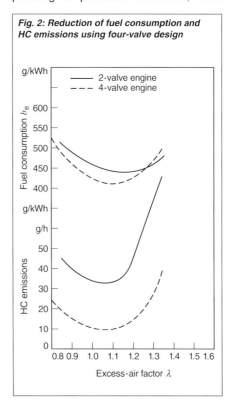

Fig. 1: Influence of spark-plug position on fuel consumption and HC emissions

g/kWh

Fuel consumption b_e

- - - Side spark-plug position
—— Central spark-plug position

600
550
500
450
400

g/kWh

g/h

HC emissions

100
80
60
40
20
0

0.8 0.9 1.0 1.1 1.2 1.3 1.4 1.5 1.6

Excess-air factor λ

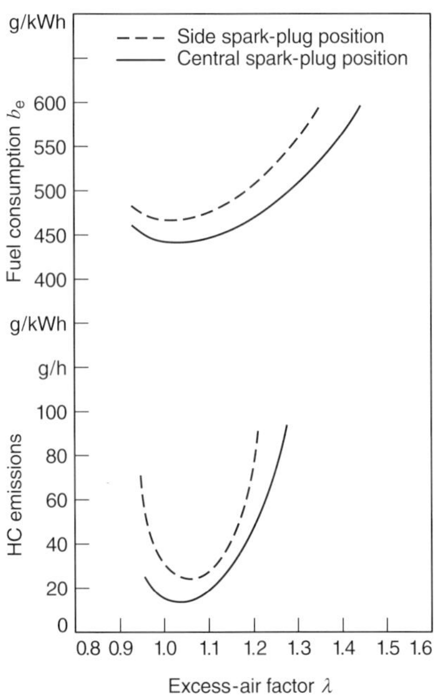

Fig. 2: Reduction of fuel consumption and HC emissions using four-valve design

g/kWh

Fuel consumption b_e

—— 2-valve engine
- - - 4-valve engine

600
550
500
450
400

g/kWh

g/h

HC emissions

50
40
30
20
10
0

0.8 0.9 1.0 1.1 1.2 1.3 1.4 1.5 1.6

Excess-air factor λ

mixture can be exhausted or exhaust gas can flow back into the intake manifold (Fig. 3). This exerts a significant influence on the level of efficiency and on emissions of unburned hydrocarbons.

It is possible to optimize the valve timing for only one engine speed. For example, at higher engine speeds, a longer opening period of the intake valves provides an increase in power. On the other hand, at lower engine speeds in the idle range, the resulting larger valve overlap can cause an increase in the emissions of unburned hydrocarbons and uneven engine running due to the higher residual-gas content. Engine-speed and load-dependent valve timing is therefore the ideal.

To do this, in engines fitted with two camshafts, the intake camshaft is turned. This allows large valve overlap at high engine speeds, resulting in high performance and good engine running. At the same time, in the lower speed range, the smaller valve overlap results in low emissions of unburned hydrocarbons.

Intake-passage design

The charge cycles are influenced not only by the valve timing, but also by the design of the intake and exhaust passages. Periodic pressure fluctuations are generated in the intake passage by the cylinder intake strokes. These pressure waves run through the intake passage and are reflected at the ends of the passage. If the intake passage is designed to harmonize with the valve timing, a pressure peak reaches the intake valve shortly before it closes. This boost effect forces a larger quantity of fresh air-fuel mixture into the cylinder (Fig. 4). A similar situation applies to the exhaust passage. If the intake and exhaust passages are designed so that there is a positive pressure difference during valve overlap, good charge cycling is obtained, with the accompanying positive effects on pollutant emissions, power and consumption.

The intake passage can be optimized

particularly effectively for good charge cycling with fuel-injection systems which spray the fuel directly onto the intake valves. The effects on fuel consumption and exhaust emissions are favourable, because it is not necessary to take into account the mixture distribution in the design of the intake passage, as is the case with carburetor engines.

An intake passage which causes intake swirl acts in a similar fashion to the turbulence in the combustion chamber. The motion of the charge makes possi-

Fig. 3: Valve timing diagram.
s Valve stroke, a Valve clearance,
b Valve overlap.
EO Exhaust valve opens
EC Exhaust valve closes
IO Intake valve opens
IC Intake valve closes

Fig. 4: Boost effect achieved by intake-passage design (oscillatory intake passage)
V_h Swept volume, V_R Intake passage volume
$(V_R \geq V_h)$, l Intake-passage length.

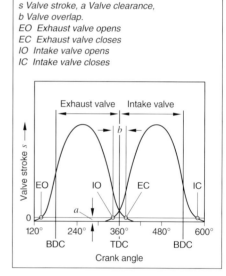

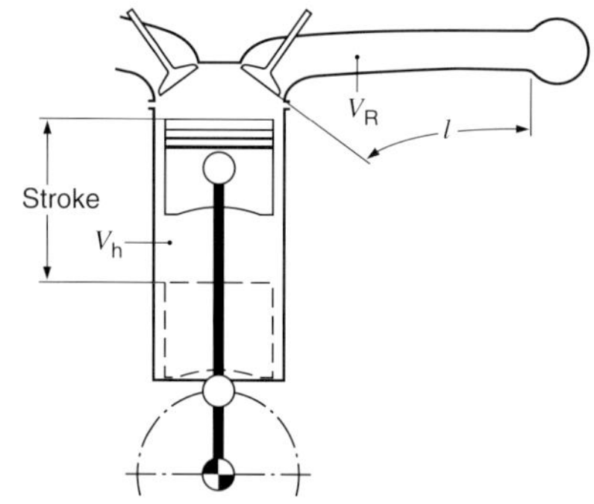

ble the rapid conversion of the air-fuel mixture in the combustion chamber. This increases efficiency and improves lean-running ability. Hence, defined intake swirl is one means of achieving lower pollutant emissions through engine design.

Charge stratification

Most spark-ignition engines are designed for a homogeneous air-fuel mixture. The combustion process can be significantly influenced with careful charge stratification.

So-called stratified-charge engines are designed so that a rich mixture forms in the vicinity of the spark plug in order to provide reliable ignition; the main combustion then takes place with a lean mixture. A particularly effective (although relatively expensive) method is to use a divided combustion chamber, with a small prechamber containing the spark plug. This prechamber is fed a rich mixture by a second fuel-induction system. Such a design has the advantage that despite a lean mixture in the main combustion chamber reliable ignition is guaranteed. This makes it possible to reach considerably lower NO_x emission values, since combustion occurs only with very rich and very lean mixtures. However, due to the greater combustion chamber surface, stratified-charge engines with divided combustion chambers have significantly higher emissions of unburned hydrocarbons than do engines with open combustion chambers. Charge stratification in the combustion chamber can also be attained through direct injection of gasoline into the combustion chamber. A rich mixture is generated in the vicinity of the spark plug despite an overall lean adjustment, similar to a diesel engine. However, such direct injection has considerable disadvantages, such as low efficiency and high costs etc.

A certain amount of charge stratification is also possible by means of suitable charge motion and swirl motion as the mixture enters the combustion cham-

ber. This form of stratification is not very well-defined and is hard to control; it changes significantly depending on the operating conditions of the engine.

Other measures in the engine

Exhaust emissions can be influenced as well by measures applied on the periphery of the engine, which reduce the power demand and thus the fuel consumption. This includes reducing the friction loss of the pistons and the valve-gear and reducing the driving power required for auxiliary systems such as fan and alternator. In such cases a reduction in the fuel consumption results in a directly proportional reduction in pollutant emissions. The opposite is the case with almost all measures which involve the thermodynamics of the engine.

During actual driving, a large percentage of the carbon monoxide emissions and the emissions of unburned hydrocarbons stem from the engine warm-up phase, in which the engine has not yet reached its operating temperature. The proper design of the coolant system and the lubrication system can shorten the warm-up phase considerably. Besides reducing the fuel consumption, this provides a superproportional reduction of pollutant emissions of carbon monoxide and unburned hydrocarbons.

Operating conditions

Engine operating range

Engine speed

A higher engine speed causes greater friction loss in the engine itself and higher power consumption in auxiliary systems. Thus, for the same energy input, there is a lower output, i.e. efficiency worsens. If a certain output is obtained at a high engine speed, it means a higher fuel consumption than would be the case if the same output were achieved at a lower engine speed. This naturally results in higher pollutant emissions.

The influence of engine speed is more or less the same for all pollutant components.

Engine load

A change in engine load has various effects on the individual components. As the load increases, so does the temperature level in the combustion chamber.

The thickness of the zone where the flame is extinguished in proximity to the combustion-chamber wall thus decreases with increasing load. In addition, the higher exhaust temperature improves post-reaction during the expansion and exhaust phases. Hence, the power-related emission of unburned hydrocarbons is reduced with increased engine load.

A similar condition applies to CO emissions, whereby the higher process temperatures likewise favor post-reaction to CO_2 during the expansion phase.

However, the reverse is the case for NO_x emissions. The increase in combustion-chamber temperature with increased engine load favors the formation of NO_x. NO_x emissions therefore increase superproportionally with engine load.

Speed

An increase in vehicle speed results in an increase in fuel consumption due to an increase in power requirements. With respect to hydrocarbons and carbon monoxide, the above-mentioned effects compensate for the effects of higher emissions through higher consumption, so that the emissions of these pollutants are basically independent of vehicle speed. However, for NO_x, emissions increase with vehicle speed.

Dynamic operation

In dynamic operation of a spark-ignition engine, there are considerably higher emission values than in steady-state operation. This results from imperfect mixture adaptation during engine-speed change. When the throttle valve is opened quickly, part of the fuel supplied from the carburetor or from the single-point (or throttle-body) injection system remains in the intake manifold. As compensation, therefore, these systems require acceleration enrichment, which in particular with a carburetor cannot be metered so that all cylinders are provided with the correct air-fuel ratio during acceleration. The result is an increase in emissions of unburned hydrocarbons and carbon monoxide.

Injection systems which spray the fuel directly onto the intake valves of the cylinders have an advantage in this respect. When the engine is at operating temperature, therefore, there is no need for acceleration enrichment in most cases. This advantage of the injection system applies in all types of dynamic operation, since there is no additional fuel accumulator – with central metering of the air-fuel mixture, the intake manifold acts as such – that must be filled and emptied. This also has its effect on fuel consumption. The more dynamically a vehicle is operated, the greater the consumption advantage of an injection system compared to a carburetor.

Mixture formation

Air-fuel ratio

Engine pollutant emissions are very dependent on the air-fuel ratio (Fig. 2). They can therefore be decisively influenced by engine management.

CO emissions

In the rich range (with air deficiency), CO emissions show an almost linear dependence on the air-fuel ratio. In the lean range (with excess air), CO emissions are very low and almost independent of the air-fuel ratio. In the range around the stoichiometric point with its excess-air factor $\lambda = 1$, CO emissions are determined by the equal distribution of the fuel to the individual cylinders. If some cylinders are operated rich and others lean, there will result a higher average CO emission than if all cylinders were operated at the same excess-air factor λ.

HC emissions

The same as CO emissions, HC emissions also fall in the rich range along with increasing Lambda. In the lean range, however, HC emissions rise again. The minimum HC emissions take place at around $\lambda = 1.1 \ldots 1.2$. This rise in HC emissions in the lean range is caused by the thicker quench zone due to the lower combustion-chamber temperature. When operating with very lean air-fuel mixtures, this effect is aggravated by delayed combustion and even misfires. This causes a drastic rise in the HC emissions. The lean misfire limit is reached under these air-fuel conditions.

NO$_x$ emissions

The dependence of NO$_x$ emissions on the excess-air factor λ is exactly the reverse: in the rich range, there is a rise with increasing Lambda as a result of the increasing concentration of oxygen. In the lean range, NO$_x$ emissions fall as the Lambda increases, because decreasing density lowers combustion-chamber temperatures.

The maximum NO$_x$ emissions with slight excess air are situated in the range around $\lambda = 1.05 \ldots 1.1$.

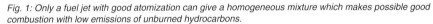

Fig. 1: Only a fuel jet with good atomization can give a homogeneous mixture which makes possible good combustion with low emissions of unburned hydrocarbons.

Fuel management

A homogeneous mixture is required to provide the best combustion characteristics in the spark-ignition engine. This requires good atomization of the fuel with the smallest possible fuel droplets (Fig. 1). Poorly prepared air-fuel mixtures show significantly higher emissions of unburned hydrocarbons (HC components) since combustion of the mixture is poorer.

Mixture distribution is associated with fuel management. This is because, with the poor mixture preparation which occurs in the upper load range in carburetors, the large fuel droplets settle at bends in the intake manifold.

This means that the fuel supply to the individual cylinders includes a large element of chance. However, poor distribution has a negative influence on pollutant emissions. HC and CO emissions are higher, power drops and consumption increases.

Injection systems which spray the fuel directly onto the intake valves provide particularly even mixture distribution. With such systems, the intake manifold is only used to transport the intake air, and the air flow is very uniform as a result. The fuel is evenly distributed to all cylinders by the injection system.

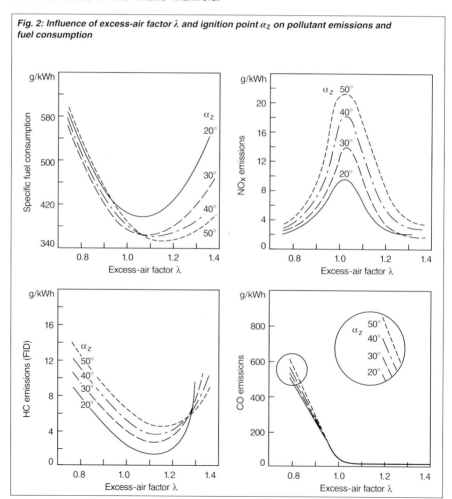

Fig. 2: Influence of excess-air factor λ and ignition point α_z on pollutant emissions and fuel consumption

Ignition

The ignition of the air-fuel mixture, i.e. the phase from spark discharge to the development of a stable flame front, has a decisive influence on the combustion process. It is determined by the point in time of spark discharge and by the ignition energy.

High excess energy provides stable ignition characteristics with positive effects on the stability of the combustion process from cycle to cycle. The low cyclic variation leads to smoother running of the engine and to lower emissions of unburned hydrocarbons. We can derive certain requirements made of the spark plug from what has been said above:

- Large electrode gap, in order to activate a large volume.
- Open spark gap, so that the air-fuel mixture can reach the spark channel easily.
- Thin electrodes and projecting spark position, in order to minimize heat dissipation through the electrodes and cylinder wall.

Under critical ignition conditions, e.g. engine idle, smoother running and considerably reduced HC emissions are obtained by increasing the spark-plug electrode gap. The same applies to ignition energy. Ignition systems with low spark duration and thereby higher energy transfer to the mixture are more suitable for the ignition of lean mixtures. Next to the air-fuel ratio, the moment of ignition has the greatest influence on pollutant emissions (Fig. 2):

HC emissions
The more the ignition is advanced, the more the emissions of unburned hydrocarbons increase, since post-reactions in the expansion phase and in the exhaust phase proceed less favorably due to the lower exhaust temperatures involved. This tendency is reversed only in the very lean range. With lean mixtures, the combustion speed is so low

that, with retarded ignition timing, combustion is not yet complete when the exhaust valve opens. The lean misfire limit (LML) of the engine is therefore reached with retarded ignition timing at a very low excess-air factor λ.

NO_x emissions
With increasingly advanced ignition, combustion-chamber temperatures increase and cause an increase of NO_x emissions throughout the whole range of the air-fuel ratio. These higher temperatures move the chemical equilibrium towards NO_x formation, and above all increase the reaction speed of NO_x formation.

CO emissions
CO emissions are almost completely independent of ignition timing, and are almost exclusively a function of the air-fuel ratio.

Fuel consumption
The influence of the ignition timing on fuel consumption is opposite to the influence it exerts on pollutant emissions. As the excess-air factor λ increases, in order to retain optimum combustion the ignition must take place earlier and earlier to compensate for the lower speed of combustion. Ignition advance therefore means lower fuel consumption and higher torque. Complicated ignition control, permitting independent optimization of the ignition point in all engine operating ranges, is necessary in order to establish a compromise in this „scissors" situation between the fuel consumption and the pollutant emission.

Fuels for spark-ignition engines

(gasoline/petrol)

The minimum requirements for these types of fuels are specified in various national standards. EN 228 defines the unleaded fuel which has been introduced in Europe ("Euro-Super").
The corresponding German specifications are contained in DIN 51600 (leaded premium gasoline) and in DIN 51607 (unleaded gasoline).

Components

Fuels for spark-ignition engines comprise hydrocarbon compounds which, to improve their characteristics, may contain supplements in the form of oxygenous organic components or other additives. A distinction is made between regular and premium (super-grade) gasolines, the latter having better anti-knock qualities as required for use in higher-compression engines.

Unleaded gasoline (DIN 51607)
Unleaded gasoline is indispensable for vehicles which employ catalytic converters to treat the exhaust gases, since lead would damage the layers of noble metals in the catalytic converter and thus render it inoperative. Unleaded fuels are a mixture of particularly high-grade, high-octane components. Anti-knock qualities can be effectively increased with nonmetallic additives. Maximum lead content is limited to 13 mg/l.

Leaded gasoline (DIN 51600)
Environmental considerations dictate that leaded fuels be restricted to engines whose exhaust valves require the combustion products of the lead-alkyl compounds for lubrication. Generally, this applies only to a relatively small number of older vehicles. Sales of leaded fuels are decreasing steadily. The "Super-Plus" which is now available on the German market has the same anti-knock qualities as leaded gasoline. In most European countries, lead content is legally restricted to maximum 0.15 g/l.

Parameters

Density (DIN 51757)
The approved density ranges for premium and regular fuels differ from each other. Because premium fuels generally include a higher proportion of aromatic compounds, they are denser than regular gasoline, and in such cases also have a slightly higher calorific value.

Anti-knock quality (octane rating)
The octane rating defines the gasoline's anti-knock quality. The higher the octane rating, the greater is the fuel's resistance to engine knock. Two different procedures are in international use for determining the octane rating: The Research Method and the Motor Method (DIN 51756; ASTM D 2699, and ASTM D 2700).

RON, MON
The octane number determined in testing according to the Research Method is termed the Research Octane Number (RON). It can be regarded as the essential index for acceleration knock.
The Motor Octane Number (MON), is derived in testing according to the Motor Method. The MON basically provides an indication of the tendency to knock at high speeds. The MON values are lower than the RON values.
Octane numbers up to 100 indicate the volumetric content of iso-octane contained in a mixture with n-heptane, at the point where the mixture's knock resistance in a test engine is identical to that of the fuel being tested.
Iso-octane, which is extremely knock-resistant, is assigned the octane number 100 (RON or MON), whereas n-heptane which has very low knock resistance is assigned the number 0.

Increasing the antiknock quality
Normal (untreated) straight-run gasoline has very little resistance to knock.

Various knock-resistant refinery products must be added to obtain a fuel with adequate anti-knock qualities, whereby the highest-possible octane level must be maintained throughout the entire boiling range.

Knock inhibitors

The most effective knock inhibitors are organic lead compounds. Depending upon their specific hydrocarbon structure, they can raise the octane number by several points. DIN 51 600 and most European national standards limit the maximum lead content to 150 mg per liter of fuel. Environmental considerations and the increasing numbers of vehicles equipped with catalytic converters have led to a steady reduction in the amounts of lead alkyls in fuels.

Volatility

To ensure satisfactory operation, fuels for SI engines must conform with stringent specifications regarding their volatility characteristics. The fuel must contain a large enough proportion of highly volatile components for good cold starts, whereas the volatility must not be so high as to impair operation and starting when the engine is hot (vapor lock). In addition, environmental considerations dictate that vaporization losses be kept to a minimum. There are a number of parameters for defining volatility.

Boiling curve

There are three areas on the boiling curve which have a particularly pronounced effect upon operation. They are defined according to the amount of fuel evaporation at three different temperatures

Vapor pressure

DIN 51 600 and DIN 51 606 limit the vapor pressure of fuels at 38 °C to 0.7 bar in summer and 0.9 bar in winter. The actual vapor-pressure characteristic curves as a function of temperature are largely determined by the composition of the gasoline concerned.

Vapor/liquid ratio

This specification provides an index of a fuel's tendency to form vapor bubbles (vapor locks). It is based upon the volume of vapor generated by a specific quantity of fuel at a set temperature, whereby the atmospheric counterpressure is significant.

Additives

Along with the structure of the hydrocarbons (refinery components), it is the additives which essentially determine the ultimate quality of a fuel. Additives are generally combined in packages containing individual components with specific attributes. Extreme care and precision are required in the testing of additives and in determining their optimal concentrations, and they must produce no undesirable side-effects. Mixing-in of the additives is thus the responsibility of the fuel manufacturer

Anti-aging additives

Such agents are added to fuels to improve their stability during storage, and are particularly important when the fuel also contains cracked components. They inhibit oxidation through atmospheric oxygen, and prevent catalytic reactions with metal ions.

Intake-system contamination inhibitors

Detergent additives ensure freedom from dirt deposits throughout the intake system (throttle valve, injectors, intake valves), as necessary for trouble-free operation and minimal emissions.

Corrosion protection

Moisture in the fuel can lead to corrosion in the fuel system. An extremely effective remedy is afforded by anti-corrosion additives which form a protective layer below the film of water.

Icing protection

Additives are available to prevent the throttle-valve from icing up. For example, alcohols dissolve ice crystals, while other agents inhibit the formation of ice deposits on the throttle valve.

Emissions-control technology

Exhaust-gas constituents

It is not possible to obtain complete combustion from the cylinders in the engine, not even by supplying an excess of oxygen. The less thorough the combustion process, the greater the proportion of pollutants in the engine's exhaust gases. It is thus necessary to improve the spark-ignition engine's exhaust pattern (for instance, with the aid of a catalytic converter) in order to reduce the load on the environment (Figures 1 and 2).

The objective of all concepts aimed at achieving reductions in the concentrations of the pollutant emissions limited by various regulations is the same: to maintain low fuel consumption, high performance and good drivability while holding the emissions of harmful substances to a minimum.

In addition to a high proportion of harmless components, exhaust gases also include secondary constituents which – at least in high concentrations – can cause damage to the environment. These pollutants represent approximately one percent of the total exhaust gas, and consist of carbon monoxide (CO), nitrous oxides (NO_X) and hydrocarbons (HC). The effects of air-fuel mixture on the concentrations of these substances is of particular interest: The response pattern for NO_X is inverted relative to that for CO and HC.

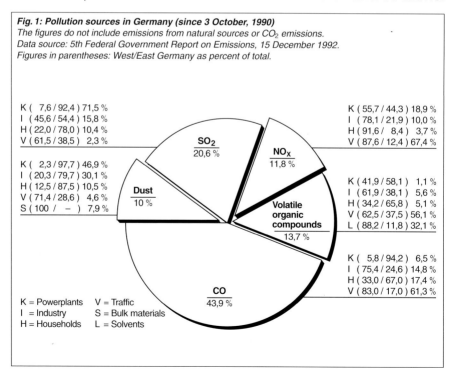

Fig. 1: Pollution sources in Germany (since 3 October, 1990)
The figures do not include emissions from natural sources or CO_2 emissions.
Data source: 5th Federal Government Report on Emissions, 15 December 1992.
Figures in parentheses: West/East Germany as percent of total.

K (7,6 / 92,4) 71,5 %
I (45,6 / 54,4) 15,8 %
H (22,0 / 78,0) 10,4 %
V (61,5 / 38,5) 2,3 %

K (2,3 / 97,7) 46,9 %
I (20,3 / 79,7) 30,1 %
H (12,5 / 87,5) 10,5 %
V (71,4 / 28,6) 4,6 %
S (100 / –) 7,9 %

$\dfrac{SO_2}{20,6\%}$

$\dfrac{NO_X}{11,8\%}$

$\dfrac{Dust}{10\%}$

Volatile organic compounds
$\dfrac{}{13,7\%}$

$\dfrac{CO}{43,9\%}$

K (55,7 / 44,3) 18,9 %
I (78,1 / 21,9) 10,0 %
H (91,6 / 8,4) 3,7 %
V (87,6 / 12,4) 67,4 %

K (41,9 / 58,1) 1,1 %
I (61,9 / 38,1) 5,6 %
H (34,2 / 65,8) 5,1 %
V (62,5 / 37,5) 56,1 %
L (88,2 / 11,8) 32,1 %

K (5,8 / 94,2) 6,5 %
I (75,4 / 24,6) 14,8 %
H (33,0 / 67,0) 17,4 %
V (83,0 / 17,0) 61,3 %

K = Powerplants V = Traffic
I = Industry S = Bulk materials
H = Households L = Solvents

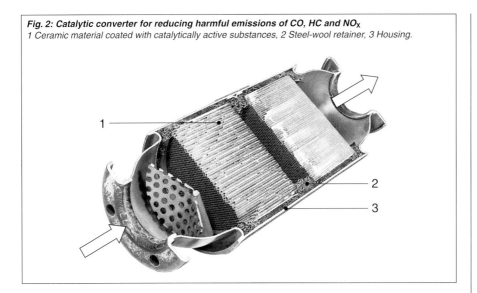

Fig. 2: Catalytic converter for reducing harmful emissions of CO, HC and NO$_X$
1 Ceramic material coated with catalytically active substances, 2 Steel-wool retainer, 3 Housing.

Main components

The main exhaust-gas components are nitrogen, carbon dioxide and water vapor. These substances are non-toxic. Nitrogen (N_2) is the element most abundant in the atmosphere. Although it is not directly involved in the combustion process, at approx. 71% it represents the major exhaust-gas component. Small amounts of nitrogen react with oxygen to form nitrous oxides.

Complete combustion converts the hydrocarbons contained in the fuel's chemical bonds into carbon dioxide (CO_2) which makes up about 14% of the exhaust gas. The hydrogen contained in the fuel's chemical structure combusts to form water vapor (H_2O), most of which condenses as it cools (producing the vapor cloud which can be seen emerging from the exhaust on cold days).

Secondary components

The secondary components carbon monoxide, hydrocarbons and incompletely-oxidized hydrocarbons are the result of incomplete combustion, while nitrous oxides form in response to secondary reactions that accompany all air combustion processes. Carbon monoxide (CO) is a colorless, odorless gas. It acts as a toxic substance by inhibiting the blood's ability to absorb oxygen. For this reason an engine should never be run in an enclosed space unless an exhaust-gas extraction system has been connected and switched on.

The hydrocarbons assume the form of unburned fuel components as well as new hydrocarbons formed during combustion. Aliphatic hydrocarbons are odorless and have a low boiling point. The closed-chain aromatic hydrocarbons (benzol, toluol, polycyclic hydrocarbons) emit a distinct odor, and are considered carcinogenic with continuous exposure. Partially-oxidated hydrocarbons (aldehydes, cetones, etc.) emit a disagreable odor. When exposed to sunlight they decay to form substances that are considered to act as carcinogens in people continually exposed to high concentrations. The term NO$_X$ is employed to identify the various oxides of nitrogen (mostly NO and NO$_2$) that result as oxygen combines with atmospheric nitrogen during high-temperature combustion.

NO is colorless and odorless and is gradually converted to NO$_2$ in the atmosphere. Pure NO$_2$ is a toxic reddish-brown gas with a pungent odor. At the levels found in air with high pollutant concentrations, NO$_2$ can irritate the mucous membranes in the respiratory system.

Exhaust-gas treatment

Lambda closed-loop control

Lambda closed-loop control in conjunction with the catalytic converter is the most effective method of cleaning spark-ignition engine exhaust gases available today. At present, there is no alternative system that can attain anywhere near the same low exhaust-gas emission levels.

Very low exhaust-gas levels can be reached with the ignition and fuel-injection systems described previously. A further reduction in the particularly harmful exhaust components hydrocarbons (HC), carbon monoxide (CO) and oxides of nitrogen (NO_x) can be achieved if the catalytic converter is used.
The so-called three-way or selective catalytic converter is particularly effective. This converter can reduce emissions of hydrocarbons, carbon monoxide and oxides of nitrogen by more than 90% if the engine is operated in a very narrow range (less than 1%) around the stoichiometric air-fuel ratio of $\lambda = 1$[1]). This very small allowable deviation applies for all engine operating conditions and cannot be maintained alone even by modern gasoline fuel-injection systems. For this reason, the so-called lambda closed-loop control is used, i.e. the composition of the mixture of fuel and air supplied to the engine (the "mixture") is continuously maintained within the optimum deviation range (the "catalytic converter window", Fig. 1) by a closed control loop. For this, the

exhaust must be measured and the injected fuel quantity immediately corrected based on this measurement. The lambda sensor is used as the measuring element. It generates a voltage jump exactly at the stoichiometric ratio ($\lambda = 1$), thus supplying a signal which shows whether the mixture is richer or leaner than $\lambda = 1$.

Lambda oxygen sensor
The lambda sensor in the exhaust pipe measures the exhaust flow evenly from all cylinders (Fig. 2). The method of operation is based on the principle of a galvanic oxygen concentration cell with solid-state electrolyte.

Construction
The solid-state electrolyte consists of a gas-tight ceramic body closed at one end. It is made of zirconium dioxide and stabilized with yttrium oxide. The surfaces have electrodes on both sides made of a thin gas-permeable platinum layer.

The platinum electrode on the outside acts as a small catalytic converter where the exhaust is subjected to catalytic aftertreatment and brought into stoichiometric equilibrium. On the side

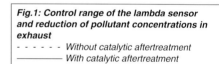

Fig.1: Control range of the lambda sensor and reduction of pollutant concentrations in exhaust
- - - - - - *Without catalytic aftertreatment*
——————— *With catalytic aftertreatment*

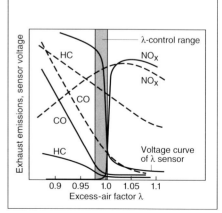

[1]) The stoichiometric air-fuel ratio is the mass ratio of 14.7 kg air to 1 kg gasoline theoretically necessary for complete combustion. The excess-air factor or air ratio λ (lambda) indicates the deviation of the actual air-fuel ratio from the theoretically required ratio:

$$\lambda = \frac{\text{actual inducted air mass}}{\text{theoretical air requirement}}$$

exposed to the exhaust gas, there is a porous ceramic layer (spinell layer) which serves as a protection against contamination. A metal tube with a number of slits protects the ceramic body against mechanical and thermal shocks. The inside open space is in contact with the exterior air as a reference gas (Fig. 3).

Method of operation
The ceramic material used for the sensor becomes conductive for oxygen ions starting at approximately 350°C. If the oxygen concentration differs on the two sides of the sensor, there results an electric voltage between the two surfaces. This serves as a measure of the difference in oxygen concentration on the two sides of the sensor. The oxygen content remaining in the exhaust of an internal-combustion engine depends greatly on the air-fuel ratio of the mixture supplied to the engine. Even with excess fuel in the mixture, there is still some oxygen in the exhaust; for example, at $\lambda = 0.95$, there is still $0.2 \ldots 0.3\%$ oxygen by volume. This relation makes it possible to use the oxygen concentration in the exhaust as a measure of the air-fuel ratio. The voltage supplied by the lambda sensor as a result of the oxygen content in the exhaust reaches $800 \ldots 1000$ mV with rich mixtures ($\lambda < 1$), but it is only about 100 mV with lean mixtures ($\lambda > 1$). The transition from the lean to the rich range lies at $450 \ldots 500$ mV.

In addition to the oxygen concentration in the exhaust, the temperature of the ceramic body also plays a decisive role, since it influences the conductivity for oxygen ions. Thus, the curve of the voltage supplied as a function of the excess-air factor λ ("static" sensor curve) is strongly influenced by the temperature. Hence, the figures given apply to a sensor working temperature of approximately 600°C. In addition, the response time for a voltage change due to a change in the mixture composition is strongly dependent on the temperature. Whereas these response times lie in the seconds range at a ceramic temperature under 350°C, at the ideal operating temperature of around 600°C, the sensor reacts after < 50 ms. For these reasons, the lambda closed-loop control is not activated until the minimum operating temperature of approximately 350°C has been reached. Until this point, the engine is operated using an open-loop control.

Fig. 2: Positioning of the lambda sensor in a dual exhaust system

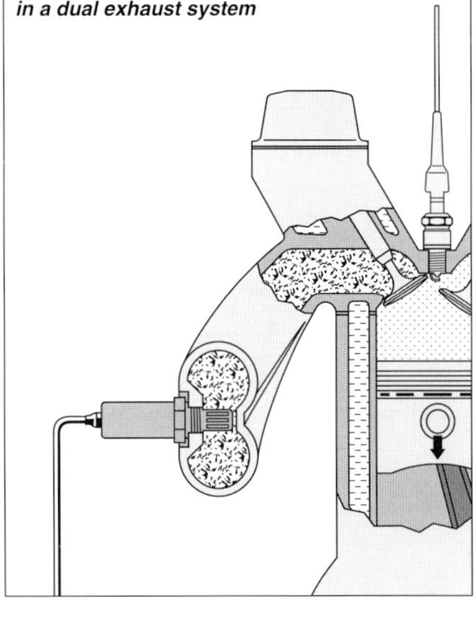

Fig. 3: Location of the lambda sensor in the exhaust pipe (schematic)
1 Sensor ceramic, 2 Electrodes, 3 Contact,
4 Electrical contacting to the housing,
5 Exhaust pipe, 6 Protective ceramic coating
(porous), 7 Exhaust gas, 8 Air.

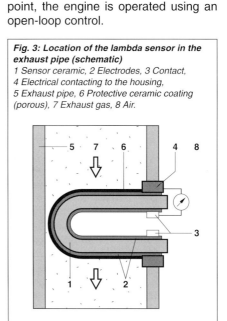

Installation

Excessive temperatures shorten service life. Therefore, the lambda sensor must be installed so that a temperature of 850°C is not exceeded during extended full-load operation; 930°C is allowable for short periods.

Heated lambda sensor

With this sensor, the ceramic temperature is determined by an electric heating element under low engine-load conditions (i.e. low exhaust temperature), and by the exhaust temperature under higher loading. The heated lambda sensor can be installed at a greater distance from the engine so that extended full-load operation is unproblematic. This internal heating means that the sensor heats up very quickly, so that, within 20 ... 30 seconds after engine start, the operating temperature has been reached and lambda closed-loop control is activated. Since the heated sensor is always at the ideal operating temperature, low exhaust emissions can be reached and maintained. Presuming correct operating conditions, the heated lambda sensors in series production today have service lives of over 100 000 km. However, in order to avoid damaging the active outer platinum electrode the engine must be operated with unleaded fuel (Figs. 4 and 6).

Operation of lambda closed-loop control

The lambda sensor transmits a voltage signal to the electronic control unit, which then signals to the fuel-management system (injection system or electronically-controlled carburetor) whether the mixture needs to be made leaner or richer, depending on the voltage output from the lambda sensor (Fig. 5). A control threshold is programmed into the control unit for this purpose. This threshold generally lies at 500 mV. If the voltage from the lambda sensor lies below this value (mixture too lean), more fuel is supplied. If the value is exceeded (mixture too rich), the quantity of fuel supplied to the engine is reduced. However, alteration of the air-fuel ratio must not be abrupt, as otherwise the vehicle will tend to buck. Therefore, the electronic control unit contains an integrator which slowly changes mixture composition via a time function.

A certain delay (dead time) passes between the time of formation of fresh mixture in the intake manifold or passages and the measurement of the combusted mixture (= exhaust) by the lambda sen-

Fig. 4: Heated lambda sensor
1 Sensor housing, 2 Protective ceramic tube, 3 Connection cable, 4 Protective tube with slots, 5 Active sensor ceramic, 6 Contact element, 7 Protective sleeve, 8 Heater, 9 Clamp terminals for heater.

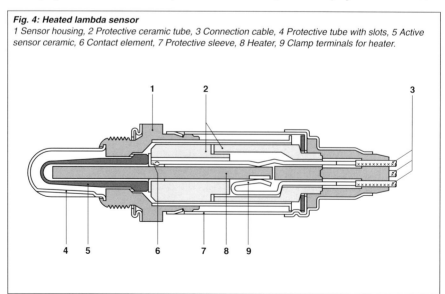

Fig. 5: Schematic diagram of lambda closed-loop control operation

1 Air-flow sensor, 2 Engine, 3 Lambda sensor, 4 Catalytic converter, 5 Fuel-injection valves (injectors), 6 Lambda closed-loop control, U_S Sensor voltage, U_V Valve-actuation voltage, V_E Injected fuel quantity.

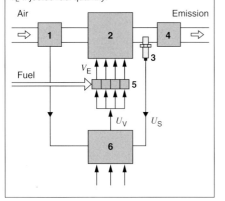

value of the air-fuel ratio remains within the "catalytic converter window", i.e. within a range where the catalytic converter reaches its highest possible conversion efficiency.

The dead time, i.e. essentially the time between formation of the mixture and measurement of the exhaust gas is, naturally, highly dependent upon the relevant load and engine speed. During idling, the dead time may be up to 1 second or more, dependent upon the distance of the lambda sensor from the engine but it is reduced to just a few hundred milliseconds at high load and engine speed. With constant regulation of the mixture as a function of time (with constant integrator slope), this would result in the amplitude of the control oscillations changing greatly with load and engine speeds. This would result in a serious increase in exhaust emissions and, at the same time, would worsen the driveability. For this reason, the characteristic of the integrator is adjusted, dependent upon load and engine speed, in such a way that a constant control amplitude, selected for optimum exhaust-gas emission and optimum driveability, is achieved on average.

sor. This is due to the time taken for the mixture to reach the engine, the time for the engine's working cycle, the time for the exhaust to reach the lambda sensor and the response time of the sensor itself. Due to this dead time, constant compliance with the exact stoichiometric ratio is impossible, instead, the air-fuel ratio constantly varies by a few percent around $\lambda = 1$. However, if the integrator is correctly matched, the average

Fig. 6: View of the unheated (front) and heated lambda sensors

Catalytic exhaust treatment

Catalytic converter systems

There are three catalytic converter systems for different exhaust designs and applications.

Oxidation catalytic converter

The oxidation catalytic converter (or single-bed oxidation catalytic converter) works with excess air and transforms hydrocarbons and carbon monoxide into water vapour and carbon dioxide through oxidation, i.e. combustion. Oxides of nitrogen (NO_x) remain practically unaffected by oxidation catalytic converters. In the case of fuel-injection engines, the oxygen necessary for oxidation is usually obtained through a lean mixture setting ($\lambda > 1$). With carburetor engines, the so-called secondary air is supplied upstream of the converter by a centrifugal pump driven by the engine or through self-inducting air valves (Fig. 7a).

Oxidation catalytic converters were first used in 1975 in vehicles for the then current US exhaust regulations.

Dual-bed catalytic converter

The dual-bed catalytic converter consists of two catalysts connected in series with each other (hence the name dual bed). With this method, the engine must be operated with a rich mixture ($\lambda < 1$), i.e. with air deficiency. The exhaust gas first flows through a reduction catalyst and then through an oxidation catalyst. Air is blown in between the two. In the first catalyst, the oxides of nitrogen are converted, and, in the second, the hydrocarbons and carbon monoxide. Due to the rich engine operation, the dual-bed design is the least favorable in terms of fuel consumption; however, it can be combined with a simple mixture-formation system without electronic control. A further disadvantage is the fact that during the reduction of oxides of nitrogen under air deficiency conditions, ammonia (NH_3) is produced, which is then partly re-oxidized to oxides of nitrogen during the subsequent addition of air.

With this design, conversion of NO_x is significantly worse than with a single-bed three-way catalytic converter with lambda closed-loop control.

The dual-bed catalytic converter is practically unused by European automakers, even for those vehicles exported to the USA or Japan. However, in the USA, it is freqently used by American automakers. The dual-bed design is also often used in the USA in conjunction with lambda closed-loop control. In these vehicles, the catalytic converter is operated with a stoichiometric mixture, whereby the fuel-consumption problems arising from rich operation are solved. However, this design is very expensive and has the disadvantages mentioned above with regard to NO_x emissions (Fig. 7b).

Three-way catalytic converter (TWC)

The three-way catalytic converter (or single-bed three-way catalytic converter) simultaneously removes all three pollutant components to a high degree (three-way).

A prerequisite is that the air-fuel mixture supplied to the engine, and thereby the exhaust, is at the stoichiometric ratio, as described in the Section "Lambda closed-loop control". The three-way catalytic converter combined with lambda closed-loop control is the most effective pollutant-reduction system presently available, for which reason it is being increasingly used to meet the strictest exhaust-gas limits. The European automakers have been using this design for years, almost exclusively for export vehicles to the USA and Japan in combination with fuel-injection systems.

In view of the strict exhaust-gas limits planned for the Federal Republic of Germany and the EEC, the vehicles for these countries will also be equipped with this technology (Fig. 7c).

Three-way catalytic converters (TWC) without lambda closed-loop control are available in the form of retrofit kits. Of course, these cannot achieve the high levels of conversion achievable when using systems with lambda closed-loop control. However, they enable a reduction in pollutants by approximately 50 %.

Fig. 7: Catalytic-converter systems
a) Single-bed oxidation catalytic converter, b) Dual-bed oxidation catalytic converter,
c) Single-bed three-way catalytic converter.
1 Mixture-formation system, 2 Secondary air, 3 Oxidation catalytic converter HC, CO,
4 Reduction catalytic converter NO_x, 5 ECU, 6 Lambda sensor,
7 Three-way catalitic converter NO_x, HC, CO.

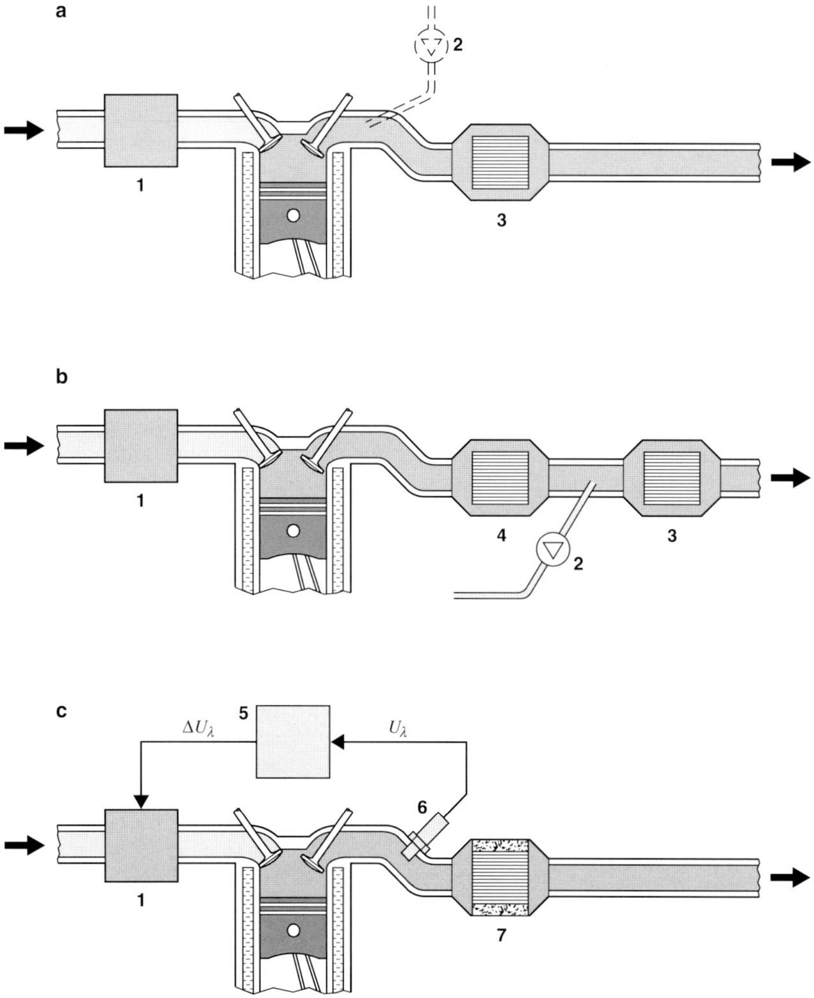

Substrate systems

The catalytic converter (or more correctly the catalytic exhaust converter) consists of a metal housing, a substrate, and the actual active catalytic layer.

There are three different substrate systems:
– pellets
– ceramic monoliths
– metallic monoliths

Pellets

The pellet type of substrate is primarily used in the USA and Japan, but is steadily loosing ground. It is practically unused by European automakers (Fig. 8a).

Ceramic monoliths

Ceramic monoliths are ceramic bodies perforated by several thousand small channels through which the exhaust flows. The ceramic material is of high-temperature-resistant magnesium-aluminum silicate.

The monolith, which is extremely sensitive to mechanical tension, is mounted in a metal housing. Between the housing walls and the substrate is an elastic metal mesh made of a high-alloy steel wire with a diameter of approximately 0.25 mm. This mesh must be adequately elastic to compensate for manufacturing tolerances, the differing expansion coefficients of housing and substrate material, mechanical stresses during vehicle operation, and the gas forces affecting the ceramic body (Fig. 8b).

Ceramic monoliths are currently the most commonly-used catalytic converter substrates. They are used by all European automakers and, in the USA and Japan, are superseding the pellet catalytic converters used previously.

Metallic monoliths

Metallic monoliths are at present only rarely used. They are primarily installed near the engine as so-called pre-catalysts or start catalysts, supplementing the main catalytic converter, in order to provide more rapid catalytic conversion after cold starts. Their application as main catalysts is primarily impeded by excessive costs compared to the ceramic monoliths.

Coating

While pellets can be directly coated with the catalytically active substances, ceramic and metallic monoliths require a substrate coating of aluminum oxide ("wash-coat"), which increases the effective surface area of the catalyst by a factor of about 7000. The effective catalytic coating applied on top of this consists in oxidation catalysts of the

---

Fig. 8: Substrate systems
a) Pellet-type catalytic converter, b) Catalytic converter with ceramic monoliths.
1 Pellets, 2 Insulation, 3 Monoliths, 4 Metal mesh.

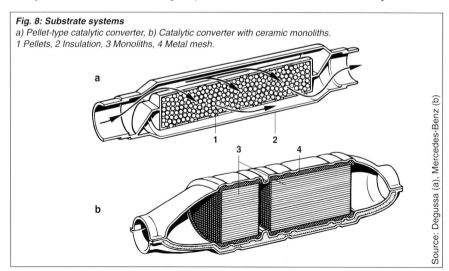

Source: Degussa (a), Mercedes-Benz (b)

noble metals platinum and palladium, and in three-way catalysts of platinum and rhodium (Fig. 9). Platinum accelerates the oxidation of the hydrocarbons and the carbon monoxide, and rhodium accelerates the reduction of the oxides of nitrogen. The content of noble metals in a catalytic converter is approximately 2 to 3 grams.

Operating conditions

As is the case with the lambda sensor, the operating temperature also plays a very important role in the function of the catalytic converter. Appreciable conversion of pollutants begins only at an operating temperature of more than about 250°C. The ideal operating conditions for high conversion rates and long service life prevail in the temperature range from approximately 400°C to 800°C. In the range from 800°C to 1000°C, thermal aging is significantly aggravated by sintering of the noble metals and the Al_2O_3 substrate coating, which leads to a reduction in the active surface area. Hence, in this temperature range, the duration of operation exerts a very great influence. Above 1000°C, thermal aging increases severely, up to the almost total ineffectiveness of the catalytic converter. These characteristics limit the possibilities for installation. Hence, it is impe-

rative that a compromise is found for the installation position of the catalytic converter in the exhaust system. In the future, this will be made easier by improved thermal stabilization of the coating (critical limit at approximately 950°C). Under ideal operating conditions, a catalytic converter can have a service life of up to 100 000 km (60 000 miles).

On the other hand, engine malfunctions, for example misfires, can cause the temperature of the catalytic converter to increase to more than 1400°C. Such high temperatures lead to the complete destruction of the catalytic converter as a result of the melting of the substrate material. In order to prevent this, in particular the ignition system on vehicles operating with catalytic converters must be very reliable and maintainance-free, and this demand is greatly facilitated by the application of electronic systems. A further prerequisite for reliable long-term operation is that the engine is operated with unleaded fuel. Otherwise, lead compounds are deposited in the pores of the active surfaces or directly on the surfaces, thus reducing them. Engine-oil residues can also "poison" the catalyst.

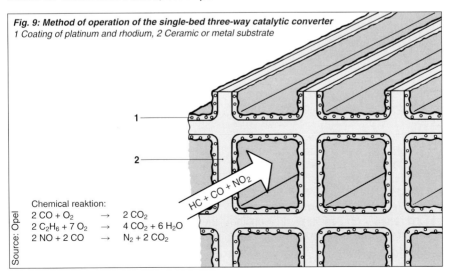

Fig. 9: Method of operation of the single-bed three-way catalytic converter
1 Coating of platinum and rhodium, 2 Ceramic or metal substrate

1 —

2 —

HC + CO + NO$_2$

Chemical reaktion:

$$2\ CO + O_2 \rightarrow 2\ CO_2$$
$$2\ C_2H_6 + 7\ O_2 \rightarrow 4\ CO_2 + 6\ H_2O$$
$$2\ NO + 2\ CO \rightarrow N_2 + 2\ CO_2$$

Source: Opel

Other measures

Lean-burn concepts

Pollutant reduction using the catalytic converter is an "external process", which does not directly influence the combustion process in the engine. In contrast, with "internal processes", which utilize appropriate combustion-chamber design, valve timing, compression ratio, exhaust-gas recirculation, ignition timing and air-fuel ratio, the combustion process itself can be influenced and as a result considerable control exerted on pollutant emissions, although not to the degree possible with catalytic exhaust aftertreatment. Such internal methods are used in lean-burn concepts.

The concentration of the pollutants hydrocarbons (HC), carbon monoxide (CO), and oxides of nitrogen (NO_x) expelled by the engine, together with fuel consumption, are dependent to a great extent on the excess-air factor lambda (λ), i.e. the air-fuel ratio at which the engine is being operated. In the rich range, the HC and CO emissions increase, while they are at a minimum in the lean range. The same is true of specific fuel consumption. Oxides of nitrogen, on the other hand, are at a maximum with a slightly lean mixture ($\lambda \approx 1.05$).

Prior to 1970, engines were operated with rich mixtures. This assured high power with problem-free driveability. However, increasingly severe emission-control legislation forced air-fuel ratios to be increased, and this meant that engines had to be run with excess air. This in the main reduces the emissions of hydrocarbons and carbon monoxide, and at the same time leads to a considerable reduction in fuel consumption. On the other hand, this lean adjustment causes NO_x to rise. It also has a derogatory effect on vehicle driveability which had to be counteracted by constant improvements on both the engines and the mixture-formation systems. It

was also necessary to adjust the ignition timing even more precisely. For all these reasons, more and more electronic ignition systems are fitted today to set the optimum spark advance for fuel economy and exhaust emissions.

Lean-burn engine

Consistent design improvements for the combustion chamber, with auxiliary support from external measures (e.g., to promote intake swirl) can be employed to obtain a lean-burn engine capable of operating at excess-air factors in the $\lambda \approx 1.4$ range. Although the lean-burn engine is characterized by low emissions and better fuel economy, it still needs a catalytic converter to comply with stringent CO and HC emission limits. Up to now, it has not been possible to meet the strict USA emissions regulations with the lean-burn engine which thus remains consigned to an outsider's role, despite the high fuel economy which makes this concept so attractive.

Thermal afterburning

Before today's catalytic treatment of exhaust emissions became standard, initial attempts to reduce emissions utilized thermal afterburning.

This method employs a specific residence time at high temperatures to burn exhaust-gas components that failed to combust in the engine's cylinders. In the rich range ($\lambda = 0.9 \ldots 1.0$), the processs must be supported with supplementary air injection. In lean operation ($\lambda = 1.1 \ldots 1.2$), the residual oxygen contained in the exhaust gas is adequate to support combustion.

Today, thermal afterburning is of no significance as it is of no value in meeting low NO_x limits. However, it can be employed to reduce emissions of HC and CO in the warm-up phase, before the catalytic converter warms to its operating temperature. Thus thermal aftertreatment can be used to achieve compliance with tomorrow's more stringent limits by reducing the emissions produced by the engine in the warm-up phase.

Secondary-air injection

Supplementary air can be injected immediately downstream from the combustion chamber to promote secondary combustion of the hot exhaust gases. This "exothermic" reaction not only reduces levels of hydrocarbons (HC) and carbon monoxide (CO), it also heats the catalytic converter.

The process substantially enhances the converter's conversion rate in the warm-up phase. The three main components of the secondary-air injection system (Fig. 10) are:
– electric secondary-air pump,
– secondary-air valve,
– non-return valve.

Thermal reactors

Thermal reactors are designed so that the exhaust-air mixture, enriched with high percentages of HC and CO during rich operation, is ignited at high temperatures and thus burns the pollutants. The reactors are optimized for the longest possible duration of the process in order to provide maximum combustion. HC emissions can be reduced by about 50 % with the help of thermal reactors; however, this increases fuel consumption by up to 15 %. For this reason, such systems using thermal reactors were only used for a short period, to be replaced by catalytic-converter technology.

Overrun fuel cutoff

Overrun fuel cutoff is another means of reducing emissions of HC and CO. When the engine is operated on overrun, a high vacuum is produced in the induction system and thereby in the combustion chamber as well. Under these conditions, the mixture is difficult to ignite as a result of its low oxygen content, so that combustion is incomplete. This leads to emissions of unburned hydrocarbons and carbon monoxide.

The complete cutoff of the fuel supply in overrun operation prevents the emission of unburned pollutants.

Overrun fuel cutoff which operates smoothly for example on the KE-Jetronic owing to continual injection from the injection valves, responds as a function of the coolant temperature. In order to avoid continual activation and deactivation at a single specific engine speed, there are differing switching points dependent upon the direction of the engine speed change. In the case of a hot engine, the switching thresholds are as low as possible in order to provide maximum fuel economy.

With the multiplicity of possibilities of reducing the pollutant emissions from spark-ignition engines, the technical solution arrived at depends on the boundary conditions, of which by no means the least significant is emission-control legislation.

Fig. 10: Secondary-air injection
1 Intake air, 2 Engine, 3 Secondary air,
4 Non-return valve, 5 Secondary-air valve,
6 Electrical secondary-air pump,
7 Lambda sensor, 8 Catalytic converter,
9 Exhaust gas.

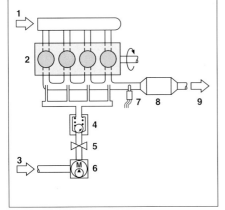

Testing exhaust and evaporative emissions

Test technology

Test program

For precise determination of a passenger car's emission levels, the vehicle must be tested in an emissions test cell under standardized conditions designed to accurately reflect real-world driving conditions. Compared with highway driving, operation in the test-cell has the advantage that precisley defined speeds can be maintained without having to take other traffic into account, and it represents the only means of ensuring that individual emissions tests remain mutually comparable.

The test vehicle is parked with its drive wheels on special rollers. The rollers' resistance to rotation can be adjusted to simulate friction losses and aerodynamic resistance, while inertial mass can be added to simulate the vehicle's weight. The required cooling is provided by a fan mounted a short distance from the vehicle.

Emissions are measured during a precisely-defined simulated driving cycle. The exhaust gases generated in testing are collected for subsequent analysis of pollutant mass (Fig. 1).

Procedures for collecting exhaust gases and determining emissions levels have been standardized at the international level, but the driving cycles remain disparate. In some countries, regulations on exhaust emissions are supplemented by limits on evaporative emissions from the fuel system.

Fig. 1: Test setups
a) for US Federal Test (here with Venturi system),
b) for Europe-Test (here with rotary-piston compressor).
1 Brake, 2 Flywheel, 3 Exhaust, 4 Air filter, 5 Dilution air, 6 Cooler, 7 Sample Venturi tube,
8 Gas temperature, 9 Pressure, 10 Venturi tube, 11 Fan, 12 Sample bag, 13 Rotary-piston blower,
14 To outlet.

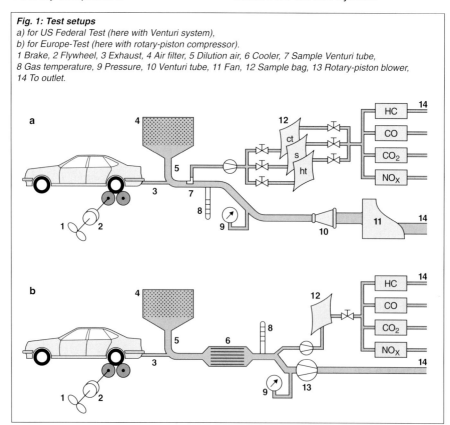

Chassis dynamometer

To ensure comparable emissions data, the time characteristics of the speeds and forces applied on the chassis dynamometer must comply precisely with those encountered during highway operation. Fluid-friction dynamometers, eddy-current brakes and DC motors simulate the inertial forces exerted by rolling and aerodynamic resistance by providing a corresponding, velocity-sensitive retarding force (the rollers' resistance to rotation). Rapid couplings are employed to connect the rollers to the various-sized inertial masses, thereby simulating vehicle mass. The progression curves for braking force must be maintained in a precise relationship to vehicle speed and inertial mass (deviations lead to test errors). Ambient conditions such as atmospheric humidity, temperature and barometric pressure also influence test results.

Test cycles

To ensure that the test results remain mutually comparable, the speeds used on the dynamometer must accurately reflect actual highway operation. Testing is based on a standardized driving cycle in which shifting, braking, idling and stationary phases have all been selected to reflect conditions encountered in the typical urban traffic of a large town. Five different test cycles are employed internationally. Usually, a driver sits in the vehicle, maintaining the speed indicated on a display screen.

Test samples and dilution procedures (CVS method)

With European adoption of the constant-volume sampling (CVS) method in 1982, there is now basically one single internationally recognized procedure for collecting exhaust gases.

Test samples and emissions analysis

The dilution process employs the following principle:
The exhaust gases emitted by the test vehicle are diluted with fresh air at a ratio of 1:10 before being extracted using a special system of pumps. These pumps are arranged to maintain a precise, consistent ratio between the flow volumes for exhaust gas and fresh air, i.e., the air feed is adjusted to reflect the vehicle's instantaneous exhaust volume. Throughout the test a constant proportion of the diluted exhaust gas is extracted for collection in one or several sample bags. Upon completion of the test cycle, the pollutant concentration in the sample bags corresponds precisely to the mean concentration in the total quantity of fresh-air/exhaust mixture which has been extracted. As it is possible to monitor the total volume of fresh-air and exhaust mixture, one can employ the pollutant concentration levels to calculate the masses of the substances emitted during the test cycle. Advantages of this procedure: Because it inhibits condensation of any water vapor contained in the exhaust gases, there is a sharp reduction in NO_x losses in the bag. In addition, dilution greatly inhibits the tendency of the exhaust components (especially hydrocarbons) to engage in mutual reactions. However, dilution does mean that pollutant concentrations decrease proportionally to the mean dilution ratio, making it necessary to use more precise analyzers.

Analyzers and dilution equipment

Standardized devices are also available for analyzing component concentrations in the test bags. Either one of two different but equally acceptable pump arrangements is generally employed to maintain the constant flow volume required for testing. In the first, a standard blower extracts the mixture of fresh air and exhaust gas through a venturi tube; the second device employs a special vane pump (Roots blower). Both methods are capable of metering flow volume with an acceptable degree of accuracy.

Determining evaporative emissions from the fuel system

In addition to and separate from the emissions generated during the engine's combustion process, motor vehicles also emit hydrocarbons (HC) in the form of evaporative emissions escaping from the tank and fuel system; these vary according to fuel-system design and temperature. Some countries (e.g., USA) already have regulations limiting the allowable levels of evaporative losses (planned for EU).

SHED test

The SHED (Sealed Housing for Evaporative Determination) test is the most common procedure for determining evaporative emissions. It comprises two test phases – employing different conditioning procedures – conducted in a gas-tight enclosure. The first part of the test is conducted with the fuel tank filled to approx. 40% of capacity. The test fuel is warmed from its initial temperature of 10 ... 14.5°C, with actual testing of HC concentrations in the enclosure starting when it reaches 15.5°C. The fuel temperature is increased by 14°C in the following hour, after which testing is concluded with a final sampling of HC concentration. Evaporative emissions levels are determined by comparing the initial and final measurements. The vehicle's windows and trunk lid remain open for the duration of the test. The vehicle is prepared for the second portion of the test by being warmed-up using the FTP 75 driving cycle before being returned to the enclosure. The increase in the HC concentration as the vehicle cools during the hour it remains parked is then measured. The sum of the results from both tests must be less than the current limit of 2 g hydrocarbon vapor. A more stringent SHED test is scheduled for introduction in the USA.

USA-FTP 75 test cycle

The FTP 75 test cycle (FTP = Federal Test Procedure) consists of three sections. The driving curve is designed to reflect conditions measured in actual morning commuter traffic in Los Angeles (Fig. 2):

Test phase		Elapsed time s
Transition phase	ct	0...505
Stabilized phase	s	506...1372
Hot test	ht	1072...2477

The test vehicle is first conditioned by being left parked for 12 hours at an ambient temperature of 20...30°C. It is then

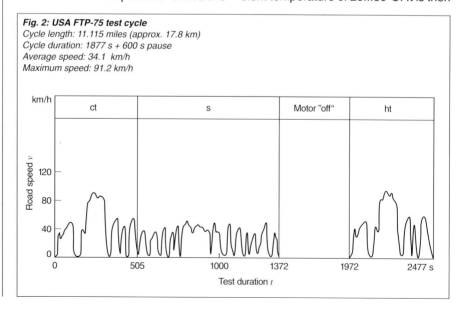

Fig. 2: USA FTP-75 test cycle
Cycle length: 11.115 miles (approx. 17.8 km)
Cycle duration: 1877 s + 600 s pause
Average speed: 34.1 km/h
Maximum speed: 91.2 km/h

started and driven through the prescribed test cycle:

Phase ct: Diluted exhaust gases are collected in bag 1 during the cold transition phase.

Phase s: Exhaust samples are diverted to bag 2 at the beginning of the stabilized phase (after 505 s) without any interruption in the program sequence. The engine is switched off for a 10-minute pause immediately following completion of the stabilized phase (after 1372 s).

Phase ht: The engine is restarted for the hot test (505 s duration). The speed sequence used in this phase is the same as the one used for the cold transition phase. The exhaust gases generated in this phase are collected in a third bag. The bag samples from the previous phases are then analyzed, as the probes should not remain in the bags for longer than 20 minutes. The exhaust-gas sample in the third bag is analyzed upon completion of the third driving sequence. The weighted sum of the pollutant emissions (HC, CO and NO_x) from all three bags is then evaluated relative to the distance covered and ex-

pressed as emissions per mile. National emissions limits vary. This test procedure is employed in the USA (incl. California – Table 1) and in several other countries (Table 2). Every passenger car registered for the first time is required to maintain compliance with these standards over a distance of 50,000 miles, regardless of vehicle weight and engine displacement. Under certain conditions, US authorities may grant waivers for specific model years. In addition, higher emissions limits apply to vehicles certified for 100,000 miles.

Among the various environmental-protection measures included in the most recent Clean Air Act is a tightening of vehicle-emissions limits to apply from 1994 onward (Table 1). California also introduced new and stricter standards in 1993, and is planning further and more radical measures.

The cold-start enrichment required when vehicles are started at low temperatures generates particularly high emissions; these are not measured in current emissions testing, which is conducted at ambient temperatures of 20 ... 30°C. The Clean Air Act aims to reduce these emissions by prescribing an emissions test at –6.7°C. However, the limit is restricted to carbon monoxide.

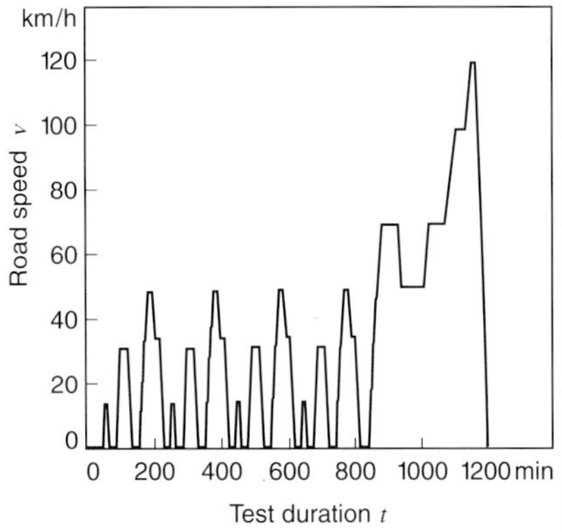

EEC and EU test cycle

The EEC/EU test cycle is based on a hypothetical driving curve designed to provide a reasonable approximation of actual driving patterns (Fig. 3).

The EEC/EU test cycle is currently obligatory in the following countries: Belgium; Denmark; France; Germany; Great Britain; Greece; Ireland; Italy; Luxembourg; the Netherlands; Portugal and Spain.

The test cycle is conducted according to the following schedule:
After initial conditioning (vehicle parked at a room temperature of 20 ... 30°C), the actual test cycle commences with a cold start and 40-second warm-up

Fig. 3: ECE/EC test cycle with expressway phase
Cycle length: 11 km
Average speed: 32.5 km/h
Maximum speed: 120.0 km/h

phase. The test cycle is run through four times in succession with no intermediate pauses. During the test, the CVS method is used to collect exhaust gases in a sample bag. In this Europe test, the pollutant masses obtained from analysis of the bag's contents are converted to reflect the test distance; one composite limit applies for hydrocarbons and nitrous oxides ($HC + NO_x$).

More stringent limits applicable for all vehicles regardless of displacement have been in effect since 1992. The corresponding regulation, 91/441 EEC, is provided in Table 3 in the section on emissions limits. This standard also prescribes limits for evaporative emissions.

Fig. 4: Japan test cycles
a) 11-mode cycle (cold test)

Cycle length:	1.021 km
No. of cycles per test:	4
Average speed:	30.6 km/h
Maximum speed:	60 km/h

b) 10•15-mode cycle (hot test)

Cycle length:	4.16 km
No. of cycles per test:	1
Average speed:	22.7 km/h
Maximum speed:	70 km/h

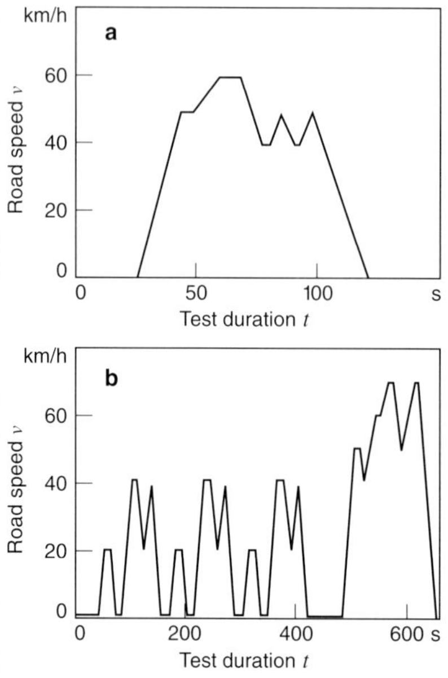

Japanese test cycle

Two test cycles with different hypothetical driving curves are included in this composite test:

Following a cold start, the 11-mode cycle is run through four times, and all four cycles are evaluated. The 10•15-mode test is absolved once as a warm test (Fig. 4).

The conditioning phase for the warm start includes the prescribed idle-emissions test, and proceeds as follows:

First, the vehicle is driven through a 15-minute warm-up phase at a speed of 60 km/h. Then the concentrations of HC, CO and CO_2 are measured at the exhaust pipe. After a further 5-minute warm-up period at 60 km/h, the 10•15-mode warm test is started. A CVS system is employed for exhaust-gas analysis in both 11-mode and 10•15-mode testing. The diluted exhaust gases are collected in bags in both tests. The emissions limits for the cold test are specified in g/test, while the limits for the warm test are expressed relative to distance, viz., converted to grams per kilometer (Table 4).

The Japanese regulations include limits on evaporative emissions, with testing using the SHED method.

Comparison of test procedures and limits

A direct comparison of the various emissions regulations is made difficult by the discrepancies between the test cycles and the associated differences in engine load. However, it can be maintained that the most stringent of current emissions limits are those applied in the USA.

Exhaust-gas analyzers

Legislation reflects govermental efforts to reduce the quantities of toxic subtances in exhaust gases by mandating regular testing for vehicles currently in service. In Germany, the CO content of the exhaust is checked at fixed intervals, in the course of the emissions test (AU) prescribed in Paragraph 29 of the StVZO (FMVSS/CUR). Exhaust-gas analyzers are indispensable service tools, necessary for both optimal mixture adjustment and for effective trouble-shooting on the engine.

Test procedures

Required is the ability to carry out precise measurements of the individual exhaust-gas components. This has led automotive service facilities to adopt the infrared method as the only suitable means for testing exhaust gases. This method bases on the fact that individual exhaust-gas components absorb infrared light at various specific rates, according to their characteristic wave lengths.
Available units include single-component analyzers (e.g., for CO) as well as multi-component devices (for CO/HC, CO/CO_2, $CO/HC/CO_2$, etc.).

Test chamber

Infrared radiation is transmitted from an emitter heated to approximately 700°C. The infrared beam passes through a measuring cell before entering the receiver chamber. If the CO content is being measured, the sealed receiver chamber contains gas with a defined CO content. This absorbs a portion of the CO-specific radiation. This absorption is accompanied by an increase in the temperature of the gas, producing a gas current which flows via the flow sensor from volume V_1 into compensating volume V_2. A rotating "chopper" disk induces a rhythmic interruption in the beam, producing an alternating flow between volumes V_1 and V_2. The flow sensor converts this motion into an alternating electrical signal. When a test

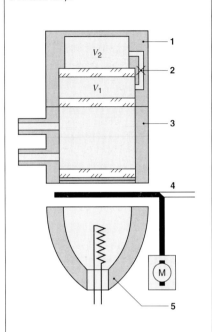

Fig. 5: Measuring chamber, infrared method (principle)
1 Receiving chamber with compensating volumes V_1 and V_2, 2 Flow sensor, 3 Test cell,
4 Rotating chopper disk with motor,
5 Infrared lamp.

gas with a variable CO content flows through the measuring cell, it absorbs radiant energy in quantities proportional to its CO content; the energy is then no longer available in the receiver chamber. The deviation from the alternating base signal serves as an index of the CO content in the test gas.

Gas path

A probe is employed to extract the test gas from the vehicle's exhaust system (1, Fig. 6). The tester's integral diaphragm pump (6) extracts the gas, drawing it through the coarse filter (2) in the water trap (3) to filter out condensation and larger particulates before subsequent treatment at the fine filter (4). The solenoid valve (5) located upstream from the diaphragm pump switches the inlet to the test chamber from exhaust gas to air, at which point the system automatically calibrates to zero. Backup filters located in both entries prevent particulates from entering the test chamber, which is also sealed against condensation of the kind that could enter the system if the water trap were not emptied. The restriction in the tank (10) serves to increase the pressure in the safety reservoir (8), inducing flow to the test chamber via bypass circuit. Gravity pulls any moisture drawn into the system back into the tank, whence it escapes back into the atmosphere. The pressure switch (7) monitors gas flow to ensure that incoming quantities are adequate. The restrictor in the safety reservoir raises the pressure at the pump outlet, activating the pressure switch. Any interruptions in gas flow will deactivate it, and the display will indicate a test error to the unit's operator (Fig. 6).

Testing the catalytic converter

A representative component can be used to obtain an indirect measurement of converter operation on vehicles with closed-loop-controlled catalytic devices. The best proxy is CO, which should not exceed 0.2% of volume downstream of the catalytic converter, whereby it is essential that lambda be maintained at exactly $\lambda = 1$ (± 0.01).

Lambda, in turn, is determined based on the composition of the exhaust gases emerging from the catalytic converter. The exhaust-gas analyzer determines lambda with the requisite accuracy using measurements based on the CO, HC, CO_2 and O_2 in the exhaust gas, with constants being employed for NO and fuel composition.

The O_2 content is determined by an electrochemical probe.

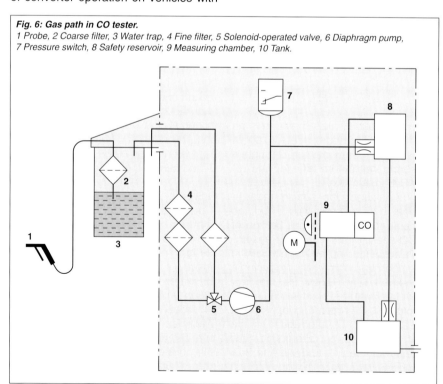

Fig. 6: Gas path in CO tester.
1 Probe, 2 Coarse filter, 3 Water trap, 4 Fine filter, 5 Solenoid-operated valve, 6 Diaphragm pump, 7 Pressure switch, 8 Safety reservoir, 9 Measuring chamber, 10 Tank.

Emission limits

Table 1.
Limits for US FED (49 states) and California.
FTP 75 test cycle.

Model year	Region	CO g/km	HC g/km	NO$_x$ g/km	Evaporation g/test
Since 1982	FED	3.41[1]	0.41	1.0[1]	2.0
	CAL	7.0	0.41	0.4[1]	2.0
1993	CAL	3.4	0.25	0.4	2.0
1994	FED	3.4	0.25	0.4	2.0

[1] Exceptions may be approved under certain conditions.

Table 2.
Limits for Switzerland, Austria, Sweden, Norway, Finland, Mexico, Brazil, Australia, South Korea.
FTP 75 test cycle.

Country	Date of introduction	CO g/km	HC g/km	NO$_x$ g/km	Evaporation g/test
Switzerland	10.87	2.1	0.25	0.62	2.0
Austria	87/88	2.1	0.25	0.62	2.0
Sweden	Model year 89	2.1	0.25	0.62	2.0
Norway	1989	2.1	0.25	0.62	2.0
Finland	1990	2.1	0.25	0.62	2.0
Mexico	1991	7.0	0.7	1.4	2.0
Brazil	1.92	12.0	1.2	1.4	–
	1.97	2.0	0.3	0.6	–
Australia	1.86	9.3	0.9	1.9	2.0
Country	Date of introduction	CO g/km	HC g/km	NO$_x$ g/km	Evaporation g/test
Canada	9.87	3.4	0.41	1.0	2.0
South Korea	Model year 88	3.4	0.41	1.0	2.0

Table 3.
Emission limits in the EC.
ECE/EEC test cycle.

Passenger car	Date of introduction		Regulation	CO g/km	HC+NO$_x$ g/km
	New Types	Initial registrations			
All swept-volume classes	1.7.92	31.12.92	91/441/EWG	2.72	0.97

Table 4.
Limits for Japan.
Japanese test cycles.

Test procedure	CO	HC	NO$_x$	Evaporation
10•15-mode (g/km)	2.1	0.25	0.25	–
11-mode (g/test)	60.0	7.0	4.4	–
SHED	–	–	–	2.0

Mixture formation

Overview

Parameters

Air-fuel mixture

The spark-ignition engine requires a specific air/fuel ratio (A/F ratio) in order to operate. The theoretical ideal for complete combustion is 14.7:1, and is referred to as the stoichiometric ratio. Mixture corrections are required to satisfy the special engine demands encountered under particular operating conditions.

The specific fuel consumption of the spark-ignition engine is largely a function of the A/F ratio. In theory, excess air is required to achieve the minimum fuel consumption that would result from complete combustion. In practice, however, latitude is restricted by factors such as mixture flammability and limits on the time available for combustion.

On contemporary engines, minimum fuel consumption is encountered at an A/F ratio corresponding to approximately 15...18 kg air for each kg of fuel. In other words, about 10,000 litres of air are required to support combustion in one litre of fuel (Figure 1).

Because automotive powerplants spend most of their time operating at part-throttle, engines are designed for minimum fuel consumption in this range. Mixtures containing a higher proportion of fuel provide better performance under other conditions such as idle and full-throttle operation. The mixture-formation system must be capable of satisfying these variegated requirements.

Excess-air factor

The excess-air factor (or air ratio) λ has been chosen to indicate how far the actual air-fuel mixture deviates from the theoretical optimum (14.7:1).

λ = Induction air mass/air requirement for stoichiometeric combustion

$\lambda = 1$: The induction air mass corresponds to the theoretical requirement.
$\lambda < 1$: Air deficiency, rich mixture. Increased output is available at $\lambda = 0.85...0.95$.
$\lambda > 1$: Excess air (lean mixture) in the range $\lambda = 1.05...1.3$. Excess-air factors in this range result in lower fuel consumption accompanied by reduced performance.
$\lambda > 1.3$: The mixture ceases to be ignitable. Ignition miss occurs, accompanied by pronounced loss of operating smoothness.

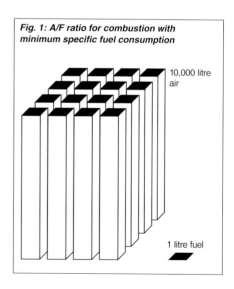

Fig. 1: A/F ratio for combustion with minimum specific fuel consumption

10,000 litre air

1 litre fuel

Spark-ignition engines achieve their maximum output at air-deficiency levels of 5...15% ($\lambda = 0.95...0.85$), while minimum fuel consumption is achieved with an air excess of 10...20% ($\lambda = 1.1...1.2$). $\lambda = 1$ provides optimum idling characteristics.

Figures 2 and 3 illustrate the effect of the excess-air factor λ on output, specific fuel consumption and exhaust emissions. It will be noted that no single excess-air factor can simultaneously generate optimal response in all areas. Air factors ranging from λ 0.9...1.1 provide the best results in actual practice.

Once the engine has reached its normal operating temperature, it is essential that $\lambda = 1$ be maintained to support subsequent exhaust treatment with a three-way catalytic converter. The preconditions for satisfying this requirement are precise determination of the induction-air quantity accompanied by an arrangement capable of providing exact fuel metering.

To ensure a satisfactory combustion process, precise fuel metering must be accompanied by homogeneous mixture formation. The fuel must be thoroughly atomized. If this condition is not satisfied, large fuel droplets will form along the walls of the inlet tract, leading to higher HC emisssions.

Adapting to specific operating conditions

Certain operating states will cause the fuel requirement to deviate considerably from that required by a stationary engine at normal operating temperature; the mixture must be corrected accordingly.

Cold starts

During cold starts, the relative amount of fuel in the mixture decreases; the mixture "goes lean." Inadequate blending of fuel and air in the intake mixture, low fuel vaporization and condensation on the walls of the intake tract due to the low temperatures, all contribute to this phenomenon. To compensate, and to assist the cold engine in "getting started," supplementary fuel must be made available for starting.

Post-start phase

After starts at low temperatures, supplementary fuel must be provided to enrich the mixture until the combustion chamber heats up and the mixture formation within the cylinder improves. The richer mixture also increases torque to provide a smoother transition to the desired idle speed.

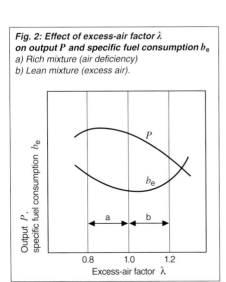

Fig. 2: Effect of excess-air factor λ on output P and specific fuel consumption b_e
a) Rich mixture (air deficiency)
b) Lean mixture (excess air).

Output P, specific fuel consumption b_e

0.8   1.0   1.2
Excess-air factor λ

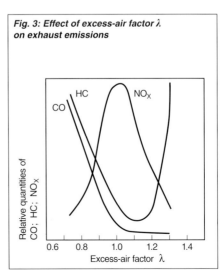

Fig. 3: Effect of excess-air factor λ on exhaust emissions

Relative quantities of CO; HC; NO$_X$

0.6   0.8   1.0   1.2   1.4
Excess-air factor λ

Warm-up phase

The starting and post-start phases are followed by the engine's warm-up phase. In this phase the engine still requires a richer mixture, as the cylinder walls are still cool, and a portion of the fuel continues to condense on them. Since the quality of mixture formation drops along with failing temperatures (due to less effective mixing of air and fuel, and large fuel droplets), condensation forms in the intake manifold, where it remains until it is vaporized as temperatures increase. These factors make it necessary to provide progressive mixture enrichment in response to decreasing temperatures.

Part-throttle operation

During part-throttle operation priority is assigned to adjusting the mixture for minimum fuel consumption. The three-way catalytic converters required to meet stringent emissions limits are making it increasingly important to control the systems for $\lambda = 1$.

Full-throttle operation

When the throttle valve has opened to its maximum aperture, the engine should respond by providing its maximum torque/output. As Figure 2 indicates, this necessitates enrichening the air-fuel mixture to $\lambda = 0.85 \ldots 0.90$.

Acceleration

When the throttle valve opens suddenly, the air-fuel mixture responds by leaning out briefly. This is due to the fuel's - restricted vaporization potential at higher manifold vacuum levels (increased tendency to form fuel layers on intake-tract walls).

To obtain good transition response, the mixture must be enriched by an amount which varies according to engine temperature. This enrichment provides good acceleration response.

Trailing-throttle (overrun) operation

The fuel-metering process can be interrupted on trailing throttle to reduce fuel consumption during descents and under braking. Another advantage is the fact that no harmful exhaust emissions are generated in this operating mode.

High-altitude adjustment

Increases in altitude (as encountered during alpine operation) are accompanied by a reduction in air density. This means that the intake air being drawn into the engine at high altitudes displays a lower mass per unit of volume. A system which fails to adjust the mixture accordingly will supply an excessively rich mixture, and the ultimate result will be higher fuel consumption and increased exhaust emissions.

Mixture-formation systems

The function of the carburetor or fuel-injection system is to supply the engine with the optimum air-fuel mixture for instantaneous operating conditions. For some years now, fuel injection has represented the preferred method, a development accelerated by the advantages that injecting the fuel provides in the areas of economy, performance, driveability and low exhaust emissions. Fuel injection can be applied for extremely precise metering, supplying exactly the correct amount of fuel for given operating and load conditions while simultaneously ensuring minimum levels of exhaust emissions. The composition of the mixture is controlled to maintain low emissions.

Multipoint fuel injection

Multipoint injection supplies the ideal starting point for meeting these objectives. The multipoint injection system uses a separate injector to inject the fuel directly through the intake valve at each individual cylinder. Examples of this type of design are the KE- and L-Jetronic in their various individual configurations (Figure 4).

Mechanical injection system

K-Jetronic is a mechanical injection system in widespread use. This driveless system injects the fuel in a continuous process.

Combined mechanical and electronic injection system

KE-Jetronic is an expanded version of the basic K-Jetronic system. It monitors an extended range of operating data for electronic open-loop control of auxiliary functions to provide more precise fuel metering under varying engine operating conditions.

Electronic injection systems

Electronically-controlled injection systems use electro-magnetic injectors to inject the fuel intermittently.
Examples:
L-Jetronic, LH-Jetronic, and the Motronic integrated fuel-injection and ignition system.

Single-point (throttle-body, central) fuel injection

Single-point fuel injection describes an electronically-controlled injection unit featuring an electromagnetic injector located directly above the throttle valve. This injector sprays fuel into the intake manifold in an intermittent pattern.
Mono-Jetronic is the brand name of the Bosch single-point injection system (Figure 5).

Advantages of fuel injection

Reduced fuel consumption

This system monitors all essential engine operating data (e.g., engine speed, load, temperature, throttle-valve aperture) for precise adaptation to stationary and dynamic operating conditions, thereby ensuring that the engine receives only the amount of fuel that it actually requires under any given circumstances.

Improved performance

K- and L-Jetronic allow greater latitude in intake-tract design for better cylinder-

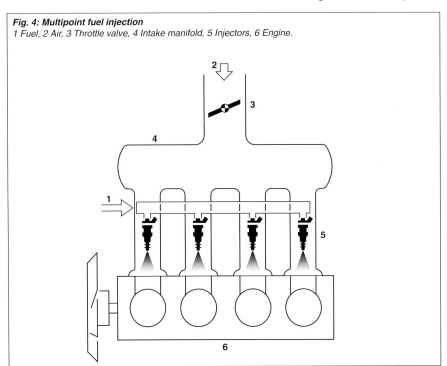

Fig. 4: Multipoint fuel injection
1 Fuel, 2 Air, 3 Throttle valve, 4 Intake manifold, 5 Injectors, 6 Engine.

filling (volumetric efficiency) and higher torque. The results are enhanced specific output and an improved torque curve. Mono-Jetronic also conforms with standard practice in incorporating separate arrangements for measuring air and metering fuel; the reduction in the length of the throttled section of the intact tract also provides higher outputs (compared with the carburetor).

Immediate acceleration response

All Jetronic units adapt to changes in load state with virtually no delay.

This applies to both the single-point and multipoint injection systems:

The multipoint systems spray the fuel directly toward the intake valves, effectively banishing virtually all problems associated with intake-tract condensation. With single-point injection, the extended mixture-transport paths make it necessary to compensate for the creation and depletion of condensate layers during transitions. This is achieved by incorporating special design features in the systems used to meter and mix the fuel.

Improved cold starting and warm-up behavior

The fuel is precisely metered according to the engine temperature and starter speed to ensure rapid starts and a rapid climb to a steady idle.

In the warm-up phase, the system supplies exactly the correct fuel quantity for combining smooth running and immediate throttle response with the lowest possible fuel consumption.

Low exhaust emissions

The air-fuel mixture exercises a direct influence on the concentration of harmful emissions in the exhaust gases. If the engine is to be operated with a minimal level of exhaust emissions, then the mixture-formation system must be capable of maintaining a specific air/fuel ratio.

The operating accuracy of the Jetronic units allow them to maintain the required levels of precise mixture formation.

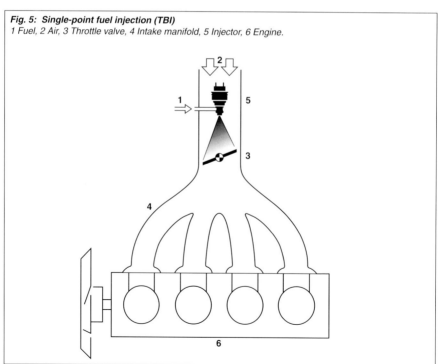

Fig. 5: Single-point fuel injection (TBI)
1 Fuel, 2 Air, 3 Throttle valve, 4 Intake manifold, 5 Injector, 6 Engine.

The story of fuel injection

The story of fuel injection extends back to cover a period of almost one hundred years.

The Gasmotorenfabik Deutz was manufacturing plunger pumps for injecting fuel in a limited production series as early as 1898.

A short time later the uses of the venturi-effect for carburetor design were discovered, and fuel-injection systems based on the technology of the time ceased to be competitive.

Bosch started research on gasoline-injection pumps in 1912. The first aircraft engine featuring Bosch fuel injection, a 1200-hp unit, entered series production in 1937; problems with carburetor icing and fire hazards had lent special impetus to fuel-injection development work for the aeronautics field. This development marks the beginning of the era of fuel injection at Bosch, but there was still a long path to travel on the way to fuel injection for passenger cars.

1951 saw a Bosch direct-injection unit being featured as standard equipment on a small car for the first time. Several years later a unit was installed in the 300 SL, the legendary production sports car from Daimler-Benz.

In the years that followed, development on mechanical injection pumps continued, and...

In 1967 fuel injection took another giant step forward: The first electronic injection system: the intake-pressure-controlled D-Jetronic!

In 1973 the air-flow-controlled L-Jetronic appeared on the market, at the same time as the K-Jetronic, which featured mechanical-hydraulic control as well as an air-flow sensor.

1979 marked the introduction of a new system: Motronic, featuring digital processing for numerous engine functions. This system combined L-Jetronic with electronic program-map control for the ignition. The first automotive microprocessor!

In 1982, the K-Jetronic model became available in an expanded configuration including an electronic closed-loop control circuit and a Lambda oxygen sensor the KE-Jetronic.

These were joined by Bosch Mono-Jetronic in 1983: This particularly cost-efficient single-point injection unit made it feasible to equip small vehicles with Jetronic.

1991 saw Bosch fuel-injection units performing in more than 37 million vehicles throughout the world.

5.6 million engine-management systems were delivered in 1992. Of this number, 2.5 million were Mono-Jetronic and Mono-Motronic systems, with 2 million Motronic systems being supplied within the same period. Today fuel-injection systems have become an essential automotive component.

*Bosch gasoline fuel injection
from the year 1954*

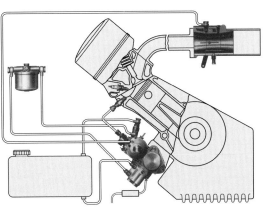

Air supply

Air filters

The air filter helps inhibit internal wear by preventing air-borne dust from being drawn into the engine.

On paved roads, the air's average dust content is about $1\,mg/m^3$; however, on unpaved roads and in construction areas it can range as high as $40\,mg/m^3$. This means that depending on roads and operating conditions, a medium-sized engine can draw in up to $50\,g$ of dust over $1000\,km$.

Passenger-car air filters

Paper elements, contained in centrally located or fender-mounted housings, serve as practical and efficient filters on passenger cars (Figures 1 and 2). In addition to filtering the intake air, these units preheat and regulate its temperature, as well as attenuating intake noise. Intake-air temperature regulation helps ensure smooth response, and also affects exhaust-gas composition. Different air temperatures may be used for part and full-throttle operation.

The hot-air intake is located adjacent to the exhaust system; a flap mechanism is employed to meter the hot air from this source into the cooler stream of fresh intake air. The regulating mechanism is usually an automatic device, and is controlled either by a pneumatic vacuum unit connected to the intake manifold or by an expansion element. The controlled (and thus constant) intake-air temperature contributes to better fuel management and improves distribution of the air-fuel mixture, paying dividends in the areas of output, fuel economy and emissions.

Commercial-vehicle air filters

Most of the air filters used in commercial vehicles are of the paper-element type, although oil-bath filters are found in some

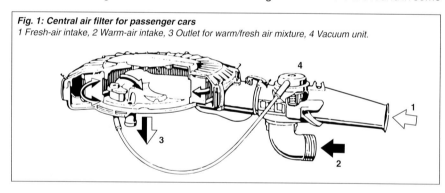

Fig. 1: Central air filter for passenger cars
1 Fresh-air intake, 2 Warm-air intake, 3 Outlet for warm/fresh air mixture, 4 Vacuum unit.

Fig. 2: Fender-mounted air filter for passenger cars
1 Fresh-air intake, 2 Warm-air intake, 3 Outlet for warm/fresh air mixture.

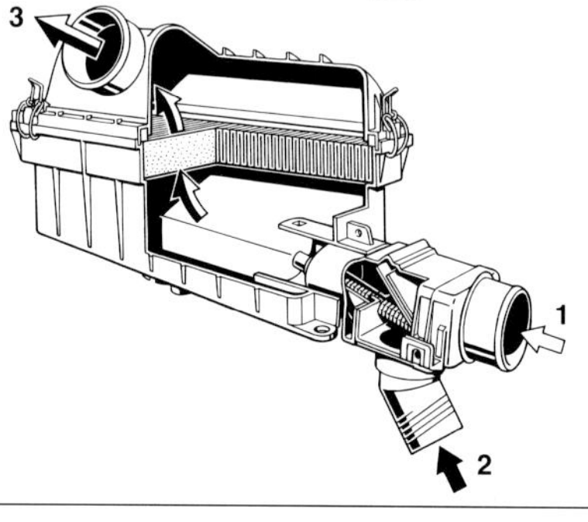

Fig. 3: Paper air filter with cyclone for commercial vehicles
1 Air inlet, 2 Air outlet,
3 Cyclone vanes,
4 Filter element,
5 Dust bowl.

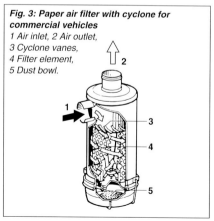

applications. Characteristic for paper filters are high filtering efficiency in all load ranges, and higher flow resistance as levels of retained contaminants increase. The paper element may be supplemented by a cyclone prefilter, incorporated in the housing to save space (Fig. 3). This combination is the current configuration of choice. Service entails replacing the element and/or emptying the dust cup.

Superchargers

Supercharger processes

An engine's output is directly proportional to the air mass that can be pumped through it. The air's mass, in turn, is a function of its density. It is therefore possible to increase output by compressing the charge before it enters the cylinder. The boost ratio is the increase in density as compared to a naturally aspirated engine. It depends upon the system used (obtainable pressure ratio) and, given a specific increase in pressure, is at a maximum when the temperature of the compressed air (charging air) is not increased, or is returned to its initial value by intercooling. On spark-ignition engines, the maximum boost is defined by the engine's knock limit – this is why supercharged (turbocharged) engines usually feature a lower compression ratio than their naturally-aspirated counterparts.

Intercoolers

Cooling the boost air reduces the thermal loading of the engine while furnishing simultaneous reductions in exhaust-gas temperature, NO_x emissions and fuel consumption. It also increases the resistance to knock on spark-ignition engines. The intercooler can employ either atmospheric air or the engine's coolant to remove heat from the charge, depending on design. Air-to-air intercoolers are the most popular for application in both passenger cars and commercial vehicles.

Dynamic supercharging

The most basic type of supercharging exploits the intake charge's own intrinsic dynamic response.
The following systems utilize these dynamic characteristics with intake manifolds designed to obtain an intake boost effect from:
– ram-effect supercharging, and
– tuned-intake (resonance) devices.
Both of these designs can be used in combination with the variable-configuration intake manifolds (Fig. 4) offered by several manufacturers.

Mechanical superchargers

The engine provides the motive power for the mechanical supercharger via a positive coupling (mechanical coupling between engine and compressor). The supercharger generally operates at a fixed ratio of engine speed. Mechanical and electromagnetic clutches are often

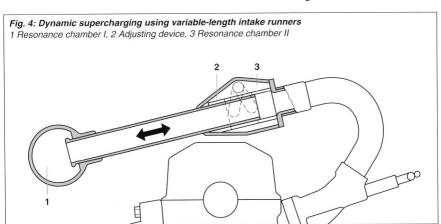

Fig. 4: Dynamic supercharging using variable-length intake runners
1 Resonance chamber I, 2 Adjusting device, 3 Resonance chamber II

2   3

1

used for selective control of supercharger operation.

If a supercharger is to be suitable for use in automotive applications, then it must deliver air at a rate characterized by a fixed, linear relationship to the unit's own speed. In other words, positive-displacement pumps using piston, rotating-vane or Roots configurations. Centrifugal turbo-compressors are not suitable for these applications.

Exhaust-gas turbocharging

The turbocharger taps the energy to power its compressor (impeller) from the engine's exhaust stream (hydrodynamic coupling between engine and compressor). This design exploits expansion energy that otherwise remains unutilized in a naturally-aspirated engine (due to expansion conditions imposed by the crank mechanism). At the same time, the turbocharger creates higher back pressure in its power source – the exhaust gases – as they leave the engine.

In today's turbocharged engines, an exhaust turbine converts the energy in the exhaust gas into mechanical energy, making it possible to use a dynamic turbo-compressor (impeller) to compress the incoming air (Fig. 5).

Pressure-wave supercharging

Pressure-wave supercharging employs a direct exchange of energy between the exhaust gas and the intake air to compress the latter (physical and hydrodynamic coupling). The concept exploits the differences in the velocities of the gas molecules and pressure waves, as well as their respective reflection properties.

The principle advantages of the pressure-wave supercharger are rapid response during load transitions and high compression rates at modest engine speeds.

Turbochargers and superchargers (self-charging)

On internal-combustion engines, turbochargers and superchargers both work by compressing the intake air used to support the fuel's combustion. This increases the amount of air an individual engine of defined displacement will process at any given engine speed, and results in increased volumetric efficiency. We distinguish between:
– superchargers,
– turbochargers, and
– pressure-wave superchargers.

Superchargers

The mechanically-driven superchargers include:
– centrifugal, and
– positive-displacement superchargers.

Fig. 5: Torque curves of naturally aspirated engine and engine with exhaust-gas turbocharging

Turbocharged engine, stationary

Naturally aspirated engine

Turbocharged engine, transient operation

Engine torque M_d

Engine speed n_n

$\frac{1}{4}$ $\frac{1}{2}$ $\frac{3}{4}$ $\frac{1}{1}$

Fig. 6: Spiral-type compressor
1 Air intake into second working chamber,
2 Drive shaft, 3 Displacer guide, 4 Air intake into primary working chamber, 5 Housing,
6 Displacer element

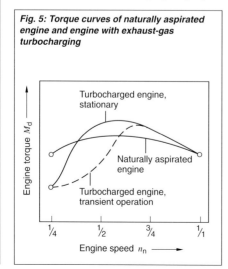

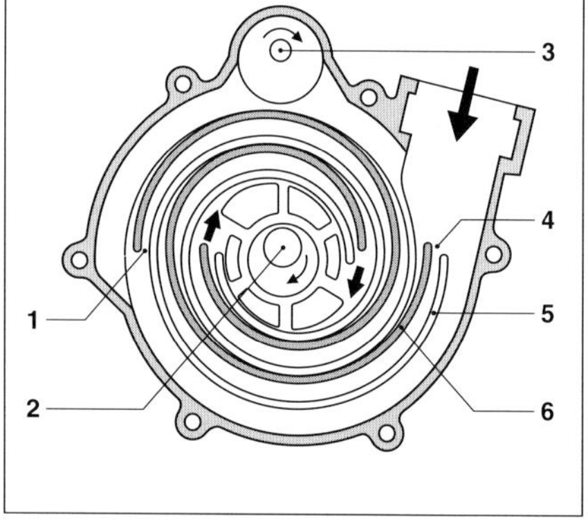

1
2
3
4
5
6

Application of mechanical centrifugal superchargers remains limited to a small number of mid-sized and larger diesel and spark-ignition engines for passenger cars.

Positive-displacement superchargers operate with and without internal compression. The internal compression designs include:
– reciprocating piston,
– screw-type,
– rotary piston,
– sliding vane, and
– spiral-type (Fig. 6).
The Roots supercharger (Fig. 7) operates without internal compression.

Superchargers on internal-combustion engines are usually belt-driven. The coupling is either direct (constant operation) or via a clutch (e.g., solenoid clutch with demand activation). Throughout the engine-speed range, the conversion ratio may be constant, or it may vary.

Mechanical positive-displacement superchargers must be substantially larger than their centrifugal counterparts to produce a given mass flow rate. Mechanical positive-displacement superchargers are generally applied on small and medium-displacement engines in passenger cars, where the ratio between flow volume and space requirements remains acceptable.

Exhaust-gas turbochargers

The exhaust-gas turbocharger consists of two turbo-elements on a common shaft: the turbine and the compressor (impeller). The turbine uses the exhaust-gas flow energy to drive the compressor. The compressor, in turn, draws in fresh air and supplies it to the cylinders in compressed form. The air and the mass flow of exhaust gases represent the only coupling between the engine and the turbocharger. There is no direct relationship between the respective rotating speeds of turbocharger and engine; the turbocharger speed is a function of the energy balance between turbine and compressor.

Exhaust-gas turbochargers are installed in passenger cars, trucks, and on industrial engines, with different designs being applied for specific applications. Despite design differences, the basic configuration remains constant. The main elements are the:
– turbine and compressor assembly,
– bearing housing, and
– compressor housing.

Depending upon the specific application, a wide variety of designs are employed for the
– turbine housing, and
– control elements (wastegate, etc.).

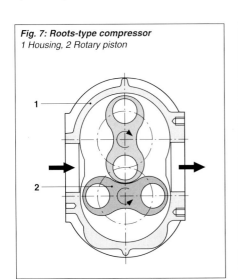

Fig. 7: Roots-type compressor
1 Housing, 2 Rotary piston

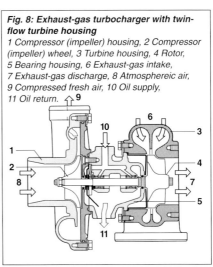

Fig. 8: Exhaust-gas turbocharger with twin-flow turbine housing
1 Compressor (impeller) housing, 2 Compressor (impeller) wheel, 3 Turbine housing, 4 Rotor, 5 Bearing housing, 6 Exhaust-gas intake, 7 Exhaust-gas discharge, 8 Atmosphereic air, 9 Compressed fresh air, 10 Oil supply, 11 Oil return.

pressure-wave propagation process (Fig. 9).

Within the rotor, the actual energy-exchange process proceeds at the speed of sound. This velocity is a function of exhaust-gas temperature, and thus of engine torque, not absolute engine speed. Because the energy exchange within the rotor occurs at the speed of sound, supercharger boost pressure responds rapidly to changes in engine demand; the precise response times are determined by the charging processes in the intake and exhaust systems.

An integral governing device regulates boost pressure to suit demand.

Intake air control

The electronic engine-management system monitors all essential operating data for its primary functions (mixture formation and ignition); the same data are thus available for integration in enhanced control systems. Such systems ensure optimum exploitation of the supercharging devices described above while discharging numerous supplementary functions. Systems that were initially independent, such as fuel injection and ignition, become integral components in an extended engine-management system featuring ever higher levels of system integration.

The most important of these integrated functions are described below:

Idle-speed control

The intake air flow, the excess-air factor λ and the ignition timing all affect the spark-ignition engine's idle speed. The idle can be adjusted by changing the air quantity (charge adjustment) and/or the ignition timing (ignition adjustment). Governing idle speed by varying the cylinder charge (idle-speed control, air adjustment) is an efficient method and has come to be accepted as standard (Fig. 10).

The control devices are designed to ensure stable, minimum idle speeds for low emissions and enhanced fuel eco-

Turbochargers for trucks feature a twin-flow housing in which the two streams merge just before reaching the impeller (Fig. 8). This housing layout is employed to achieve pulse turbocharging, in which the primary pressure of the exhaust gas is supplemented by its kinetic energy.

The turbochargers installed on passenger cars generally feature single-channel turbine housings. However, some form of turbocharger-governing mechanism is required to maintain relatively constant pressure levels throughout the car engine's wide rpm range. Control for this device (wastegate, bypass valve) is generally either pneumatic-mechanical or electronic.

Pressure-wave supercharger

The pressure-wave supercharger exploits the dynamic properties of gases, using pressure waves to convey energy from the exhaust gas to the intake air. This exchange takes place within the cells of a rotor. This cell-type rotor depends upon an engine-driven belt for synchronization, and for maintaining the

nomy throughout the vehicle's service life (maintenance-free systems).

Sensors monitor engine speed, coolant temperature and throttle position; and furthermore the system can also monitor the loads imposed by such devices as automatic transmission, air conditioning, power steering, and other influencing quantities. The electronic controller compares the actual current idle speed with the desired (setpoint) speed. It then transmits a signal to the idle actuator, which adjusts to the desired idle speed by increasing or decreasing the flow of air.

Electronic Throttle Control (ETC)

ETC ("E gas," "drive-by-wire") represents a departure from the conventional mechanical linkages that rely on levers and bowden cables to control throttle-valve position. Instead, it uses an ECU and an electric motor. The system is thus capable of controlling throttle-valve position with reference to numerous operating parameters, and can also assume tasks such as torque reduction for electronic traction control (ASR).

A travel sensor monitors the position of the accelerator pedal and transmits a corresponding signal to the ECU. The ECU refers to input signals from other sources (e.g., ASR, Motronic) in proces-

sing this travel-sensor signal as the basis for its control signal back to the throttle actuator. A potentiometer located within the throttle actuator provides the ECU with feedback, making it possible to apply a position control loop to ensure precise throttle-angle adjustment (Fig. 11).

The ECU constantly monitors all components to ensure that the system is operating correctly. Dual sensors are complemented by two ECU processor circuits; this system redundancy facilitates signal comparisons for a supplementary systems check.

In addition to those systems in which the connection between accelerator pedal and actuator is exclusively electrical, there also exist arrangements in which a supplementary transfer element (such as a bowden cable) is provided to supply a backup mechanism, allowing continued vehicle operation if a system error leads to actuator switch-off.

Because it controls the throttle valve electronically, the Electronic Throttle Control (ETC) can assume various supplementary functions to enhance driving safety and convenience and provide more efficient engine management. The safety features include both ASR and engine drag-torque control (MSR), which employs programmed throttle openings

Fig. 10: Idle-speed control using cylinder-charge adjustment
1 Idle actuator, 2 Electronic idle controller, 3 Throttle valve.
U_B *supply voltage,* n *Engine speed,*
T_M *Engine temperature,* α_{DK} *Throttle position,*
D/AC Signal from automatic transmission/air-conditioner.

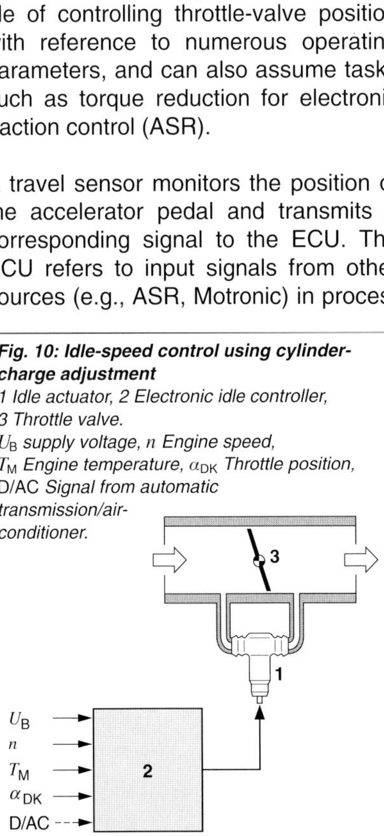

Fig. 11: Electronic engine-power control (EMS)
1 Accelerator pedal, 2 Pedal-position sensor, 3 ECU with 3a microcomputer, and 3b data bus, 4 Throttle actuator.

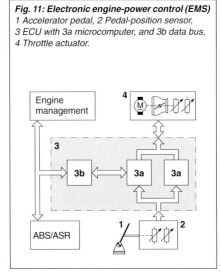

to reduce engine braking to uncritical levels and help prevent traction loss at the drive wheels.

Comfort and convenience features include cruise control and the option of using ETC to smooth the vehicle's transient response characteristics during sudden acceleration and deceleration.

Electronic boost-pressure control

Turbochargers must attain their specified boost pressures, but they should also provide good response (pressure build-up) at low engine speeds. The design objects are high low-speed boost, balanced pressure – and thus torque – characteristics at all engine speeds and pedal positions, and optimum levels of volumetric efficiency. The ability of the mechanically-regulated turbocharger to achieve these objectives is limited.

In contrast, an electronic wastegate mechanism, together with the appropriate turbocharger, combines a virtually ideal boost curve, extending throughout the engine's operating range, with good transition response. The boost-pressure data for all engine loads and speeds are stored in program maps; the load index can be supplied by manifold pressure, or this data can be derived from the intake-air flow or mass.

To ensure consistently efficient operation, the boost-pressure control device always works in tandem with a knock-control system. This allows the engine to run on maximum timing advance while remaining immune to knock damage (Fig. 12). Should the system determine that excessively retarded timing is posing a threat to the turbo-charger, it starts by enriching the air-fuel mixture to protect the turbocharger from excessive exhaust-gas temperatures. Should this prove insufficient, the system lowers the boost pressure.

Fig. 12: Combined knock and boost control
1 Intake air, 2 Compressor, 3 Turbine, 4 To exhaust system , 5 Waste-gate control valve, 6 Throttle valve, 7 Throttle-valve potentiometer, 8 Temperature sensor, 9 Knock sensor, 10 Control valve, 11 ECU. p_1 Pressure before compressor, p_2 Boost pressure, p_2' Intake-manifold pressure, p_3 Exhaust back pressure, S_K Knock-sensor signal, S_R Engine-speed signal, T_L Boost-air temperature, V_A Exhaust-gas volumetric flow, V_T Volumetric flow through turbine, V_W Volumetric flow through wastegate, α_D Throttle-valve angle, α_Z Ignition advance angle.

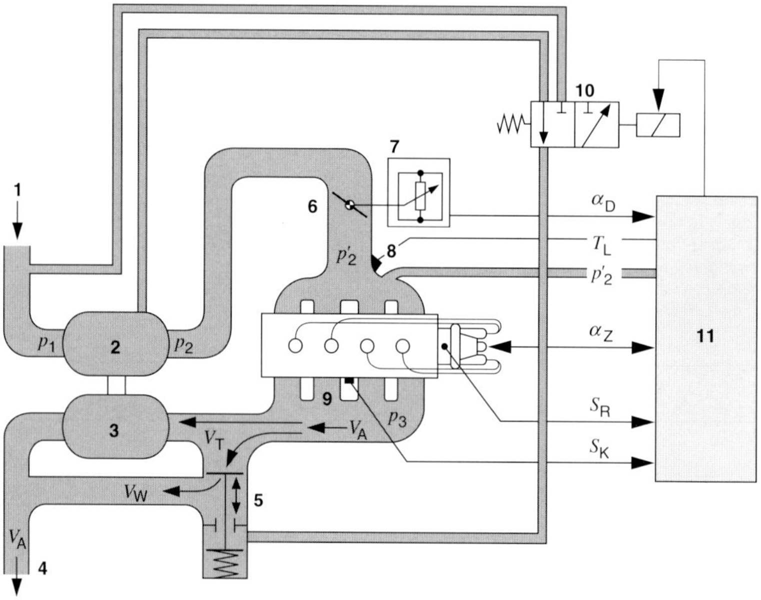

Exhaust-gas recirculation (EGR)

Exhaust-gas recirculation (EGR) provides an effective means of reducing nitrous oxide emissions. The system adds (combusted) exhaust gases to the fresh air-fuel mixture in order to reduce peak combustion temperatures. This reduces heat-related emissions of nitrous-oxides.

A degree of "internal" exhaust-gas recirculation, occurring during overlap between intake and exhaust valves, is an inherent design feature of all internal-combustion engines. A certain amount of residual exhaust gas – determined by the degree of overlap – is re-inducted along with the fresh air-fuel mixture. On engines with variable valve timing, it would theoretically be possible to influence NO_x emissions by varying the rate of internal exhaust-gas recirculation.

Virtually all of the EGR systems used on today's cars operate according to the principles of "external" exhaust-gas recirculation. A specific proportion of the engine's exhaust gas is extracted and returned to the fresh air-fuel mixture via control valve. The recirculation of exhaust gases is generally governed by a pneumatic or mechanical system designed to meter exhaust gases according to factors such as engine speed, manifold pressure and engine temperature. In some systems (e.g., Motronic) the ECU employs an electropneumatic transducer to activate the EGR valve.

EGR can be used to reduce emissions of NO_x by up to 40%. Increases in HC emissions combine with rougher engine operation to impose an upper limit on the recirculation rate. Thus the EGR is deactivated at idle, when no significant NO_x emissions are generated in any case.

Exhaust-gas recirculation is generally activated during part-throttle operation, where it is most effective. Unfavorable pressure conditions limit the application of EGR at extreme load factors.

Evaporative-emissions control systems

As fuel in the tank evaporates, hydrocarbons escape into the atmosphere. The rate at which this occurs increases as a function of temperature. Compliance with official regulations governing evaporative emissions is achieved by installing activated charcoal canisters to store the vapors emanating from the tank, which is then vented exclusively via the canister. However, the canister's limited storage volume means that the charcoal must be continually regenerated.

With the engine running, air is drawn through the charcoal canister and into the engine for combustion. To ensure smooth operation and maintain compliance with the regulations governing exhaust emissions, the engine-management system governs the recirculation rate using a so-called canister-purge valve.

Variable-length intake manifold

The torque curve for any engine is proportional to the mass of the inducted air over speed.

Design modifications embracing the configuration of the intake manifold are one way to influence torque; and particularly multipoint fuel injection greatly increases the latitude for applying this concept. Standard intake manifolds consist of individual runners (length adjustment) combined with plenum chambers and throttle valves (volume adjustment). A virtually ideal torque curve can be obtained using a variable-length intake manifold. Such a device can react to engine load factor, engine speed and throttle-valve aperture to provide the following options:

– Infinitely-variable adjustment of intake-runner length,

– Ability to switch between various intake-runner lengths,

– Ability to switch between different intake-runner diameters,

– Ability to deactivate a single channel per cylinder on multi-tract runners,

– Ability to adjust the plenum chamber's volume.

These options mean that the variable-length intake manifold can be employed to improve operating dynamics or to reduce fuel consumption without any sacrifice in response.

Fuel supply

Fuel-supply system

The system for the supply of fuel to the engine comprises the following main components:
– Fuel tank
– Fuel lines
– Electric fuel pump
– Fuel filter
– Fuel rail (only for multipoint fuel injection)
– Fuel-pressure regulator.

Together, it is the task of these components to provide the engine with sufficient fuel no matter what operating conditions are concerned (cold-start, hot-fuel delivery, idle, and full-load).

An electrically driven fuel pump pumps the fuel from the fuel tank and through the fuel filter to the injection valve (injector). The electromagnetically controlled injector injects a precisely metered quantity of fuel into the engine's intake manifold. Surplus fuel flows back to the fuel tank via a fuel-pressure regulator which provides for constant fuel pressure in the system (Fig. 1).

On single-point fuel-injection (SPI) systems, fuel is injected through a single injector situated directly above the throttle valve.

In the case of multipoint fuel-injection (MPI) systems, each cylinder is allocated its own injector which is situated in the intake manifold directly before the intake valve concerned. Fuel is supplied to the individual injectors through a so-called fuel rail.

Fuel tank

According to the German equivalent of the FMVSS/CUR, the fuel tank must be corrosion-resistant and not leak even at a pressure defined as double the normal operating pressure, but at least at 0.3 bar overpressure. Suitable openings, safety valves etc. must be provided to permit excess pressure to escape. Fuel must not escape past the filler cap, nor through the pressure-equalization devices. This also applies in the case of road shocks, or in curves, or when the vehicle is tilted. The fuel tank must be remote from the engine so that the ignition of the fuel is not to be expected even in the event of an accident. Further, more stringent regulations apply in the case of vehicles with open cabs, and for tractors and buses.

Fuel lines

Fuel lines must be installed so that they cannot be adversely effected by torsional motion, engine movement, or similar phenomena.

They can be manufactured from seamless flexible metal tubing, or flame- and fuel-resistant synthetic hose. They must be protected against mechanical damage.

All fuel-conducting components must be protected against heat which could otherwise impair correct operation. They must be positioned so that the possibility of dripping or evaporating fuel accumulating on hot components, or being ignited by electrical devices, is ruled out. Fuel lines on buses are not to pass through the passenger or driver compartment, and gravity-feed systems are forbidden.

Electric fuel pump

The use of electric pumps in passenger cars places particularly stringent demands on the pumps regarding their function, noise, size, and service life. Having a variety of different pump sizes available means that under every possible operating condition (cold start, hot-fuel delivery, idle, and full load), these demands can be fulfilled for a very wide range of different injection systems and engines. Electric fuel pumps are available as in-line (Fig. 1a), or in-tank versions (Fig. 1b).

The in-line pump is situated outside the fuel tank in the line between tank and fuel filter, and is attached to the vehicle's body platform.

Fig. 1: Fuel-supply system (Example using multipoint fuel injection)
With electric fuel pump: a) In-line, b) In-tank.
1 Fuel tank, 2 Electric fuel pump, 3 Fuel filter, 4 Fuel rail, 5 Fuel injector, 6 Fuel-pressure regulator.

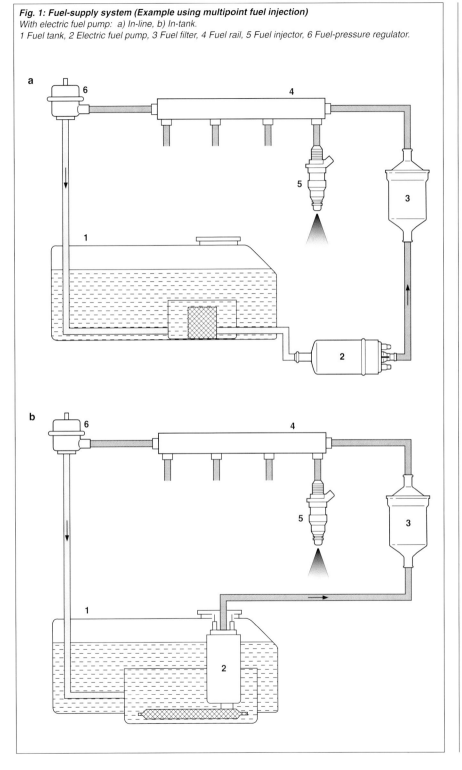

cost of increased fuel consumption. It allows economical engines to be designed, featuring high power-output per liter, whilst at the same time displaying good flexibility coupled with excellent driveability.

Fuel supply

The fuel supply system comprises
– electric fuel pump (Fig. 2),
– fuel accumulator,
– fuel filter (Fig. 4),
– primary-pressure regulator and
– fuel-injection valves.

With regard to the components used, the KE-Jetronic fuel system differs only slightly from that of the K-Jetronic system. An electric roller-cell pump feeds fuel from the tank to the pressure accumulator at a pressure of over 5 bar, and, from there, through the fuel filter to the fuel distributor. From the fuel distributor, the fuel flows to the fuel-injection valves. The fuel-injection valves inject the fuel continuously into the intake ports of the engine. This is why the system is designated KE (taken from the German for continuous and electronic). When the intake valves open, the mixture is drawn into the cylinders.

The primary-pressure regulator maintains the supply pressure in the system constant, and returns the surplus fuel to the tank. Due to the constant flow of fuel through the fuel-supply system, cool fuel is always available. This prevents the formation of vapor bubbles and ensures good hot-starting characteristics.

Electric fuel pump

The electric fuel pump is a roller-cell pump driven by a permanent-magnet electric motor.

The rotor plate which is eccentrically mounted in the pump housing is fitted with metal rollers in notches around its circumference which are pressed against the pump housing by centrifugal force and act as rolling seals. The fuel is carried in the cavities which form be-

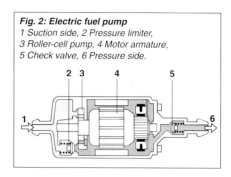

Fig. 2: Electric fuel pump
1 Suction side, 2 Pressure limiter, 3 Roller-cell pump, 4 Motor armature, 5 Check valve, 6 Pressure side.

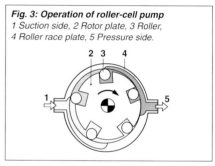

Fig. 3: Operation of roller-cell pump
1 Suction side, 2 Rotor plate, 3 Roller, 4 Roller race plate, 5 Pressure side.

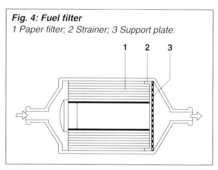

Fig. 4: Fuel filter
1 Paper filter; 2 Strainer; 3 Support plate.

tween the rollers. The pumping action takes place when the rollers, after having closed the inlet bore, force the trapped fuel around in front of them until it can escape from the pump through the outlet bore (Figure 3). The fuel flows directly around the electric motor. There is no danger of explosion, however, because there is never an ignitable mixture in the pump housing.

The electric fuel pump always delivers more fuel than the engine needs, so that there is always sufficient pressure in the fuel system under all conditions. A check valve in the pump decouples the fuel system from the fuel tank by preventing return flow of fuel to the fuel tank.

The electric fuel pump starts to run immediately when the ignition and starting switch is operated and remains switched on continuously after the engine has started. A safety circuit is incorporated to stop the pump running and fuel being delivered if the ignition is switched on but the engine has stopped turning (for instance as might occur in the case of an accident). The fuel pump is located in the direct vicinity of the fuel tank and requires no maintenance.

Fuel accumulator

The fuel accumulator maintains the pressure in the fuel system for a certain time after the engine has been switched off in order to facilitate restarting, particularly when the engine is hot. The special design (Figure 5) of the accumulator housing is such that it deadens the sound of the electric fuel pump.

The interior of the fuel accumulator is divided into two chambers by means of a diaphragm. One chamber serves as the accumulator for the fuel, whilst the other represents the compensation volume and is connected to the atmosphere by means of a vent fitting, either directly or through the fuel-tank ventilation system. During operation, the accumulator chamber is filled with fuel and the diaphragm is caused to bend back against the force of the spring until it is halted by the stops in the spring chamber. The diaphragm remains in this position, which corresponds to the maximum accumulator volume, as long as the engine is running.

Fuel filter

The fuel filter retains particles of dirt which are present in the fuel and which would otherwise adversely effect the functioning of the injection system. The filter contains a paper element with a medium pore size of 10 μm, which is backed up by a fluff strainer (Figure 4). This combination of filter element and fluff strainer ensures a high degree of filtration.

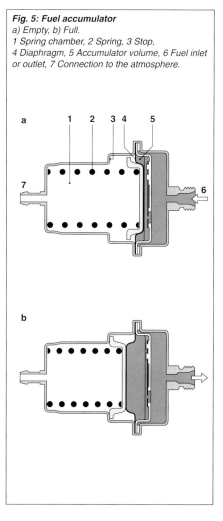

Fig. 5: Fuel accumulator
a) Empty, b) Full.
1 Spring chamber, 2 Spring, 3 Stop,
4 Diaphragm, 5 Accumulator volume, 6 Fuel inlet or outlet, 7 Connection to the atmosphere.

A support plate secures the filter in its metal housing. The filter life depends on the fuel's purity. The filter is installed in the fuel line downstream of the fuel accumulator. When the filter is changed, it is imperative to observe the throughflow direction as indicated by the arrow on the housing.

Primary-pressure regulator

The primary-pressure regulator keeps the supply pressure constant.

In contrast to the K-Jetronic, in which a warm-up regulator regulates the control pressure, the hydraulic counterpressure acting upon the control plunger in the KE-Jetronic is identical to the primary pressure. The control pressure must be held constant since any variation of the control pressure has a direct effect upon the air-fuel ratio. This also applies particularly even if fuel delivery from the supply pump, and injected fuel quantity, vary considerably.

Figure 6 shows a section through the primary-pressure regulator. The fuel enters on the left. The return fuel connection from the fuel distributor is located at the right. The return line to the tank is connected at the top. As soon as the fuel pump starts and generates pressure, the control diaphragm of the pressure accumulator moves downwards. The pressure of the counterspring forces the valve body to follow the diaphragm until, after a very short distance, it encounters a stop and the pressure-controlled function starts. The fuel returning from the fuel distributor, comprising the fuel flowing through the pressure actuator plus the control-plunger leakage can now flow back through the open valve seat to the fuel tank together with the excess fuel. When the engine is switched off, the electric fuel pump also stops. If the system pressure then drops, the valve plate moves back up again and subsequently pushes the valve body upwards against the force of the counterspring until the seal closes the return line to the tank.

The pressure in the fuel supply system then sinks rapidly to below the injection-valve opening pressure so that the injection valves then close tightly due to the force excerted by the valve-needle spring. The system pressure then increases again to the value determined by the fuel accumulator (Fig. 7).

Fuel-injection valves

At a certain pressure, the injection valves open against the pressure from the valve-needle spring and inject fuel into the intake ports. The fuel is atomized by the operation of the valve needle. They inject the fuel allocated by the fuel distributor into the intake port directly onto the cylinder intake valves. The injection valves are secured in a special holder in order to insulate them from the engine heat. The insulation prevents vapor bubbles forming in the fuel-injection lines which would otherwise lead to poor starting behavior when the engine is hot.

The injection valves have no metering function. They open of their own accord when the opening pressure of, for instance, 3.5 bar is exceeded. They are fitted with a needle valve (Figure 9) whose needle vibrates ("chatters")

Fig. 6: Primary-pressure regulator
1 Return line from fuel distributor
2 To fuel tank
3 Adjustment screw
4 Counterspring
5 Seal
6 Inlet
7 Valve plate
8 Diaphragm
9 Control spring
10 Valve body

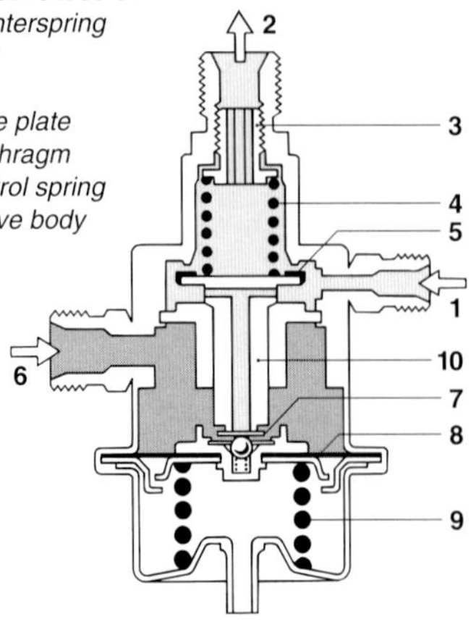

Fig. 7: Pressure curve after engine switch-off
First of all, the pressure drops from the normal primary pressure (1) to the closing pressure of the pressure regulator (2). It then rises again, due to the effect of the fuel accumulator, to the value (3) which is still below the injection-valve opening pressure (4).

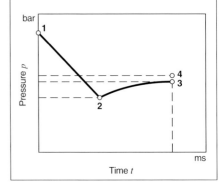

audibly at high frequency when fuel is being injected. This results in excellent fuel atomization, even with the smallest of injected quantities.

When the engine is switched off, the fuel-injection valves close tightly as soon as the fuel-system pressure drops below their opening pressure. This means that no more fuel can enter the intake ports and thus reach the intake valves of the engine, once the engine has been switched off.

Air-shrouded fuel-injection valves

Air-shrouded fuel-injection valves improve fuel induction particularly at idle. The air-shrouding principle is based upon the fact that a portion of the air drawn in by the engine enters through the fuel-injection valves (Figure 10) with the result that fuel is particularly well atomized at the point of exit. Air-shrouded valves reduce fuel consumption and lower the level of toxic emissions.

Fig. 8: KE-Jetronic fuel-injection valve (injector): Spray patterns with and without air-shrouding
With air shrouding (shown on the right) the air has a permanent effect and atomizes the fuel even better than in the conventional injector without air-shrouding (shown on the left).

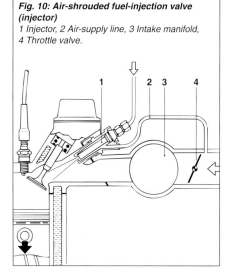

Fig. 9: Fuel-injection valve (injector)
a) Closed
b) Open
1 Valve housing
2 Filter
3 Valve needle
4 Valve seat

Fig. 10: Air-shrouded fuel-injection valve (injector)
1 Injector, 2 Air-supply line, 3 Intake manifold, 4 Throttle valve.

Fuel metering

The task of fuel induction is to meter to the engine a quantity of fuel corresponding to the inducted air quantity.
Basically, fuel metering takes place through the air-flow sensor and the fuel distributor. In a number of operating conditions, however, the amount of fuel required deviates greatly from the "standard" quantity and it becomes necessary to intervene in the mixture-formation system.

Air-flow sensor

The quantity of air drawn in by the engine is a precise measure of its operating load. The air-flow sensor operates according to the suspended-body principle, and measures the amount of air drawn in by the engine (Figure 12).
The intake air quantity serves as the main actuating variable for determining the basic injection quantity. It is the appropriate physical quantity for deriving the fuel requirement, and changes in the induction characteristics of the engine have no effect upon the formation of the air-fuel mixture. Since the air

Fig. 12: Principle of the air-flow sensor
a) Small amount of air drawn in: Sensor plate only lifted slightly. b) Large amount of air drawn in: Sensor plate is lifted considerably further.

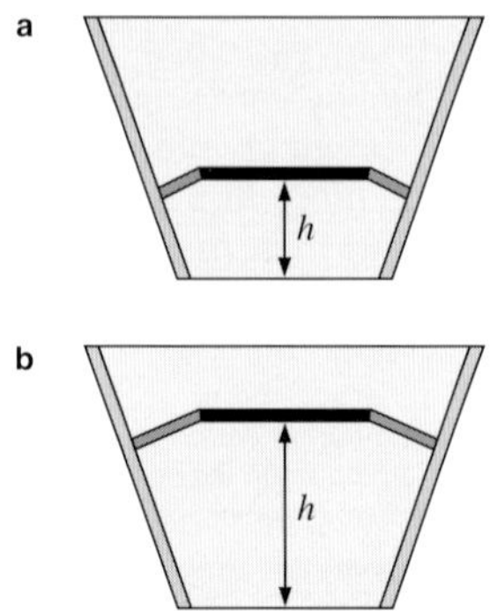

drawn in by the engine must pass through the air-flow sensor before it reaches the engine, this means that it has been measured and the control signal generated before it actually enters the engine cylinders. The result is that, in addition to other measures described below, the correct mixture adaptation takes place at all times.

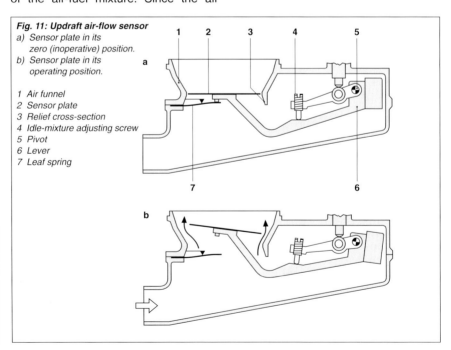

Fig. 11: Updraft air-flow sensor
a) Sensor plate in its zero (inoperative) position.
b) Sensor plate in its operating position.

1 Air funnel
2 Sensor plate
3 Relief cross-section
4 Idle-mixture adjusting screw
5 Pivot
6 Lever
7 Leaf spring

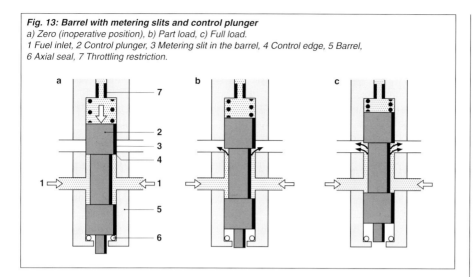

Fig. 13: Barrel with metering slits and control plunger
a) Zero (inoperative position), b) Part load, c) Full load.
1 Fuel inlet, 2 Control plunger, 3 Metering slit in the barrel, 4 Control edge, 5 Barrel,
6 Axial seal, 7 Throttling restriction.

The air-flow sensor is located upstream of the throttle valve so that it measures all the air which enters the engine cylinders.

The air-flow sensor comprises an air funnel in which the sensor flap (suspended body) is free to pivot. The air flowing through the funnel deflects the sensor plate by a given amount out of its zero position (Figure 11).

The movements of the sensor plate are transmitted by a lever system to a control plunger which determines the basic injection quantity required for the basic functions. Considerable pressure shocks can occur in the intake system if backfiring takes place in the intake manifold. For this reason, the air-flow sensor is so designed that the sensor plate can swing back in the opposite direction in event of misfiring, and past its zero position to open a relief cross-section in the funnel.

A rubber buffer limits the downward stroke (the upward stroke on the downdraft air-flow sensor).

A counterweight compensates for the weight of the sensor plate and lever system (this is performed by means of an extension spring on the downdraft air-flow sensor).

An adjustable leaf spring is fitted to ensure the correct zero position in the switched-off phase.

Fuel distributor
Depending upon the position of the plate in the air-flow sensor, the fuel distributor meters the basic injection quantity to the individual engine cylinders.

The position of the sensor plate is a measure of the amount of air drawn in by the engine. The position of the plate is transmitted to the control plunger by a lever. Depending upon its position in the barrel with metering slits, the control plunger opens or closes the slits to a greater or lesser extent. The fuel flows through the open section of these slits to the differential-pressure valves and then to the fuel-injection valves (Figure 13).

If sensor-plate travel is only very small, the control plunger is lifted only slightly and, as a result, only a small section of the slit is opened for the passage of fuel. On the other hand, with a larger plunger travel, the plunger opens a larger section of the slits and more fuel can flow. There is a linear relationship between sensor-plate travel and the slit section in the barrel which is opened for fuel flow.

A hydraulic force is applied to the control plunger, and acts in opposition to the movement resulting from the sensor-plate deflection. A constant air-pressure drop at the sensor plate is the result, and this ensures that the control plunger always follows the movement of the sensor-plate lever. In some versions, a pressure spring is used to assist this hydraulic force (Figure 14). It prevents the control plunger from being drawn up due to vacuum effects when the system cools down.

It is imperative that the primary pressure be accurately controlled, otherwise variations would have a direct effect upon the air-fuel ratio (or λ value). A damping throttle (Figure 14) serves to damp oscillations that could be caused by sensor-plate forces. When the engine is switched off, the control plunger sinks until it comes to rest against an axial seal ring (Figures 13 to 15). This is secured by an adjustable screw and can be set to the correct height to ensure that the metering slits are closed correctly by the plunger when it is in its zero position.

Whereas with the K-Jetronic, the zero position of the plunger is determined by its abutting against the sensor-plate lever, with the KE-Jetronic, the plunger rests upon the axial seal ring due to the force applied to it by the residual primary pressure. This measure serves to prevent pressure loss due to leakage

past the control plunger, and thus prevents the fuel accumulator from emptying through the control-plunger gap. The fuel accumulator must remain full, because it has the job of maintaining the primary pressure above the fuel-vapor pressure which is applicable for the particular fuel temperature prevailing when the engine is switched off.

Differential-pressure valves

The differential-pressure valves in the fuel distributor serve to generate a given pressure drop at the metering slits.

The air-flow sensor has a linear characteristic. This means that if double the quantity of air is drawn in, the sensor-plate travel is also doubled. If this (linear) travel is to result in a change of the basic injection quantity in the same relationship, then a constant pressure drop must be guaranteed at the metering slits regardless of the amount of fuel flowing through them (Figure 13).

The differential-pressure valves maintain the drop in pressure between the upper and lower chambers constant, regardless of fuel throughflow. The diffe-

---

Fig. 14: Fuel distributor with differential-pressure valves

1 Fuel inlet (primary pressure), 2 Upper chamber of differential-pressure valve, 3 Line to the fuel-injection valve (injector), 4 Control plunger, 5 Control edge and metering slit, 6 Valve spring, 7 Valve diaphragm, 8 Lower chamber of differential-pressure valve, 9 Axial seal ring, 10 Pressure spring, 11 Fuel from the electro-hydraulic pressure actuator, 12 Throttling restriction, 13 Return line.

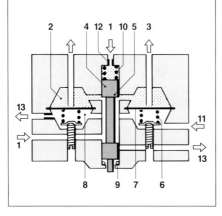

Fig. 15: Differential pressure valve

a) Operating position with small injected fuel quantity
b) Operating position with large injected fuel quantity

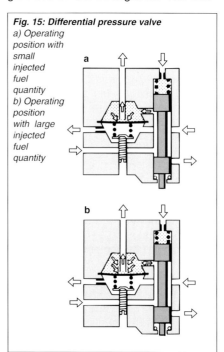

rential pressure is usually 0.2 bar. This ensures a high degree of metering accuracy.

The differential-pressure valves are of the flat-seat type and are located in the fuel distributor. They are each allocated to one control slit. A diaphragm separates the upper chamber from the lower chamber of the valve (Figures 14 and 15). The lower chambers of all valves are interconnected by means of a ring main, as well as to the electro-hydraulic pressure actuator. The valve seat is located in the upper chamber. Each upper chamber is connected to a metering slit and its corresponding fuel-injection line. The upper chambers are completely sealed off from each other. The pressure differential at the metering slit is determined by the force of the helical spring in the lower chamber, together with the effective diaphragm diameter and the electro-hydraulic pressure actuator.

If a large basic injection quantity flows into the upper chamber, the diaphragm bends downwards and opens the outlet cross-section of the valve until the set

differential pressure is reached again. If throughflow quantity drops, the valve cross-section is reduced due to the equilibrium of forces at the diaphragm until a pressure differential of 0.2 bar prevails again. This means that an equilibrium of forces exists at the diaphragm which can be maintained for every basic injection quantity by controlling the valve cross-section (Figure 15).

An additional fine filter with a separator for ferromagnetic contamination is fitted in the fuel line to the electro-hydraulic pressure actuator.

Mixture formation

The formation of the air-fuel mixture takes place in the intake ports and cylinders of the engine.

The continually injected fuel coming from the injection valves is "stored" in front of the intake valves. When the intake valve is opened, the air drawn in by the engine carries the waiting "cloud" of fuel with it into the cylinder. An ignitable air-fuel mixture is formed during the induction stroke due to the swirl effect.

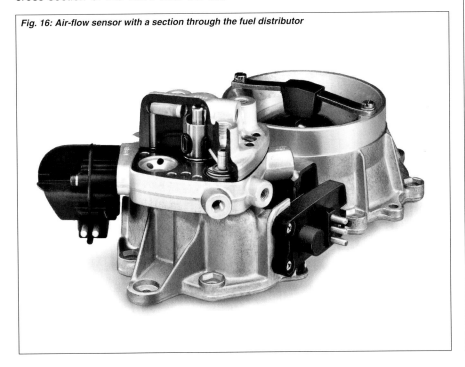

Fig. 16: Air-flow sensor with a section through the fuel distributor

Adaptation to operating conditions

In addition to the basic functions described up to now, the mixture has to be adapted during particular operating conditions. These adaptations (corrections) are necessary in order to optimize the power delivered, to improve the exhaust-gas composition and to improve the starting behavior and driveability. Thanks to additional sensors for the engine temperature and the throttle valve position (load signal), the control unit of the KE-Jetronic can perform these matching tasks better than a mechanical system.

Basic adaptation

The basic adaptation of the air-fuel mixture to the operating modes of idle, part load and full load is by appropriately shaping the air funnel in the air-flow sensor (Fig. 17).

If the funnel had a purely conical shape, the result would be a mixture with a constant air-fuel ratio throughout the whole of the sensor plate range of travel (metering). However, it is necessary to meter to the engine an air-fuel mixture which is optimal for particular operating modes such as idle, part load and full load. In practice, this means a richer mixture at idle and full load and a leaner mixture in the part-load range. This adaptation is achieved by designing the air funnel so that it becomes wider in stages (Fig. 18).

If the funnel is flatter than the basic form (which was specified for a given mixture, e.g. at $\lambda = 1$), then the mixture is leaner. If, on other hand, the funnel walls are steeper than in the basic form, the mixture is richer because the sensor plate deflects further for the same air throughflow and the control plunger meters more fuel. Consequently, this means that the air funnel can be shaped so that it is possible to meter mixtures to the engine which have different air-fuel ratios depending upon the sensor-plate position in the funnel (which in turn corresponds to the particular engine

operating mode i.e. idle, part load and full load). In the case of the KE-Jetronic, the air funnel is preferably so shaped that an air-fuel mixture with $\lambda = 1$ results across the whole operating range.

Electronic control unit (ECU)

The electronic control unit evaluates the data delivered by the various sensors concerning the engine operating condition, and, from the status, generates a control signal for the electro-hydraulic pressure actuator (Fig. 19).

Registration of operating data
Additional criteria, above and beyond the information coming from the intake-air quantity, are required in order to determine the optimum fuel quantity

---

Fig. 17: Influence of funnel-wall angle upon the sensor-plate deflection for identical air throughput
a) The basic funnel shape results in stroke "h",
b) Steep funnel walls result in increased stroke "h" for identical air throughput,
c) Flatter funnel shape results in reduced deflection "h" for identical air throughput.

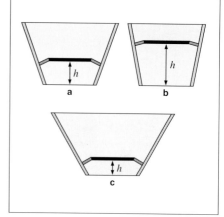

Fig. 18: Adaptation of the air-funnel shape
1 For maximum power, 2 For part load, 3 For idle.

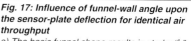

required by the engine. These must be registered by sensors and signalled to the electronic control unit.

Table 1. Adaptations

Performance characteristics	Sensor
Full load idle	Throttle-valve switch
Engine speed	Ignition-triggering system (usually in the ignition distributor
Start	Ignition and starting switch
Engine temperature	Engine temperature sensor
Air pressure	Aneroid-box sensor
Air-fuel mixture	Lambda sensor

The sensors are described in conjunction with the relevant adaptation function.

Design and function
Depending upon the functional scope, the electronic circuitry uses either analog techniques or mixed analog/digital techniques. Starting with the "Europe" unit, the module for idle-mixture control and for lambda closed-loop control can be added. ECUs with a more extensive range of functions are designed using digital techniques. The electronic components are installed on a PC board and include ICs (e.g. operational amplifiers, comparators and voltage stabilizers), transistors, diodes, resistors and capacitors. The PC boards are inserted in the ECU housing which can be equipped with a pressure-equalization element. The ECU is connected to the battery, to the sensors and to the actuator by a 25-pole plug.
The ECU processes the incoming signals from the different sensors and, on the basis of this, calculates the control current for the electro-hydraulic pressure actuator.

Voltage stabilization
The ECU must be powered by a stable voltage which remains constant regardless of the voltage of the vehicle electrical system. The current applied to the pressure actuator, which depends upon the incoming sensor signals carrying the data on the engine operating conditions, is generated from this stabilized voltage, the stabilization of which takes place in a special IC.

Input filters
Input filters filter out any interference which may be present in the incoming signals from the sensors.

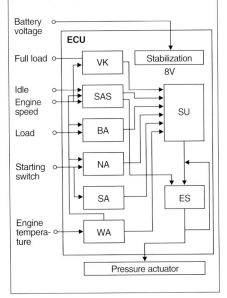

Fig. 19: Block diagram of the KE-Jetronic ECU, using analog techniques
The correcting signals from the individual blocks are combined in an adder stage.
They are then amplified in the output stage and transmitted to the electro-hydraulic pressure actuator.
VK   *Full-load correction*
SAS *Overrun fuel cutoff*
BA   *Acceleration enrichment*
NA   *Post-start enrichment*
SA   *Voltage increase for starting*
WA   *Warm-up enrichment*
SU   *Adder stage*
ES   *Output stage*

Adder

Here, the evaluated sensor signals are combined. The electrically processed corrective signals are added in an operational circuit and then transmitted to the current regulator.

Output stage

The output stage generates the control signal for the pressure actuator, whereby it is possible to input opposing currents into the pressure actuator in order to increase or decrease the pressure drop.

The magnitude of the current in the pressure actuator can be adjusted at will in the positive direction by means of a permanently triggered transistor. The current is reversed during "overrun" (overrun fuel cut-off), and influences the differential pressure at the differential-pressure valves so that the flow of fuel to the injection valves is interrupted.

Additional output stages

If necessary, additional output stages can be included. These can trigger the valves for EGR, and control the bypass cross-section around the throttle valve as required for idle-mixture control, to mention but two applications.

Electro-hydraulic pressure actuator

Depending upon the operating mode of the engine and the resulting current signal received from the ECU, the electro-hydraulic pressure actuator varies the pressure in the lower chambers of the differential-pressure valves. This changes the amount of fuel delivered to the injection valves.

Design

The electro-hydraulic pressure actuator (Figure 20) is mounted on the fuel distributor. The actuator is a differential-pressure controller which functions according to the nozzle/baffle-plate principle, and its pressure drop is controlled by the current input from the ECU. In a housing of non-magnetic material, an armature is suspended on a frictionless taut-band suspension element, between two double magnetic poles. The armature is in the form of a diaphragm plate made from resilient material.

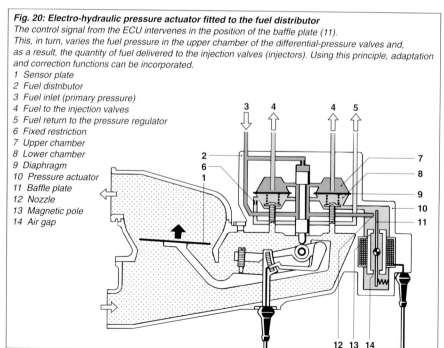

Fig. 20: Electro-hydraulic pressure actuator fitted to the fuel distributor
The control signal from the ECU intervenes in the position of the baffle plate (11).
This, in turn, varies the fuel pressure in the upper chamber of the differential-pressure valves and, as a result, the quantity of fuel delivered to the injection valves (injectors). Using this principle, adaptation and correction functions can be incorporated.

1 *Sensor plate*
2 *Fuel distributor*
3 *Fuel inlet (primary pressure)*
4 *Fuel to the injection valves*
5 *Fuel return to the pressure regulator*
6 *Fixed restriction*
7 *Upper chamber*
8 *Lower chamber*
9 *Diaphragm*
10 *Pressure actuator*
11 *Baffle plate*
12 *Nozzle*
13 *Magnetic pole*
14 *Air gap*

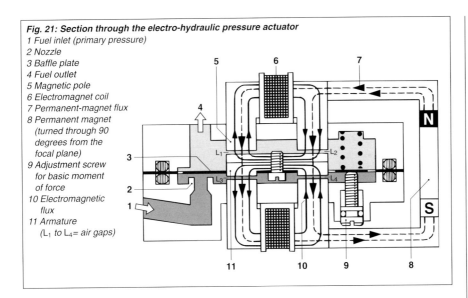

Fig. 21: Section through the electro-hydraulic pressure actuator
1 Fuel inlet (primary pressure)
2 Nozzle
3 Baffle plate
4 Fuel outlet
5 Magnetic pole
6 Electromagnet coil
7 Permanent-magnet flux
8 Permanent magnet
   (turned through 90
   degrees from the
   focal plane)
9 Adjustment screw
   for basic moment
   of force
10 Electromagnetic
   flux
11 Armature
   (L_1 to L_4 = air gaps)

Function

The magnetic flux of a permanent magnet (broken lines in Figure 21) and that of an electromagnet (unbroken lines) are superimposed upon each other in the magnetic poles and their air gaps. The permanent magnet is actually turned through 90 degrees referred to the focal plane. The paths taken by the magnetic fluxes through the two pairs of poles are symmetrical and of equal length, and flow from the poles, across the air gaps to the armature, and then through the armature.

In the two diagonally opposed air gaps (Figure 21 L_2, L_3), the permanent-magnet flux, and the electro-magnet flux resulting from the incoming ECU control signal are added, whereas in the other two air gaps (Figure 21 L_1, L_4) the fluxes are subtracted from each other. This means that, in each air gap, the armature, which moves the baffle plate, is subjected to a force of attraction proportional to the square of the magnetic flux.

Since the permanent-magnet flux remains constant, and is proportional to the control current from the ECU flowing in the electromagnet coil, the resulting torque is proportional to this control current. The basic moment of force applied to the armature has been selected so that, when no current is applied from the ECU, there results a basic differential pressure which corresponds preferably to $\lambda = 1$. This also means that, in the case of control current failure, limp-home facilities are available without any further correction measures being necessary.

The jet of fuel which enters through the nozzle attempts to bend the baffle plate away against the prevailing mechanical and magnetic forces. Taking a fuel throughflow which is determined by a fixed restriction located in series with the pressure actuator, the difference in pressure between the inlet and outlet is proportional to the control current applied from the ECU. This means that the variable pressure drop at the nozzle is also proportional to the ECU control current, and results in a variable lower-chamber pressure. At the same time, the pressure in the upper chambers changes by the same amount. This, in turn, results in a change in the difference at the metering slits between the upper-chamber pressure and the primary pressure and this is applied as a means for varying the fuel quantity delivered to the injection valves.

As a result of the small electromagnetic time constants, and the small masses which must be moved, the pressure actuator reacts extremely quickly to variations in the control current from the ECU.

If the direction of the control current is reversed, the armature pulls the baffle plate away from the nozzle and a pressure drop of only a few hundredths of a bar occurs at the pressure actuator. This can be used for auxiliary functions such as overrun fuel cutoff and engine-speed limitation. The latter function is performed by interrupting the flow of fuel to the injection valves.

Cold-start enrichment

Depending upon the engine temperature, the cold-start valve injects an additional quantity of fuel for a limited period of time during starting.

This is carried out in order to compensate for the losses resulting from condensation on the cylinder walls and in order to facilitate starting the cold engine. For this purpose, due to the fact that during starting the pronounced variations in the engine speed would result in a false air-flow signal, it is necessary for the ECU to provide a fixed load signal during cranking which is weighted with an engine-temperature factor.

This additional quantity of fuel is injected by the cold-start valve into the intake manifold. The "on" period of the cold-start valve is limited by a thermotime switch as a function of the engine temperature.

This process is known as cold-start enrichment and results in a "richer" air-fuel mixture, i.e. the excess-air factor λ is temporarily less than 1.

Cold-start valve

The cold-start valve (Figure 22) is a solenoid-operated valve. The solenoid coil is located inside the valve, and when the valve is closed, it is sealed off by its movable armature being pressed against the seal by a spring.

When the solenoid is energized, the armature is lifted from its seat and permits fuel to flow into a so-called swirl nozzle which causes it to rotate. The result is that the fuel is atomized extremely finely and enriches the mixture in the intake manifold downstream of the throttle valve. The cold-start valve is so

---

Fig. 22: Cold-start valve in operated state
1 Electrical connection, 2 Fuel supply with strainer, 3 Valve (electromagnet armature), 4 Solenoid winding, 5 Swirl nozzle, 6 Valve seat.

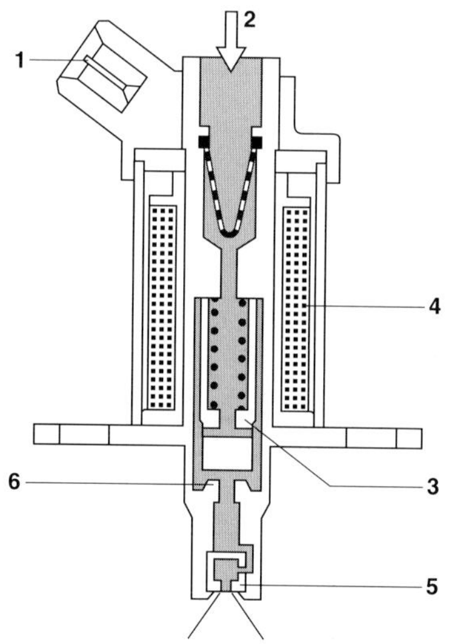

Fig. 23: Thermo-time switch
1 Electrical connection, 2 Housing, 3 Bimetal strip, 4 Heating filaments, 5 Electrical contact.

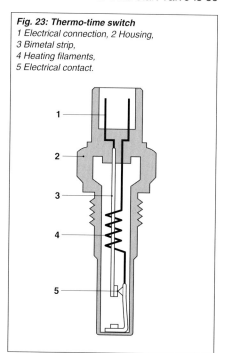

positioned in the inlet manifold that a favorable distribution of the air-fuel mixture to all cylinders is ensured.

Thermo-time switch

The thermo-time switch limits the duration of cold-start valve operation, depending upon temperature.

The thermo-time switch (Figure 23) consists of an electrically heated bimetal strip which, depending upon its temperature, opens or closes a contact. It is brought into operation by the ignition/starter switch, and is mounted at a spot which is representative of engine temperature.

During a cold start, it limits the "on" period of the cold-start valve. In case of repeated start attempts, or when starting takes too long, the cold-start valve ceases to inject. Its "on" period is determined by the thermo-time switch which is heated by engine heat as well as by its own built-in heater. Both these heating effects are necessary in order to ensure that the "on" period of the cold-start valve is limited under all conditions, and engine flooding is prevented.

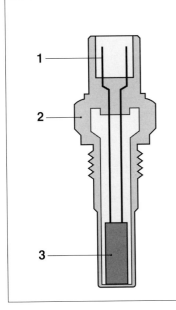

Fig. 24: Engine-temperature sensor
*1 Electrical connection, 2 Housing,
3 NTC resistor.*

During an actual cold start, the heat generated by the built-in heater is mainly responsible for the "on" period (switch off, for instance, at –20°C after 7.5 seconds).

With a warm engine, the thermo-time switch has already been heated up so far by engine heat that it remains open and prevents the cold-start valve from going into action.

Post-start enrichment

Enrichment with additional fuel improves the post-start performance at low temperatures.

This function is calibrated to give satisfactory throttle response at all temperatures together with minimum fuel consumption.

Post-start enrichment is dependent upon temperature and time and, starting from a temperature-dependent initial value, is decreased practically as a linear function of time. This means that the enrichment duration is a function of the initial temperature.

The ECU maintains the temperature-dependent mixture enrichment at its maximum level for about 4.5 seconds and then reduces to zero. For instance, following a start at 20°C, the reduction to zero takes 20 seconds.

Engine-temperature sensor

The engine temperature is measured by the engine-temperature sensor which provides the ECU with a corresponding electric signal.

The engine-temperature sensor (Figure 24) is mounted in the engine block on air-cooled engines. With water-cooled engines, it projects into the coolant.

The sensor "reports" the particular engine temperature to the ECU in the form of a resistance value. The ECU then controls the electro-hydraulic pressure actuator which carries out the appropriate adaptation of the injected fuel quantity during the post-start and warm-up periods. The temperature sensor consists of an NTC resistor embedded in a threaded sleeve.

NTC stands for Negative Temperature Coefficient, the decisive characteristic of this resistor. When the temperature increases, the electrical resistance of the semiconductor resistor decreases.

Warm-up enrichment

During warm-up, the engine receives extra fuel depending upon the temperature, the load and the engine speed.

The engine-temperature sensor registers the coolant temperature and reports this to the ECU which then converts this data into a control signal for the electro-hydraulic pressure actuator. The mixture adaptation through the pressure actuator is arranged such that perfect combustion is achieved at all temperatures while, at the same time, keeping the fuel enrichment as low as possible.

Acceleration enrichment

During acceleration, the KE-Jetronic meters additional fuel to the engine as long as it is still cold.

If the throttle is opened abruptly, the air-fuel mixture is momentarily leaned-off, and a short period of mixture enrichment is needed to ensure good transitional response.

As a result of the change in the load signal (referred to time), the ECU recognizes when acceleration is taking place and, as a result, triggers the acceleration enrichment. This prevents the familiar "flat spot". When the engine is cold, it requires additional enrichment due to the less than optimum air-fuel mixing and due to the possibility of fuel being deposited on the intake-manifold walls.

The maximum value for acceleration enrichment is a function of the temperature. The acceleration enrichment is triggered at $\leq 80°C$ by a needle-shaped enrichment pulse with a duration of 1 second. The enrichment quantity is higher the colder the engine, and is also dependent upon changes in load.

The speed with which the pedal is depressed when accelerating is determined from the deflection of the air-flow sensor. This has only a very slight lag referred to the throttle-plate movement. This signal, which corresponds to the change in the intake-air quantity and therefore approximately to the engine power, is registered by the potentiometer in the air-flow sensor and passed to the ECU which controls the pressure actuator accordingly. The potentiometer curve is non-linear, so that the acceleration signal is at maximum when accelerating from idle. It decreases along with the increase in engine power. The result is a reduction in the ECU circuit complexity.

Sensor-plate potentiometer

The potentiometer in the air-flow sensor (Figure 25) is manufactured using film techniques on a ceramic base.

A brush-type wiper moves across the potentiometer track. The brushes consist of a number of fine wires which are welded to a lever. The individual wires apply only a very low pressure to the potentiometer track with the result that wear is extremely low. Due to the large number of wires in the brush, excellent electrical contact is guaranteed even on a rough track surface and also when the wiper moves quickly.

The potentiometer lever is attached to the sensor-plate shaft but is electrically insulated from it. The wiper voltage is tapped off by a second wiper brush which is electrically connected to the main wiper.

The wiper is designed to travel past the ends of the tracks in both directions so far that damage is ruled out when backfiring occurs in the intake manifold. A fixed film resistor is included in series with the wiper to prevent damage in the case of short-circuit.

Full-load enrichment

The engine delivers its maximum power at full load, when the air-fuel mixture must be enriched compared with that at part-load.

In contrast to part load, where the calibration is for minimum fuel consumption and low emissions, at full load it is necessary to enrich the air-fuel mixture. This enrichment is programmed to be engine-speed dependent. It provides maximum possible torque over the entire engine-speed range, and this ensures optimum fuel-economy figures during full-load operation.

At full load, e.g. in the engine-speed ranges between 1500 and 3000 min^{-1} and above 4000 min^{-1}, the KE-Jetronic enriches the air-fuel mixture. The full-load signal is delivered by a full-load switch on the throttle valve, or by a microswitch on the accelerator-lever linkage. The information on engine speed is taken from the ignition. From this data, the ECU calculates the additional fuel quantity needed, and this is put into effect by the pressure actuator.

Throttle-valve switch

The throttle-valve switch communicates the "idle" and "full load" throttle positions to the ECU.

The throttle-valve switch (Figure 26) is mounted on the throttle body and actuated by the throttle-valve shaft.

Attached to this shaft is a contoured switch guide that closes the idle contacts at one end of its travel and the full-load contacts at the other. Recognition of these two engine-operating modes is

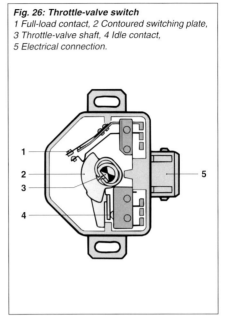

Fig. 26: Throttle-valve switch
1 Full-load contact, 2 Contoured switching plate,
3 Throttle-valve shaft, 4 Idle contact,
5 Electrical connection.

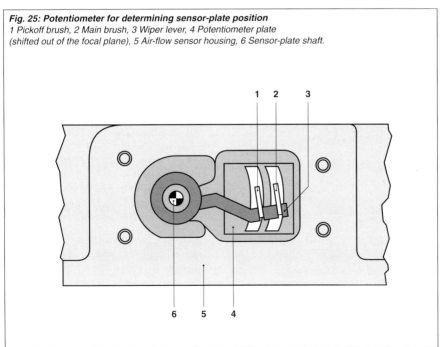

Fig. 25: Potentiometer for determining sensor-plate position
1 Pickoff brush, 2 Main brush, 3 Wiper lever, 4 Potentiometer plate
(shifted out of the focal plane), 5 Air-flow sensor housing, 6 Sensor-plate shaft.

Fig. 27: Auxiliary-air device (section)
1 Plate opening, 2 Pivot, 3 Electrical heating,
4 Air passage, 5 Perforated plate.
Top: Air passage partially opened by the perfora-
ted plate.
Bottom: Perforated plate blocks off the air pas-
sage since the engine has reached the appro-
priate operating temperature.

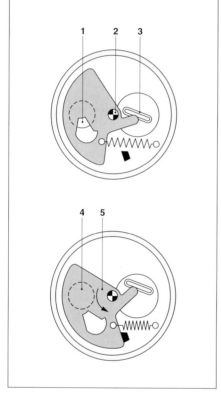

Fig. 28: Electrically heated auxiliary-air device
1 Electrical connection, 2 Electrical heating,
3 Bimetal strip, 4 Perforated plate.

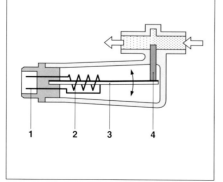

essential for the engine-management system.

Controlling the idle speed by means of the auxiliary-air device

In order to achieve smoother running at idle, the idle-speed is increased. This also leads to a more rapid warm-up of the engine. Depending upon engine temperature, an auxiliary-air device in the form of a bypass around the throttle plate allows the engine to draw in more air. This auxiliary air is also measured by the air-flow sensor, and leads to the KE-Jetronic providing the engine with more fuel. Precise adaptation is by means of the electrical heating facility. The engine temperature then determines how much auxiliary air is fed in initially through the bypass, and the electrical heating is mainly responsible for subsequently reducing the auxiliary air as a function of time.

Auxiliary-air device

The auxiliary-air device incorporates a perforated plate (Figures 27, 28 and 30) which is actuated by the bimetallic strip and which controls the cross-section of the bypass passage. Initially, the by-pass cross-section opened by the perforated plate is determined by the engine temperature, so that during a cold start, the bypass opening is adequate for the auxiliary air required. The opening closes steadily along with increasing engine temperature until, finally, it is closed completely. The bimetal strip is electrically heated and this limits the opening time, starting from the initial setting which is dependent upon engine temperature. The auxiliary-air device is fitted in the best possible position on the engine for it to assume engine temperature. It does not function when the engine is warm.

Closed-loop idle-speed control by rotary idle actuator

The air quantity or charge is the best correcting variable for closed-loop idle-speed control. Closed-loop idle-speed control via the charge (also termed idle-mixture control) permits a stable, low and, thus, economical idle speed which does not vary throughout the service life of the vehicle.

Excessive idle speed increases the fuel consumption at idle and, as a result, the vehicle's overall fuel consumption. This problem is solved by the closed-loop idle-speed control which always provides exactly the right amount of mixture in order to maintain the idle speed, regardless of the engine load (e.g. cold engine with increased frictional resistance). Furthermore, the emission figures remain constant in the long term without having to adjust the idle speed. To a certain extent, closed-loop idle-speed control also compensates for changes in the engine which are attributable to aging. It also stabilizes the idle speed throughout the entire service life of the engine (Fig. 29).

The rotary idle actuator opens a bypass around the throttle valve. Depending upon the signal applied to it, the actuator adjusts a given opening in the bypass. Due to the fact that KE-Jetronic registers the resulting extra air with its sensor plate, the injected fuel quantity changes accordingly. By contrast with other idle-speed controls on the market, this closed-loop idle-speed control controls the idle speed efficiently due to it actually carrying out a comparison between the desired and actual values and, in case of deviation, correcting accordingly.

Rotary idle actuator

Depending upon the deviation of the idle speed from the set value, the rotary idle actuator supplies the engine with more or less intake air through a bypass around the throttle valve. It assumes the function of the auxiliary-air device which is no longer needed.

The rotary idle actuator of the KE-Jetronic (Figures 30 and 31) receives its control signal from the ECU. This control signal depends upon engine speed and temperature, and causes the rotating plate in the idle actuator to change the bypass opening.

The rotary idle actuator is powered by a rotary-magnet drive comprising a winding and a magnetic circuit. Its rotational range is limited to 60 degrees. The rotating slide is attached to the armature shaft and opens the bypass passage far enough for the specified idle speed to be maintained independent of the engine loading. The closed-loop control circuit in the ECU, which is provided by the engine-speed sensor with the ne-

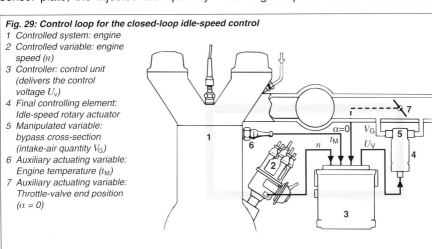

Fig. 29: Control loop for the closed-loop idle-speed control
1 Controlled system: engine
2 Controlled variable: engine speed (n)
3 Controller: control unit (delivers the control voltage U_V)
4 Final controlling element: Idle-speed rotary actuator
5 Manipulated variable: bypass cross-section (intake-air quantity V_G)
6 Auxiliary actuating variable: Engine temperature (t_M)
7 Auxiliary actuating variable: Throttle-valve end position ($\alpha = 0$)

the lambda sensor is processed in the control unit which is already fitted, and the required control intervention for correction of the fuel allocation is carried out via the pressure actuator.

Electrical circuitry

If the engine stops but the ignition remains switched on, the electrical fuel pump is switched off by a safety circuit. The KE-Jetronic system is equipped with a number of electrical components such as electric fuel pump, auxiliary-air device, cold-start valve and thermo-time switch. All these components are controlled by the control relay which, itself,

is switched by the ignition and starting switch. Apart from its switching functions, the control relay also has a safety function. A commonly used circuit is described below.

Function

When cold-starting the engine, voltage is applied to the cold-start valve and the thermo-time switch through terminal 50 (Figs. 36 and 37). If the cranking process takes longer than between 8 and 15 seconds, the thermo-time switch switches off the start valve in order that the engine does not "flood". In this case, the thermo-time switch performs a time-switch function.

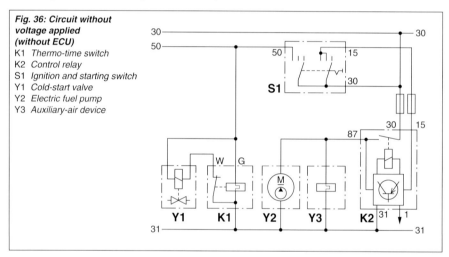

Fig. 36: Circuit without voltage applied (without ECU)
K1 *Thermo-time switch*
K2 *Control relay*
S1 *Ignition and starting switch*
Y1 *Cold-start valve*
Y2 *Electric fuel pump*
Y3 *Auxiliary-air device*

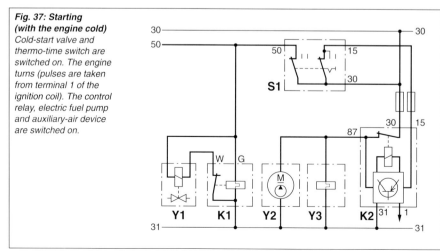

Fig. 37: Starting (with the engine cold)
Cold-start valve and thermo-time switch are switched on. The engine turns (pulses are taken from terminal 1 of the ignition coil). The control relay, electric fuel pump and auxiliary-air device are switched on.

If the temperature of the engine is above approximately + 35°C when the starting process is commenced, the thermo-time switch will have already open-circuited the connection to the start valve which, as a result, does not inject extra fuel. In this case, the thermo-time switch functions as a temperature switch.

Voltage from the ignition and starting switch is still present at the control relay which switches on as soon as the engine runs. The engine speed reached when the starting motor cranks the engine is high enough to generate the "engine running" signal which is taken from the ignition pulses coming from terminal 1 of the ignition coil.

An electronic circuit in the control relay evaluates these pulses. After the first pulse, the control relay switches on and applies voltage to the electric fuel pump and the auxiliary-air device. The control relay remains switched on providing the ignition is switched on and the engine is running (Fig. 38).

If the pulses from terminal 1 of the ignition coil stop because the engine has stopped turning (for instance in the case of an accident), the control relay switches off approximately 1 second after the last pulse is received. This safety circuit prevents the fuel pump from pumping fuel when the ignition is switched on but the engine is not turning (Fig. 39).

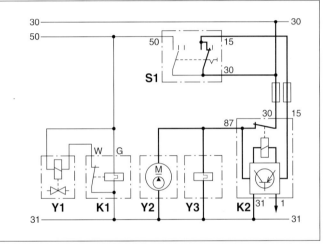

Fig. 38: Operation
Ignition on and engine running. Control relay, electric fuel pump and auxiliary-air device are switched on.

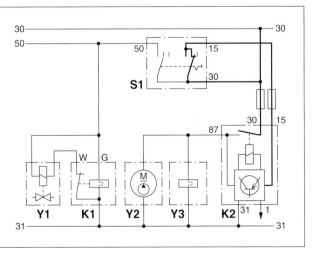

Fig. 39: Ignition on but engine stopped
No pulses can be taken from terminal 1 of the ignition coil. The control relay, electric fuel pump and auxiliary-air device are switched off.

L-Jetronic

Outline of system

The L-Jetronic is an electronically controlled fuel-injection system which injects fuel intermittently into the intake ports. It does not require any form of drive. It combines the advantages of direct air-flow sensing and the special capabilities afforded by electronics.

As is the case with the K-Jetronic system, this system detects all changes resulting from the engine (wear, deposits in the combustion chamber and changes in valve settings), thus guaranteeing a uniformly good exhaust gas quality.

The task of the gasoline injection system is to supply to each cylinder precisely the correct amount of fuel as is necessary for the operation of the engine at that particular moment. A prerequisite for this, however, is the processing of as many influencing factors as possible relevant to the supply of fuel. Since, however, the operating condition of the engine often changes quite rapidly, a speedy adaptation of the fuel delivery to the driving situation at any given moment is of prime importance. Electronically controlled gasoline injection is particularly suitable here. It enables a variety of operational data at any particular location of the vehicle to

be registered and converted into electrical signals by sensors. These signals are then passed on to the control unit of the fuel-injection system which processes them and calculates the exact amount of fuel to be injected. This is influenced via the duration of injection.

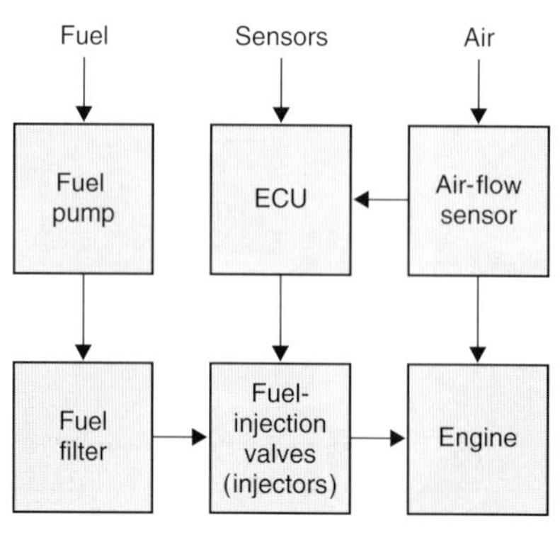

Function

A pump supplies the fuel to the engine and creates the pressure necessary for injection. Injection valves inject the fuel into the individual intake ports and onto the intake valves. An electronic control unit controls the injection valves.

The L-Jetronic consists principally of the following function blocks:
– fuel supply system,
– operating-data sensing system and
– fuel-metering system.

Fuel-supply system

The fuel system supplies fuel from the fuel tank to the injection valves, creates the pressure necessary for injection and maintains it at a constant level.

Operating-data sensing system

The sensors register the measured variables which characterize the operating mode of the engine.

The most important measured variable is the amount of air drawn in by the engine and registered by the air-flow sensor. Other sensors register the position of the throttle, the engine speed, the air temperature and the engine temperature.

Fuel-metering system

The signals delivered by the sensors are evaluated in the electronic control unit (ECU) where they are used to generate the appropriate control pulses for the injection valves.

Advantages of the L-Jetronic system

Low fuel consumption

In carburetor systems, due to segregation processes in the intake manifold, the individual cylinders of the engine do

Fig. 1: Principle of the L-Jetronic (simplified)

not all receive the same amount of air-fuel mixture. Optimum fuel distribution cannot be achieved if a mixture is created which is suitable for supplying sufficient fuel even to the worst-fed cylinder. This would result in high fuel consumption and unequal stressing of the cylinders.

In L-Jetronic systems, each cylinder has its own injection valve. The injection valves are controlled centrally; this ensures that each cylinder receives precisely the same amount of fuel, the optimum amount, at any particular moment and under any particular load.

Adaptation to operating conditions

The L-Jetronic system adapts to changing load conditions virtually immediately since the required quantity of fuel is computed by the control unit (ECU) within milliseconds and injected by the injection valves onto the engine intake valves.

Low-pollution exhaust gas

The concentration of pollutants in the exhaust gas is directly related to the air-fuel ratio. If the engine is to be operated with the least pollutant emission, then a fuel-management system is necessary which is capable of maintaining a given air-fuel ratio. The L-Jetronic works so precisely that the precise mixture formation necessary for observing the present-day exhaust regulations is guaranteed.

Higher power output per litre

The fact that there is no carburetor enables the intake passages to be designed aerodynamically in order to achieve optimum air distribution and cylinder charge and, thus, greater torque. Since the fuel is injected directly onto the intake valves, the engine receives only air through the intake manifold. This results in a higher power output per litre and a torque curve appropriate to practice.

Fig. 2: Schematic diagram of an L-Jetronic system with lambda closed-loop control
1 Fuel tank, 2 Electric fuel pump, 3 Fuel filter, 4 ECU, 5 Fuel-injection valve (injector),
6 Fuel rail and fuel-pressure regulator, 7 Intake manifold, 8 Cold-start valve, 9 Throttle-valve switch,
10 Air-flow sensor, 11 Lambda sensor, 12 Thermo-time switch, 13 Engine-temperature sensor,
14 Ignition distributor, 15 Auxiliary-air device, 16 Battery, 17 Ignition and starting switch.

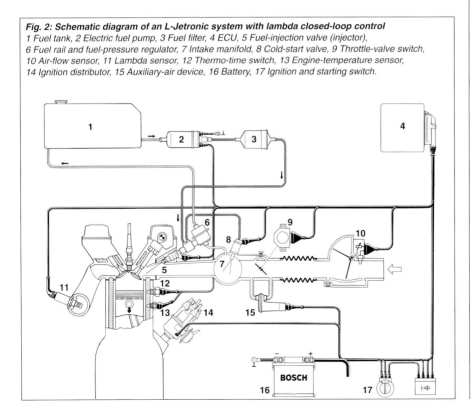

Fuel supply system

The fuel supply system comprises the following components:
– electric fuel pump,
– fine filter,
– fuel rail,
– pressure regulator and
– fuel-injection valves.

An electrically driven roller-cell pump pumps the fuel from the fuel tank at a pressure of approximately 2.5 bar through a filter into the fuel rail. From the fuel rail, fuel lines diverge to the injection valves. At the end of the fuel rail is a pressure regulator which maintains the injection pressure at a constant level (Figure 3). More fuel circulates in the fuel system than is needed by the engine even under the most extreme conditions. The excess fuel is returned to the fuel tank by the pressure regulator but not under pressure. The constant flushing through of the fuel system enables it to be continually supplied with cool fuel. This helps to avoid the formation of fuel vapour bubbles and guarantees good hot-starting characteristics.

Electric fuel pump

The electric fuel pump is a roller-cell pump driven by a permanent-magnet electric motor. The rotor plate which is eccentrically mounted in the pump housing is fitted with metal rollers in notches around its circumference which are pressed against the pump housing by centrifugal force and act as seals. The fuel is carried in the cavities which form between the rollers. The pumping action takes place when the rollers, after having closed the inlet port, force the trapped fuel around in front of them until it can escape from the pump through the outlet port (Figure 5). The fuel flows directly around the electric motor. There is no danger of explosion, however, because there is never an ignitable mixture in the pump housing.

The electric fuel pump delivers more fuel than the maximum requirement of the engine so that the pressure in the fuel system can be maintained under all operating conditions. A check valve in the pump disconnects the fuel system from the fuel tank by preventing return flow of fuel to the fuel tank.
The electric fuel pump starts immediately when the ignition and starting switch is operated and remains switched on continously after the engine has started. A safety circuit prevents fuel from being delivered when the ignition is switched on, but when the engine is stationary (e.g. after an accident). The fuel pump is located in the direct vicinity of the fuel tank and requires no maintenance.

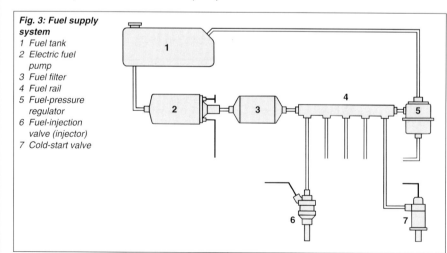

Fig. 3: Fuel supply system
1 Fuel tank
2 Electric fuel pump
3 Fuel filter
4 Fuel rail
5 Fuel-pressure regulator
6 Fuel-injection valve (injector)
7 Cold-start valve

Fuel filter

The fuel filter filters off impurities in the fuel which could impair the function of the injection system. The filter contains a paper element with an average pore size of 10 µm, which is backed up by a fluff strainer (Figure 6). This combination ensures a high degree of filtration. A support plate secures the filter in its metal housing. The filter is installed in the fuel line downstream of the fuel accumulator.

When the filter is changed, it is imperative that the throughflow direction as indicated by the arrow on the housing be observed.

Fuel rail

The fuel rail supplies all injection valves with an equal quantity of fuel and ensures the same fuel pressure at all injection valves.

The fuel rail has a storage function. Its volume, compared with the amount of fuel injected during each working cycle of the engine, is large enough to prevent variations in pressure. The injection valves connected to the fuel rail are therefore subjected to the same fuel pressure.

The fuel rail also facilitates easy fitting of the injection valves.

Pressure regulator

The pressure regulator keeps the pressure differential between the fuel pressure and manifold pressure constant. Thus, the fuel delivered by the electromagnetic injection valve is determined solely by the valve opening time.

The pressure regulator is a diaphragm-controlled overflow pressure regulator which controls pressure at 2.5 or 3 bar, dependent upon the system in question. It is located at the end of the fuel rail and consists of a metal housing, divided into two spaces by a flanged diaphragm: a chamber for the spring that preloads the diaphragm, and a chamber for the fuel (Figure 7). When the preset pressure is exceeded, a valve operated by the diaphragm opens the return line for the excess fuel to flow back,

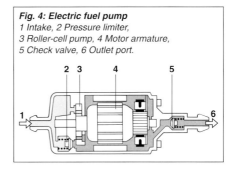

Fig. 4: Electric fuel pump
1 Intake, 2 Pressure limiter,
3 Roller-cell pump, 4 Motor armature,
5 Check valve, 6 Outlet port.

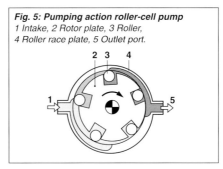

Fig. 5: Pumping action roller-cell pump
1 Intake, 2 Rotor plate, 3 Roller,
4 Roller race plate, 5 Outlet port.

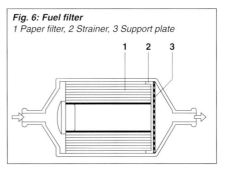

Fig. 6: Fuel filter
1 Paper filter, 2 Strainer, 3 Support plate

not under pressure, to the fuel tank. The spring chamber is connected by a tube with the intake manifold downstream of the throttle valve. This has the effect that the pressure in the fuel system is dependent upon the absolute manifold pressure; therefore, the pressure drop across the fuel-injection valves is the same for any throttle position.

Fuel-injection valves

The electronically controlled fuel-injection valves inject precisely metered fuel into the intake ports and onto the intake valves.

Each engine cylinder has its own fuel-injection valve. The valves are solenoid-operated and are opened and closed by means of electric pulses from the electronic control unit. The fuel-injection valve consists of a valve body and the needle valve with fitted solenoid armature. The valve body contains the solenoid winding and the guide for the needle valve. When there is no current flowing in the solenoid winding, the needle valve is pressed against its seat on the valve outlet by a helical spring. When a current is passed through the solenoid winding, the needle valve is lifted by approximately 0.1 mm from its seat and the fuel can be injected through the precision annular orifice. The front end of the needle valve has a specially ground pintle for atomizing the fuel (Figure 8). The pickup and release times of the valve lie in the range of 1 to 1.5 ms. To achieve good fuel distribution together with low condensation loss, it is necessary that wetting of the intake-manifold walls be avoided.

The means that a particular spray angle in conjunction with a particular distance of the injection valve from the intake valve must therefore be maintained, specific to the engine concerned. The fuel-injection valves are fitted with the help of special holders and are mounted in rubber mouldings in these holders. The insulation from the heat of the engine thereby achieved prevents the formation of fuel-vapour bubbles and guarantees good hot-starting characteristics. The rubber mouldings also ensure that the fuel-injection valves are not subjected to excessive vibration.

Fig. 7: Fuel-pressure regulator
1 Intake-manifold connection, 2 Spring, 3 Valve holder, 4 Diaphragm, 5 Valve, 6 Fuel inlet, 7 Fuel return.

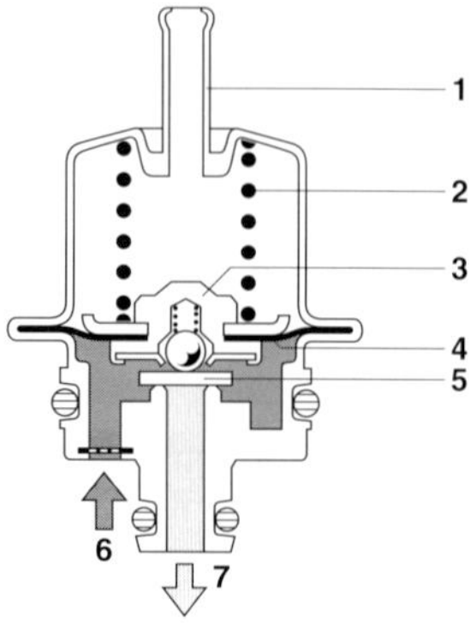

Fig. 8: Solenoid-operated fuel-injection valve (injector)
1 Filter in fuel inlet, 2 Electrical connection, 3 Solenoid winding, 4 Valve housing, 5 Armature, 6 Valve body, 7 Valve needle.

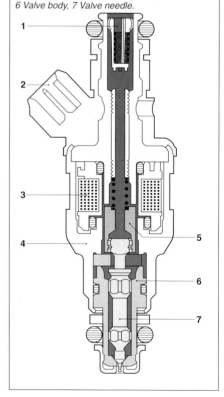

Operating-data sensing system

Sensors detect the operating mode of the engine and signal this condition electrically to the control unit. The sensors and ECU form the control system. The sensors are described in conjunction with the relevant main function or compensation function.

Measured variables
The measured variables characterizing the operating mode of the engine are as follows:
– main measured variables
– measured variables for compensation
– measured variables for precise compensation.
The ECU evaluates all measured variables together so that the engine is always supplied with exactly the amount of fuel required for the instantaneous operating mode. This achieves optimum driveability.

Main measured variables
The main measured variables are the engine speed and the amount of air drawn in by the engine. These determine the amount of air per stroke which then serves as a direct measure for the loading condition of the engine.

Measured variables for compensation
For operating conditions such as cold start and warm-up and the various load conditions which deviate from normal operation, the mixture must be adapted to the modified conditions. Starting and warm-up conditions are detected by sensors which transmit the engine temperature to the control unit. For compensating various load conditions, the load range (idle, part-load, full-load) is transmitted to the control unit via the throttle-valve switch.

Measured variables for precision compensation
In order to achieve optimum driving behavior, further operating ranges and in-

fluences can be considered: the sensors mentioned above detect the data for transition response when accelerating, for maximum engine-speed limitation and during overrun. The sensor signals have a particular relationship to each other in these operating ranges. The control unit recognizes these relationships and influences the control signals of the injection valves accordingly.

Calculating engine speed
Information on engine speed and the start of injection is passed on to the L-Jetronic ECU in breaker-triggered ignition systems by the contact-breaker points in the ignition distributor, and, in breakerless ignition systems, by terminal 1 of the ignition coil.

Measuring the air flow
The amount of air drawn in by the engine is a measure of its loading condition. The air-flow measurement system allows for all changes which may take place in the engine during the service life of the vehicle, e.g. wear, combustion-chamber deposits and changes to the valve setting.
Since the quantity of air drawn in must first pass through the air-flow sensor before entering the engine, this means that, during acceleration, the signal leaves the sensor before the air is actually drawn into the cylinder. This

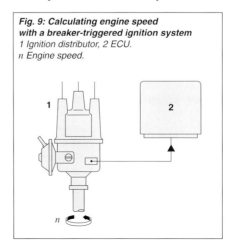

Fig. 9: Calculating engine speed with a breaker-triggered ignition system
1 Ignition distributor, 2 ECU.
n Engine speed.

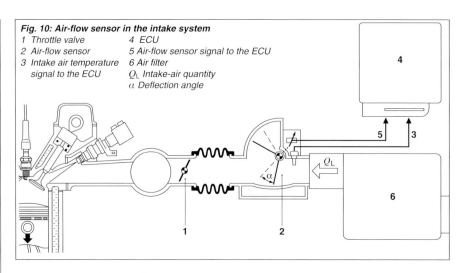

Fig. 10: Air-flow sensor in the intake system

1 Throttle valve	4 ECU
2 Air-flow sensor	5 Air-flow sensor signal to the ECU
3 Intake air temperature	6 Air filter
signal to the ECU	Q_L Intake-air quantity
	α Deflection angle

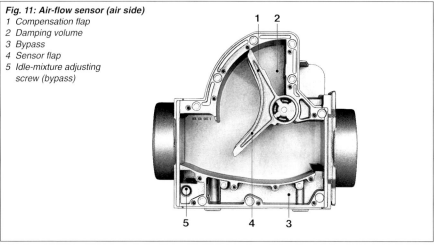

Fig. 11: Air-flow sensor (air side)
1 Compensation flap
2 Damping volume
3 Bypass
4 Sensor flap
5 Idle-mixture adjusting
   screw (bypass)

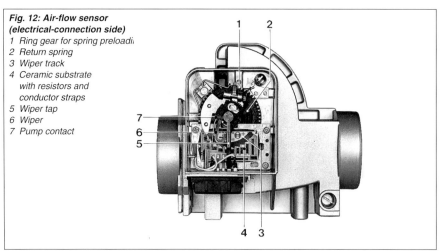

**Fig. 12: Air-flow sensor
(electrical-connection side)**
1 Ring gear for spring preloadi
2 Return spring
3 Wiper track
4 Ceramic substrate
   with resistors and
   conductor straps
5 Wiper tap
6 Wiper
7 Pump contact

permits correct mixture adaptation at any time during load changes.

The sensor flap in the air-flow sensor measures the entire air quantity inducted by the engine, thereby serving as the main controlled variable for determining the load signal and basic injection quantity.

Air-flow sensor

The principle is based on the measurement of the force emanating from the stream of air drawn in by the engine. This force has to counteract the opposing force of a return spring acting upon the air-flow sensor flap. The flap is deflected in such a manner that, together with the profile of the measurement channel, the free cross-section increases along with the rise in the quantity of air passing through it (Figs. 10, 11 and 12).

The change in the free air-flow sensor cross-section, depending on the position of the sensor flap, was selected so that a logarithmic relationship results between flap angle and air throughput. The result is that, at low air throughput, where measurement precision must be particularly high, the sensitivity of the air-flow sensor is also high. In order to prevent the oscillations in the intake system caused by the engine intake strokes from having more than a minimum effect upon the sensor-flap position, a compensation flap is attached rigidly to the sensor flap. The pressure oscillations have the same effects upon both flaps and the moments of force therefore cancel each other out so that the measurement is not affected. The angular position of the sensor flap is transformed by a potentiometer into a voltage. The potentiometer is calibrated such that the relationship between air throughput and voltage output is inversely proportional. In order that aging and the temperature characteristic of the potentiometer have no effect upon the accuracy, only resistance values are evaluated in the ECU. In order to set the air-fuel ratio at idle, an adjustable by-pass channel is provided.

Fuel metering

As the central unit of the system, the ECU evaluates the data delivered by the sensors on the operating mode of the engine. From this data, control pulses for the injection valves are generated, whereby the quantity to be injected is determined by the length of time the injection valves are opened.

Electronic control unit (ECU)

Configuration

The L-Jetronic ECU is in a splash-proof sheet-metal housing which is fitted where it is not affected by the heat radiated from the engine. The electronic components in the ECU are arranged on printed-circuit boards; the output-stage power components are mounted on the metal frame of the ECU thus assuring good heat dissipation. By using integrated circuits and hybrid modules, it has been possible to reduce the number of parts to a minimum. The reliability of the ECU was increased by combining functional groups into integrated circuits (e.g. pulse shaper, pulse divider and division control multivibrator) and by combining components into hybrid modules.

A multiple plug is used to connect the ECU to the injection valves, the sensors and the vehicle electrical system. The input circuit in the ECU is designed so that the latter cannot be connected with the wrong polarity and cannot be short-circuited. Special Bosch testers are available for carrying out measurements on the ECU and on the sensors. The testers can be connected between the wiring harness and the ECU with multiple plugs.

Operating data processing

Engine speed and inducted air quantity determine the basic duration of injection.

The timing frequency of the injection pulses is determined on the basis of the engine speed.

The pulses delivered by the ignition

system for this purpose are processed by the ECU. First of all, they pass through a pulse-shaping circuit which generates square-wave pulses from the signal "delivered" in the form of damped oscillations, and feeds these to a frequency divider.

The frequency divider divides the pulse frequency given by the ignition sequence in such a manner that two pulses occur for each working cycle regardless of the number of cylinders. The start of the pulse is, at the same time, the start of injection for the injection valves. For each turn of the crankshaft, each injection valve injects once, regardless of the position of the intake valves. When the intake valve is closed, the fuel is stored and the next time it opens the fuel is drawn into the combustion chamber together with the air. The duration of injection depends on the amount of air measured by the air-flow sensor and the engine speed.

The ECU also evaluates the signal supplied by the potentiometer. Fig. 14 shows the interrelationships between intake air quantity, flap angle, potentiometer voltage and injected quantity. Assuming a specific intake-air quantity Q_L flowing through the air-flow sensor (point Q), we thus obtain the theoreti-

cally required injection quantity Q_K (point D). In addition, a specific flap angle (point A) is established as a function of the air intake quantity. The potentiometer actuated by the air-flow sensor flap supplies a voltage signal U_S to the ECU (point B) which controls the injection valves, whereby point C represents the injected fuel quantity V_E. It can be seen that the fuel quantity injected in practice and the theoretically required injection quantity are identical (line C–D).

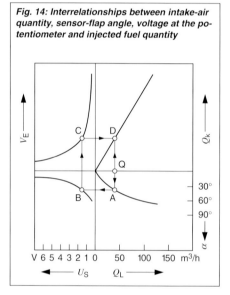

Fig. 14: Interrelationships between intake-air quantity, sensor-flap angle, voltage at the potentiometer and injected fuel quantity

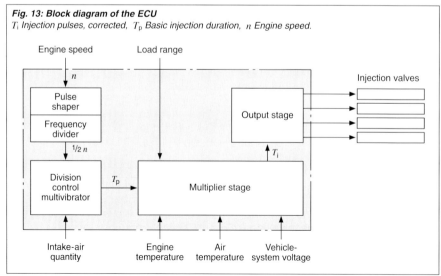

Fig. 13: Block diagram of the ECU
T_i Injection pulses, corrected, T_p Basic injection duration, n Engine speed.

Generation of injection pulses (Fig. 15)
The generation of the basic injection duration is carried out in a special circuit group in the ECU, the division control multivibrator.

The division control multivibrator (DSM) receives the information on speed n from the frequency divider and evaluates it together with the air-quantity signal U_S. For the purpose of intermittent fuel injection, the DSM converts the voltage U_S into square-wave control pulses. The duration T_p of this pulse determines the basic injection quantity, i.e. the quantity of fuel to be injected per intake stroke without considering any corrections. T_p is therefore regarded as the "basic injection duration". The greater the quantity of air drawn in with each intake stroke, the longer the basic injection duration.

Two border cases are possible here: if the engine speed n increases at a constant air throughput Q, then the abso-

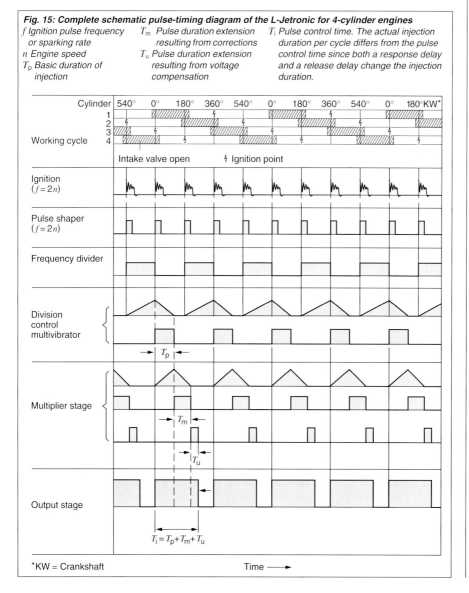

Fig. 15: Complete schematic pulse-timing diagram of the L-Jetronic for 4-cylinder engines

f Ignition pulse frequency or sparking rate
n Engine speed
T_p Basic duration of injection

T_m Pulse duration extension resulting from corrections
T_u Pulse duration extension resulting from voltage compensation

T_i Pulse control time. The actual injection duration per cycle differs from the pulse control time since both a response delay and a release delay change the injection duration.

Cylinder 540° 0° 180° 360° 540° 0° 180° 360° 540° 0° 180°KW*

Working cycle 1 2 3 4

Intake valve open   ⌇ Ignition point

Ignition $(f = 2n)$

Pulse shaper $(f = 2n)$

Frequency divider

Division control multivibrator

T_p

Multiplier stage

T_m

T_u

Output stage

$T_i = T_p + T_m + T_u$

*KW = Crankshaft   Time ⟶

lute pressure sinks downstream of the throttle valve and the cylinders draw in less air per stroke, i.e. the cylinder charge is reduced. As a result, less fuel is needed for combustion and the duration of the pulse T_p is correspondingly shorter. If the engine output and thereby the amount of air drawn in per minute increase and providing the speed remains constant, then the cylinder charge will improve and more fuel will be required: the pulse duration T_p of the DSM is longer (Figs. 15 and 16).

During normal driving, engine speed and output usually change at the same time, whereby the DSM continually calculates the basic injection duration T_p. At a high speed, the engine output is normally high (full load) and this results ultimately in a longer pulse duration T_p and, therefore, more fuel per injection cycle.

The basic injection duration is extended by the signals from the sensors depending on the operating mode of the engine.

Adaptation of the basic injection duration to the various operating conditions is carried out by the multiplying stage in the ECU. This stage is controlled by the DSM with the pulses of duration T_p. In addition, the multiplying stage gathers information on various operating modes of the engine, such as cold start, warm-up, full-load operation etc. From this information, the correction factor k is calculated. This is multiplied by the basic injection duration T_p calculated by the division control multivibrator. The resulting time is designated T_m. T_m is added to the basic injection duration T_p, i.e. the injection duration is extended and the air-fuel mixture becomes richer. T_m is therefore a measure of fuel enrichment, expressed by a factor which can be designated "enrichment factor". When it is very cold, for example, the valves inject two to three times the amount of fuel at the beginning of the warm-up period (Figures 13 and 15).

Fig. 16: Signals and controlled variables at the ECU
Q_L Intake air quantity, ϑ_L Air temperature, n Engine speed, P Engine load range, ϑ_M Engine temperature, V_E Injection quantity, Q_{LZ} Auxiliary air, V_{ES} Excess fuel for starting, U_B Vehicle-system voltage.

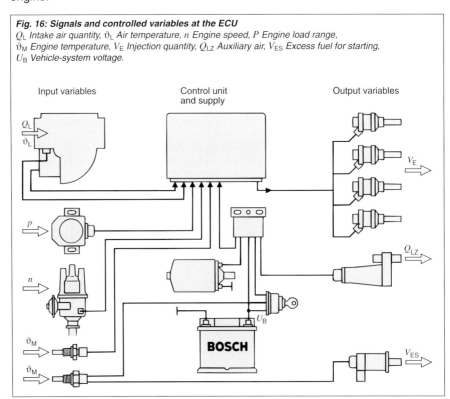

Input variables   Control unit and supply   Output variables

Voltage correction

The pickup time of the fuel-injection valves depends very much on the battery voltage. Without electronic voltage correction, the response delay which results from a low-voltage battery would cause the injection duration to be too short and, as a result, insufficient fuel would be injected. The lower the battery voltage, the less fuel the engine would receive. For this reason, a low battery voltage, i.e. after starting with a heavily discharged battery, must be compensated for with an appropriate extension T_u of the pre-calculated pulse time in order that the engine receives the correct fuel quantity. This is known as "voltage compensation". For voltage compensation, the effective battery voltage is fed into the control unit as the controlled variable. An electronic compensation stage extends the valve control pulses by the amount T_u which is the voltage-dependent pickup delay of the injection valves. The total duration of the fuel-injection pulses T_i is thus the sum of T_p, T_m and T_u (Fig. 15).

Amplification of the injection pulses

The fuel-injection pulses generated by the multiplying stage are amplified in a following output stage. The injection valves are controlled with these amplified pulses.

All the fuel-injection valves in the engine open and close at the same time. With each valve, a series resistor is wired into the circuit and functions as a current limiter. The output stage of the L-Jetronic supplies 3 or 4 valves simultaneously with current. Control units for 6 and 8-cylinder engines have two output stages with 3 and 4 injection valves respectively. Both output stages operate in unison. The injection cycle of the L-Jetronic is selected so that for each revolution of the camshaft (= 1 working cycle) half the amount of fuel required by each working cylinder is injected twice.

In addition to controlling the fuel-injection valves through the series resistors, some control units have a regu-

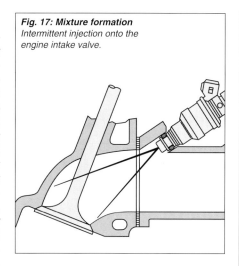

Fig. 17: Mixture formation
Intermittent injection onto the engine intake valve.

lated output stage. In these control units, the fuel-injection valves are operated without series resistors. Control of the fuel-injection valve takes place then as follows: as soon as the valve armatures have picked up at the beginning of the pulse, the valve current is regulated for the rest of the pulse duration to a considerably reduced current, the holding current. Since these valves are switched on at the start of the pulse with a very high current, short response times are the result. By means of the reduction in current strength after switching on, the output stage is not subjected to such heavy loading. In this way, up to 12 fuel-injection valves can be switched with only one output stage.

Mixture formation

Mixture formation is carried out in the intake ports and in the engine cylinder. The fuel-injection valve injects its fuel directly onto the engine intake valve and, when this opens, the cloud of fuel is entrained along with the air which is drawn in by the engine and an ignitable mixture is formed by the swirling action which takes place during the intake cycle (Fig. 17).

Adaptation to operating modes

In addition to the basic functions described up to now, the mixture has to be adapted during particular operating modes.

These adaptations (corrections) are necessary in order to optimize the power delivered by the engine, to improve the exhaust-gas composition and to improve the starting behavior and driveability. With additional sensors for the engine temperature and the throttle-valve position (load signal), the L-Jetronic ECU can perform these adaptation tasks. The characteristic curve of the air-flow sensor determines the fuel-requirement curve, specific to the particular engine, for all operating ranges.

Cold-start enrichment

When the engine is started, additional fuel is injected for a limited period depending on the temperature of the engine. This is carried out in order to compensate for fuel condensation losses in the inducted mixture and in order to facilitate starting the cold engine.

This extra fuel is injected by the cold-start valve into the intake manifold. The injection duration of the cold-start valve is limited by a thermo-time switch depending upon the engine temperature.

This process is known as cold-start enrichment and results in a "richer" air-fuel mixture, i.e. the excess-air factor λ is temporarily less than 1.

There are two methods of cold-start enrichment:
– start control with the aid of the ECU and injection valves (Figure 18) or
– cold-start enrichment via thermo-time switch and cold-start valve (Figure 19).

Start control

By extending the period during which the fuel-injection valves inject, more fuel can be supplied during the starting phase. The electronic control unit controls the start procedure by processing the signals from the ignition and starting switch and the engine-temperature sensor (Figure 18). The construction and method of operation of the temperature sensor are described in Chapter "Warm-up enrichment".

Cold-start valve

The cold-start valve (Figure 20) is a solenoid-operated valve. The solenoid winding is located in the valve. In neutral position, a helical spring presses the movable solenoid armature against a seal, thereby shutting off the valve.

When a current is passed through the solenoid, the armature, which now rises from the valve seat, allows fuel to flow along the sides of the armature to a nozzle where it is swirled. The swirl nozzle atomizes the fuel very finely and as a result enriches the air in the intake

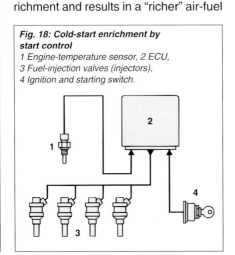

Fig. 18: Cold-start enrichment by start control
1 Engine-temperature sensor, 2 ECU,
3 Fuel-injection valves (injectors),
4 Ignition and starting switch.

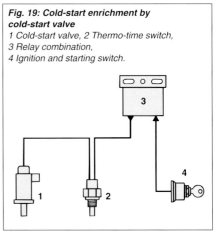

Fig. 19: Cold-start enrichment by cold-start valve
1 Cold-start valve, 2 Thermo-time switch,
3 Relay combination,
4 Ignition and starting switch.

Fig. 20: Cold-start valve operated
1 Electrical connection, 2 Fuel inlet with filter strainer, 3 Valve (solenoid armature), 4 Solenoid winding, 5 Swirl nozzle, 6 Valve seat.

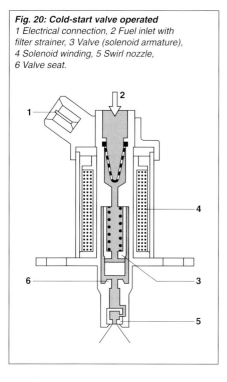

Fig. 21: Thermo-time switch
1 Electrical connection, 2 Housing, 3 Bimetal, 4 Heating winding, 5 Electrical contact.

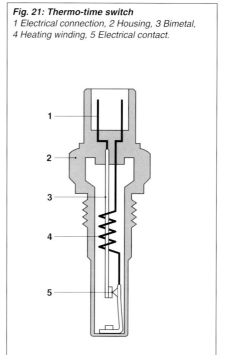

manifold downstream of the throttle valve with fuel. The cold-start valve is mounted on the intake manifold in such a way as to provide a favourable distribution of the air-fuel mixture to all engine cylinders.

Thermo-time switch
The thermo-time switch limits the duration of injection of the cold-start valve depending on the temperature of the engine.

The thermo-time switch (Figure 21) is an electrically heated bimetal switch which opens or closes a contact depending on its temperature. It is controlled via the ignition and starting switch. The thermo-time switch is attached in a position representative of the engine temperature. During a cold start, it limits the "on" period of the cold-start valve. In the case of repeated start attempts, or when starting takes too long, the cold-start valve ceases to inject.

The "on" period is determined by the thermo-time switch which is heated by the heat of the engine as well as by its own built-in electric heater. The electrical heating is necessary in order to ensure that the "on" period of the cold-start valve is limited under all conditions, and engine flooding is prevented. During an actual cold start, the heat generated by the built-in heating winding is mainly responsible for the "on" period (switch-off, for instance, at –20 °C after approx. 7.5 s). With a warm engine, the thermo-time switch has already been heated so far by engine heat that it remains open and prevents the cold-start valve from going into action.

Post-start and warm-up enrichment
During warm-up, the engine receives extra fuel.

The warm-up phase follows the cold-start phase of the engine. During this phase, the engine needs substantially more fuel since some of the fuel condenses on the still cold cylinder walls. In addition, without supplementary fuel enrichment during the warm-up period, a major drop in engine speed would be noticed after the additional fuel from the cold-start valve has been cut off.

For example, at a temperature of –20 °C, depending on the type of engine, two to three times as much fuel must be injected immediately after starting compared with when the engine is at normal operating temperature. In this first part of the warm-up phase (post-start), there must be an enrichment dependent on time. This is the so-called post-start enrichment. This enrichment has to last about 30 s and, dependent upon temperature, results in between 30 % and 60 % more fuel.

When the post-start enrichment has finished, the engine needs only a slight mixture enrichment, this being controlled by the engine temperature. The diagram (Figure 22) shows a typical enrichment curve with reference to time with a starting temperature of 22 °C. In order to trigger this control process, the electronic control unit must receive information on the engine temperature. This comes from the temperature sensor.

Engine-temperature sensor

The engine-temperature sensor (Figure 23) measures the temperature of the engine and converts this into an electrical signal for the ECU.

It is mounted on the engine block on air-cooled engines. With water-cooled engines, it projects into the coolant.

The sensor "reports" the particular engine temperature to the ECU in the form of a resistance value. The ECU then adapts the quantity of fuel to be injected during post-start and during warm-up. The temperature sensor consists of an NTC resistor embedded in a threaded sleeve.

NTC stands for Negative Temperature Coefficient, the decisive characteristic of this resistor. When the temperature increases, the electrical resistance of the semiconductor resistor decreases.

Part-load adaptation

By far the major part of the time, the engine will be operating in the part-load range. The fuel-requirement curve for this range is programmed in the ECU and determines the amount of fuel supplied. The curve is such that the fuel

Fig. 22: Warm-up enrichment curve
Enrichment factor F as a function of time:
a) Proportion mainly dependent on time,
b) Proportion mainly dependent on engine temperature.

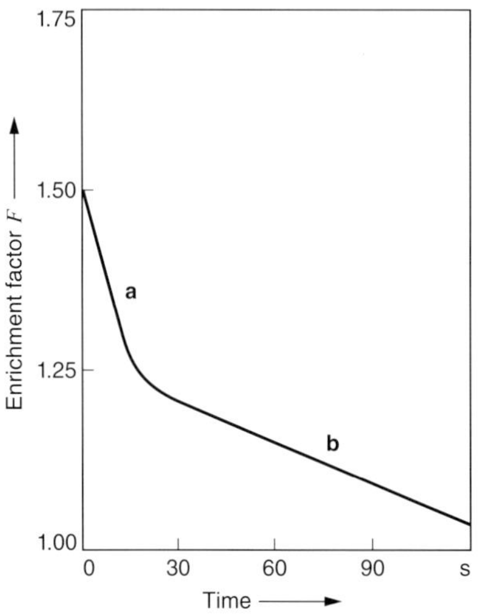

Fig. 23: Engine-temperature sensor
1 Electrical connection, 2 Housing,
3 NTC resistor.

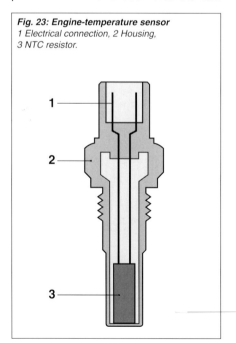

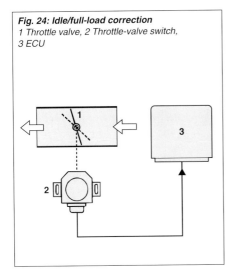

Fig. 24: Idle/full-load correction
1 Throttle valve, 2 Throttle-valve switch,
3 ECU

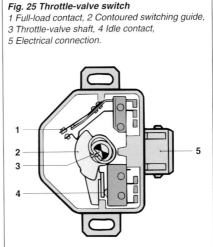

Fig. 25 Throttle-valve switch
1 Full-load contact, 2 Contoured switching guide,
3 Throttle-valve shaft, 4 Idle contact,
5 Electrical connection.

consumption of the engine is low in the part-load range.

Acceleration enrichment

During acceleration, the L-Jetronic meters additional fuel to the engine.

If the throttle is opened abruptly, the air-fuel mixture is momentarily leaned-off, and a short period of mixture enrichment is needed to ensure good transitional response.

With this abrupt opening of the throttle valve, the amount of air which enters the combustion chamber, plus the amount of air which is needed to bring the manifold pressure up to the new level, flow through the air-flow sensor. This causes the sensor plate to "overswing" past the wide-open-throttle point. This "overswing" results in more fuel being metered to the engine (acceleration enrichment) and ensures good acceleration response.

Since this acceleration enrichment is not adequate during the warm-up phase, the control unit also evaluates a signal representing the speed at which the sensor flap deflects during this operating mode.

Full-load enrichment

The engine delivers its maximum torque at full load, when the air-fuel mixture must be enriched compared to that at part-load.

In contrast to part-load where the calibration is for minimum fuel consumption and low emissions, at full load it is necessary to enrich the air-fuel mixture. This enrichment is programmed in the electronic control unit, specific to the particular engine. The information on the load condition is supplied to the control unit by the throttle-valve switch.

Throttle-valve switch

The throttle-valve switch (Figure 25) communicates the "idle" and "full load" throttle positions to the control unit.

It is mounted on the throttle body and actuated by the throttle-valve shaft. A contoured switching guide closes the "idle" contact at one end of switch travel and the "full-load" contact at the other.

Controlling the idle speed

The air-flow sensor contains an adjustable bypass via which a small quantity of air can bypass the sensor flap.

The idle-mixture-adjusting screw in the bypass permits a basic setting of the air-fuel ratio or mixture enrichment by varying the bypass cross-section (Figure 26). In order to achieve smoother running even at idle, the idle-speed control increases the idle speed. This also leads to a more rapid warm-up of the engine. Depending upon engine temperature, an electrically heated auxiliary-air device in the form of a bypass around the throttle plate allows the engine to draw in more air (Figure 26).

This auxiliary air is measured by the air-flow sensor, and leads to the L-Jetronic providing the engine with more fuel. Precise adaptation is by means of the electrical heating facility. The engine temperature then determines how much auxiliary air is fed in initially through the bypass, and the electrical heating is mainly responsible for subsequently reducing the auxiliary air as a function of time.

Auxiliary-air device

The auxiliary-air device incorporates a perforated plate (Figure 27) which is actuated by the bimetallic strip and which controls the cross-section of the bypass passage.

Initially, the bypass cross-section opened by the perforated plate is determined by the engine temperature, so that during a cold start the bypass opening is adequate for the auxiliary air required. The opening closes steadily along with increasing engine temperature until, finally, it is closed completely. The bimetal strip is electrically heated and this limits the opening time, starting from the initial setting which is dependent upon the engine temperature.

The auxiliary-air device is fitted in the best possible position on the engine for it to assume engine temperature. It does not function when the engine is warm.

Adaptation to the air temperature

The quantity of fuel injected is adapted to the air temperature. The quantity of air necessary for combustion depends upon the temperature of the air drawn in. Cold air is denser. This means that with the same throttle-valve position the volumetric efficiency of the cylinders drops as the temperature increases.

To register this effect, a temperature sensor is fitted in the intake duct of the air-flow sensor. This sensor measures the temperature of the air drawn in and passes this information on to the control unit which then controls the amount of fuel metered to the cylinders accordingly.

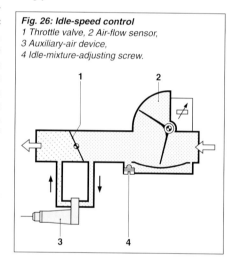

Fig. 26: Idle-speed control
*1 Throttle valve, 2 Air-flow sensor,
3 Auxiliary-air device,
4 Idle-mixture-adjusting screw.*

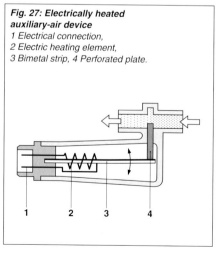

**Fig. 27: Electrically heated
auxiliary-air device**
*1 Electrical connection,
2 Electric heating element,
3 Bimetal strip, 4 Perforated plate.*

Supplementary functions

Lambda closed-loop control
By means of the lambda closed-loop control, the air-fuel ratio can be maintained precisely at $\lambda = 1$. In the control unit, the lambda-sensor signal is compared with an ideal value (setpoint), thus controlling a two-position controller. The intervention in fuel-metering is accomplished through the opening time of the fuel-injection valves.

Overrun fuel cutoff
Overrun fuel cutoff is the interruption of the supply of fuel to the engine in order to reduce consumption and emissions during downhill driving and braking. When the driver takes his foot off the accelerator pedal while driving, the throttle-valve switch signals "throttle-valve closed" to the ECU and fuel injection is interrupted. The engine-speed switching threshold for injection-pulse cutoff, as well as that for the resumption of fuel injection, depend upon engine temperature.

Engine-speed limiting
When the maximum permissible engine speed is reached, the engine-speed limiting system suppresses the injection signals and interrupts the supply of fuel to the injection valves.

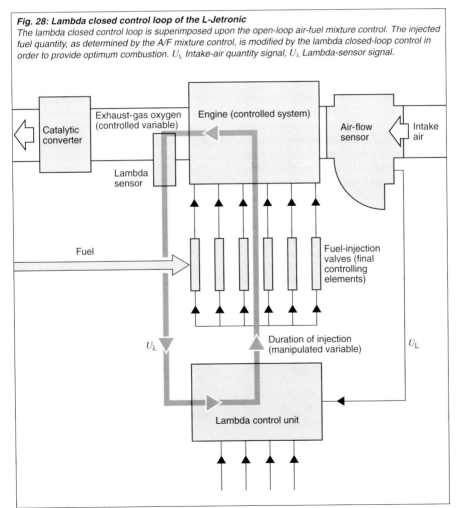

Fig. 28: Lambda closed control loop of the L-Jetronic
The lambda closed control loop is superimposed upon the open-loop air-fuel mixture control. The injected fuel quantity, as determined by the A/F mixture control, is modified by the lambda closed-loop control in order to provide optimum combustion. U_L Intake-air quantity signal, U_λ Lambda-sensor signal.

Fig. 29: Components of the L-Jetronic
1 Air-flow sensor, 2 ECU, 3 Fuel filter, 4 Fuel pump, 5 Fuel pressure regulator, 6 Auxiliary-air device,
7 Thermo-time switch, 8 Temperature sensor, 9 Throttle-valve switch, 10 Cold-start valve,
11 Fuel-injection valves (injectors).

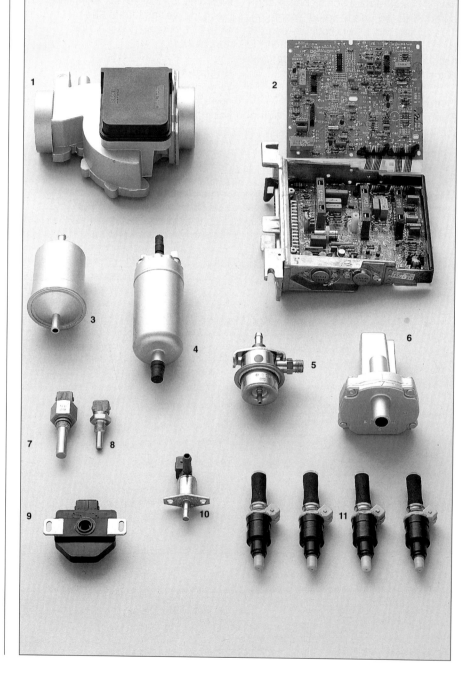

Electric circuitry

The complete circuitry of the L-Jetronic has been designed so that it can be connected to the vehicle electrical system at a single point.

At this point, you will find the relay combination which is controlled by the ignition and starting switch, and which switches the vehicle voltage to the control unit and the other Jetronic components.

The relay combination has two separate plug connections, one to the vehicle electrical system and one to the Jetronic.

Safety circuit

In order to prevent the electric fuel pump from continuing to supply fuel following an accident, it is controlled by means of a safety circuit. When the engine is running, the air passing through the air-flow sensor causes a switch to be operated. This switch controls the relay combination which in turn switches the electric fuel pump. If the engine stops with the ignition still on, air is no longer drawn in by the engine and the switch interrupts the power supply to the fuel pump. During starting, the relay combination is controlled accordingly by terminal 50 of the ignition and starting switch.

Terminal diagram

The example shown here is a typical terminal diagram for a vehicle with a 4-cylinder engine. Please note with the wiring harness that terminal 88z of the relay combination is connected directly and without a fuse to the positive pole (terminal post) of the battery in order to avoid trouble and voltage drops caused by contact resistances. Terminals 5, 16 and 17 of the control unit, as well as terminal 49 of the temperature sensor, must be connected with separate cables to a common ground point.

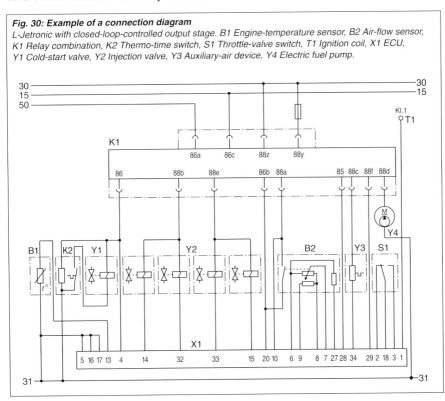

Fig. 30: Example of a connection diagram
L-Jetronic with closed-loop-controlled output stage. B1 Engine-temperature sensor, B2 Air-flow sensor, K1 Relay combination, K2 Thermo-time switch, S1 Throttle-valve switch, T1 Ignition coil, X1 ECU, Y1 Cold-start valve, Y2 Injection valve, Y3 Auxiliary-air device, Y4 Electric fuel pump.

L3-Jetronic

Specific systems for specific markets have in the meantime been developed on the basis of the L-Jetronic. These systems include the LE-Jetronic without lambda closed-loop control for Europe and the LU-Jetronic system with lambda closed-loop control for countries with strict exhaust gas emission legislation (e.g. the USA). The most recent stage of development is the L3-Jetronic which differs from its predecessors in respect of the following details:

– the control unit, which is suitable for installation in the engine compartment, is attached to the air-flow sensor and thus no longer requires space in the passenger compartment,

– the combined unit of control unit and air-flow sensor with internal connections simplifies the cable harness and reduces installation expense,

– the use of digital techniques permits new functions with improved adaptation capabilities to be implemented as compared with the previous analog techniques used.

The L3-Jetronic system is available both with and without lambda closed-loop control. Both versions have what is called a "limp-home" function which enables the driver to drive the vehicle to the nearest workshop if the microcomputer fails. In addition the input signals are checked for plausibility, i.e. an implausible input signal (e.g. engine temperature lower than –40°C) is ignored and a default value stored in the control unit is used in its place.

Fuel supply

On this system, the fuel is supplied to the injection valves in the same way as on the L-Jetronic system via an electric fuel pump, fuel filter, fuel rail and pressure regulator.

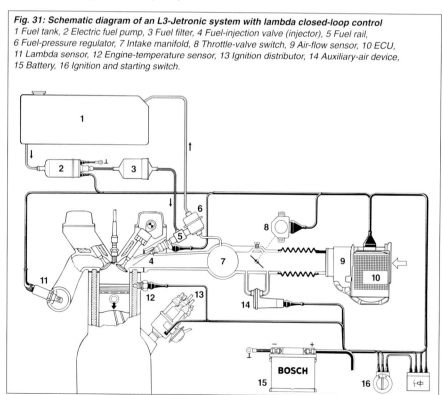

Fig. 31: Schematic diagram of an L3-Jetronic system with lambda closed-loop control
*1 Fuel tank, 2 Electric fuel pump, 3 Fuel filter, 4 Fuel-injection valve (injector), 5 Fuel rail,
6 Fuel-pressure regulator, 7 Intake manifold, 8 Throttle-valve switch, 9 Air-flow sensor, 10 ECU,
11 Lambda sensor, 12 Engine-temperature sensor, 13 Ignition distributor, 14 Auxiliary-air device,
15 Battery, 16 Ignition and starting switch.*

Operating-data sensing system

The ignition system supplies the information on engine speed to the control unit. A temperature sensor in the coolant circuit measures the engine temperature and converts it to an electrical signal for the control unit. The throttle-valve switch signals the throttle-valve positions "idle" and "full load" to the control unit for controlling the engine in order to allow for the different optimization criteria in the various operating conditions. The control unit senses the fluctuations in the electrical vehicle supply and compensates for the resultant response delays of the fuel-injection valves by correcting the duration of injection.

Air-flow sensor

The air-flow sensor of the L3-Jetronic system measures the amount of air drawn in by the engine using the same measuring principle as the air-flow sensor of the conventional L-Jetronic system. Integrating the control unit with the air-flow sensor to form a single measuring and control unit requires a modified configuration however. The dimensions of the potentiometer chamber in the air-flow sensor and of the control unit have been reduced to such an extent that the overall height of the entire unit does not exceed that of the previous air-flow sensor alone. Other features of the new air-flow sensor include the reduced weight due to the aluminum used in place of the zinc material for the housing, the extended measuring range and the improved damping behavior in the event of abrupt changes in the intake air quantity. Thus, the L3-Jetronic incorporates clear improvements both in respect of electronic components and in respect of mechanical components whilst requiring less space (Figs. 32 and 33).

Fuel metering

Fuel is injected onto the intake valves of the engine by means of solenoid-operated injection valves. One solenoid valve is assigned to each cylinder and is operated once per crankshaft revolution. In order to reduce the circuit complexity, all valves are connected electrically in parallel. The differential pressure between the fuel pressure and

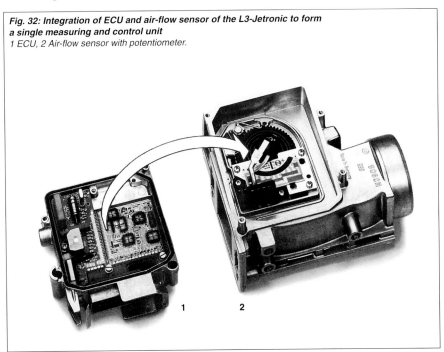

Fig. 32: Integration of ECU and air-flow sensor of the L3-Jetronic to form a single measuring and control unit
1 ECU, 2 Air-flow sensor with potentiometer.

1   2

intake-manifold pressure is maintained constant at 2.5 or 3 bar so that the quantity of fuel injected depends solely upon the opening time of the injection valves. For this purpose, the control unit supplies control pulses, the duration of which depends upon the inducted air quantity, the engine speed and other actuating variables which are detected by sensors and processed in the control unit.

Electronic control unit (ECU)

By contrast with the L-Jetronic system, the digital control unit of this system adapts the air-fuel ratio by means of a load/engine-speed map. On the basis of the input signals from the sensors, the control unit computes the injection duration as a measure of the amount of fuel to be injected. The microcomputer system of the control unit permits the required functions to be influenced. The control unit for attachment to the air-flow sensor must be very compact and must have very few plug connections in addition to being resistant to heat, vibration and moisture. These conditions are met by the use of a special-purpose hybrid circuit and a small PC board in the control unit. In addition to accommodating the microcomputer, the hybrid circuit also accommodates 5 other integrated circuits, 88 film resistors and 23 capacitors. The connections from the ICs to the thick-film board comprise thin gold wires which are a mere 33 thousandths of a millimeter in thickness.

Adaptation to operating conditions

During certain operating conditions (cold start, warm-up, acceleration, idle and full load), the fuel requirement differs greatly from the normal value so that it is necessary to intervene in mixture formation.

Throttle-valve switch

This switch is operated by the throttle-valve shaft and has a switching contact for each of the two end positions of the throttle valve. When the throttle valve is closed (idle) or fully open (full load), the

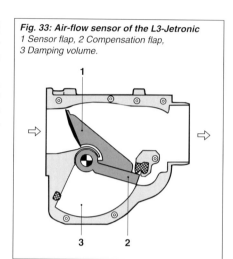

Fig. 33: Air-flow sensor of the L3-Jetronic
1 Sensor flap, 2 Compensation flap,
3 Damping volume.

switch issues a switching signal to the control unit.

Auxiliary-air device

A plate which is moved by a bimetallic spring or expansion element supplies extra air to the engine during the warm-up phase. This results in the higher idle speed which is required during the warm-up phase for smooth running of the engine.

A closed-loop idle-speed control system, in the form of a separate system, can be used instead of the auxiliary-air device to control the idle speed.

Engine-temperature sensor

The engine-temperature sensor, a temperature-dependent resistor, controls warm-up enrichment. The overrun fuel cutoff function, and the speed limiting function at maximum permissible engine speed, permit fuel economy and a reduction in pollutant emission.

Lambda closed-loop control

In the control unit, the signal from the lambda sensor is compared with an ideal value (setpoint), thus controlling a two-position controller. Dependent upon the result of the comparison, either an excessively lean air-fuel mixture is enriched or an excessively rich mixture is leaned. Fuel metering is influenced via the opening time of the injection valves.

LH-Jetronic

The LH-Jetronic is closely related to the L-Jetronic. The difference lies in the hot-wire air-mass meter which measures the air mass inducted by the engine. The result of measurement is thus independent of the air density which is itself dependent upon temperature and pressure.

Fuel supply

The fuel is supplied to the injection valves through the same components as with the L-Jetronic.

Operating-data sensing system

The information on engine speed is supplied to the control unit by the ignition system. A temperature sensor in the coolant circuit measures the engine temperature and converts it to an electronic signal for the control unit. The throttle-valve switch signals the throttle-valve positions "idle" and "full load" to the control unit for engine control in order to allow for the different optimization criteria in the various operating conditions. The control unit detects the fluctuations in the vehicle electrical supply and compensates for the resultant response delays of the injection valves by correcting the duration of injection.

Air-mass meters

The hot-wire and hot-film air-mass meters are "thermal" load sensors. They are installed between the air filter and the throttle valve and register the air-mass flow [kg/h] drawn in by the engine. Both sensors operate according to the same principle.

Hot-wire air-mass meter

With the hot-wire air-mass meter, the electrically heated element is in the form of a 70 µm thick platinum wire. The intake-air temperature is registered by a temperature sensor. The hot wire and the intake-air temperature sensor are part of a bridge circuit in which they function as

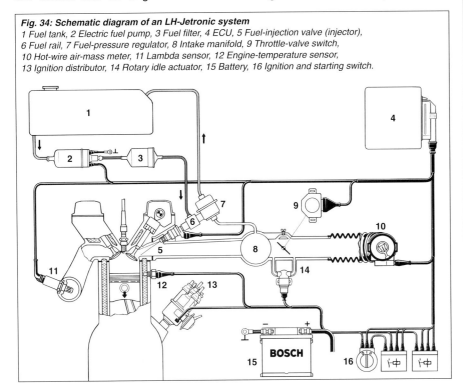

Fig. 34: Schematic diagram of an LH-Jetronic system
1 Fuel tank, 2 Electric fuel pump, 3 Fuel filter, 4 ECU, 5 Fuel-injection valve (injector),
6 Fuel rail, 7 Fuel-pressure regulator, 8 Intake manifold, 9 Throttle-valve switch,
10 Hot-wire air-mass meter, 11 Lambda sensor, 12 Engine-temperature sensor,
13 Ignition distributor, 14 Rotary idle actuator, 15 Battery, 16 Ignition and starting switch.

temperature-dependent resistances. A voltage signal which is proportional to the air-mass flow is transmitted to the ECU (Figs. 35 and 36).

Hot-film air-mass meter

With the hot-film air-mass meter, the electrically heated element is in the form of a platinum film resistance (heater). The heater's temperature is registered by a temperature-dependent resistor (throughflow sensor). The voltage across the heater is a measure for the air-mass flow. It is converted by the hot-film air-mass meter's electronic circuitry into a voltage which is suitable for the ECU (Fig. 37).

Fuel metering

Fuel is injected by means of solenoid-operated injection valves onto the intake valves of the engine. A solenoid valve is assigned to each cylinder and is operated once per crankshaft revolution. In order to reduce the circuit complexity, all valves are connected electri-

cally in parallel. The differential pressure between the fuel pressure and intake-manifold pressure is maintained constant at 2.5 or 3 bar so that the quantity of fuel injected depends solely upon the opening time of the injection valves. For this purpose, the control unit supplies control pulses, the duration of which are dependent upon the inducted air quantity, the engine speed and other actuating variables which are detected by sensors and processed in the control unit.

Electronic control unit (ECU)

By comparison with the L-Jetronic system, the digital control unit of this system adapts the air-fuel ratio by means of a load/engine-speed map. On the basis of the input signals from the sensors, the control unit computes the injection duration as a measure of the quantity of fuel to be injected. The microcomputer system of the control unit permits the required functions to be influenced.

Fig. 35: Hot-wire air-mass meter. The 70 μm thin platinum wire is suspended inside the measuring venturi.

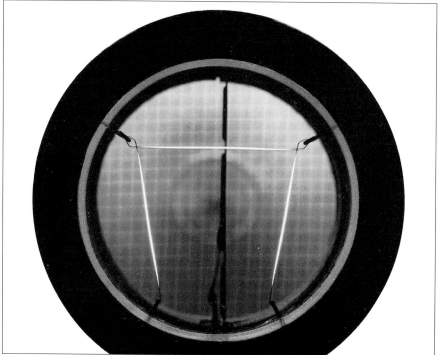

Adaptation to operating conditions

During certain operating conditions (cold start, warm-up, acceleration, idle and full load), the fuel requirement differs greatly from the normal value, thus necessitating an intervention in mixture formation.

Throttle-valve switch

This switch has a switching contact for each of the two end positions of the throttle valve. It issues a switching signal to the control unit when the throttle valve is closed (idle) or fully open (full load).

Rotary idle actuator

The idle speed can be reduced and stabilized with the idle-speed control function. For this purpose, the rotary idle actuator opens a bypass line to the throttle valve and supplies the engine with more or less air. Since the hot-wire air-mass meter senses the extra air, the injected fuel quantity also changes as required.

Engine-temperature sensor

The engine-temperature sensor, a temperature-dependent resistor, controls warm-up enrichment.

Supplementary functions

The overrun fuel cutoff function, and the speed limiting function at maximum permissible engine speed, permit fuel economy and a reduction in pollutant emission.

Lambda closed-loop control

The lambda sensor supplies a signal which represents the instantaneous mixture composition. In the control unit, the signal of the lambda sensor is compared with an ideal value (setpoint), thus controlling a two-position controller. Dependent upon the result of comparison, either an excessively lean air-fuel mixture is enriched or an excessively rich mixture is leaned. Fuel metering is influenced via the opening time of the injection valves.

Fig. 36: Hot-wire air-mass meter
1 Hybrid circuit, 2 Cover, 3 Metal insert,
4 Venturi with hot wire, 5 Housing, 6 Screen,
7 Retaining ring.

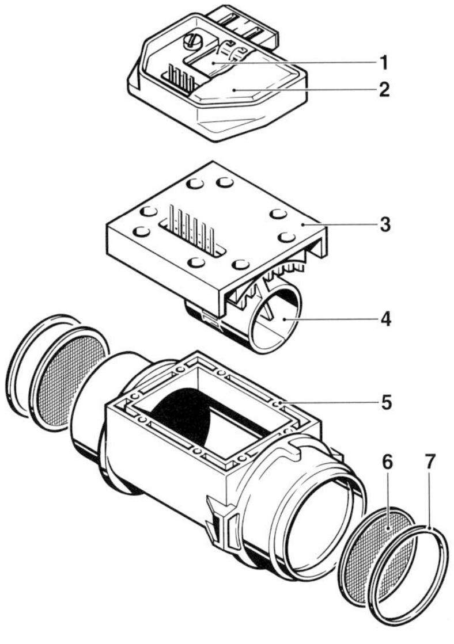

Fig. 37: Hot-film air-mass meter
a) Housing, b) Hot-film sensor (fitted in the middle of the housing).
1 Heat sink, 2 Intermediate module, 3 Power module, 4 Hybrid circuit, 5 Sensor element.

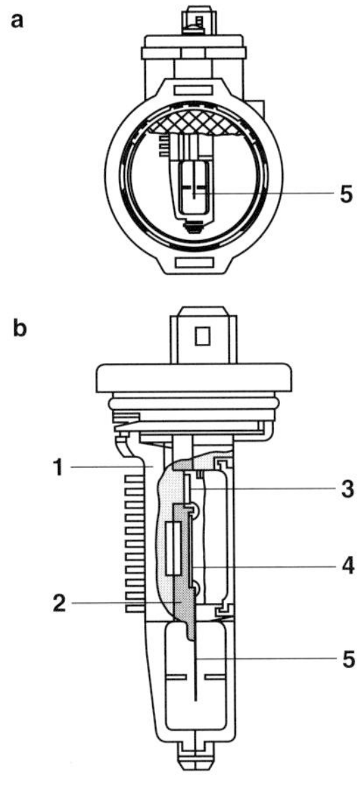

Mono-Jetronic fuel-injection system

System overview

Mono-Jetronic is an electronically controlled, low-pressure, single-point injection (SPI) system for 4-cylinder engines. While port injection systems such as KE and L-Jetronic employ a separate injector for each cylinder, Mono-Jetronic features a single, centrally-located, solenoid-controlled injection valve for the entire engine.

The heart of the Mono-Jetronic is the central injection unit (described in the following). It uses a single solenoid-operated injector for intermittent fuel injection above the throttle valve.

The intake manifold distributes the fuel to the individual cylinders.

A variety of different sensors are used to monitor engine operation and furnish the essential control parameters for optimum mixture adaptation. These include:

- throttle-valve angle,
- engine speed,
- engine and intake-air temperature,
- throttle-valve positions (idle/full-throttle),
- residual oxygen content of exhaust gas, and (depending on the vehicle's equipment level):

Fig. 1: Mono-Jetronic schematic diagram
1 Fuel tank, 2 Electric fuel pump, 3 Fuel filter, 4 Fuel-pressure regulator, 5 Solenoid-operated fuel injector, 6 Air-temperature sensor, 7 ECU, 8 Throttle-valve actuator, 9 Throttle-valve potentiometer, 10 Canister-purge valve, 11 Carbon canister, 12 Lambda oxygen sensor, 13 Engine-temperature sensor, 14 Ignition distributor, 15 Battery, 16 Ignition-start switch, 17 Relay, 18 Diagnosis connection, 19 Central injection unit.

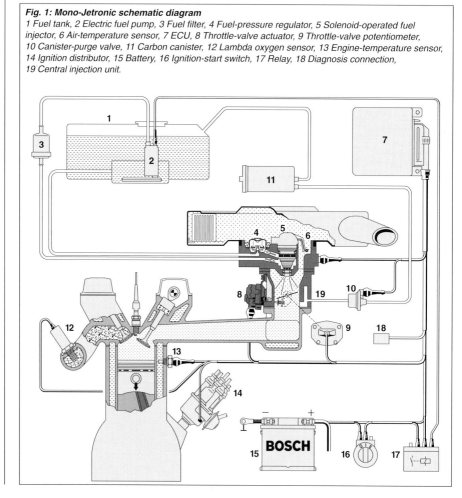

– automatic transmission, air-conditioner settings, and a/c compressor clutch status (engaged-disengaged).
Input circuits in the ECU convert the sensor data for transmission to the microprocessor, which analyzes the operating data to determine current engine operating conditions; this information, in turn, provides the basis for calculating control signals to the various final-control elements (actuators). Output amplifiers process the signals for transmission to the injector, throttle-valve actuator and canister-purge valve.

Versions

The following text and illustrations describe a typical Mono-Jetronic installation (Figure 1). Other versions are available to satisfy any specific individual requirements that the manufacturers define for fuel-injection systems.
The Mono-Jetronic system discharges the following individual functions (Fig. 2):
– fuel supply,
– acquisition of operating data, and
– processing of operating data.

Basic function
Mono-Jetronic's essential function is to control the fuel-injection process.

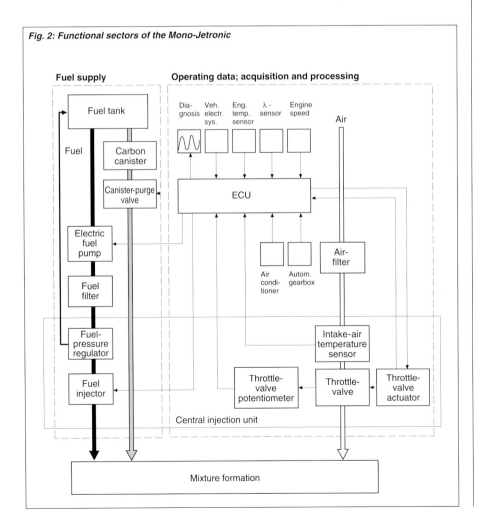

Fig. 2: Functional sectors of the Mono-Jetronic

Fuel supply

Operating data; acquisition and processing

Fuel tank

Dia-gnosis Veh. electr. sys. Eng. temp. sensor λ-sensor Engine speed

Air

Fuel

Carbon canister

Canister-purge valve

ECU

Electric fuel pump

Air condi-tioner Autom. gearbox Air-filter

Fuel filter

Fuel-pressure regulator

Intake-air temperature sensor

Fuel injector

Throttle-valve potentiometer Throttle-valve Throttle-valve actuator

Central injection unit

Mixture formation

Supplementary functions

Mono-Jetronic also incorporates a number of supplementary closed-loop and open-loop control functions with which it monitors operation of emissions-relevant components. These include idle-speed control, Lambda closed-loop control, and open-loop control of the evaporative-emissions control system.

Fuel supply

The fuel system supplies fuel from the tank to the solenoid-operated injector.

Fuel delivery

The electric fuel pump continuously pumps fuel from the tank and through the fuel filter to the central injection unit. Fuel pumps are available as in-line or in-tank versions.

In-line fuel pumps are situated outside the fuel tank, in the fuel line on the vehicle body platform between the fuel tank and the fuel filter.

Usually, the Mono-Jetronic has an in-tank fuel pump. As the name implies, this pump is located inside the tank. It is held in a special holder which normally incorporates an additional fuel filter on the intake side, a fuel-level gauge, a fuel-swirl pot which serves as a fuel reservoir, and the electrical and hydraulic connections to the outside (Figures 3 and 4).

Electric fuel pump

The electric motor and the pump itself are encased in a common housing. Fuel circulates around both pump and motor for continuous cooling. No complex sealing arrangements are required between pump and motor, so the motor's performance is better. There is no danger of explosion because an ignitable mixture can never form in the electric motor. The pump's output-end cover contains the electrical connections, the check valve, and the hydraulic pressure connection. The check valve also maintains primary pressure in the system for some time after the fuel pump is deactivated; this inhibits formation of vapor bubbles in warm fuel. In addition, the output-end cover can also incorporate the interference-suppression devices (Fig. 5).

The electric fuel pump described above is the most common type used in Mono-Jetronic applications. It provides ideal

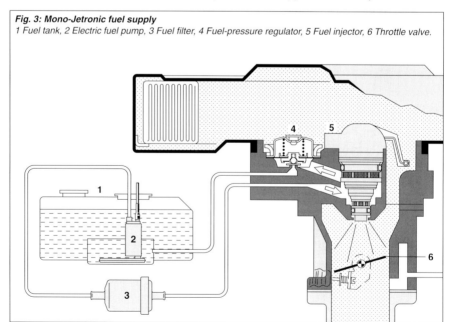

Fig. 3: Mono-Jetronic fuel supply
1 Fuel tank, 2 Electric fuel pump, 3 Fuel filter, 4 Fuel-pressure regulator, 5 Fuel injector, 6 Throttle valve.

performance with this system's low primary pressure. It is a two-stage flow-type pump: a side-channel pump being used as the preliminary stage (pre-stage) and a peripheral pump as the main stage. Both stages are integrated in a single impeller wheel.

The pre-stage circuit features a side channel on each side of the impeller blade ring, that is, one in the pump cover and one in the pump housing. The fuel, which is accelerated by the blade ring of the rotating impeller, converts its velocity energy into pressure energy in these two side channels, at the end of which the fuel is then transferred to the outside (as viewed from the end along the center axis) main pump stages. A degassing vent is provided in the over-flow channel between the preliminary stage and the main stage. Through it, excess fuel, together with any vapor bubbles which may have formed, is continuously returned to the fuel tank.

The main stage and pre-stage function identically. The main difference is in the design of the impeller wheel and the shape of the channel which encloses the blade ring at the side and around its periphery (peripheral principle). There is

a device for rapid venting of the main stage at the end of the peripheral channel. This takes the form of a diaphragm plate which closes an opening in the intake cover and functions as a discharge valve (Fig. 6).

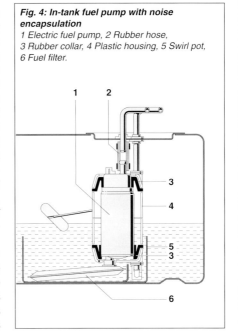

Fig. 4: In-tank fuel pump with noise encapsulation
1 Electric fuel pump, 2 Rubber hose,
3 Rubber collar, 4 Plastic housing, 5 Swirl pot,
6 Fuel filter.

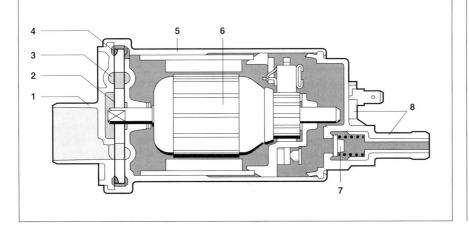

Fig. 5: Two-stage electric fuel pump, in-tank version. With side-channel pump (pre-stage) and peripheral pump (main stage)
1 Input-end cover with intake connection, 2 Impeller wheel, 3 Side-channel pump, 4 Peripheral pump, 5 Pump housing, 6 Armature, 7 Check valve, 8 Output-end cover with pressure connection.

With the discharge valve closed, the fuel is forced into the pump's electric-motor chamber from where it flows through the check valve into the fuel-supply line.

At high fuel temperatures, since the fuel-vapor bubbles have already been removed, this pump is distinguished by its excellent delivery characteristic and outstanding quietness.

A further advantage of the flow-pump principle lies in its fuel delivery, which is almost completely free of pressure pulsations. This fact also contributes to the pump's quiet operation.

Fuel filtration

Fuel-borne contaminants and impurities can prevent the injectors and fuel-pressure regulator from operating correctly. A filter is therefore fitted in the fuel line between the electric fuel pump and the central injection unit, preferably in a position underneath the vehicle protected against stone-throw.

Fuel filter

The filter's paper element has a mean pore size of 10 μm and comprises a paper tube with sealing rim. In order to completely separate the filter element's contaminated side from its clean side, the sealing rim is welded to the inside of the housing, which is made of impact-resistant plastic material. The paper tube is held axially by a plug and by support ribs in the filter cover (Fig. 7).

Depending on fuel-contamination levels and filter volume, filter service life is usually between 30,000 and 80,000 km.

Fuel-pressure control

It is the task of the fuel-pressure regulator to maintain the differential between line pressure and the local pressure at the injector nozzle constant at 100 kPa. In the Mono-Jetronic, the pressure regulator is an integral part of the central injection unit's hydraulic circuit.

Fig. 6: Components of the two-stage electric fuel pump
a) Input-end cover (seen from the impeller wheel), b) Impeller wheel,
c) Pump housing (seen from the impeller wheel).
1 Venting valve, 2 Degassing vent, 3 Inlet port for the side channel, 4 Side channel (pre-stage),
5 Peripheral channel (main stage), 6 Blade ring for side-channel pump (pre-stage),
8 Outlet port for peripheral channel.

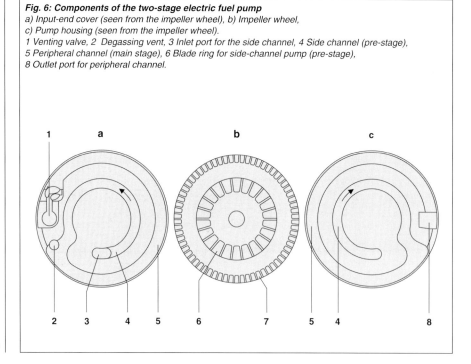

Fuel-pressure regulator

A rubber-fabric diaphragm divides the fuel-pressure regulator into the lower (fuel) chamber and the upper (spring) chamber. The pressure from the helical spring is applied to the diaphragm. A movable valve plate which is connected to the diaphragm through the valve holder is pressed onto the valve seat by spring pressure (flat-seat valve).

When the force generated by the fuel pressure against the diaphragm's area exceeds the opposing spring force, the valve plate is lifted slightly from its seat and the excess fuel can flow back to the tank through the open valve. In this state of equilibrium, the differential pressure between the upper and lower chambers of the pressure regulator is 100 kPa.

Vents maintain the spring chamber's internal pressure at levels corresponding to those at the injector nozzle. The valve-plate lift varies depending upon the delivery quantity and the actual fuel quantity required.

The spring characteristics and the diaphragm area have been selected to provide constant, narrow-tolerance pressure over a broad range of fuel-delivery rates. When the engine is switched off, fuel delivery also stops. The check valve in the electric fuel pump then closes, as does the pressure-regulator valve, maintaining the pressure in the supply line and in the hydraulic section for a certain period (Fig. 8).

Because this design configuration effectively inhibits the formation of vapor bubbles which can result from fuel-line heat build-up during pauses in operation, it helps ensure trouble-free warm starts.

Fig. 7: Fuel filter
*1 Filter cover, 2 Sealing rim, 3 Filter housing,
4 Plug, 5 Support ribs, 6 Paper element,
7 Paper tube.*

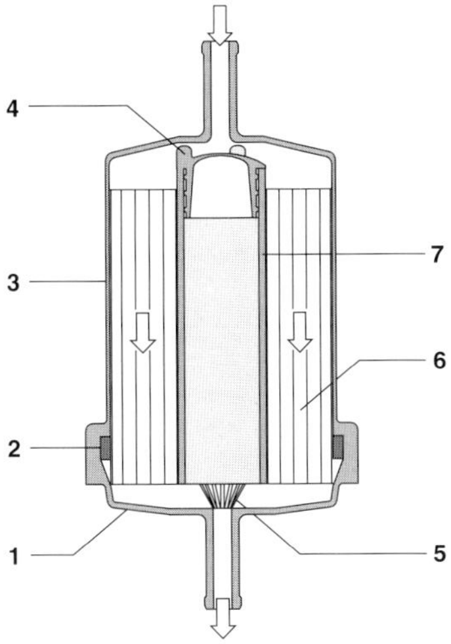

Fig. 8: Fuel-pressure regulator
*1 Venting ports, 2 Diaphragm, 3 Valve holder,
4 Compression spring, 5 Upper chamber,
6 Lower chamber, 7 Valve plate.*

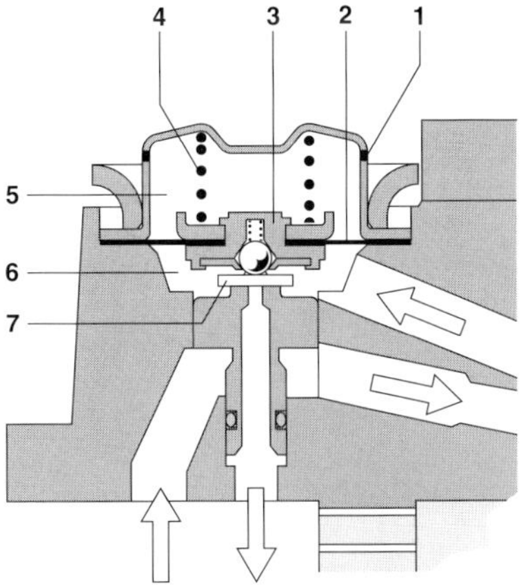

Evaporative-emissions control

In order to reduce the emissions of hydrocarbon compounds, legislation in a number of countries forbids the escape of fuel vapors from the fuel tank into the atmosphere.

Vehicles must be equipped with an evaporative-emissions control system in which the fuel tank is connected to a carbon canister. The carbon in the canister absorbs the fuel contained in the vapors passed through it. In order to transport the fuel from the canister to the engine, the fresh air drawn in by the engine is passed through the canister to reabsorb the fuel. From the canister, the intake air which is now enriched with hydrocarbons is passed through the intake manifold to the engine for combustion (Fig. 9).

Carbon canister

The dimensions of the carbon canister have been selected to maintain a state of equilibrium between the quantity of fuel absorbed and the quantity removed by the fresh air passing through the canister. To minimize canister size, the regenerative air stream is maintained at the highest possible level under all operating conditions (from idle to full throttle).

The level of the regeneration air flow is essentially determined by the difference between intake-manifold and ambient pressure. Because the differential is considerable at idle, the flow volume must be minimized to prevent driveability problems. At higher engine load factors, conditions are exactly the opposite because the regeneration-gas flow may be quite high, although the available pressure difference is only slight.

An ECU-controlled canister-purge valve provides precise metering of the fuel vapor flow.

Fig. 9: Evaporative-emissions control system
1 Line from fuel tank to carbon canister, 2 Carbon canister, 3 Fresh air, 4 Canister-purge valve, 5 Line to intake manifold, 6 Throttle valve.
p_S *Intake-manifold pressure,* p_u *Atmospheric pressure,* Δp *Difference between intake-manifold pressure and atmospheric pressure.*

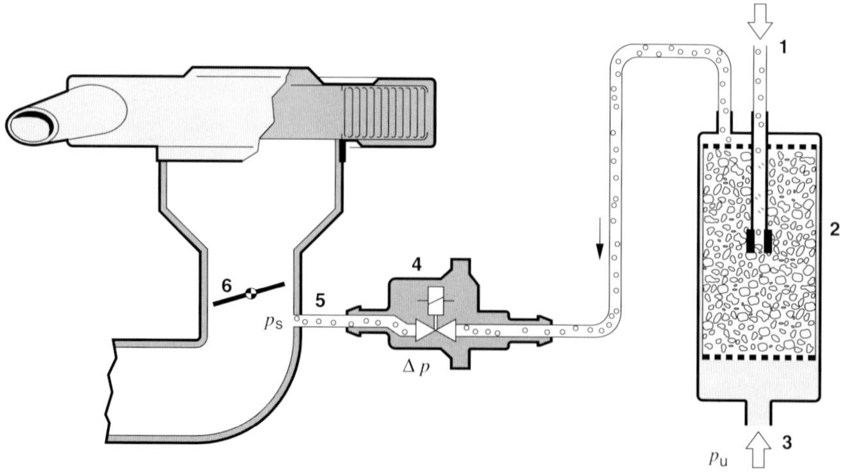

Acquisition of operating data

Sensors monitor all essential operating data to furnish instantaneous information on current engine operating conditions. This information is transmitted to the ECU in the form of electric signals, which are converted to digital form and processed for use in controlling the various final-control elements.

Air charge

The system derives the data required for maintaining the required air-fuel mixture ratio by monitoring the intake-air charge for each cycle. Once this air mass (referred to as air charge in the following) has been measured, it is possible to adapt the injected fuel quantity by varying injection duration.

With the Mono-Jetronic, the air charge is determined indirectly, using coordinates defined by the throttle-valve angle α and engine speed n. For this design to function, the relationship between throttle-valve angle and flow area within the throttle-valve housing must be maintained within very close tolerances on all production units.

The driver controls the engine's intake-air stream with the accelerator pedal, this determines throttle opening and load factor. The throttle-valve angle α is registered by the throttle-valve potentiometer. Engine speed n and intake-air density supplement the throttle-valve position α as additional variables for determining the intake-air mass.

Air charge as a function of α and n is determined for a given engine on the engine dynamometer. Figure 10 shows a typical set of curves for an engine program; it illustrates the relative air-charge factors for various throttle-valve apertures α and engine speeds n. If the engine response data are already available, and assuming constant air density, air charge can be defined precisely using α and n exclusively (α/n system).

The Mono-Jetronic throttle-valve assembly is an extremely precise air-

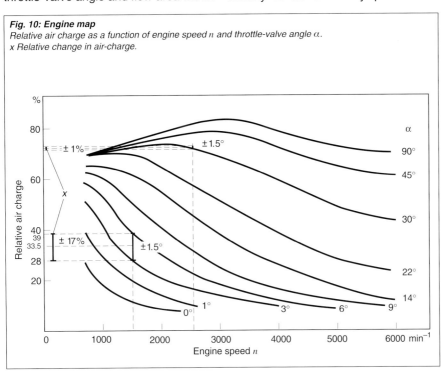

Fig. 10: Engine map
Relative air charge as a function of engine speed n and throttle-valve angle α.
x Relative change in air-charge.

measuring device and provides the ECU with a very accurate signal for the throttle-valve angle. The engine-speed information is provided by the ignition system. Because the differential between internal fuel pressure within the injector and air pressure at the nozzle is maintained at a constant level, injected fuel quantities are determined solely by the length of time (injection duration) the injector remains open for each triggering pulse.

This injection duration must be proportional to the monitored air charge to maintain a specific air-fuel ratio. In other words: The injection duration is a direct function of α and n. In the Mono-Jetronic, this relationship is governed by a Lambda program map with input variables α and n. The system is programmed to compensate for fluctuations in air density, which is a function of the intake-air temperature and the air pressure. The intake-air temperature, measured as the air enters the central injection unit, provides the ECU with the basic data required to determine the corresponding correction factor.

To enable it to comply with the stringent US exhaust-gas regulations, the Mono-Jetronic is always equipped with the Lambda closed-loop control, designed to maintain the air-fuel ratio at precisely $\lambda = 1$. In addition, the Lambda closed-loop control is used to implement adaptive mixture adaptation, in other words, the system learns to adapt itself to the changing operating conditions.

Correction factors for variations in atmospheric pressure (especially those associated with altitude changes) are supplemented by correction factors designed to compensate for differences in production tolerances and ongoing wear. When the engine is switched off, the system stores the correction factors so that they are effective immediately once the engine is started again.

This system of indirect determination of intake-air mass – with control based on the α/n control parameters – operates with adaptive mixture control and super-

imposed Lambda closed-loop control to accurately maintain a constant mixture, without any need for direct measurement of air mass.

Throttle-valve angle

The ECU employs the throttle-valve angle α to calculate the throttle-valve's position and angular velocity. Throttle-valve position is an important input parameter for determining intake-air volume, the basic factor in calculating injection duration. When the throttle is closed, the idle switch provides the throttle-valve actuator with a supplementary position signal.

Data on the throttle valve's angular velocity are used mainly for the transition compensation. The resolution of the α signal is determined by the air-charge measurement. To ensure good driveability and low emissions, the resolution of the air-charge measurement and injection duration must take place in the smallest-possible digital steps (quantization), to maintain the air-fuel ratio within a tolerance range of 2 %.

The program range that displays the largest intake-charge variations relative to α is defined by minimal apertures α and low engine speeds n, i.e., at idle and low part load. Within this range – as illustrated in Figure 10 – a change of ±1.5° in throttle-valve angle shifts the air-charge/lambda factor by ±17 %, whereas outside this range, with higher throttle-valve angles, a similar increment has an almost negligible effect. This means that a high angular resolution is necessary at idle and low part load.

Throttle-valve potentiometer

The potentiometer wiper arm is fastened to the throttle-valve shaft. The potentiometer resistance tracks and the electrical connection are on a plastic plate screwed onto the underside of the fuel-injection assembly. Power supply is from a stabilized 5 V source.

The required high level of signal resolution is achieved by distributing the throttle-valve angle for the range between idle and full-throttle between two resistance tracks.

Voltage drop is linear across each section of track. In parallel with each resistance track is a second (collector) track. The resistance tracks and the collector tracks are manufactured using thick-film techniques.

The wiper arm carries four wipers, each of which contacts one of the potentiometer tracks. The wipers for each resistance and collector-track pair are connected, the signal from the resistance track is thus transmitted to the collector track (Fig. 11).

Track 1 covers the angular range from 0° ... 24°, and track 2 the range from 18° ... 90°. The angle signals (α) from each track are converted separately in the ECU, each in its own analog/digital converter circuit. The ECU also evaluates the voltage ratios, using this data to compensate for wear and temperature fluctuations at the potentiometer. The potentiometer plate features a seal ring in a circumferential groove to prevent moisture and contamination from entering the unit. The potentiometer chamber is connected to the atmosphere by means of a venting device.

Engine speed

The engine-speed information required for α/n control is obtained by monitoring the periodicity of the ignition signal. These signals from the ignition system are then processed in the ECU. The ignition signals are either T_D pulses already processed by the ignition trigger box, or the voltage signal available at Terminal 1 (U_S) on the low-voltage side of the ignition coil. At the same time, these signals are also used for triggering the injection pulses, whereby each ignition pulse triggers an injection pulse (Fig. 12).

Engine temperature

Engine temperature has a considerable influence on fuel consumption. A temperature sensor in the engine coolant circuit measures the engine temperature and provides the ECU with an electrical signal.

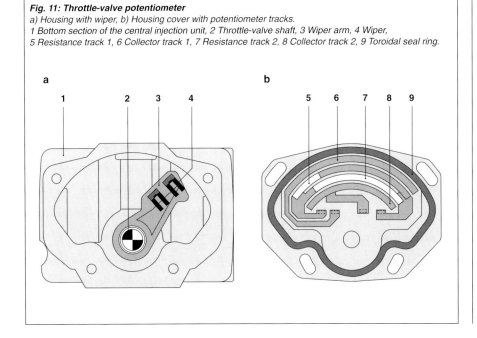

Fig. 11: Throttle-valve potentiometer
a) Housing with wiper, b) Housing cover with potentiometer tracks.
1 Bottom section of the central injection unit, 2 Throttle-valve shaft, 3 Wiper arm, 4 Wiper,
5 Resistance track 1, 6 Collector track 1, 7 Resistance track 2, 8 Collector track 2, 9 Toroidal seal ring.

a   b

1   2   3   4   5   6   7   8   9

Engine-temperature sensor

The engine-temperature sensor consists of a threaded sleeve with an integral NTC semiconductor resistor (NTC = Negative Temperature Coefficient). The sensor's resistance changes with temperature, and the ECU evaluates this change (Fig. 13).

Intake-air temperature

Intake-air density varies according to temperature. To compensate for this influence, a temperature sensor on the intake side of the throttle body monitors the temperature of the intake air for transmission to the ECU.

Air-temperature sensor

The air-temperature sensor incorporates a NTC resistor element. So that changes in intake-air temperature can be registered immediately, the resistor protrudes from the end of a trunk-shaped moulding into the area of maximum air-flow speed. The 4-pole plug-and-socket connection includes the plug for the fuel injector (Fig. 14).

Operating modes

Idle and full-throttle must be registered accurately so that the injected fuel quantity can be optimized for these operating modes, and in order that full-load enrichment and overrun fuel cutoff can function correctly.

The idle operating mode is registered from the actuated idle contact of a switch in the throttle-valve actuator, which is closed by a small plunger in the actuator shaft (Fig. 15). The ECU recognizes full-throttle operation based on the electrical signal from the throttle-valve potentiometer.

Battery voltage

The solenoid fuel injector's pickup and release times vary according to battery voltage. If system voltage fluctuates during operation, the ECU adjusts the injection timing to compensate for delays in injector response times.

In addition, the ECU responds to the low system voltages encountered during starting at low temperatures by extending injection duration.

The extended duration compensates for voltage-induced variations in the pumping characteristic of the electric fuel pump, which does not achieve maximum system pressure under these conditions.

Fig. 12: Engine-speed signals from the ignition system
1 Ignition distributor, 2 Trigger box, 3 Ignition coil, n Engine speed, T_D Conditioned pulses from ECU, U_S Voltage signal.

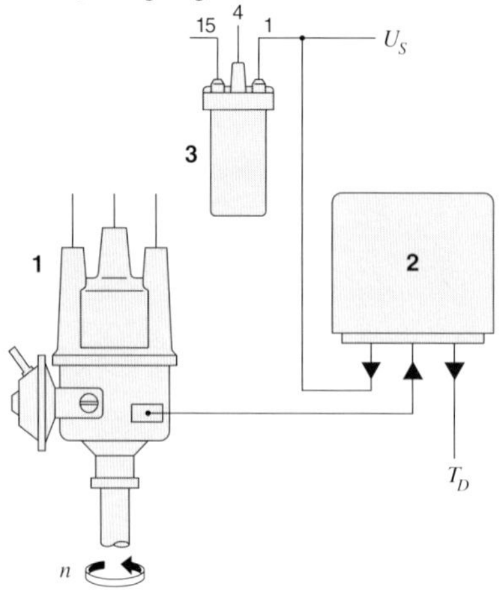

Fig. 13: Engine-temperature sensor
1 Electrical connection, 2 Housing, 3 NTC resistor.

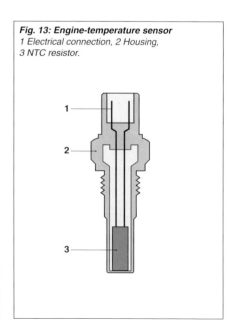

The ECU receives the battery voltage in the form of a continuous signal transmitted to the microprocessor via the A/D converter.

Control signals from the air-conditioner and/or automatic transmission

When the air conditioner is switched on, or the automatic transmission is placed in gear, the resulting engine load would normally cause the idle speed to drop. To compensate, the air-conditioner modes "air-conditioner ON" and "compressor ON," as well as the "Drive" position on the automatic gearbox, are registered by the ECU as switching signals. The ECU then modifies the idle-speed control signal to compensate. It may be necessary to increase the idle speed to ensure that the air conditioner continues to operate effectively, and reductions in idle speed are often required when "Drive" is selected on automatic-transmission vehicles.

Mixture composition

Due to the exhaust-gas aftertreatment using a three-way catalytic converter, the correct air-fuel mixture composition must be precisely maintained. A Lambda oxygen sensor in the exhaust-gas flow provides the ECU with an electric signal indicating the current mixture composition. The ECU then uses this signal for the closed-loop control of the mixture composition to obtain a stoichiometric ratio. The Lambda oxygen sensor is installed in the engine's exhaust system at a position which ensures that it is kept at the temperature required for correct functioning across the complete engine operating range.

Lambda oxygen sensor
The Lambda oxygen sensor protrudes into the exhaust-gas stream and is designed so that the outer electrode is surrounded by the exhaust gas while the inner electrode remains in contact with the atmosphere (Fig. 16).
The Lambda sensor consists of a special-ceramic housing, the surfaces of which are covered by gas-permeable platinum electrodes. The sensor's operation is based on the fact that the ceramic material is porous and permits the diffusion of the oxygen present in the air (solid electrolyte). At higher temperatures the ceramic becomes conductive, and if the oxygen concentration at one of the electrodes differs from that at the

Fig. 14: Intake-air temperature sensor
1 Intake air, 2 Trunk-shaped moulding, 3 Guard, 4 NTC resistor, 5 Fuel injector.

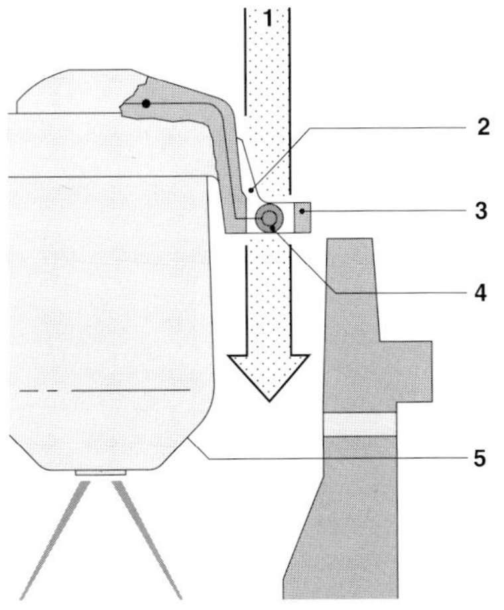

Fig. 15: Idle switch
1 Actuation by throttle-valve lever, 2 Idle contact, 3 Electrical connections.

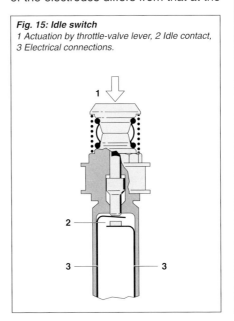

other, a voltage is generated between them. At a stoichiometric air-fuel ratio $\lambda = 1.0$, a jump takes place in the sensor's output voltage. This voltage is used as the measuring signal (Fig. 17). The sensor ceramic body is held in a threaded mounting and provided with a protective tube and electrical connections. The sensor-ceramic surface is covered by a microporous platinum layer which on the one hand has a decisive effect on the sensor's characteristic while on the other serving as an electrical contact. A highly adhesive and highly porous ceramic coating has been applied over the platinum layer at the end of the sensor ceramic which is in contact with the exhaust gas. This serves to protect the platinum layer against erosion due to the solid particles in the exhaust gas.

The exhaust-gas end of the sensor is provided with a protective tube to keep combustion deposits away from the sensor ceramic. This tube is slotted, so that the exhaust gases and the combustion particles they contain cannot reach the sensor ceramic. In addition to the mechanical protection provided by this tube, it also effectively reduces the temperature changes at the sensor during transitions from one operating mode to the other.

A protective metal sleeve is fitted over the electrical contact end of the sensor. As well as serving as the support for a disc spring, it has a bore which ensures pressure compensation in the sensor interior. The electrical connection cable exits the sensor through an insulating sleeve.

The voltage and internal resistance of the sensor depend upon its temperature. Efficient closed-loop control is possible with exhaust-gas temperatures above 350°C (unheated sensor) and above 200°C (heated sensor).

Heated Lambda oxygen sensor

To a large extent, the design principle of the heated Lambda sensor (Fig. 18) is identical to that of the unheated version. The sensor's active ceramic body is heated internally by a ceramic heating element to maintain its temperature above the 350°C operating limit, even if the exhaust gas is cooler. The heated Lambda sensor features a protective tube with a reduced flow opening. Among other things, this prevents the sensor ceramic cooling off when the exhaust gas is cold.

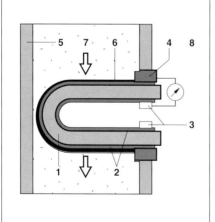

Fig. 16: Installation of Lambda oxygen sensor in intake manifold (schematic)
1 Sensor ceramic, 2 Electrodes, 3 Contact, 4 Housing contact, 5 Exhaust pipe, 6 Ceramic protective layer (porous), 7 Exhaust gas, 8 Air.

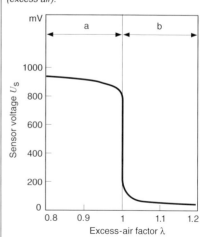

Fig. 17: Voltage characteristic of the Lambda oxygen sensor at a working temperature of 600°C
a) Rich mixture (air deficiency), b) Lean mixture (excess air).

The advantages of the heated Lambda sensor are reliable closed-loop control at low exhaust-gas temperatures (e.g., at idle); almost complete independence from variations in exhaust-gas temperature; rapid response to minimize delays before effective Lambda control can be implemented after cold starts; low exhaust emissions due to improved sensor reaction time; and greater flexibility in selecting the installation location (because the sensor does not depend upon the exhaust gas to reach operating temperature).

Processing of operating data

The ECU processes the engine operating data received from the sensors. From this data, it uses the programmed ECU functions to generate the triggering signals for the fuel injector, the throttle-valve actuator, and the canister-purge valve.

Electronic control unit (ECU)

The ECU is housed in a fiberglass-reinforced, polyamide plastic casing. To insulate it from the engine's heat, it is located either in the passenger compartment or the ventilation plenum chamber between the engine and passenger compartments.

All of the ECU's electronic components are installed on a single printed-circuit board. The output amplifiers and the voltage regulator responsible for maintaining 5V supply to the electronic components are installed on heat sinks for better thermal dissipation.

A 25-pin plug connects the control unit to the battery, the sensors and the actuators (final-control elements).

Fig. 18: Heated Lambda oxygen sensor
1 Sensor housing, 2 Ceramic support tube, 3 Electrical connections, 4 Protective tube with slots, 5 Active sensor ceramic, 6 Contact element, 7 Protective sleeve, 8 Heating element, 9 Clamp-type connections for heating element.

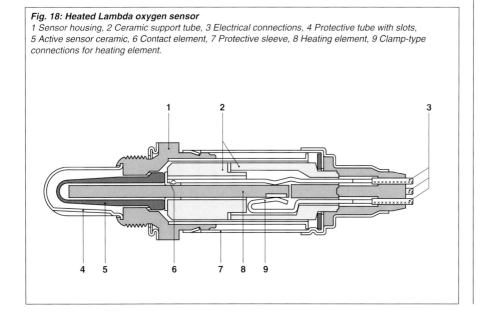

Analog-digital converter (A/D)

The signals from the throttle-valve potentiometer are continuous analog signals; as are the Lambda-sensor signal; the engine-temperature signal; the intake-air signal; the battery voltage; and a voltage-reference signal generated in the ECU. These analog signals are converted to data words by the analog-digital converter (A/D) and transmitted to the microprocessor via the data bus. An analog-digital input is used so that, depending upon the input voltage, various data records in the read memory can be addressed (data coding). The engine-speed signal provided by the ignition is conditioned in an integrated circuit (IC) and transmitted to the microprocessor. The engine-speed signal is also used to control the fuel-pump relay via an output stage.

Microprocessor

The microprocessor is the heart of the ECU (Fig. 19). It is connected through the data and address bus with the programmable read-only memory (EPROM) and the random-access memory (RAM). The read memory contains the program code and the data for the definition of operating parameters. In particular, the random-access memory serves to store the adaptation values (adaptation: adapting to changing conditions through self-learning). This memory module remains permanently connected to the vehicle's battery to maintain the adaptation data contained in the random-access memory when the ignition is switched off.

A 6 MHz quarz oscillator provides the stable basic clock rate needed for the arithmetic operations. A signal interface adapts the amplitude and shape of the

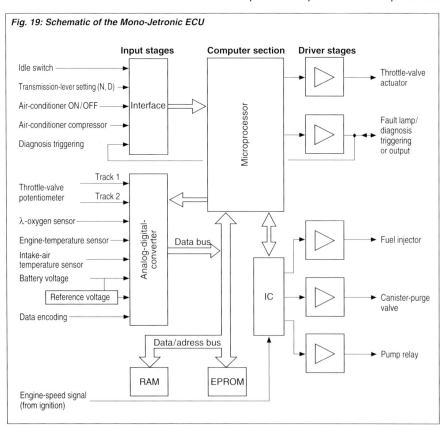

Fig. 19: Schematic of the Mono-Jetronic ECU

control signals before transmitting them to the microprocessor for processing. These signals include the idle-switch setting, diagnosis activation, the position of the selector lever on automatic-transmission vehicles (Neutral, Drive), and a signal for "Air-conditioner ON" and "Compressor ON/OFF" in vehicles with air-conditioning.

Output stages
A number of different driver stages generate the control signals for the fuel injector, the throttle-valve actuator, the canister-purge valve, and the fuel-pump relay. A fault lamp is installed in some vehicles to warn the driver in case of sensor or actuator faults. The fault lamp's output also serves as an interface for diagnosis activation and read-outs.

Lambda program map
The Lambda map is used for precise adaptation of the air-fuel ratio at all static operating points once the engine is warm. This map is stored electronically in the digital circuit section of the ECU; the reference data are determined empirically through tests on the engine dynamometer. For a Lambda closed-loop-controlled engine-management concept such as the Mono-Jetronic, this testing is employed to determine optimum injection timing and duration for a specific engine under all operating conditions (idle, part or full-throttle). The resulting program consistently maintains an ideal (stoichiometric) air-fuel mixture throughout the operating range.
The Mono-Jetronic Lambda program map consists of 225 control coordinates; these are assigned to 15 reference coordinates for the parameters throttle-valve angle α and n for engine speed n. Because the α/n curves are extremely non-linear, necessitating high resolution accuracy at idle and in the lower part-load range, the data points are situated very closely together in this area of the map (Fig. 20). Control coordinates located between these reference coordinates are determined in the ECU using linear interpolation.

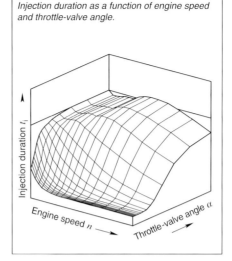

Fig. 20: Lambda map
Injection duration as a function of engine speed and throttle-valve angle.

Because the Lambda map is designed for the engine's normal operating and temperature range, it becomes necessary to correct the basic injection timing when engine temperatures deviate or when special operating conditions are encountered.

If the ECU registers deviations from $\lambda = 1$ in the signals from the Lambda sensor, and as a result is forced to correct the basic injection duration for an extended period of time, it generates mixture correction values and stores them in an internal adaptation process. From then on, these values are effective for the complete map and are continually up-dated.
This layout ensures consistent compensation for individual tolerances and for permanent changes in the response characteristics of engine and injection components.

Fuel injection
The fuel-injection system must be able to accurately meter to the engine the minimum amount of fuel required (at idle or zero-load), as well as the maximum (at full throttle). The control coordinates for these conditions must be situated within the linear range on the injector curves (Fig. 21).

One of the Mono-Jetronic's most important assignments is the uniform distribution of the air-fuel mixture to all cylinders. Apart from intake-manifold design, the distribution depends mainly upon the fuel injector's location and position, and the quality of its air-fuel mixture preparation. The ideal fuel-injector position within the Mono-Jetronic housing was determined in the research and development phase. Special adaptations for operation in individual engines are not required.

The central injection unit's housing is centered in the intake-air flow by a special bracket, and has been designed for maximum aerodynamic efficiency. The housing contains the injector, which is installed directly above the throttle valve for intensive mixing of the injected fuel with the intake air. To this end, the injector finely atomizes the fuel and injects it in a cone-shaped jet between the throttle valve and the throttle-valve housing into the area with the highest air-flow speed.

The fuel injector is sealed-off to the outside by seal rings. The central injection unit is closed off at the top by a semicircular plastic cap which not only contains the injector's electrical connections but also ensures correct axial positioning.

Injector

The fuel injector (Fig. 22) comprises the valve housing and the valve group. The valve housing contains the solenoid winding and the electrical connections. The valve group includes the valve body which holds the valve needle and its solenoid armature.

When no voltage is applied to the solenoid winding, a helical spring assisted by the primary system pressure forces the valve needle onto its seat. With voltage applied and the solenoid energized, the needle lifts about 0.06 mm (depending upon valve design) from its seat so that fuel can exit through an annular gap. The pintle on the front end of the valve needle projects from the valve-needle bore, and its shape ensures excellent fuel atomization.

The size of the gap between the pintle and the valve body determines the valve's static fuel quantity. In other words, the maximum fuel flow with the

Fig. 21: Fuel-injector characteristic curve
At an engine speed of 900 min⁻¹ (corresponds to a 33ms injection pulse train). 1 Voltage-dependent fuel-injector delay time, 2 Non-linear characteristic section, 3 Injection-duration section at idle or no-load operation.

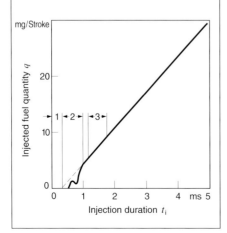

Fig. 22: Fuel injector
1 Electrical connection, 2 Fuel return, 3 Fuel inlet, 4 Solenoid winding, 5 Solenoid armature, 6 Valve needle, 7 Pintle.

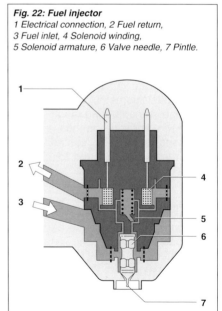

Fig. 23: Fuel deposits in the cold engine
1 Fuel injector, 2 Metered fuel, 3 Throttle valve, 4 Fuel deposits, 5 Fuel film on manifold walls
(exaggerated for presentation), 6 Fuel-vapor stream, 7 Evaporation from the fuel film on the manifold
walls.

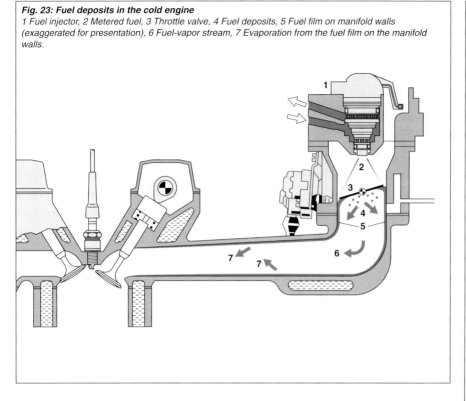

valve permanently open. The dynamic fuel quantity injected during intermittent operation depends also on the valve spring, the valve-needle mass, the magnetic circuit and the ECU driver stage. Because the fuel pressure is constant, the amount of fuel actually injected by the fuel injector depends solely upon the valve's opening time (injection duration).

Due to the frequency of the injection pulse train (every ignition pulse triggers an injection pulse) the fuel injector must feature extremely short switching times. Its pick-up and release times are kept to below one millisecond by the low mass of armature and needle, as well as by the optimized magnetic circuit. Precise metering of even the smallest amount of fuel is therefore guaranteed.

Mixture adaptation

Starting phase

When the engine is cold, effective fuel vaporization is inhibited by the following factors:
– cold intake air,
– cold manifold walls,
– high manifold pressure,
– low air-flow velocity in the intake manifold, and
– cold combustion chambers and cylinder walls.

These factors mean that part of the fuel metered to the engine condenses on the cold manifold walls and covers them with a film of fuel (Fig. 23).

To ensure that the fuel leaving the injector reaches the engine for combustion, this condensation process must be terminated as soon as possible. To do so, more fuel is metered to the engine when starting than would otherwise be needed for the combustion of the intake air. Being as the amount of fuel condensation mainly depends upon the intake-manifold temperature, the injection times for starting are specified by the ECU according to engine temperature (Fig. 24a).

The fuel condensation rate not only depends upon the manifold-wall temperature but also on the air velocity in the intake manifold. The higher the air-flow velocity, the less fuel is deposited on the manifold walls. The injection duration is reduced as engine speed increases (Fig. 25a).

In order to achieve very short starting times, the build-up of the fuel film on the manifold walls must take place as quickly as possible, in other words a large quantity of fuel must be metered to the engine in a short period. At the same time, precautions must be taken to prevent flooding the engine.

These demands are in opposition to each other, but are complied with by reducing the injection duration the longer engine cranking continues (Fig. 25b). The engine is considered to have started as soon as the so-called end-of-starting speed, which is dependent upon engine temperature, is exceeded (Fig. 24b).

Post-start and warm-up phase

As soon as the engine has started, and depending upon throttle-valve position

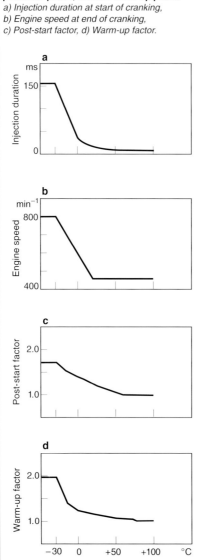

Fig. 24: Corrections as a function of engine temperature. During the cranking phase, the post-start phase, and the warm-up phase
a) Injection duration at start of cranking,
b) Engine speed at end of cranking,
c) Post-start factor, d) Warm-up factor.

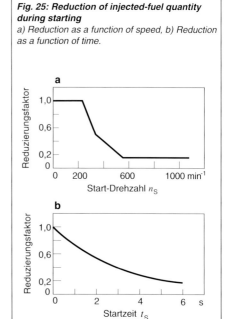

Fig. 25: Reduction of injected-fuel quantity during starting
a) Reduction as a function of speed, b) Reduction as a function of time.

and engine speed, the fuel injector is triggered with the injection durations stored in the Lambda map. From this point on, and until engine operating temperature has been reached, fuel enrichment continues to be necessary due to the fuel condensation on the combustion chamber and manifold walls, which are still cold.

Immediately following a successful start, the enrichment must be increased briefly, but this increase is then followed by normal enrichment which depends solely on the engine temperature.

Two functions determine the engine's fuel requirement in the phase between end-of-start and reaching operating temperature:

– Post-start enrichment is stored as an engine-temperature-dependent correction factor. This post-start factor is used to correct the injection durations calculated from the Lambda map. The reduction of the post-start factor to the value 1 is time-dependent (Fig. 24c).

– The warm-up enrichment is also stored as an engine-temperature-dependent correction factor. Reduction of this factor to value 1 depends solely on engine temperature (Fig. 24d).

Both functions operate simultaneously; the injection durations calculated from the Lambda map are adapted with the post-start factor as well as with the warm-up factor.

Mixture adaptation as a function of intake-air temperature

The air mass required for the combustion is dependent upon the intake air's temperature. Taking a constant throttle-valve setting, this means that cylinder charge reduces along with increasing air temperature. The Mono-Jetronic central injection unit therefore is equipped with a temperature sensor which reports the intake-air temperature to the ECU which then corrects the injection duration, e.g., the injected fuel quantity, by means of an intake-air-dependent enrichment factor (Fig. 26).

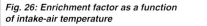

Fig. 26: Enrichment factor as a function of intake-air temperature

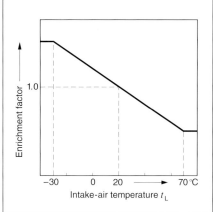

Transition compensation

The dynamic mixture correction which is necessary to compensate for the load changes due to throttle-valve movements is provided by the transition compensation. This facility is required in order to achieve best-possible driveability and exhaust-gas behavior, and in the case of a single-point fuel-injection system its functional complexity is somewhat higher than with a multipoint system. This is due to the fact that mixture distribution is via the intake manifold in a single-point system, which means that for transition compensation three different factors must be taken into consideration with regard to the transportation of the fuel:

– Fuel vapor in the central injection unit or in the intake manifold, or which forms on the manifold walls due to the evaporation of the fuel film. This vapor is transported very quickly at the same speed as the intake air.

– Fuel droplets, which are transported at different speeds, but nevertheless at about the same speed as the intake-air. Some of these droplets are flung against the intake-manifold walls though, where they contribute to the evaporation of the fuel film.

– Liquid fuel, transported to the combustion chamber at reduced speed, stemming from the fuel film on the intake-manifold walls. There is a time lag in the availability of this portion of the fuel for combustion.

At low intake-manifold pressures, that is at idle or lower part load, the fuel in the intake manifold is almost completely in vaporous form and there is practically no fuel film on the manifold walls. When the manifold pressure increases though, i.e. when the throttle valve is opened (or when speed drops), the proportion of fuel in the wall film increases. The result is that when the throttle valve is operated during a transition, the balance between the increase and decrease in the amount of fuel in the wall film is disturbed. This means that when the throttle valve is opened, some form of compensation is necessary in order to prevent the mixture leaning-off due to the increase in the amount of fuel deposited on the manifold walls. This compensation is provided by the acceleration-enrichment facility. Correspondingly, when the throttle valve is closed, the wall film reduces by releasing some of its fuel, and without some form of compensation this would lead to mixture enrichment at the cylinders during the transitional phase. Here, the deceleration lean-off facility comes into effect.

In addition to the tendency of the fuel to evaporate as a result of the intake-manifold pressure, the temperature also plays an important role. Therefore, when the intake manifold is still cold, or with low intake-air temperatures, there is a further increase in the amount of fuel held in the wall film.

In the Mono-Jetronic, complex electronic functions are applied to compensate for these dynamic mixture-transportation effects, and these functions ensure that the air-fuel ratio remains as near as possible to $\lambda = 1$ during transition modes.

The acceleration enrichment and deceleration lean adjustment functions are based on throttle-valve angle, engine speed, intake-air temperature, engine temperature and the throttle-valve's angular velocity.

Acceleration enrichment and trailing-throttle lean adjustment are triggered when the throttle valve's angular velocity exceeds the respective trigger threshold. For acceleration enrichment, the trigger threshold is in the form of a characteristic curve based on the throttle valve's angular velocity, and for deceleration lean adjustment it is constant (Fig. 27).

Also based on the throttle valve's rate of travel are the two dynamic-response correction factors for acceleration enrichment and trailing-throttle lean adjustment. Both of these dynamic mixture-correction factors are stored as characteristic curves (Fig. 28).

To reduce the tendency for fuel to condense along the intake tracts, the intake

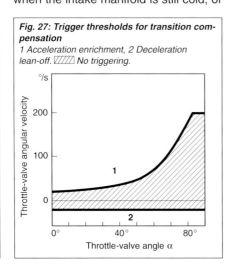

Fig. 27: Trigger thresholds for transition compensation
1 Acceleration enrichment, 2 Deceleration lean-off. ▨ No triggering.

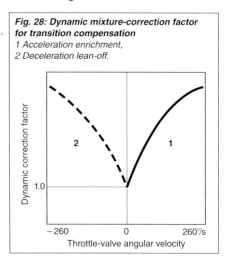

Fig. 28: Dynamic mixture-correction factor for transition compensation
1 Acceleration enrichment,
2 Deceleration lean-off.

manifold is heated by including it in the engine's cooling circuit. Meanwhile, a heat-riser warms the intake air to facilitate formation of a homogeneous air-fuel mixture. These influences are taken into account by using correction curves which modify the dynamic mixture-correction factors to compensate for variations in engine and intake-air temperature (Figures 29 and 30a).

To compensate for the variations in manifold vacuum and their effect on the rate at which fuel condenses along the intake tracts, yet another program containing supplementary evaluation factors adapts the dynamic correction factors in response to changes in throttle-valve angle and engine speed (Fig. 31).

When the throttle valve's angular velocity drops below one of the control thresholds, or if the ECU responds to the current sensor signals by prescribing a series of radical reductions in mixture-correction factor, the system adapts by phasing out the last dynamic correction factors for acceleration enrichment and trailing-throttle lean correction. The process periodicity coincides with that of the ignition pulse, and is based on an engine-temperature factor of less than 1. Each of the reduction factors, that is, acceleration enrichment and trailing-throttle lean correction, is defined in

a separate program curve (Fig. 30b). The program's compensation mode thus functions as a comprehensive transition factor for adapting both injection timing and duration.

Because changes in load factor can be quite rapid relative to injection periodicity, the system is also capable of generating a supplementary injection pulse to provide additional compensation.

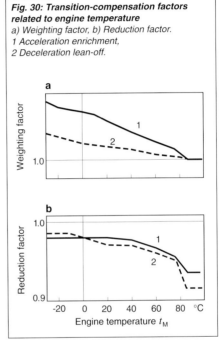

Fig. 30: Transition-compensation factors related to engine temperature
a) Weighting factor, b) Reduction factor.
1 Acceleration enrichment,
2 Deceleration lean-off.

Fig. 29: Transition-compensation map
Weighting factors as a function of engine speed and throttle-valve angle.

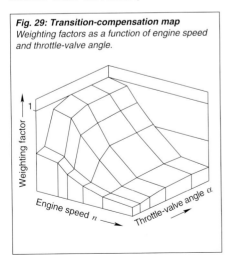

Fig. 31: Transition-compensation weighting factor related to intake-air temperature

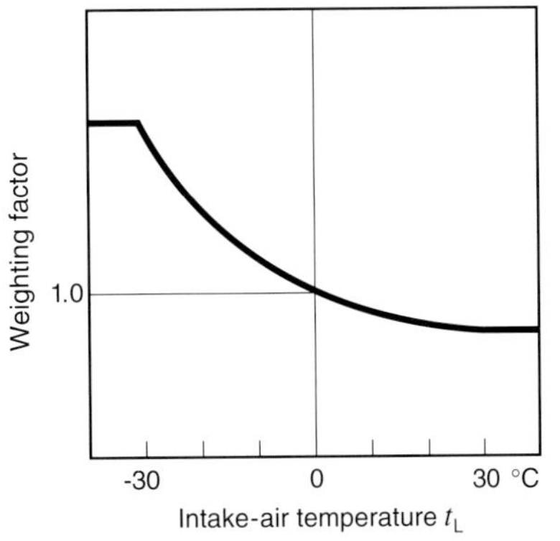

Lambda closed-loop control

The Lambda closed-loop control circuit maintains an air-fuel mixture of precisely $\lambda = 1$. The ECU receives continuous signals from the Lambda oxygen sensor located in the exhaust-gas stream. Using this signal, the ECU monitors the instantaneous level of the residual oxygen in the exhaust gas. The ECU employs these signals to monitor the current mixture ratio and to adjust injection duration as required.

The Lambda closed-loop control is superimposed on the basic mixture-control system. It ensures that the system is always optimally matched to the 3-way catalytic converter (Fig. 32).

Fig. 32: Lambda closed control loop
1 Fuel, 2 Air, 3 Central injection unit,
4 Fuel injector, 5 Engine, 6 Lambda oxygen
sensor, 7 Catalytic converter, 8 ECU with
Lambda closed-loop control, 9 Exhaust gas.
U_λ Sensor voltage, U_v Injector triggering pulse.

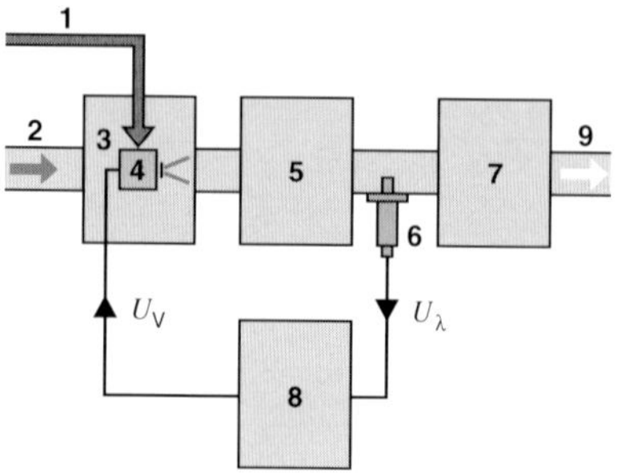

Lambda closed-loop control circuit

Deviations from the stoichiometric air-fuel ratio are detected and corrected with the aid of the Lambda oxygen sensor. The control principle is based on the Lambda sensor measuring the level of residual oxygen in the exhaust gas. This residual oxygen is a measure for the composition of the air-fuel mixture supplied to the engine. The Lambda sensor is installed so that it extends into the exhaust gas and acts as a probe which delivers information as to whether the mixture is richer or leaner than $\lambda = 1$. If the mixture deviates from $\lambda = 1$, the sensor output voltage changes abruptly and this change is evaluated by the ECU control circuit. A high (approx. 800 mV) sensor output voltage indicates a mixture which is richer than $\lambda = 1$, and a low output signal (approx. 200 mV) a mixture which is leaner. The Lambda sensor's signal periodicity is illustrated in Figure 33. The Lambda control stage receives a signal for every transition from rich to lean mixture and from lean to rich.

The Lambda correction factor is applied to adjust injection duration. At Lambda values above 1.0 (low sensor voltage) the injection quantity is increased, at values below 1.0, it is decreased. When a sensor voltage jump occurs, in order to generate a correction factor as soon as possible, the air-fuel mixture is changed immediately by a given amount. The manipulated variable then follows a programmed adaptation function until the next Lambda-sensor voltage jump takes place. The result is that within a range very close to $\lambda = 1$, the air-fuel mixture permanently changes its composition either in the rich or in the lean direction. If it were possible to adapt the Lambda map to the ideal value $\lambda = 1$, the manipulated variable for the Lambda control stage (the Lambda correction factor) would control permanently to the neutral value $\lambda = 1$.

Unavoidable tolerances make this impossible though, so the Lambda closed-loop control follows the deviations from the ideal value and controls each map point to $\lambda = 1$. In this manner, the fuel is metered so precisely that the air-fuel ratio is an optimum for all operating conditions. The system compensates for the effects of production tolerances and engine wear. Without this continuous, practically instantaneous adjustment of the mixture to $\lambda = 1$, efficient treatment of the exhaust gas by the downstream catalytic converter would be impossible. The Lambda oxygen sensor needs a temperature above about 350°C before it delivers a signal which can be evaluated. There is no closed-loop control below this temperature.

Mixture adaptation

The mixture-adaptation function provides separate, individual mixture adjustment for specific engine-defined operating environments. It also furnishes the mixture-control circuits with reliable compensation for variations in air density. The mixture adaptation program is designed to compensate for the effects of production tolerances and wear on engine and injection-system components.

The system must compensate for three variables:
– Influences due to air-density changes when driving at high altitudes (air-flow multiplicative influence).
– Influences related to vacuum leakage in the intake tract. Leakage downstream from the throttle valve can also vary as deposits reseal the affected areas (air-flow additive influence).
– Influences due to individual deviations in the injector response delay (injection-duration additive influence).
As there are certain map sectors where these influences have a very marked effect, the map is subdivided into three mixture-adaptation sectors:
– Air-density changes which have the same effect over the complete map.

The mixture-adaptation sector for the adaptation variable which takes the air density into account (air-flow multiplicative value) therefore applies to the complete map.
– Changes in the leakage-air rate have a pronounced effect at low air-flow rates (e.g. in the vicinity of idle). An additional adaptation value is therefore calculated in a second sector (airflow-additive value).
– Changes in the injected fuel quantity for every injection pulse are particularly effective when the injection duration is very short. A further adaptation value is therefore calculated in a third sector (injection-duration additive value).

The mixture-adaptation variable is calculated as follows:
The Lambda control-stage manipulated variable is a defined quantity. When a mixture fault is detected, this variable is changed until the mixture has been corrected to $\lambda = 1$. Here the mixture correction for the Lambda controller is defined by the deviation from the Lambda control value. For mixture adaptation, these Lambda controller parameters are evaluated using a weighting factor before being added to the adaptation variables for the individual ranges. The ad-

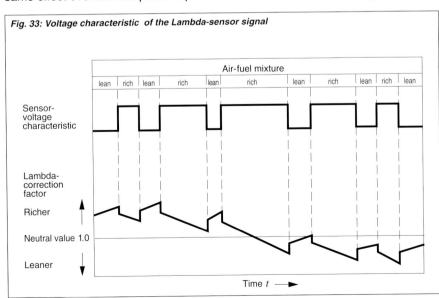

Fig. 33: Voltage characteristic of the Lambda-sensor signal

Air-fuel mixture

lean | rich | lean | rich | lean | rich | lean | rich | lean | rich | lean

Sensor-voltage characteristic

Lambda-correction factor

Richer

Neutral value 1.0

Leaner

Time *t* ⟶

aptation variable thus varies in fixed increments, with the size of the increments being proportional to the current Lambda mixture-correction factor. Each increment provides compensation for another segment of the mixture correction (Figure 34).

Depending upon the engine load and speed, the incremental periodicity is between 1 s and 100 ms. The adaptation variables are updated so quickly that any effects of tolerance and drift on driveability and exhaust-gas composition are compensated for completely.

Idle-speed control
The idle-speed (closed-loop) control is used to reduce and stabilize the idle speed, and maintains a consistent idle speed throughout the whole of the vehicle's service life. The Mono-Jetronic system is maintenance-free, because no idle speed or idle mixture adjustments are required. In this type of idle-speed control, the throttle-valve actuator, which opens the throttle valve by means of a lever, is so controlled that the stipulated idle speed is maintained exactly under all operating conditions. This applies no matter whether the vehicle electrical system is heavily loaded, or the air-conditioner is switched on, or

the automatic gearbox is at "Drive", or the power-assisted steering is at full lock etc. Engine temperature also has no effect, nor do high altitudes, where larger throttle-valve angles are required to compensate for lower barometric pressure.
The idle-speed control adapts the idle speed to the engine operating condition. In most cases, the idle speed is reduced, which is a decisive contribution to a reduction in fuel consumption and exhaust-gas emissions.

For the idle-speed control facility there are two engine-temperature-dependent curves stored in the ECU (Fig. 35a):

– Curve 1 for automatic-transmission vehicles when "Drive" is engaged.
– Curve 2 for manually-shifted transmissions, or automatic gearboxes if "Drive" is not engaged (Neutral).

The idle speed is usually reduced on automatic vehicles in order to reduce their tendency to creep when "Drive" is engaged. When the air-conditioner is switched on, the idle speed is often increased to maintain a defined minimum idle and ensure adequate cooling (Curve 3). In order to prevent engine-speed fluctuations when the air-con-

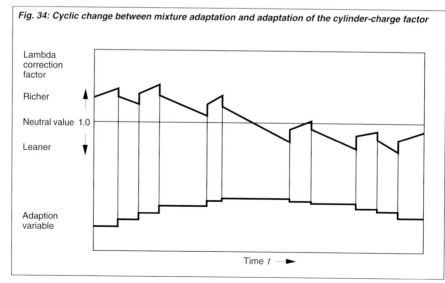

Fig. 34: Cyclic change between mixture adaptation and adaptation of the cylinder-charge factor

ditioner compressor engages and disengages, the high idle speed is maintained even when the compressor is not engaged.

From the difference between the actual engine speed and the set speed (n_{set}), the engine-speed control stage calculates the appropriate throttle-valve setting.

With the idle switch closed, the control signal to the throttle-valve actuator comes from a position controller. This generates the control signal from the difference between the actual throttle-valve setting as registered by the throttle-valve potentiometer, and the desired throttle-valve setting as calculated by the engine-speed control stage.

In order to avoid sudden drops in engine speed during transitions, for instance, in the transition from overrun to idle, the throttle valve must not be closed too far. This is ensured by applying pilot control characteristics which electronically limit the minimum correcting range of the throttle-valve actuator. This necessitates the ECU containing a temperature-dependent throttle-valve pilot-control characteristic for "Drive" and for "Neutral" (Fig. 35b).

In addition, a number of different pilot-control corrections come into effect when the air-conditioner is switched on, dependent on whether the compressor is engaged or not. So that the pilot control is always at optimum value, pilot-control corrections are also adapted to cover all possible combinations resulting from the input signals for Transmission setting (Drive/Neutral), "Air-conditioner ready" (YES/NO), and "Compressor engaged" (YES/NO). It is the object of this adaptation to select the overall effective pilot-control value so that at idle this is at a specified number of degrees in advance of the actual throttle-valve setting.

In order that the correction of the pilot-control values becomes effective before the first idle phase when driving at high-altitudes, an additional air-density-dependent pilot-control correction is applied. The possibility of also being able to operate the throttle-valve outside the idle range (if the driver is not pressing the accelerator pedal) is taken advantage of and applied as a vacuum-limiting function. During overrun, this function opens the throttle valve in accordance with an engine-speed-dependent characteristic curve (Fig. 35b), just far

Mono-Jetronic

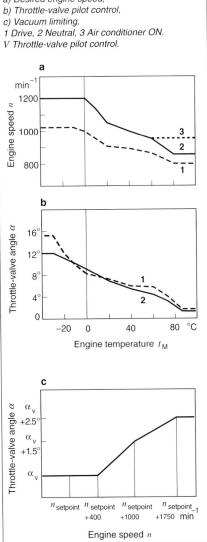

Fig. 35: Idle-speed control
a) Desired engine speed,
b) Throttle-valve pilot control,
c) Vacuum limiting.
1 Drive, 2 Neutral, 3 Air conditioner ON.
V Throttle-valve pilot control.

133

enough to avoid operating points which have a very low cylinder charge (incomplete combustion).

Throttle-valve actuator

Through its control shaft, the throttle-valve actuator can adjust the throttle-valve lever and thereby influence the amount of air available to the engine. The actuator is powered by a DC motor which drives the setting shaft through a worm and roller gearset. Depending upon the motor's direction of rotation (which in turn depends upon the polarity applied to it), the setting shaft either extends and opens the throttle valve or retracts and reduces the throttle-valve angle. The control shaft incorporates a switching contact which closes when the shaft abuts against the throttle-valve lever and provides the ECU with the idle signal.

A rubber bellows device between the control shaft and the throttle-valve actuator housing prevents the intrusion of dirt and damp (Fig. 36).

Full-load enrichment

The driver presses the accelerator pedal to the floor to obtain maximum power from the engine. An IC engine develops maximum power with an air-fuel mixture which is about 10...15% richer than the stoichiometric air-fuel ratio. The degree of enrichment is stored in the ECU in the form of a factor which is used to multiply the injection duration figures calculated from the Lambda map. Full-load enrichment comes into effect as soon as a specified throttle-valve angle is exceeded (this is a few degrees before the throttle-valve stop).

Engine-speed limiting

Extremely high rotational speeds can destroy the engine (valve gear, pistons). The limiting circuit prevents the engine from exceeding a given maximum speed. This speed n_0 can be defined for every engine, and as soon as it is exceeded the ECU suppresses the injection pulses. When the engine speed drops below n_0, the injection pulses are resumed again. This cycle is repeated in rapid succession within a tolerance band centered around the maximum permitted engine speed (Fig. 37).

The driver notices a sharp reduction in engine response, which also signals that an upshift is due.

Fig. 36: Throttle-valve actuator
1 Housing with electric motor, 2 Worm,
3 Wormwheel, 4 Setting shaft, 5 Idle contact,
6 Rubber bellows.

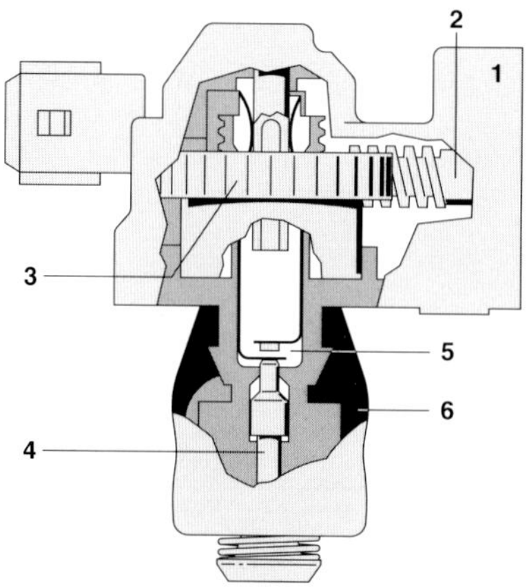

Fig. 37: Limitation of engine speed n_0 by means of injection-pulse suppression
a Area of fuel cut-off.

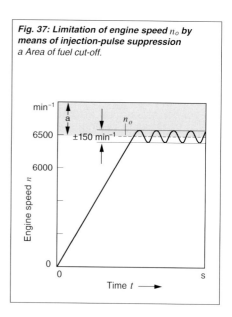

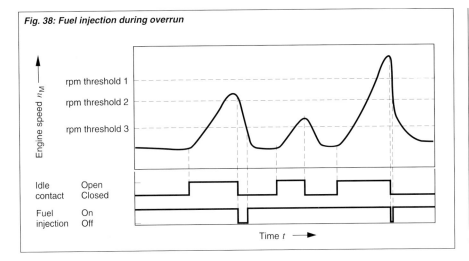

Fig. 38: Fuel injection during overrun

Engine speed n_M

rpm threshold 1
rpm threshold 2
rpm threshold 3

Idle contact — Open / Closed

Fuel injection — On / Off

Time t

Overrun (trailing throttle)

When the driver takes his foot off of the accelerator pedal while driving the vehicle, the throttle valve closes completely, and the vehicle is driven by its own kinetic energy. This operating mode is termed overrun or trailing throttle.

In order to reduce exhaust emissions and to improve driveability, a number of functions come into operation during overrun:

If the engine speed is above a given threshold (rpm threshold 2) when the throttle valve is closed, injector triggering stops, the engine receives no more fuel, and its speed falls. Once the next threshold is reached (rpm threshold 3), fuel injection is resumed. If the engine speed drops abruptly during overrun, as can occur when the clutch is pressed, fuel injection is resumed at a higher engine speed (rpm threshold 1), otherwise the engine speed could fall below idle or the engine could even stall (Fig. 38).

If the throttle valve is closed at high engine speeds, on the one hand the vehicle is decelerated abruptly due to the braking effect of the motored engine. On the other, the emission of hydrocarbons increases because the drop in manifold pressure causes the fuel film on the manifold walls to evaporate. This fuel though cannot combust completely because there is insufficient combustion air. To counteract this effect, during overrun the throttle-valve actuator opens the throttle valve slightly as a function of engine speed. This is described above under engine-speed limiting. If on the other hand the engine-speed drop is very abrupt during overrun, the throttle-valve opening angle is no longer a function of the fall in engine speed but instead the reduction in opening angle is slower and follows a time function.

During overrun the film of fuel deposited on the intake-manifold walls evaporates completely and the intake manifold dries-out. When the overrun mode is completed, fuel must be made available to build up this fuel film on the manifold walls again. This results in a slightly leaner air-fuel mixture in the transitional period until equilibrium returns. Fuel-film buildup is aided by an additional injection pulse, the length of which depends upon the overrun duration.

System voltage compensation

Fuel-injector voltage compensation

A feature of the solenoid-operated fuel injector is that due to self-induction it tends to open more slowly at the beginning of the injection pulse and to close more slowly at the end. Opening and closing times are in the order of 0.8 ms. The opening time depends heavily on the battery voltage, whereas the closing time depends only slightly on this factor. Without electronic voltage correction, the resulting delay in injector pickup would mean a far too short injection duration and therefore insufficient fuel would be injected.

In other words, the lower the battery voltage, the less fuel is metered to the engine. Therefore, a reduction in battery voltage must be counteracted by a voltage-dependent increase in injection duration, the so-called additive injector correction factor (Fig. 39a). The ECU registers the actual battery voltage and increases the injector-triggering pulse by the voltage-dependent injector pickup delay.

Fig. 39: Correction of injection duration as a function of battery voltage
a) Voltage compensation, fuel injector
b) Voltage compensation, electric fuel pump:
1 Flow-type pump, 2 Positive-displacement pump.

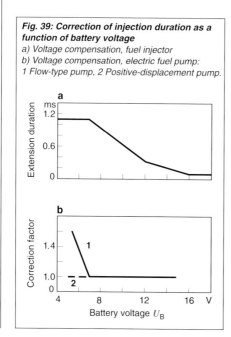

Fuel-pump voltage compensation

The speed of the fuel-pump motor is very sensitive to variations in battery voltage. For this reason, if the battery voltage is low (for instance during a cold start), the fuel pump, which functions according to the hydrodynamic principle, is unable to bring the primary pressure up to its specified level. This would result in insufficient fuel being injected. To compensate for this effect, particularly at very low battery voltages, a voltage-correction function is applied to correct the injection duration (Fig. 39b). If a positive-displacement electric fuel pump is used, this voltage correction function is unnecessary. The ECU is provided with a coding input, therefore, which enables the voltage-correction function to be activated depending upon pump type.

Controlling the regeneration-gas flow

When fresh air is drawn through the carbon in the carbon canister (purging), it transports the fuel trapped in the carbon to the engine for combustion.

The canister-purge valve between the carbon canister and the central injection unit controls the regeneration-gas flow. The control ensures that under all operating conditions as much of the trapped fuel as possible is transported away to the engine for burning. In other words, the regeneration-gas flow is kept as high as possible, without driveability being impaired. In general, the limit for the regeneration-gas flow is reached when the fuel contained in the regeneration-gas flow is about 20% of the fuel required by the engine at the given operating point.

In order to ensure the correct functioning of the mixture adaptation it is imperative that a cyclic change is made between normal operation, which makes mixture adaptation possible, and regeneration operation. Furthermore, it is necessary during the regeneration phase to ascertain the fuel content in the regeneration gas and to use this value for adaptation. The same as with the mixture adaptation, this takes place by evaluating the Lambda control stage's deviation from the $\lambda = 1$ value. Once the fuel content is known, the injection duration can be increased or decreased accordingly when the cycle changes so that during transition the mixture is maintained within tight limits around $\lambda = 1$.

To specify the fuel content in the regeneration-gas stream as a function of the engine operating mode, as well as to adapt the proportion of fuel in the regeneration-gas stream, the relationship between the regeneration-gas stream and the amount of air drawn in by the engine via the throttle valve must be determined. Both partial streams are practically proportional to the open cross-section areas through which they flow.

Whereas it is relatively simple to calculate the cross-section area in the throttle housing from the throttle-valve angle, the open cross-section area of the canister-purge valve changes according to the applied differential pressure.

The differential pressure applied at the canister-purge valve depends upon the engine's operating point and can be derived from the injection durations stored in the Lambda map.

The ratio of regeneration-gas stream to air stream drawn in by the engine can be calculated for each engine operating point as defined by the throttle-valve angle and the engine speed. The regeneration-gas stream can be further reduced by cycling the canister-purge valve and in this manner adjusted precisely to the required ratio necessary to ensure acceptable driveability.

Canister-purge valve

Due to the canister-purge valve's throughflow characteristic, it is possible to have a large regeneration stream for relatively small pressure differentials (operation near to WOT), and a small regeneration stream for large pressure differentials (idle operation). With switched-mode operation, the throughflow values can be further reduced by increasing the valve's on-off ratio. It is provided with two hose fittings for connection to the carbon canister and to the intake manifold (Fig. 40).

With a signal applied, the solenoid winding draws in the armature so that its sealing element (rubber seal) is pressed against the seal seat and closes the valve's outlet. The armature is fastened with a thin leaf spring which is secured at one end. When no current flows through the solenoid winding, this spring lifts the armature and seal element from the seal seat so that the throughflow cross section is open.

When the differential pressure between valve inlet and valve outlet increases, the forces acting on the leaf spring cause it to bend in the direction of the stream flow and in doing so bring the seal element nearer to the seal seat so that the effective throughflow cross section is reduced.

A check valve is provided in the valve-inlet area to prevent fuel vapors entering the intake manifold from the carbon canister when the engine is switched off.

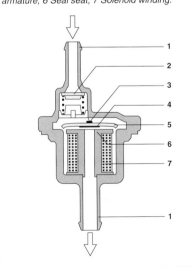

Fig. 40: Canister-purge valve
1 Hose connection, 2 Non-return valve, 3 Leaf spring, 4 Sealing element, 5 Solenoid armature, 6 Seal seat, 7 Solenoid winding.

Limp-home and diagnosis

All sensor signals are continuously checked for their plausibility by monitoring functions incorporated in the ECU. If one of the sensor signals deviates from its defined, plausible range, this means that either the sensor itself is defective or there is a fault in one of its electrical connections.

If one of the sensor signals fails or is no longer plausible, it must be replaced with a substitute signal in order that the vehicle does not break down completely but can still safely reach the next specialist workshops under its own power even though with some restrictions in driveability and comfort.

For instance, if temperature signals fail, signals are substituted which normally prevail when the engine is at its operating temperature: for the intake air 20°C and for the engine coolant 100°C. If a fault occurs in the Lambda closed-loop control, the complete Lambda control facility is closed down, that is, the injection durations from the Lambda map are only corrected with the mixture-adaptation value (if available).

If the signals from the throttle-valve potentiometer are not plausible, this means that one of the main controlled variables is missing. In other words, access is no longer possible to the injection durations stored in the Lambda map. In this case. the fuel injector is triggered with defined constant-length pulses. Two different injection durations are available, and switching between them depends upon engine speed.

In addition to the sensors, the throttle-valve actuator (idle-speed control) is also monitored continuously.

Fig. 41: Central injection unit (Section drawing)
1 Fuel-pressure regulator, 2 Intake-air temperature sensor, 3 Fuel injector, 4 Upper section (hydraulic section), 5 Fuel-inlet channel, 6 Fuel-return channel, 7 Thermal-insulation plate, 8 Throttle valve, 9 Lower section.

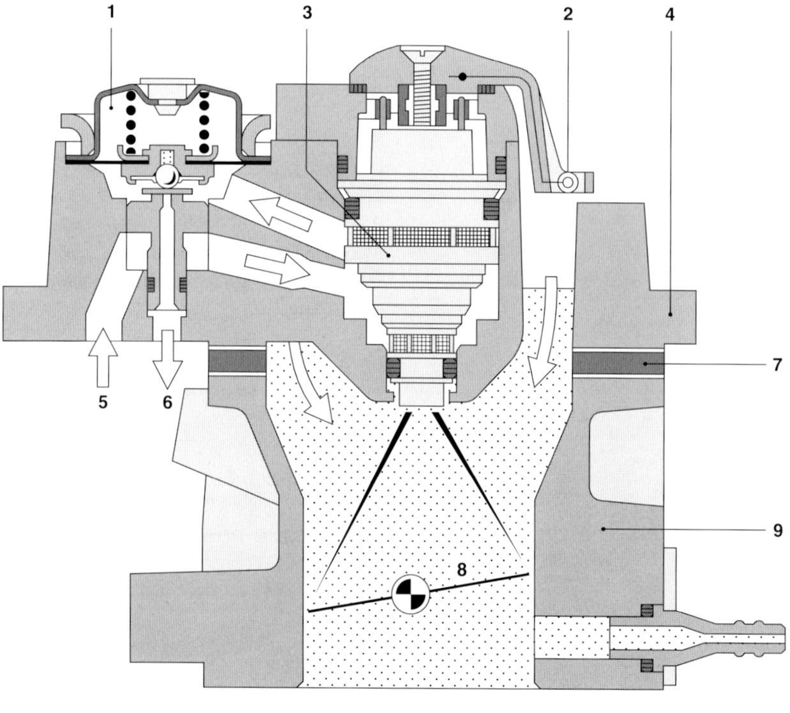

Fault memory

As soon as a sensor failure or throttle-valve actuator malfunction is registered, a corresponding entry is made in the fault memory. This entry remains accessible for a number of operating cycles (that is, even when the engine is switched off and the vehicle is left standing overnight a number of times) so that the workshop is able to localize the fault. This also applies to sporadic faults such as loose contacts etc.

Fault diagnosis

When diagnosis is triggered, the contents of the fault memory are made available to the workshop in the form of a flashing code, or with the aid of a diagnostic tester. As soon as the fault has been repaired, the Mono-Jetronic system operates again normally.

Central injection unit

The Mono-Jetronic central injection unit is bolted directly to the intake manifold. It supplies the engine with finely atomized fuel, and is the heart of the Mono-Jetronic system. Its design is dictated by the fact that contrary to multipoint fuel injection (e.g., L-Jetronic), fuel-injection takes place at a central point, and the intake-air quantity is measured indirectly through the two factors throttle-valve angle α and engine speed n, as already described, (Figures 41 and 42).

Lower section

The lower section of the central injection unit comprises the throttle valve together with the throttle-valve potentiometer for measuring the throttle-valve

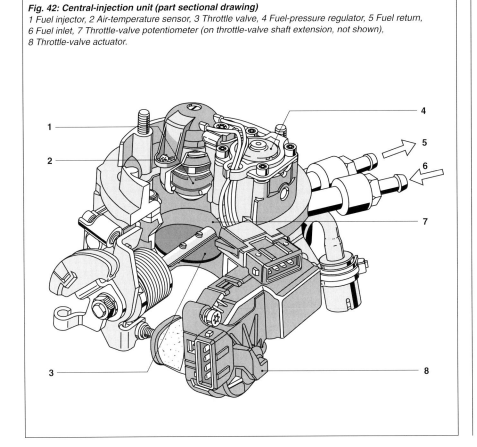

Fig. 42: Central-injection unit (part sectional drawing)
1 Fuel injector, 2 Air-temperature sensor, 3 Throttle valve, 4 Fuel-pressure regulator, 5 Fuel return, 6 Fuel inlet, 7 Throttle-valve potentiometer (on throttle-valve shaft extension, not shown), 8 Throttle-valve actuator.

angle. The throttle-valve actuator for the idle-speed control is mounted on a special bracket on the lower section.

Upper section

The complete fuel system for the central injection unit is in the upper section, consisting of the fuel injector, the fuel-pressure regulator, and the fuel channels to the fuel injector which are incorporated in the injector bracket. Two passages descend through the housing to supply the injector with fuel. The fuel flows to the injector via the lower passage.

The upper passage is connected to the lower chamber of the pressure regulator. From the fuel-pressure regulator, excess fuel enters the fuel-return line via the plate valve. This fuel-channel arrangement was selected so that even when the formation of fuel-vapor bubbles increases (as can occur for instance when the fuel-injection assembly heats up after the engine is switched off), enough fuel collects at the injector metering area to ensure trouble-free starting.

The open cross-section area between the return channel and the inlet channel is limited to a defined dimension by a shoulder on the fuel-injector strainer. This ensures that excessive fuel that has not been injected is divided into two partial streams, one of which flows through the injector and the other around it. This form of intensive flushing cools the fuel injector, and the fuel-channel arrangement with fuel circulating around the injector as well as through it, results in the Mono-Jetronic's excellent hot-starting characteristics. The temperature sensor for measuring the intake-air temperature is fitted in the central injection unit's cover cap.

Power supply

Battery

The battery supplies the complete electrical system with electrical energy.

Ignition/starter switch

The ignition switch is a multipurpose switch. It is used for starting the engine, and from here, electric power is switched to most of the vehicle's electrical circuits, including the ignition and the fuel-injection system.

Relay

The relay is controlled by the ignition switch, and switches the vehicle system voltage to the ECU and the other electrical components.

Electrical circuitry

The ECU is connected through a 25-pole plug-and-socket connection to all the Mono-Jetronic components as well as to the vehicle electrical system (Fig. 43).

The ECU is connected to the vehicle system voltage through two connections:

– One connection is used to permanently connect the ECU to the battery positive pole (Terminal 30). This permanent connection to the battery maintains the stored data (adaptation values, diagnostic fault memory) even when the ignition is switched off.

– The other connection connects the ECU to the battery when the ignition is switched on. In order to avoid voltage peaks which can be caused by the ignition coil's self-inductance, instead of connecting the ECU directly to Terminal 15 it may be necessary to connect it to the battery via a relay (main relay) which is controlled by Terminal 15 on the ignition switch.

ECU ground

Two separate lines are also used for connecting the ECU to ground:

– The ECU electronic circuitry requires a separate ground connection in order to correctly process the sensor signals (Lambda oxygen sensor, potentiometer, NTC sensors).

– The high currents from the ECU driver stages for triggering the actuators flow through the second ground line.

Lambda oxygen sensor connection

In order to screen the Lambda oxygen sensor line from interference due to voltage peaks, it is surrounded by a wire-mesh sheath in the wiring harness.

Fuel-pump safety cicuit

The fuel-pump relay is directly controlled from the ECU. This ensures that the fuel-pump stops delivering fuel if the engine has ceased running, for instance in case of an accident. Switching on the ignition activates the fuel pump for about 1 second and so does each ignition pulse. This is termed dynamic pump control. If the engine stops with the ignition still switched on, the fuel-pump relay releases and open-circuits the power supply to the fuel pump.

Fig. 43: Mono-Jetronic diagram
B1 Intake-air temperature sensor, B2 Lambda oxygen sensor, B3 Engine-temperature sensor, B4 Throttle-valve potentiometer, F1 + F2 Fuses, H1 Diagnosis lamp and tester connection, K1 Pump relay, K2 Main relay, Kl.1/TD engine-speed information, R1 Dropping resistor, S1 Air-conditioner ON, S2 Air-conditioner compressor, S3 Gearbox switch, W1 t_v-coding, W2 pump coding, X1 ECU, Y1 Canister-purge valve, Y2 Electric fuel pump, Y3 Fuel injector, Y4 Throttle-valve actuator with idle switch.

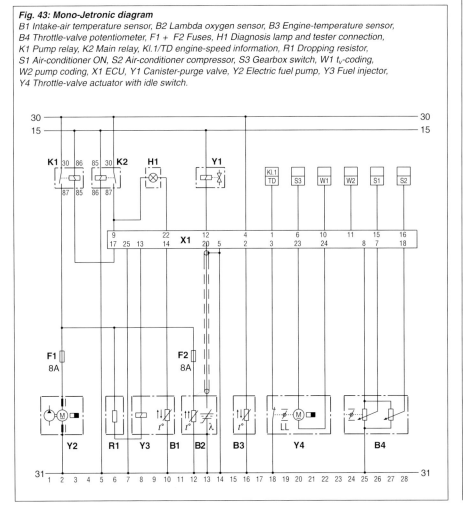

Ignition

Ignition in the spark-ignition engine

The design of the ignition system for the spark-ignition engine varies according to how ignition is triggered, how the timing is adjusted and how the high voltage is distributed.

Table 1 shows a classification of various ignition systems.

Ignition point (timing)

The ignition point is essentially dependent on the variables "engine speed" and "load." It is dependent upon the engine speed since the time taken for complete combustion of the mixture at constant charge and air-fuel ratio is constant and, thus, the ignition point (timing) must be shifted forward as engine speed increases, in other words it must take place earlier. The dependence upon load is due to the leaner mixtures, higher proportions of residual gas and less dense cylinder charges that accompany low load factors. This influence causes a longer ignition delay and lower combustion rates in the mixture; the timing must be advanced to compensate (Fig. 1).

Spark advance

Variable ignition timing allows the ignition to respond to variations in engine speed and load factor. On simple systems, timing is adjusted by a centrifugal advance mechanism and a vacuum control unit. Manifold vacuum provides a reasonably accurate index of engine load.

Semiconductor ignition systems also allow for other influences of the engine, e.g., temperature or changes in the mixture composition. The values of all ig-

Table 1. Definition of the ignition system.
An ignition system must perform at least the following functions:

Function	Ignition system			
	Ci	TI	SI	DLI
	Coil ignition	Transistorized ignition	Semiconductor ignition	Distributorless semiconductor ignition
Ignition triggering (pulse generator)	mechanical	electronic	electronic	electronic
Determining the ignition angle on the basis of the speed and load condition of the engine	mechanical	mechanical	electronic	electronic
High-tension generation	inductive	inductive	inductive	inductive
Distribution and assignment of the ignition spark to the correct cylinder	mechanical	mechanical	mechanical	electronic
Power section	mechanical	electronic	electronic	electronic

nition timing functions are linked either mechanically or electronically in order to determine the ignition point. The energy storage device must be fully charged before the actual ignition point. This requires the formation of a dwell period or dwell angle in the ignition system. The energy is generally stored in an inductive storage device, and, in rare cases, in a capacitive storage device. High voltage is generated by disconnecting the primary inductor from the power supply followed by transformation. The high voltage is applied to the cylinder currently performing the working stroke. When an ignition distributor is used, the crankshaft position information required for this is provided by an appropriate mechanism via the ignition distributor drive.

In the case of stationary voltage distribution, an electrical signal from the crankshaft or the camshaft provides the position signal. The connecting elements (plugs and high-tension cable) convey the high voltage to the spark plug. The spark plug must function reliably in all engine operating ranges in order to ensure consistent ignition of the mixture.

Ignition voltage

The excess-air factor λ and the cylinder pressure which is determined by charge and compression have, together with the spark-plug electrode gap, a crucial influence upon the required ignition voltage and, thus, upon the required secondary available voltage of the ignition system.

Ignition of the mixture

Ignition energy
Approximately 0.2 mJ of energy is required per individual ignition for igniting an air-fuel mixture by electric spark, providing the mixture (static, homogeneous) has a stoichiometric composition. Rich and lean mixtures (turbulent) require over 3 mJ. This amount of energy is but a fraction of the total energy contained in the ignition spark, the ignition energy.

If insufficient ignition energy is available, ignition does not occur; the mixture cannot ignite and there are combustion misses. This is why adequate ignition energy must be provided to ensure that, even under worst-case external conditions, the air-fuel mixture always ignites. It may suffice for a small cloud of explosive mixture to move past the spark. The cloud of mixture ignites and, in turn, ignites the rest of the mixture in the cylinder, thus initiating fuel combustion.

Influences on ignition characteristics
Good induction and easy access of the mixture to the ignition spark improve the ignition characteristics as do long spark duration and a long spark or large electrode gap. Intense turbulence of the mixture also has a similarly favourable effect providing that adequate ignition energy is available. The spark position and spark length are determined by the dimensions of the spark plug. The spark duration is determined by the type and design of ignition system and the instantaneous ignition conditions. The spark position and accessibility of the

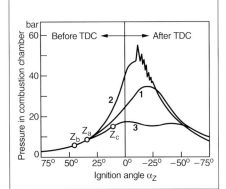

Fig. 1: Pressure curve in combustion chamber for different ignition points
1 Ignition (Z_a) at correct time
2 Ignition (Z_b) too soon (ignition knock)
3 Ignition (Z_c) too late

mixture to the spark plug influence the exhaust gas, especially in the idle range.

Particularly high ignition energy and a long spark duration are favourable in the case of lean mixtures. This can be demonstrated using an engine at idle. During idle, the mixture may be very inhomogeneous. Valve overlap results in a high residual exhaust-gas component. If we compare a normal breaker-triggered coil ignition system and a high-energy transistorized ignition system, we can see that the spark of the transistorized ignition system clearly reduces and stabilizes HC emission. Smooth running of the engine is also stabilized at the same time.

Fouling of the spark plug is also an important factor. If spark plugs are badly fouled, energy is discharged from the ignition coil via the spark-plug shunt path during the period in which the high voltage is being built up. This shortens the spark duration, thus affecting the exhaust gas and, in critical cases (if the spark plugs are badly fouled or wet) may result in complete misfiring. A certain amount of misfiring is normally not noticed by the driver but does result in higher fuel consumption and may damage the catalytic converter.

Pollutant emission

The ignition angle α_z or the ignition point has an important influence on the exhaust-gas values, the torque, the fuel consumption and the driveability of the spark-ignition engine. The most important pollutants in the exhaust gas are the unburned hydrocarbons (HC), oxides of nitrogen (NO_x) and carbon monoxide (CO).

The emission of unburned hydrocarbons increases the more the ignition is advanced.

NO_x emission also increases when the ignition is advanced across the entire air-fuel ratio range. The reason for this is the rise in combustion-chamber temperature associated with increasing ignition advance.

CO emission is practically independent of the ignition point and is virtually exclusively a function of the air-fuel ratio.

Fuel consumption

The influence of the ignition point on fuel consumption conflicts with the influence on pollutant emission. With increasing excess-air factor λ, ignition must occur earlier in order to compensate for the lower combustion rate and thus maintain an optimum combustion process. Thus, an advanced ignition point means lower fuel consumption and high torque but only if the mixture is controlled accordingly.

Knocking tendency

One further important interrelationship is that between ignition point and the engine's tendency to knock. This is demonstrated by the effect of a too early or too late ignition point (by comparison with the correct ignition point) on the pressure in the combustion chamber (Fig. 1). If the ignition point is too early, mixture at various points in the combustion chamber also ignites owing to the ignition pressure wave. This means that the mixture burns irregularly and intense pressure fluctuations occur with high combustion-pressure peaks. This effect, called knocking, can be heard clearly at low engine speeds. At high engine speeds, the noise is smothered by the engine noise. But it is precisely in this range that knocking may lead to engine damage and it must thus be avoided by finding an optimum combination of suitable fuel and ignition point.

Conventional coil ignition CI

The conventional coil-ignition system is breaker-triggered. This means that the current flowing through the ignition coil is switched on and off mechanically via a contact in the ignition distributor (contact breaker).

The breaker-triggered coil-ignition system is the simplest version of an ignition system in which all functions are implemented. In addition to the ignition distributor, there are a whole number of other components, as shown in Table 2 together with their functions.

Operating principle

Synchronization and high-voltage distribution

Synchronization with the crankshaft and, thus, with the position of the individual pistons is guaranteed by the mechanical coupling of the ignition distributor to the camshaft or to another shaft which turns at only half the speed of the crankshaft. Thus, if the ignition distributor is turned, this will also result in a shift in the ignition point or, in other words, turning the ignition distributor permits setting a prescribed ignition point.

The mechanical rotor arm which is also permanently coupled to the upper section of the ignition-distributor shaft ensures correct distribution of the high voltage, in conjunction with routing of the high-voltage cables to the individual spark plugs.

Ignition sequence

When the system is operating, voltage from the battery (1) flows through the starter/ignition switch (2) and to terminal 15 on the ignition coil (3) (Figures 1 and 2). When the contact breaker (6) is closed, the current flows through the primary winding of the ignition coil to ground. This builds up a magnetic field in the ignition coil, thus storing the ignition energy. The current rise is exponential owing to the inductance and the primary resistance of the primary winding. The charging time is determined by the dwell angle. In turn, the dwell angle is determined by the design of the cam which actuates the contact breaker via the cam follower. At the end of the dwell period, the ignition-distributor cam opens the ignition contact and thus interrupts the coil current.

Table 2
Components of the conventional ignition system

A coil-ignition system is composed of various components and subassemblies, the actual design and construction of which depend mainly on the engine with which the system is to be used.

Component	Function
Ignition coil	Stores the ignition energy and delivers it in the form of a high voltage surge through the HT ignition cable to the distributor
Ignition and starting switch	A switch in the primary circuit of the coil, manually operated with the ignition key
Ballast resistor	This is shorted during starting for starting-voltage boosting
Contact breaker	Opens and closes the primary circuit of the ignition coil for the purposes of energy storage and voltage conversion
Ignition condenser/ capacitor	Provides for low-loss interruption of the primary current and suppresses most of the arcing between the contact points
Ignition distributor	At the instant of ignition, distributes the firing voltage to the spark plugs in a pre-set sequence
Centrifugal advance mechanism	Automatically shifts the ignition timing depending on the engine speed
Vacuum advance mechanism	Automatically shifts the ignition timing depending on the engine load
Spark plug	Contains the electrodes which are the most important parts required to generate the ignition spark and seals off the combustion chamber

The current, the off time and the number of windings in the secondary circuit of the ignition coil essentially determine the ignition voltage induced in the secondary circuit. Since the current tends to carry on flowing, an arc would form at the ignition contact. In order to prevent this, the ignition capacitor (5) is connected in parallel with the contact breaker. This means that the primary current flows to the capacitor and charges it until the ignition voltage discharges disruptively. This means that voltages of a few hundred V occur briefly at terminal 1 of the ignition coil in the primary circuit (Figures 1 and 2).

The high tension generated in the secondary circuit charges the connection to the center tower of the ignition distributor, causes a disruptive discharge between the rotor arm and outer electrode, then charges the high-voltage cable to the relevant spark plug and finally causes disruptive discharge at the spark plug, i.e. causes the ignition spark.

After this, the magnetic energy stored in the ignition coil is discharged constantly as electrical energy to the spark. This causes a spark voltage of approxima-

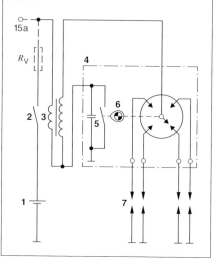

Fig. 2: Circuit diagram of the coil ignition system
1 Battery, 2 Ignition and starting switch, 3 Ignition coil, 4 Ignition distributor, 5 Ignition capacitor, 6 Contact breaker, 7 Spark plugs, R_v ballast resistor.

tely 400 V at the spark plug. The spark duration is generally 1 to 2 ms. After the ignition coil is discharged, the cam of the ignition distributor switches the contact breaker back on and the ignition coil is recharged.

Fig. 1: Ignition system with conventional coil ignition
1 Battery, 2 Ignition and starting switch, 3 Ignition coil, 4 Ignition distributor, 5 Ignition capacitor, 6 Contact breaker, 7 Spark plugs, R_v ballast resistor for boosting the starting voltage (not always fitted).

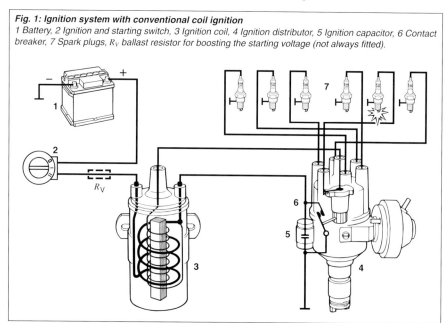

The rotor arm which carries on moving in the meantime transfers the high tension to the next spark plug during the next ignition.

Ignition coil

Construction

The ignition coil consists of a metal case which accommodates metal plate jackets for reducing stray magnetic fields. The secondary winding is wound directly onto the laminated iron core and connected electrically to the center tower in the cap of the ignition coil via the core.

Since the high voltage is applied to the iron core, the core must be insulated by the cap and an additional insulator inserted in the base. The primary winding is located near to the outside around the secondary winding (Fig. 3).

The insulated ignition coil cap contains the terminals 15 and 1 for the battery voltage and the connection to the contact breaker, arranged symmetrically with the high-tension tower, terminal 4. The windings are insulated and mechanically locked in position by potting with asphalt. Oil-filled ignition coils are also available.

The power loss occurs chiefly in the primary winding. The heat is dissipated through the metal plate jackets to the case. This is why the ignition coil is secured to the bodywork with such a wide clamp so that as much heat as possible is dissipated via this metal band.

Function

The primary current which is switched on and off by the ignition distributor flows through the ignition-coil primary winding. The magnitude of the current is determined by the battery voltage at terminal 15 and the ohmic resistance of the primary winding. The primary resistance may lie between 0.2 and 3 Ω, dependent upon use of the ignition coil. The primary inductance L1 is a few mH. The following formula applies to the energy

stored in the magnetic field of the ignition coil

$$W_{Sp} = \frac{1}{2} L_1 \cdot i_1^2$$

W_{Sp} stored energy, L_1 inductance of the primary winding, i_1 current which flows in the ignition distributor at the moment at which the contact breaker opens.

At the ignition point, the voltage at terminal 4 (high-voltage tower of the ignition coil) rises approximately sinusoidally. The rate of rise is determined by the capacitive load at terminal 4. When the spark-plug breakdown voltage is

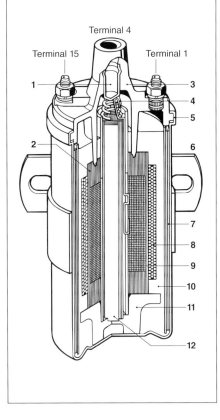

Fig. 3: Section through an ignition coil
1 High-tension connection on the outside,
2 Winding layers with insulating paper,
3 Insulating cap, 4 High-tension connection on the inside via spring contact, 5 Case, 6 Mounting bracket, 7 Metal plate jacketing (magnetic),
8 Primary winding, 9 Secondary winding,
10 Sealing compound, 11 Insulator, 12 Iron core.

Terminal 4

Terminal 15   Terminal 1

1
3
4
5
2
6
7
8
9
10
11
12

reached, the voltage drops to the spark voltage of the spark plug and the energy stored in the ignition coil flows to the ignition spark. As soon as the energy no longer suffices to maintain the glow discharge, the spark breaks down and the remaining energy decays in the secondary circuit of the ignition coil.

The high voltage is polarized such that the center electrode of the spark plug is negative with respect to the vehicle chassis or ground. If the polarity were the reverse, this would mean a slightly higher required voltage. The ignition coil is designed as an auto-transformer such that the secondary side is connected to terminal 1 or 15.

In the same way as the primary inductance and the primary resistance determine the stored energy, the secondary inductance determines the high-voltage and spark characteristic. A typical turns-ratio of primary to secondary winding is 1:100. The induced voltage, the spark current and the spark duration are dependent upon both the stored energy and the secondary inductance.

Internal resistance

One further important value is the ignition-coil internal resistance since it is one of the factors which determine the rate of voltage rise and is thus a measure of how much energy is discharged from the ignition coil via shunt resistances at the moment of spark discharge. A low internal resistance is advantageous in the case of fouled or wet spark plugs. The internal resistance is dependent upon the secondary inductance.

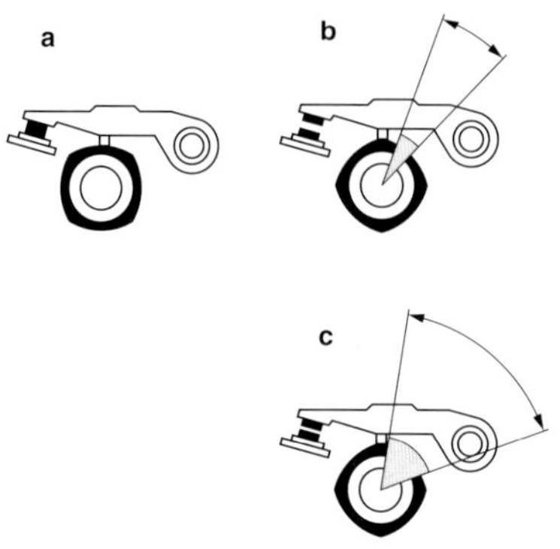

Contact breaker

The contact breaker is triggered via the breaker cam which has as many lobes as the number of cylinders in the engine. The breaker cam can be turned on the ignition distributor shaft. It is adjusted dependent upon the engine-speed-dependent ignition-timing adjustment input from the centrifugal advance mechanism. The cam is configured such that there results a dwell angle corresponding to the ignition coil and the sparking rate (Fig. 4).

This means that the dwell angle is permanently preset for a breaker-triggered ignition system and is invariable throughout the entire engine-speed range. However, the dwell angle does change throughout the service life of the engine owing to wear of the cam follower on the breaker lever. The abrasion which is thus produced means that the contact breaker opens at a later point. The resultant ignition retard generally results in higher fuel consumption. This is one of the reasons why the contact breaker needs to be renewed regularly and the dwell angle checked. Another reason why maintenance is required is contact erosion (pitting). The contact must switch currents of up to 5 A and break voltages of up to 500 V. On a 4-cylinder engine with an engine speed of 6000 min^{-1} the contact switches 12000 times per minute, corresponding to a frequency of 200 Hz.

Defective contacts mean inadequate charging of the ignition coil, undefined ignition points and, thus, higher fuel consumption and poorer exhaust-gas values.

Fig. 4: Contact breaker (schematic diagram)
a) Contact closed,
b) Large point gap, small dwell angle,
c) Small point gap, large dwell angle.

Ignition distributor

The ignition distributor is the component of the ignition system which performs most functions. It rotates at half the crankshaft speed. A 4-cylinder distributor has, for instance, 4 outputs which each generate an ignition pulse each time the rotor turns (Fig. 5).

Features

The main exterior features are the pot-shaped ignition-distributor housing and the distributor cap made of insulating material with the towers for the high-voltage connections. On some versions of shaft distributors, the drive shaft projects into the engine. It is then driven via a gearing system or a coupling. Another design, the short-type distributor, simplifies direct attachment to the camshaft. In this case, there is no drive shaft and the drive coupling is located directly at the base of the ignition-distributor housing. The stringent requirements in respect of ignition-distributor accuracy require very good bearing support. On shaft distributors, the shaft itself provides an adequately long bearing section. Short-type distributors require an additional bearing above the triggering system.

Construction

The ignition-distributor housing accommodates the centrifugal advance mechanism, the actuation system for the vacuum advance system and the ignition triggering system. The ignition capacitor and the vacuum control unit are secured on the outside of the ignition-distributor housing. In addition, the outside of the housing also has the catches for securing the distributor cap and the electrical connection. The dust-protection cover protects the triggering system against dirt deposits and moisture. There is a slot on the distributor shaft above the breaker cam. This slot serves to define the installation position of the distributor rotor. This is why, when fitting, it must be ensured that the rotor arm is fitted in the correct position. The distributor rotor and distributor cap are made of a high-grade plastic which is required to meet very stringent requirements in respect of dielectric strength, climatic resistance, mechanical strength and flammability. The high voltage generated in the ignition coil is fed to the ignition distributor via the central tower.

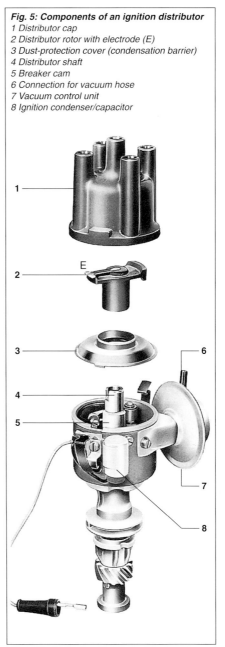

Fig. 5: Components of an ignition distributor
1 Distributor cap
2 Distributor rotor with electrode (E)
3 Dust-protection cover (condensation barrier)
4 Distributor shaft
5 Breaker cam
6 Connection for vacuum hose
7 Vacuum control unit
8 Ignition condenser/capacitor

There is a small, spring-loaded carbon pin between the distributor rotor and central tower. This pin establishes contact between the fixed cap and the rotating distributor rotor. The ignition energy flows from the centerpoint of the distributor rotor through the interference-suppression resistor with a rating of $\geq 1\,k\Omega$ to the distributor-rotor electrode, and, from there, sparks over to the respective outer electrode which is recessed in the outer tower. The voltage required for this is in the kV region. The resistor in the distributor rotor limits the peak currents when the sparks are being built up and thus serves to suppress interference. With the exception of the contact breaker, all parts of the ignition distributor require virtually no maintenance.

Spark-advance mechanism

The centrifugal advance mechanism advances ignition timing as a function of the engine speed. Assuming constant charge and fuel induction, this results in a fixed duration for ignition and complete combustion of the mixture. This fixed duration means that it is necessary to produce the ignition spark correspondingly earlier at high engine speeds. However, the progression of an ignition-distributor characteristic curve is also influenced in practice by the knock limit and the variation in composition of the mixture.

The vacuum advance mechanism takes the load condition of the engine into account since the ignition and combustion rate of the fresh gas in the cylinder is highly dependent upon the charge in the cylinder.

The engine-speed or centrifugal advance mechanism, and the vacuum advance mechanism or load adjustment, are interconnected mechanically in such a way that both adjustments are added (Fig. 6).

Centrifugal advance mechanism

The centrifugal advance mechanism adjusts the ignition point as a function of engine speed. The support plate which

Fig. 6: Example of an overall timing-control system comprising adjustment dependent upon engine-speed and upon intake-manifold pressure
1 Part load on road
2 Full load

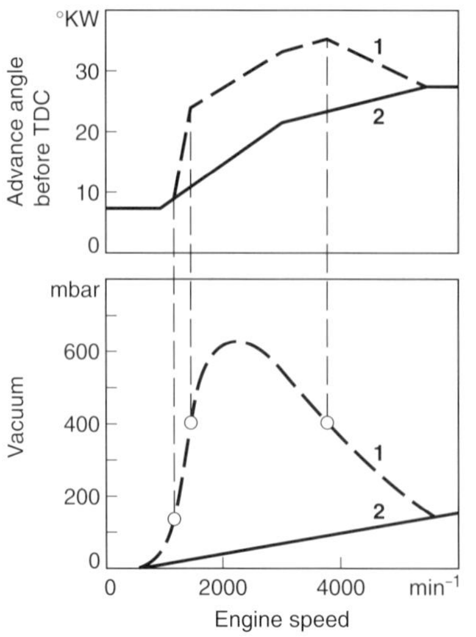

Fig. 7: Centrifugal advance mechanism in rest position (top) and in operating position (below)
1 Support plate
2 Distributor cam
3 Rolling contact path
4 Flyweight
5 Ignition-distributor shaft
6 Yoke

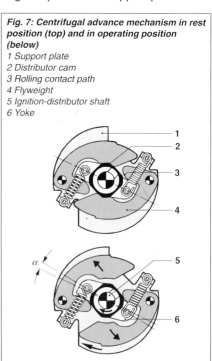

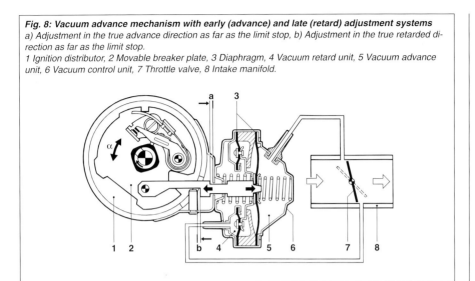

Fig. 8: Vacuum advance mechanism with early (advance) and late (retard) adjustment systems
a) Adjustment in the true advance direction as far as the limit stop, b) Adjustment in the true retarded direction as far as the limit stop.
1 Ignition distributor, 2 Movable breaker plate, 3 Diaphragm, 4 Vacuum retard unit, 5 Vacuum advance unit, 6 Vacuum control unit, 7 Throttle valve, 8 Intake manifold.

rotates with the distributor shaft bears the flyweights. As engine speed increases, the flyweights move outwards. By means of their contact path, they rotate the yoke in the direction of shaft rotation but relative to the shaft. The result is that the distributor cam also rotates relative to the shaft by the same angle, the advance angle α_z, and thus advances the ignition point by this angle (Fig. 7).

Vacuum advance mechanism

The vacuum advance mechanism adjusts the ignition point as a function of the engine power or engine load. The vacuum in the intake manifold near to the throttle valve serves as a measure for this vacuum advance. The vacuum is measured by one or two aneroid capsules (Fig. 8).

"Early" (advance) adjustment system

The lower the load, the earlier the air-fuel mixture needs to be ignited since it burns more slowly. The percentage of burned but non-exhausted residual gases in the combustion chamber increases and the mixture becomes leaner.

The vacuum for adjustment in the advance direction is taken off at the intake manifold. As the engine load decreases, the vacuum in the vacuum advance unit increases, causing the diaphragm and the vacuum advance arm to move to the right (Fig. 8). The vacuum advance arm turns the movable breaker plate in the opposite direction to the direction of rotation of the distributor shaft. The ignition point is advanced further, i.e. in the "early" direction.

"Late" (retard) adjustment system

The vacuum in the intake manifold is, in this case, taken off downstream of the throttle valve. With the aid of the annular "vacuum retard unit", the ignition point is retarded, i.e. moved in the "late" direction, under specific engine conditions (e.g., idle, overrun) in order to improve the exhaust-gas values. The ring diaphragm moves, together with the vacuum advance arm, to the left as soon as there is a vacuum. The vacuum advance arm turns the movable breaker plate, including the contact breaker, in the direction of rotation of the ignition distributor shaft. The late adjustment system is subordinate to the early adjustment system: simultaneous vacuum in both aneroid capsules means an ignition-timing shift in the advance direction for part-load operation.

Breaker-triggered transistorized ignition TI-B

The ignition distributor of the breaker-triggered transistorized ignition system (TI-B) is identical to the ignition distributor of the breaker-triggered coil ignition system (CI). However, the contact breaker no longer needs to switch the primary current but only the control current for the transistorized ignition system. The transistorized ignition system itself plays the role of a current amplifier and switches the primary current via an ignition transistor (generally a Darlington transistor). In order to facilitate understanding, the wiring of the contact and the function of a simple TI-B are compared below to a breaker-triggered coil-ignition system.

Operating principle

Figures 2 and 3 clearly show that the breaker-triggered transistorized ignition system is a further development of the conventional, non-electronic coil-ignition system: the transistor T is used as the circuit breaker in place of the contact breaker and assumes its switching function in the primary circuit of the ignition system. However, since the transistor has a relay characteristic, it must be caused to switch in the same way as the relay. This can be done, for instance, as shown in Fig. 2, with a control switch. Such transistorized ignition systems are thus termed breaker-triggered.

In Bosch transistorized ignition systems, the cam-operated breaker performs the function of this control switch. When the contact is closed, a control current I_s flows to the base B and the transistor is electrically conductive between the emitter E and the collector C. In this condition, it corresponds to a switch in the "On" position and current can flow through the primary winding L_1 of the ignition coil. However, if the

contact of the breaker is open, no control current flows through to the base and the transistor is electrically non-conductive. It thus blocks the primary current and, in this condition, corresponds to a switch in the "Off" position.

Advantages

The breaker-triggered transistorized ignition system has two essential advantages over the breaker-triggered coil-ignition system:

– An increase in the primary current and
– considerably longer service life of the breaker contact.

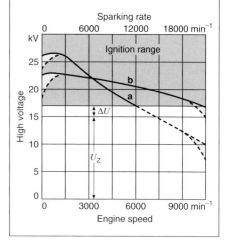

Fig.1: Secondary available voltage of the ignition coil for the spark plug as a function of the sparking rate or engine speed (4-cylinder engine).
a) Ignition coil with maximum sparking rate 12 000 min⁻¹,
b) High-performance ignition coil with maximum sparking rate 21 000 min⁻¹.
U_z Ignition voltage, ΔU Minimum voltage reserve.
Shaded area: Area for operation free of misfiring.

The primary current can be increased if using a switching transistor since a mechanical contact can switch currents of only up to 5 A for long periods and with the required frequency. Since the stored energy is proportional to the square of the primary current, the power of the ignition coil increases and, thus, also all high-voltage data such as secondary available voltage, spark duration and spark current. Thus, a breaker-triggered transistorized ignition system also requires a special ignition coil in addition to the ignition trigger box.

A far longer service life of the TI-B results from the fact that the contact breaker is not required to switch high currents. In addition, the TI-B is also not subject to two other problems which indefinably reduce the secondary available voltage of contact-triggered coil-ignition systems: Contact chatter and the contact-breaking spark which results from the inductance of the ignition coil. The contact-breaking spark reduces the

available energy and delays the high-voltage rise, particularly at low engine speed and when starting. Conversely, contact chatter occurs at high engine speeds owing to the high switching frequency of the contact and is a disturbing influence. The contact bounces when closing and thus charges the ignition coil less intensely, precisely at a point in time at which the dwell period is reduced anyway. The first negative characteristic of the contact breaker is not applicable to the breaker-triggered transistorized ignition system, the second is.

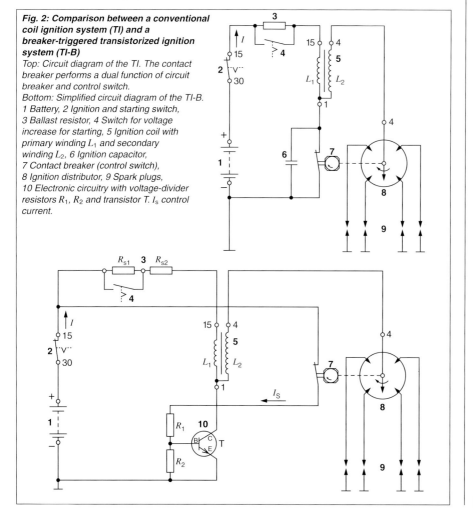

Fig. 2: Comparison between a conventional coil ignition system (TI) and a breaker-triggered transistorized ignition system (TI-B)
Top: Circuit diagram of the TI. The contact breaker performs a dual function of circuit breaker and control switch.
Bottom: Simplified circuit diagram of the TI-B.
1 Battery, 2 Ignition and starting switch, 3 Ballast resistor, 4 Switch for voltage increase for starting, 5 Ignition coil with primary winding L_1 and secondary winding L_2, 6 Ignition capacitor, 7 Contact breaker (control switch), 8 Ignition distributor, 9 Spark plugs, 10 Electronic circuitry with voltage-divider resistors R_1, R_2 and transistor T. I_s control current.

Circuit

On a breaker-triggered transistorized ignition system, the ignition trigger box (control unit) is connected between terminal 1 of the ignition distributor (i.e. the contact breaker) and terminal 1 of the ignition coil (Fig. 3). In addition, the ignition trigger box requires one further terminal 15 for its power supply and a ground connection 31. The primary circuit of the ignition coil is powered via a pair of ballast resistors which are normally connected in series. When starting, the left-hand ballast resistor is bypassed by terminal 50 at the starter. This means that a higher supply voltage is applied to the ignition coil via the right-hand ballast resistor. It compensates for the disadvantages which result from the starting operation and the resulting reduction in battery voltage. Ballast resistors serve to limit the primary current in the case of low-resistance, rapidly chargeable ignition coils. They thus prevent overload of the ignition coil, particularly at low engine speeds, and thus protect the ignition contact breaker

since the dwell angle is still determined by the distributor cam. Since the ignition coil actually requires a constant period for charging but does not operate with a fixed dwell angle, there is too much time available at low engine speeds for charging and too little at high engine speeds. Ballast resistors and a rapidly chargeable ignition coil permit an optimum situation over the entire operating range.

On older vehicles, the TI-B was an original equipment item. It has now been displaced by the transistorized ignition with maintenance-free trigger systems. However, as a retrofit-equipment set, the TI-B is still well-suited for substantially improving the ignition characteristics on vehicles with breaker-triggered coil-ignition systems fitted as standard. This is why it is advisable to retrofit such a system in the case of general ignition problems, specifically in the case of starting difficulties, and if the vehicle is to be used largely for stop-and-go driving.

Fig. 3: Components and connection diagram of the TI-B
1 Battery, 2 Ignition and starting switch, 3 Ignition trigger box, 4 Ballast resistors, 5 Cable connection to the starter, 6 Ignition coil, 7 Ignition distributor, 8 Spark plugs, I primary current, I_s control current.

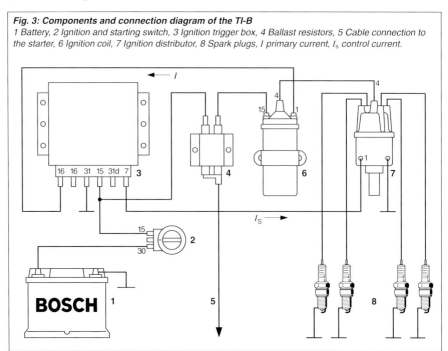

Transistorized ignition with Hall generator TI-H

In addition to the breaker-triggered transistorized ignition system (TI-B), there are two other versions of transistorized ignition with Hall triggering system (TI-H).

On one version, the dwell angle is determined by the shape of the rotor in the ignition distributor. The other version contains a control unit incorporating hybrid circuitry and which automatically regulates the dwell angle. An additional current limiter with a highly efficient ignition coil make this version a particularly high-performance ignition system.

Hall effect

If electrons move in a conductor to which the lines of force of a magnetic field are applied, the electrons are deflected perpendicularly to the current direction and perpendicularly to the direction of the magnetic field: an excess of electrons occurs at A_1 and a deficiency of electrons occurs at A_2, i.e. the Hall voltage occurs across A_1 and A_2. This so-called Hall effect is particularly prominent in the case of semiconductors (Fig. 1).

Hall generator

When the ignition-distributor shaft turns, the vanes of the rotor move through the air gap of the magnetic barrier without touching it. When the air gap is unobstructed the incorporated IC and the Hall layer are subjected to the magnetic field (Fig. 2).

At the Hall layer, the magnetic flux density B is high and the Hall voltage U_H is maximum. The Hall IC is activated. As soon as one of the rotor vanes enters the air gap, most of the magnetic flux runs through the vane area and is thus largely prevented from reaching the Hall layer. The flux density at the Hall layer is reduced to a virtually negligible level, resulting from the leakage field. Voltage U_H is at minimum.

Fig.1: Hall effect
B Flux density of the magnetic field, I_H Hall current, I_V Supply current, U_H Hall voltage, d Thickness.

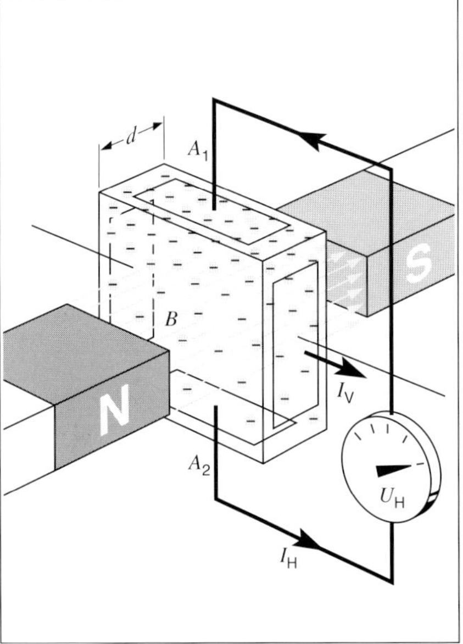

Fig.2 Hall generator in the ignition distributor
Top: Principle. Below: Generator voltage U_G (converted Hall voltage).
1 Vane with width b, 2 Soft magnetic conductive elements with permanent magnet, 3 Hall IC, 4 Air gap.

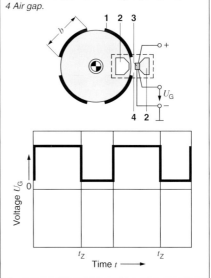

The Hall generator is accommodated in the ignition distributor. The magnetic barrier is mounted on the movable carrying plate.

The Hall IC is located on a ceramic substrate and is potted in plastic together with one of the conductive elements in order to protect it against moisture, dirt and mechanical damage. The conductive elements and trigger wheel are of a soft magnetic material. The trigger wheel and distributor rotor comprise one component on the retrofit version. The number of vanes is equal to the number of cylinders. The width b of the individual vanes can determine the maximum dwell angle of the ignition system, dependent upon the ignition trigger box. The dwell angle consequently remains constant throughout the entire service life of the Hall generator; thus, there is no need to set it. The mode of operation and design of the Hall generator permit the ignition system to be set with the engine switched off providing peak-coil-current cut-off is incorporated. If the technical prerequisites are fulfilled, and the installation instructions are observed precisely, it is an easy matter to convert from conventional ignition to breakerless ignition (Fig. 4). Bosch service stations will be able to provide you with further information.

Current regulation and dwell-angle closed-loop control

High-performance ignition systems operate with ignition coils which charge very rapidly. For this purpose, the ohmic resistance of the primary winding is reduced to less than 1Ω. The information content of the signal of a Hall vane switch in the ignition distributor corresponds to the signal of an ignition contact breaker. In one case, the dwell angle is determined by the distributor cam and, in the other, the pulse duty factor is determined by the rotor vane. A rapidly chargeable ignition coil cannot operate with a fixed dwell

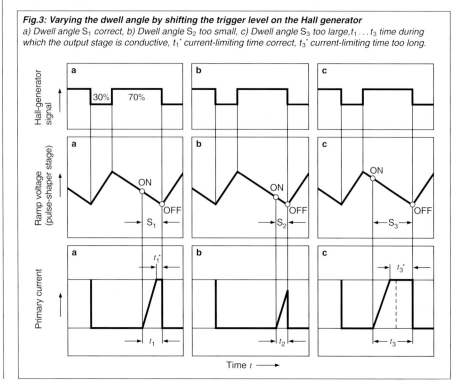

Fig.3: Varying the dwell angle by shifting the trigger level on the Hall generator
a) Dwell angle S_1 correct, b) Dwell angle S_2 too small, c) Dwell angle S_3 too large, $t_1 \ldots t_3$ time during which the output stage is conductive, t_1^* current-limiting time correct, t_3^* current-limiting time too long.

angle. This is why two measures must be taken to protect the ignition coil: a primary-current regulation system and a dwell-angle closed-loop control system (Fig. 3).

Current-regulation function

The primary-current regulation system serves to limit the current through the ignition coil and, thus, to limit the build-up of energy to a specific amount. A certain lead time is required in order to cope with the dynamic conditions applicable when the engine accelerates. This means that the ignition coil should reach its nominal value before the ignition point. During this current regulation phase, the ignition transistor operates in its active range. More voltage than in the pure switch mode drops across the transistor. This means a high power loss which may lie between 20 and 30 W. In order to minimize this, and in order to set the appropriate dwell angle, a dwell-angle closed-loop control system is required (which is actually a dwell-period closed-loop control system since the coil is charged as a function of time).

Function of the dwell-angle closed-loop control system

Since control processes in analog systems are carried out simply by shifting voltage threshold values, the square-

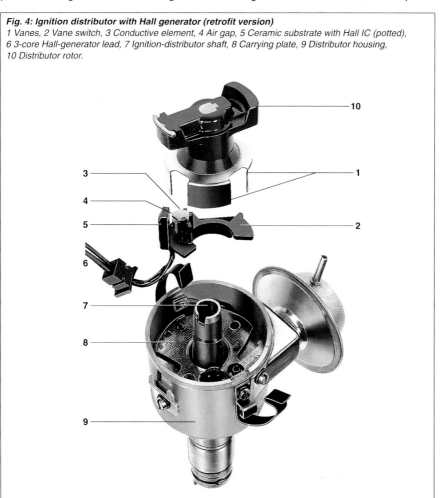

Fig. 4: Ignition distributor with Hall generator (retrofit version)
1 Vanes, 2 Vane switch, 3 Conductive element, 4 Air gap, 5 Ceramic substrate with Hall IC (potted), 6 3-core Hall-generator lead, 7 Ignition-distributor shaft, 8 Carrying plate, 9 Distributor housing, 10 Distributor rotor.

Fig. 5: Control unit (trigger box) with output stage for current regulation and dwell-angle closed-loop control

wave signal of the Hall generator is first converted to a ramp signal by charging and discharging capacitors. The pulse duty factor of the Hall generator is 30:70 between two ignition points.

The ignition point determined by adjustment of the ignition distributor lies at the end of the vane width corresponding to 70 % . The closed-loop control system is set such that the current control time t_1 corresponds precisely to the required dynamic lead. A voltage is formed on the basis of value t_1 and is compared with the trailing ramp of the ramp voltage. The primary current is switched on at the intersection point "ON" and the dwell angle starts. In this way, the switch-on point of the dwell angle can be varied as required by shifting the in-

tersection point on the ramp voltage and by varying the voltage derived from the current control time. This means that the correct dwell angle is always formed for every operating range. Since current regulation and dwell-angle closed-loop control are dependent directly upon current and time, this eliminates the effects of varying battery voltage and temperature effects or other ignition-coil tolerances. This renders these ignition systems particularly suitable for cold starting. Since primary current can flow owing to the waveform of the Hall signal with the engine switched off and with the ignition-starting switch switched on, the control units can be equipped with an auxiliary circuit which switches off this "peak-coil current" after a certain period.

Control unit (ECU)

Transistorized ignition systems with current regulation and dwell-angle closed-loop control, virtually all comprise hybrid circuits. This makes it possible to combine the compact and lightweight control units (Fig. 5), for instance with the ignition coil, to form one assembly. Owing to the power loss which occurs in the ignition coil and in the transistorized-ignition control unit, adequate cooling and good thermal contact with the bodywork are required.

Fig. 6: ECU circuitry using hybrid techniques

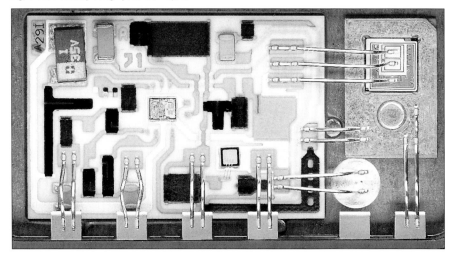

Transistorized ignition with induction-type pulse generator TI-I

The transistorized ignition system with induction-type pulse generator (TI-I) is a high-performance ignition system like the Hall-generator ignition system, and there are only slight differences between the two systems. As compared with the TI-H, the TI-I has a greater phase displacement between the actual ignition point and the off-edge of the pulse-generator voltage at high engine speeds. This is attributable to the induction-type pulse generator in the TI-I which represents an electrical AC generator and has an additional phase displacement owing to the load of the control unit. In certain cases, this effect is even desirable in order to correct the characteristic curves to prevent knocking. Owing to the symmetrical pulse-generator construction, the TI-I is characterized by less spark oscillation in comparison to the Hall barrier of the TI-H which is arranged asymmetrically with respect to the axis of rotation.

Induction-type pulse generator

The permanent magnet, inductive winding and the core of the induction-type pulse generator form a self-contained unit, the "stator". The trigger wheel which is located on the ignition distributor shaft, termed the "rotor" turns with respect to this fixed assembly. The core and rotor are made of soft magnetic steel. They have tooth-shaped extensions (stator teeth, rotor teeth).

The operating principle is based upon the fact that the air gap between the rotor and stator teeth changes periodically when the rotor rotates. This also changes the magnetic flux. The change in flux induces an AC voltage in the inductive winding. The peak voltage $\pm \hat{U}$ is dependent upon the engine speed: approximately 0.5 V at low engine speed and ap-

proximately 100 V at high engine speed. The frequency f of this AC voltage corresponds to the sparking rate.
It is as follows,

$$f = z \cdot \frac{n}{2}$$

f Frequency or sparking rate (min^{-1}),
z Number of cylinders,
n Engine speed (min^{-1}).

Design features

The induction-type pulse generator is accommodated in the housing of the ignition distributor in place of the contact breaker (Fig. 1). When viewed from the outside, only the plug-in two-core generator lead indicates that this ignition distributor has an induction-type pulse generator. The soft magnetic core of the inductive winding is in the form of a circular disc, called the "pole piece". On the outside, the pole piece has stator teeth which, for instance, may be bent upwards perpendicularly. Consequently the rotor has teeth which are bent downwards.

The trigger wheel, which is comparable with the distributor cam of the contact

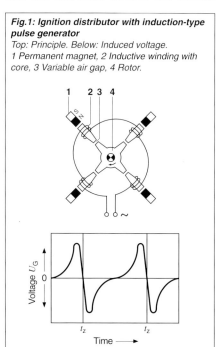

Fig.1: Ignition distributor with induction-type pulse generator
Top: Principle. Below: Induced voltage.
1 Permanent magnet, 2 Inductive winding with core, 3 Variable air gap, 4 Rotor.

breaker, is permanently connected to the hollow shaft which encloses the distributor shaft. The number of teeth on the trigger wheel and on the pole piece generally correspond to the number of cylinders in the engine. The fixed and moving teeth, when positioned directly opposite each other, have a spacing of approximately 0.5 mm.

Current regulation and dwell-angle closed-loop control

Current regulation and dwell-angle closed-loop control on the TI-I are similar to those on the TI-H. However, they are generally less complex since, normally, it is not necessary to generate a ramp voltage for shifting the on-time of the dwell angle. Instead, the signal of the induction-type pulse generator itself can be used as the voltage ramp on the basis of which the on-time of the dwell angle is determined by comparison with a voltage signal corresponding to the current control time (Fig. 2).

Current regulation function
The current regulation system detects the current by measuring the voltage drop across a low-resistance resistor in the emitter lead of the ignition transistor. The driver stage of the ignition transistor (Darlington transistor) is driven directly via a closed-loop current-limiting circuit.

Function of the dwell-angle closed-loop control system
The dwell-angle closed-loop control system operates with the same measuring-circuit voltage but routes it to its own closed-loop control circuit. Any necessary correction of the dwell angle can be determined by assessing the time during which the current of the transistor is being controlled.

Control unit (ECU)

Control units of TI-I high-performance ignition systems virtually all comprise hybrid circuits since they combine a high packing density with low weight and high reliability.

Fig. 2: Varying the dwell angle by shifting the trigger level on the induction-type pulse generator
a) Dwell angle S_1 correct, b) Dwell angle S_2 too small, c) Dwell angle S_3 too large, $t_1 \ldots t_3$ time during which the output stage is conductive, $t_1{}^*$ current-limiting time correct, $t_3{}^*$ current-limiting time too long.

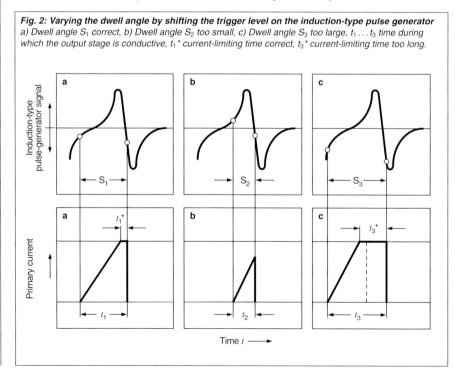

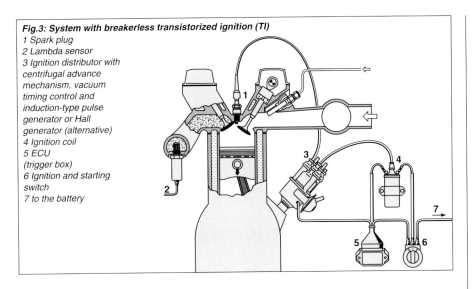

Fig.3: System with breakerless transistorized ignition (TI)
1 Spark plug
2 Lambda sensor
3 Ignition distributor with
centrifugal advance
mechanism, vacuum
timing control and
induction-type pulse
generator or Hall
generator (alternative)
4 Ignition coil
5 ECU
(trigger box)
6 Ignition and starting
switch
7 to the battery

If less stringent performance data are permitted, it may be possible to dispense with dwell-angle closed-loop control and, possibly even current regulation. Since the control load ratio of the evaluated pulse-generator signal on TI-I systems drops with decreasing engine speed, TI-I control units may be designed more compactly for specific applications and are thus particularly well-suited for direct attachment to the ignition distributor housing. Similar to combining the ECU with the ignition coil, this permits a reduction in the number of components in the ignition system which must be connected with leads (Fig. 4).

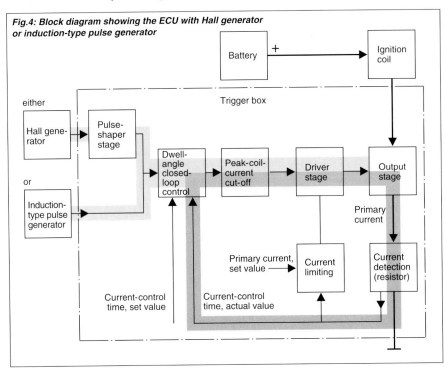

**Fig.4: Block diagram showing the ECU with Hall generator
or induction-type pulse generator**

Semiconductor ignition SI

On transistorized ignition systems, the conventional ignition distributor with centrifugal advance and vacuum advance mechanisms is capable of implementing only very simple advance characteristic curves. This means they can only approximately meet the demands imposed by optimum engine operation.

On the "semiconductor ignition system" (SI, Fig. 1), there is no mechanical spark-advance system in the distributor. Instead, a pulse-generator signal, in the form of an engine-speed signal, is used to trigger the ignition. An additional pressure sensor supplies the load signals. The microcomputer computes the required ignition-point adjustment and modifies the output signal issued to the trigger box accordingly.

Advantages

– Spark advance can be matched better to the individual and diverse requirements made of the engine.
– It is possible to include other control parameters (e.g. engine temperature).
– Good starting behaviour, improved idle control and lower fuel consumption.
– Extended operating-data acquisition.
– It is possible to implement knock control.

The advantages of the semiconductor ignition system are most clearly demonstrated by the ignition-advance map which contains the ignition angle for every given engine operating point. This ignition angle was selected during engine design as the best compromise for every engine speed and for every load condition. The ignition angle for a specific operating point is selected on the basis of the following aspects: fuel consumption, torque, exhaust gas, safety margin from the knock limit, engine temperature and driveability etc. Dependent upon the optimization criterion, one of

Fig. 1: Semiconductor ignition system (SI)
1 Ignition coil with attached ignition output stage, 2 High-tension distributor, 3 Spark plug, 4 ECU, 5 Engine-temperature sensor, 6 Throttle-valve switch, 7 Rotational-speed sensor and reference-mark sensor, 8 Ring gear, 9 Battery, 10 Ignition and starting switch.

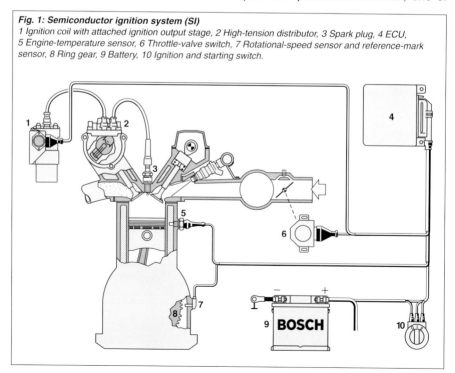

these aspects will be more important. This is why the ignition-advance map of a semiconductor spark-advance system frequently appears very rugged and jagged by comparison with the ignition map of a system with centrifugal and vacuum advance mechanisms. If, in addition, the generally non-linear influence of temperature or of another correction function is also to be represented, this would require a four-dimensional ignition map which would be impossible to depict.

Operating principle

The signal issued by the vacuum sensor is used as the load signal for the ignition system. A three-dimensional ignition-advance map is, so to speak, stretched over this signal and the engine speed. This map permits the best ignition point (angle) (in the vertical plane) to be programmed for every engine speed and load condition (horizontal plane) in respect of the exhaust gas and fuel consumption. The entire ignition-advance map contains approximately

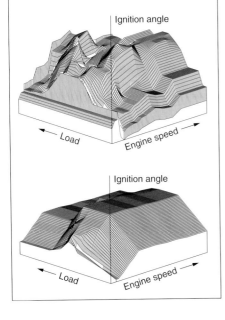

Fig. 2: Optimized electronic ignition-advance map (top) compared with the ignition-advance map of a mechanical spark-advance system (below)

Ignition angle

Load
Engine speed

Ignition angle

Load
Engine speed

1000 ... 4000 individual recallable ignition points, dependent upon requirements (Fig. 2).

When the throttle valve is closed, the special idle/overrun characteristic curve is selected. The ignition point can be "advanced" for engine speeds below the nominal engine idle speed in order to achieve idle stabilization by increasing the torque. Ignition points matched in respect of exhaust gas, handling and driveability are programmed for overrun operation. At full load, the full-load curve is selected. This curve contains the best programmed ignition parameters allowing for the knock limit.

In the case of specific systems, for starting, a progression of the ignition point, independent of the ignition-advance map, can be programmed as a function of engine speed and engine temperature. This permits high engine torque during starting without the occurrence of countertorques.

Dependent upon requirements, it is possible to implement ignition-advance maps of various degrees of complexity or only a few programmable advance curves. Electronic spark advance is possible within the framework of various semiconductor ignition systems. For instance the Motronic system incorporates fully integrated spark advance. However, it is also possible to implement a spark-advance system as an addition to a transistorized ignition system (in the form of an additional advance system) or as a device with integrated output stage.

Engine-speed sensing

There are two possible methods of engine-speed sensing in order to determine the engine speed and for synchronization with the crankshaft: the signal can be tapped-off directly at the crankshaft or camshaft, or at an ignition distributor equipped with a Hall ignition vane switch. The advantages afforded by an ignition-advance map with the form already discussed can be utilized to maximum accuracy with an engine-speed sensor on the crankshaft.

Input signals

Engine speed/crankshaft position and intake-manifold pressure are the two main control variables for the ignition point.

Engine speed and crankshaft position

An induction-type pulse generator which scans the teeth of a special-purpose gear wheel on the crankshaft serves to sense the engine speed. The resulting change in magnetic flux induces an AC voltage which is evaluated by the control unit. This gear wheel has a gap which is sensed by the pulse generator and the signal is then processed in a special circuit for clear assignment of the crankshaft position. Triggering with the aid of a Hall generator in the ignition distributor can also be used. In the case of symmetrical engines, it is also possible to trigger pulses inductively via segments on the crankshaft. The number of segments in this case corresponds to half the number of cylinders (Figures 3 to 5).

Load (intake-manifold pressure)

The pressure in the intake manifold acts upon the pressure sensor via a hose.
In addition to the intake-manifold pressure for only indirect load measurement, the air mass or the air quantity per unit of time are also particularly suitable as load signals since they provide a better indication of the charge of the cylinder which is the actual load. On engines equipped with an electronic fuel-injection system, it is thus possible to utilize the load signal not only for the fuel management but also for the ignition as well.

Throttle-valve position

A throttle-valve switch supplies a switching signal during engine idle and full load (Fig. 5).

Temperature

A water-temperature sensor in the engine block (Fig. 5) supplies the control unit with a signal corresponding to the engine temperature. The intake-air temperature can also be sensed by a further sensor either in addition to or instead of the engine temperature.

Battery voltage

The battery voltage is also a correcting quantity which is detected by the control unit.

Signal processing

Intake-manifold pressure, engine temperature and battery voltage, in the form of analog variables, are digitized in the analog-to-digital converter. Engine

Fig. 3: Ring gear (on the crankshaft) with induction-type pulse generator

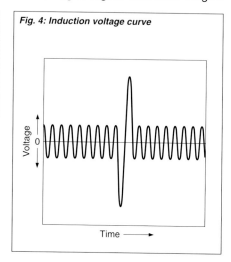

Fig. 4: Induction voltage curve

Voltage

0

Time ⟶

speed, crankshaft position and throttle-valve stops are digital variables and are routed directly to the microcomputer. Signal processing is carried out in the microcomputer, which comprises the microprocessor with quartz oscillator crystal for clock-pulse generation. In the computer, the updated values for the ignition angle and the dwell period are calculated anew for each ignition in order that the optimum ignition point is always available to the engine for every operating point.

Ignition output signal

The primary circuit of the ignition coil is switched by means of a power output stage in the electronic control unit. The dwell period is controlled such that the secondary voltage remains practically constant regardless of engine speed and battery voltage.

Since the dwell period or dwell angle is determined anew for each engine speed and battery voltage condition, this requires a further ignition map: the dwell-angle map (Fig. 6). It contains a network of data points between which interpolation is carried out as is the case with the ignition-advance map. Using such a dwell-angle map permits the energy stored in the ignition coil to be metered just as precisely as with a dwell-angle closed-loop control system.

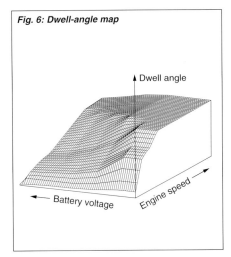

Fig. 6: Dwell-angle map

Dwell angle

Battery voltage

Engine speed

However, there are also semiconductor ignition systems in which a dwell-angle closed-loop control is superimposed upon the dwell-angle map. This closed-loop control system optimizes the dwell angle for each cylinder independently.

Control unit (ECU)

As can be seen on the block diagram, the heart of the control unit for a semiconductor ignition system is a microcomputer which contains all data, including the ignition maps, in addition to the programs for detecting the input variables and for computing the output variables. Since the sensors are largely

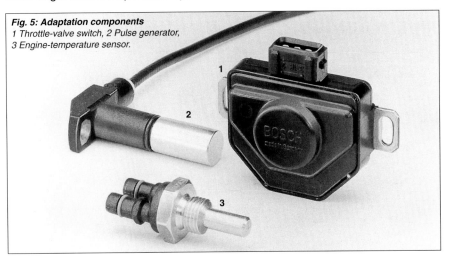

Fig. 5: Adaptation components
1 Throttle-valve switch, 2 Pulse generator,
3 Engine-temperature sensor.

electromechanical components matched to the tough operating conditions of the engine, it is necessary to process the signals for the computer.

Pulse-shaping circuits convert the pulsating signals from the sensors (such as those from the rpm sensor) into defined digital signals. As a further example, temperature and pressure sensors frequently transmit their signals in analog form. This analog signal is converted in an analog-to-digital converter and routed to the computer in digital form. The analog-to-digital converter may also be integrated in the microcomputer (Fig. 7).

In order to permit ignition-map data to be changed until shortly before the start of series production, there are control units available with an electronically programmable memory, generally in the form of an EPROM (electronically programmable read-only memory).

Ignition output stage

The ignition output stage may either be incorporated in the control unit itself (as shown in the block diagram) or may be accommodated externally, generally in combination with the ignition coil. In the case of external ignition output stages, the control unit is generally fitted in the passenger compartment. This is also the case less frequently on control units with integrated ignition output stage.

If control units with integrated ignition output stage are accommodated in the engine compartment, they require particularly good heat dissipation. This is achieved by the use of hybrid circuitry. Semiconductor devices and, thus, also the output stage, are then fitted directly to the heat sink which ensures good thermal contact to the bodywork. This means that such control units can be operated at ambient temperatures of over 100°C. Hybrid units have the further advantage of being compact and lightweight.

Fig. 7: Signal processing in the ECU (block diagram)
1 Engine speed, 2 Switch signals, 3 CAN (serial Bus), 4 Intake-manifold pressure, 5 Engine temperature, 6 Intake-air temperature, 7 Battery voltage, 8 A/D converter, 9 Microcomputer, 10 Ignition output stage.

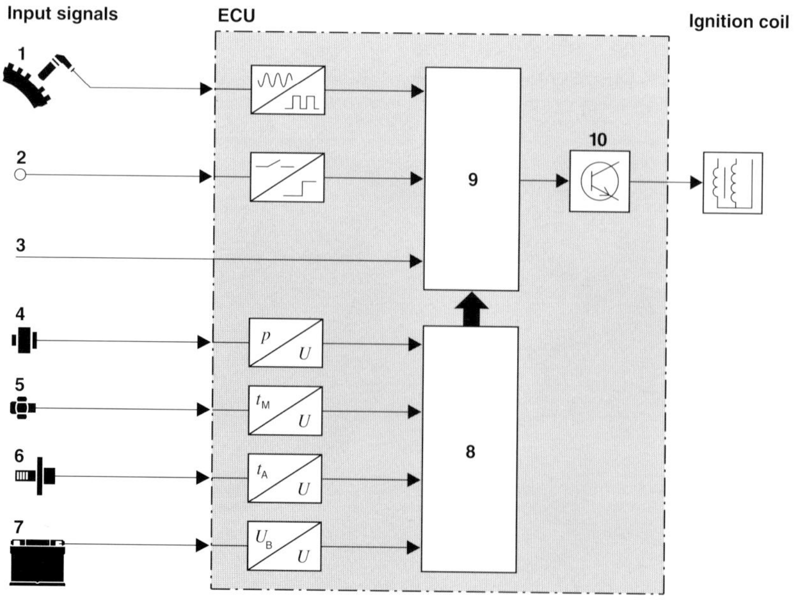

Other output variables

In addition to the ignition output stage, there are controls for further output variables, dependent upon the particular application. Examples of these are outputs for engine-speed signals and status signals for other control units such as injection, diagnostic signals, switching signals for actuating injection pumps or relays etc.

The semiconductor ignition system is particularly suitable for combining with other engine-management functions (Figures 8 and 9). Combined with an electronic fuel-ignition system, this means that the basic version of a Motronic system is realized in a single control unit.

One equally popular form is combining the semiconductor ignition system with a knock-control system. This combination is particularly advantageous since retarding the ignition point is the fastest and most reliable method of intervention to avoid engine knocking.

Fig.9: Semiconductor-ignition ECU using hybrid techniques
The load sensor is located in the cover.

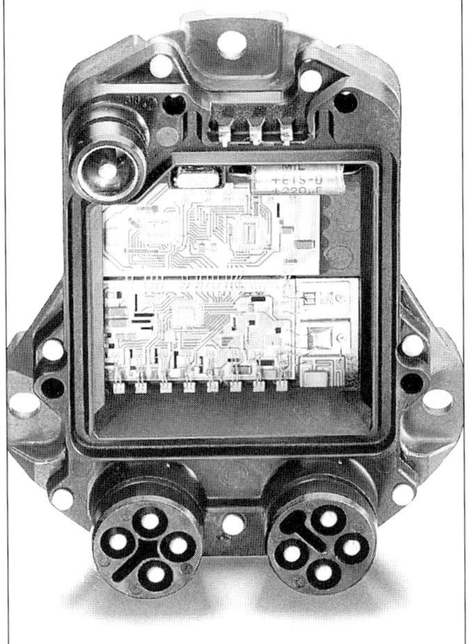

Fig. 8: Semiconductor-ignition ECU with knock control, using printed-circuit-board techniques
The aneroid box (D) serves to measure the intake-manifold pressure.

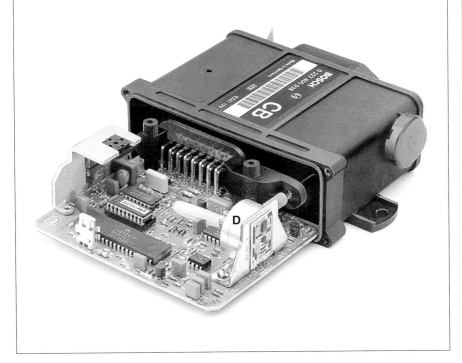

Distributorless semi-conductor ignition DLI

The distributorless semiconductor ignition system (DLI, Fig. 1) is characterized by two features: it performs the functions of a semiconductor ignition system, but has no rotating high-voltage distribution system using an ignition distributor.

Advantages

Although it has no advantages regarding weight, stationary high-voltage distribution does have the following advantages:
– Far lower electromagnetic interference level since no open sparks occur,
– no rotating components,
– noise reduction,
– less high-voltage connections and
– design advantages for the engine manufacturer.
The performance data of a distributorless semiconductor ignition system are comparable to those of a conventional semiconductor ignition system.

High-voltage distribution

High-voltage distribution with double-spark ignition coils

In the simplest case, e.g., on the 4-cylinder engine, two double-spark ignition coils are used instead of the ignition distributor. These are energized alternately via an ignition output stage. At the ignition point for a given cylinder, which is determined by the microcomputer-controlled ignition map in the same way as with a conventional semiconductor ignition system, the corresponding double-spark ignition coil generates two ignition sparks simultaneously. The two spark plugs at which the sparks are produced are each electrically connected in series with this ignition coil so that one spark plug is connected to each of its high-voltage outputs. These two spark plugs must be arranged so that one spark plug fires in the working stroke of the cylinder in question and the other in the exhaust stroke of the cylinder which is offset by 360°. One rotation of the crankshaft later, these two cylinders are two working strokes further and the spark plugs fire again, but now with reversed roles.

Fig. 1: Distributorless semiconductor-ignition system (DLI)
1 Spark plug, 2 2 x Double-spark ignition coils, 3 Throttle-valve switch, 4 Control unit with integrated driver stages, 5 Lambda sensor, 6 Engine-temperature sensor, 7 Engine-speed and reference-mark sensor, 8 Ring gear, 9 Battery, 10 Ignition and starting switch.

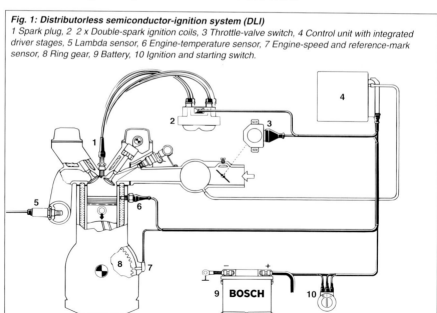

The second double-spark ignition coil also generates two sparks but offset by 180° (crankshaft) with respect to the first. Using the 4-cylinder engine as an example again, we see that cylinders 1 and 4 always fire simultaneously as do cylinders 3 and 2.

In addition, the double-spark ignition coil which is the next to be fired requires a signal identifying the start of a revolution. In the example shown, the TDC signal signals that firing must occur in cylinder group 1/4. The computer establishes when the crankshaft has turned a further 180° and then initiates ignition in cylinder group 3/2 with the other double-spark ignition coil. At the start of the second revolution, the TDC signal is issued again and, once again, causes ignition in cylinder group 1/4.

This forced synchronization system also ensures that the correct firing sequence is maintained even in the event of malfunctions of any kind. Only engines with an even number of cylinders (e.g. 2, 4, 6) are suitable for this type of stationary, or fully-electronic, high-tension distribution. The number of ignition coils required can be calculated in each case by halving the number of cylinders.

The schematic diagram of the distributorless semiconductor-ignition system shows a system with distribution by two double-spark ignition coils. The reference-mark sensor on the crankshaft also serves to trigger the correct ignition coil, in addition to calculating the ignition angle.

High-voltage distribution with single-spark ignition coils

A distributorless semiconductor-ignition system for an odd number of cylinders (e.g. 3, 5) requires its own ignition coil for each cylinder (single-spark ignition coils are also suitable for engines with an even number of cylinders, in conjunction with distributorless semiconductor ignition systems). The actual distribution of the high voltage to the ignition coils is performed in the low-voltage circuit in a power module with distributor logic. In the case of engines with an odd number of cylinders, one cycle covers two revolutions of the crankshaft. For this reason, a TDC signal from the crankshaft is not sufficient in this case. One signal per camshaft revolution must be triggered by the camshaft for synchronization purposes.

Distributorless semiconductor ignition

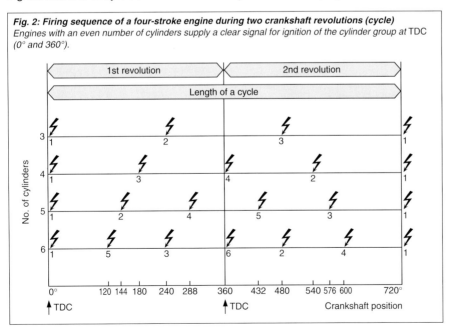

Fig. 2: Firing sequence of a four-stroke engine during two crankshaft revolutions (cycle)
Engines with an even number of cylinders supply a clear signal for ignition of the cylinder group at TDC (0° and 360°).

High-voltage distribution with four-spark ignition coils

One further method of stationary high-voltage distribution is a four-spark ignition coil which has two primary windings and one secondary winding. The two primary windings are energized by two ignition output stages. The high-voltage winding has two diodes at each output. From each of these diodes, one high-voltage cable is routed to each spark plug. This means that two sparks are produced alternately, decoupled by the diodes, as is the case on the double-spark ignition coil.

Required ignition voltage

Since two spark plugs are connected in series on double-spark and four-spark ignition coils, the required voltage increases by a few kV owing to the spark plug which fires in the low pressure of the exhaust stroke. However, this additional required voltage is compensated for by the fact that there is no ignition-distributor spark gap. In addition, one spark plug is "incorrectly" polarized in each cylinder group. This means that the center electrode is positive and not negative as is normally the case. This also causes the required voltage to be slightly higher.

Ignition coils

Design

Double-spark and four-spark ignition coils, are designed as plastic-molded coils. The resulting squat and compact design, together with the large area on the upper side, permit two separate high-voltage towers to be provided on these ignition coils. The coil is cooled and secured by the iron core which is led out externally (Fig. 3).

Mode of operation

If we consider the cycle of a single-cylinder four-stroke engine (two revolutions), we can see how the ignition sparks of a double-spark ignition coil occur during the engine strokes. The first revolution starts shortly after IO (intake valve opens) and lasts until TDC (top dead

---

Fig. 3: Double-spark ignition coil

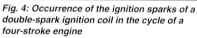

Fig. 4: Occurrence of the ignition sparks of a double-spark ignition coil in the cycle of a four-stroke engine
1 Switch-on range (start) of the primary current,
2 Ignition range of the first ignition spark,
3 Ignition range of the second ignition spark.
TDC Top dead center, BDC Bottom dead center,
IO Intake valve opens,
IC Intake valve closes, EO Exhaust valve opens,
EC Exhaust valve closes.

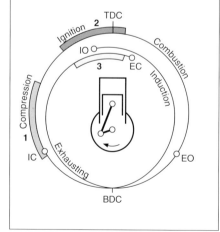

center). The second revolution starts at TDC and ends shortly before EC (exhaust valve closes). During the working stroke, firing occurs in the area marked red before and shortly after TDC, dependent upon the position of the ignition-advance map point (Fig. 4).

The dwell angle starts in the hatched area, i.e. the ignition-coil primary current is switched on. Depending upon engine speed and battery voltage the switch-on point in this area shifts with the ignition point. At the same time, it also shifts relative to the ignition point in accordance with the dwell-angle map (rotational speed and battery voltage).

Since the two ignition sparks of a double-spark ignition coil are produced simultaneously, i.e. with the same angular crankshaft position, the second ignition spark occurs at the end of the exhaust stroke of the other cylinder (offset by 360° crankshaft) supplied by the given coil. This means that the spark in this cylinder can flash over when the intake valve is starting to open again, and this is critical particularly in the case of large valve overlap (overlap in the open periods of intake and exhaust valves). Stationary high-voltage distribution with single-spark ignition coils (Fig. 5) requires the same number of ignition output stages and ignition coils as there are cylinders. In such cases, it is practical to combine the power output stage with the ignition coil. This minimizes the number of cables for the high voltage and the medium-high voltage between ignition transistor and ignition coil.

Control unit (ECU)

The electronic control unit of the distributorless semiconductor-ignition system is largely identical to that of the semiconductor ignition system. The ignition output stage can be integrated in the control unit (e.g., in the case of double-spark or four-spark ignition coils) or can be accommodated externally, in a power module with distributor logic or in combination with the relevant ignition coil (e.g., in the case of single-spark ignition coils).

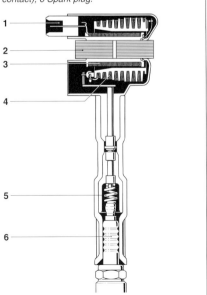

Fig. 5: Single-spark ignition coil
1 External low-voltage terminal, 2 Laminated iron core, 3 Primary winding, 4 Secondary winding, 5 Internal high-voltage connection (via spring contact); 6 Spark plug.

1
2
3
4
5
6

Danger of accident

All electronic ignition systems are inherently dangerous. Before working on these systems, therefore, always switch off the ignition or disconnect the battery. Such work includes:

– Replacing such components as spark plugs, ignition coil or transformer, distributor, high-voltage cables, etc.

– Connecting engine test equipment such as stroboscopic timing light, dwell angle/engine-speed tester, ignition oscilloscope, etc.

Dangerous voltages are present when the ignition is switched on. Testing should therefore be performed by qualified personnel only.

Knock control

Basic functions

Knock limit

Operation with a catalytic converter requires that the engine be operated with unleaded gasoline with an excess-air factor of $\lambda = 1.0$. Previously, lead was mixed into gasoline as an antiknock agent, in order to make possible knock-free operation at high compression ratios ε . With unleaded gasoline, a low compression ratio and higher fuel consumption can be expected.

"Knocking" or "pinking", a form of uncontrolled combustion, can lead to engine damage if it occurs too frequently and violently. For this reason, the spark advance is normally designed so that there is always a safety margin before the knock limit is reached. However, since the knock limit is also dependent upon fuel quality, engine condition and environmental conditions, the ignition point demanded by this safety margin is too far retarded and the result is a worsening of fuel consumption in the order of several percent. This disadvantage can be avoided if the knock limit is determined continuously during operation, and the ignition angle adjusted to it in a closed loop under the assumption that the ignition angle as specified by the ignition-advance map is already within the knock range. This is carried out by knock control (Fig. 1).

Knock sensor

It is so far impossible to determine the knock limit without the actual occurrence of knocking. Therefore, during closed-loop control along the knock limit there will always be scattered knocking. However, the system is adjusted to the individual type of vehicle concerned so that the knocking is not audible and so that damage is precluded with absolute certainty. The measuring device is the knock sensor which registers the typical noises associated with knocking, turns these into electrical signals and relays them to the electronic control unit (Figures 2 to 4).

The knock sensor is arranged so that knocking from any cylinder can be recognized without difficulty under all conditions. The mounting position is generally on the side of the engine block. With six or more cylinders, one knock sensor is usually inadequate to determine knocking from all cylinders. In such cases, two knock sensors are used per engine, and these are switched corresponding to the firing sequence.

Fig. 1: Schematic diagram of knock control

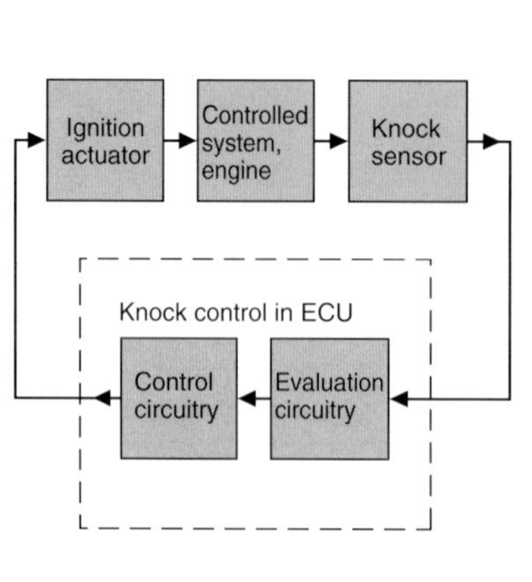

Ignition actuator → Controlled system, engine → Knock sensor

Knock control in ECU

Control circuitry ← Evaluation circuitry

Fig. 2: Knock sensor: A wide-band acceleration sensor with a natural frequency above 25 kHz.

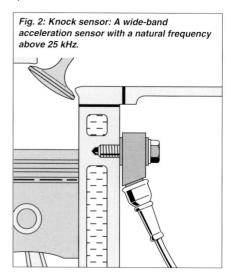

Control unit (ECU)

The sensor signals are evaluated in the electronic control unit. A reference level is individually formed for each cylinder, this level then continuously and automatically adapting itself to operating conditions.

A comparison with the useful signal obtained from the sensor signal after filtering and integration within a crank angle section shows for every combustion process in every cylinder whether knocking is occurring. If this is the case, the ignition point is retarded by a fixed amount, for example 3° crankshaft, for the cylinder involved. This process is repeated for every cylinder for every combustion process recognized as knocking. If there is no more knocking, the ignition point is slowly advanced in small steps until it has returned to its map value.

Since the knock limit varies from cylinder to cylinder within an engine and changes dramatically within the operating range, the result in actual operation at the knock limit is an individual ignition point for every cylinder. This type of "cylinder-selective" knock recognition and control makes possible the best optimization of engine efficiency and fuel consumption. If the vehicle is designed for operation with unleaded premium fuel, it can also be operated with regular unleaded fuel without damage when provided with knock control. In dynamic operation, knock frequency will increase under such conditions. In order to avoid this, an individual spark-advance map can be stored in the electronic control unit for each of the two fuel types. The engine is then operated after starting with the "premium" map and switched over to the "regular" map if the frequency of knocking exceeds a predetermined limit. The driver is not aware of this switchover; only power and fuel consumption are slightly worsened. A vehicle designed for premium gasoline and using a conventional ignition system cannot be operated with regular gasoline without danger of knock damage, while a vehicle designed for use with regular gasoline shows no advantages in consumption and power when it is operated with premium gasoline.

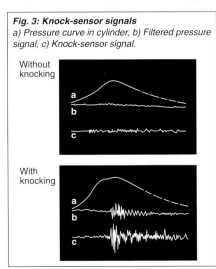

Fig. 3: Knock-sensor signals
a) Pressure curve in cylinder, b) Filtered pressure signal, c) Knock-sensor signal.

Without knocking

With knocking

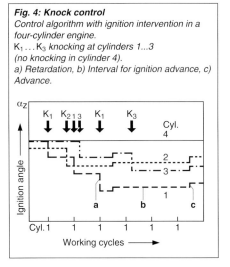

Fig. 4: Knock control
Control algorithm with ignition intervention in a four-cylinder engine.
$K_1 \ldots K_3$ knocking at cylinders 1...3
(no knocking in cylinder 4).
a) Retardation, b) Interval for ignition advance, c) Advance.

Knock control with turbocharged engines

Boost pressure is controlled via the drive power of the exhaust turbine. Intervention is by the opening cross-section of the exhaust wastegate, which is acted upon with control pressure via a solenoid-operated valve.

A map contains the control values for the solenoid-operated valve. By means of the map, the charge pressure is built up only to the level required by the engine as dictated by the driver (accelerator-pedal position).

The advantages as compared to conventional turbocharged engines are: Less turbocharger work in the part-load range, less exhaust backpressure, less residual exhaust gas in the cylinders, lower charge-air temperature, freely selectable full-load curve of boost pressure as a function of engine speed, softer turbo response, better performance and driveability (Fig. 5).

With closed-loop map control of boost pressure, a control loop is superimposed on the pilot control. A pressure sensor measures intake-manifold pressure which is compared with the values of a stored map. In the case of deviations between the setpoint and actual values the pressure is levelled via the solenoid-operated valve.

Advantages of boost-pressure closed-loop control as compared to open-loop control: Component tolerances and wear, particularly in the exhaust wastegate and turbocharger, do not affect the level of boost pressure. In addition, if an absolute-pressure sensor is used, the boost pressure can be maintained within a wide range independent of the level of atmospheric pressure (altitude correction).

In case of knocking, ignition timing is retarded for the knocking cylinder just as with a naturally-aspirated engine. In addition, boost pressure is lowered when the ignition retardation of at least 1 cylinder exceeds a prescribed value. This value is stored in the electronic control unit as an engine-speed-dependent characteristic curve. Its quantity is set depending on the maximum allowable

Fig. 5: Knock control through combination of semiconductor ignition and boost-pressure control
1 Intake air, 2 Turbocharger, 3 Turbine, 4 Exhaust, 5 Wastegate, 6 Knock sensor, 7 Timing valve, 8 ECU, 9 Ignition coil with attached ignition final stage.
Signals: a Throttle-valve position, b Intake-manifold pressure, c Knock signals, d Ignition pulses, e Engine temperature, f Timing-valve position, g Ignition point.

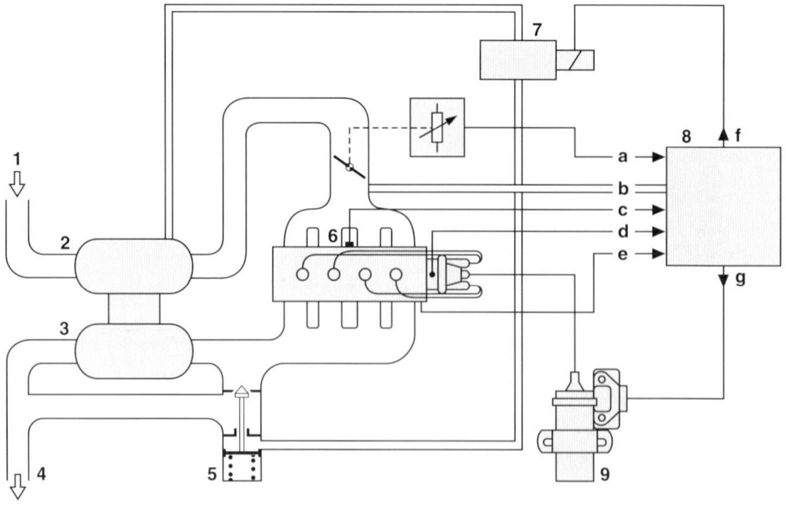

exhaust temperature at the turbine inlet. The ignition-timing algorithm (Algorithm: Defined, step-by-step procedure for obtaining mathematical solutions), with fast pressure decrease and slow step-by-step increase up to the nominal value, is similar to the algorithm for ignition timing, but has significantly larger time constants.

The two control algorithms are coordinated taking into consideration the knocking frequency, dynamic behaviour of the engine, exhaust wastegate, and turbocharger, exhaust temperature, driveability, and control stability.

Advantages of this combined control as compared to pure ignition-timing control: Improvement in engine dwell-angle efficiency, reduction in temperature loading of engine and turbocharger, reduction of charge-air temperature.

Advantages compared with pure boost-pressure control: Rapid control response in case of knocking, good dynamic engine behaviour, control stability and driveability.

Special functions

The basic functions of knock-detection and control, ignition-timing, dwell-angle and, where applicable, boost-pressure map, are processed in the control unit. In addition, the intake-manifold pressure as measured by a pressure sensor in the control unit provides information on the load and can be processed in the control unit as can a load signal made available from the gasoline fuel-injection system. Coolant and intake-air temperatures can be taken into account as correction quantities.

If required, overrun fuel cut-off, idle stabilization, and engine-speed limitation can be achieved by switching off ignition or fuel pump and with a fuel-pump control. In addition, should the computer fail – the driver will be informed of this condition – limp-home operation is possible, so that the vehicle must not be left standing.

With turbocharged engines, an engine-speed-dependent full-load signal can be generated and sent to the ignition, in the same way as a signal can be sent to reduce the boost pressure in case of knocking.

Safety and diagnosis

All the functions of knock control, failure of which could lead to engine damage make monitoring a necessity. This must trigger conversion to safe operation should a malfunction arise. The driver can be alerted to the switch to the safety mode by a display on the instrument panel. The exact defect can then be read out via a pulse code when the vehicle is inspected.

The following are monitored:
1. Knock sensor, including wiring harness, continually during operation above a certain engine speed. If a defect is detected, ignition timing in the map range where knock control is active is retarded by a fixed angle; with turbocharged engines, the boost pressure is also decreased.
2. Evaluation circuitry, including the computer, below a certain engine speed. Detection of a defect leads to the same reaction as described above.
3. The load signal, continuously during operation. In the event of defect, the full-load spark advance is used with simultaneous continuous activation of knock control.

Depending upon application, other sensors and signals are monitored and the appropriate reactions determined (e.g., temperature sensor).

Electrical connecting elements

The task of the electrical connecting elements is to reliably transmit the high voltage from the ignition coil through the ignition distributor to the spark plug. Various connection techniques are used, dependent upon the requirements made of the engine and, thus, of the ignition.

Plugs and sockets

Basic versions

One example of the available connection techniques is the plug connection at the high-voltage terminal towers of the ignition distributor. Socket version A (Fig. 1) has only a relatively low high-voltage strength and is thus encountered only in isolated cases in original equipment applications. Versions B and C are

the main versions. Both are characterized by having locking pins deep in the terminal tower and by their guaranteeing a substantially higher electric contacting strength owing to the long leakage path. Enlargement in the geometry (as is the case on version C) creates the necessary reserve for guaranteeing the 30 kV required for lean-burn engines. Furthermore, the insertion forces and water-tightness are carefully optimized to each other.

Service life

The related mean service life in operating hours is shown by the curves beneath the relevant plug versions. Fig 2 demonstrates their significance: If a voltage U_x is applied to new parts, they initially withstand the stress. However, the insulating capability slowly decreases and, as from time t_1, isolated disruptive discharges must be anticipated. The process advances and, at time t_2, 63% of the parts are destroyed. At low volta-

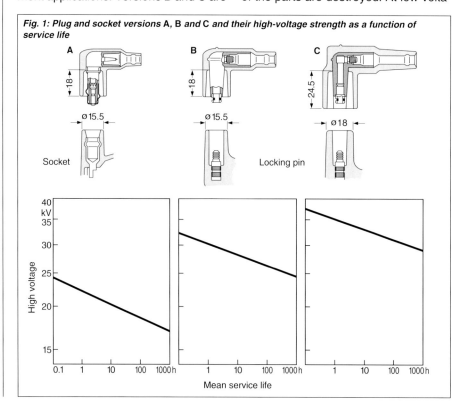

Fig. 1: Plug and socket versions **A**, **B** and **C** and their high-voltage strength as a function of service life

ges, the parts withstand the stress substantially longer than at high voltages (logorithmic scales). This also approximately corresponds to the statistical distribution of the engine voltage curve. The very high required voltage occurs only rarely, referred to the total number of ignitions. The accumulation point lies at values below 25 kV and this is why versions B and C, in conjunction with a maintenance-free ignition system, sturdy high-voltage cables with metal core and regular spark-plug replacement, provide an ignition system which poses no problems throughout the vehicle's service life.

Special versions

One particularly carefully designed connection technique comprises watertight spark-plug connectors, high-quality ignition cables, watertight ignition-distributor and ignition-coil connectors and protective hoods for the ignition distributor and the ignition coil. These protective

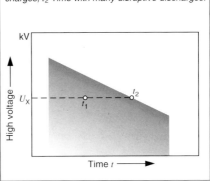

Fig. 2: Insulating capability of plug connectors as a function of time
U_x Voltage, t_1 Time with isolated disruptive discharges, t_2 Time with many disruptive discharges.

hoods provide additional protection against hose water and against dirt. In addition, the ignition-distributor hood improves the interference suppression (Fig. 3).

Fig. 3: Ignition-system cable connections
Protective caps prevent the penetration of dirt and moisture.

Ignition-system testing

The ignition system must function perfectly for the engine to function correctly. The importance of this is indicated by the fact that, in Germany, a periodic inspection of the ignition setting and dwell angle is obligatory on every passenger vehicle with SI engine. This is conducted during the emissions inspections (AU). The following equipment can be used for inspection:

– Stroboscopic timing light for ignition setting,

– Engine analyzer with stroboscope, oscilloscope and voltmeter etc. for checking the complete ignition system,

– Trouble-shooting chart specifying the correct procedure (as specified by the relevant vehicle manufacturer).

Stroboscopic timing light

This tester is powered by the vehicle battery. The incorporated timing strobe flashes, triggered by the ignition pulse of cylinder 1, analogously to the engine speed. The flywheel housing and crankcase marks are set so that they coincide by illuminating the ignition marks on the flywheel with the stroboscopic timing light and adjusting the setting on the timing light. The ignition angle can now be read off directly on the scale of the stroboscopic timing light and the ignition system can be set correctly.

On modern vehicle engines, the ignition angle can be measured and indicated directly by the engine analyzer even without the stroboscopic timing light, using a TDC sensor (TDC = top dead center).

Fig. 1: Pocket engine analyzer with integrated stroboscopic timing light

Engine analyzers

The range of engine analyzers extends from the pocket analyzer (Fig. 1) through to the diagnostic system with a wide variety of functions (Fig. 2). These engine analyzers (dependent upon their equipment level), permit measurement of engine speed, dwell angle and various voltages through to compression testing during the cranking period.

The engine analyzer shown contains an oscilloscope for displaying and evaluating various voltage curves, e.g., the high voltage at the spark plug. Top-flight models have wire-less remote control and programmable, microprocessor-controlled test programs.

Since, when measuring an ignition system, the testers only display actual values, it is necessary to adjust to the values specified for the vehicle and engine analyzer in order to set the ignition. If the ignition system is defective, a systematic procedure is required when searching for the cause. Workshops use a specific schedule for trouble-shooting in order to quickly locate sources of faults even on complex systems. This method permits the mechanic to detect defective components in a minimum of time and carry out the required repair work with suitable test equipment and tools.

An ignition map test is not possible on semiconductor ignition systems which, in some cases, have very finely structured ignition maps. Measurement and assessment of the high voltage is becoming increasingly important and is superseding the check of dwell angle and ignition angle.

Fig. 2: Engine analyzer with a variety of functions

Spark plugs

Spark-ignition engine and externally supplied ignition

Ignition energy

High-voltage generation

Ignition in the spark-ignition engine is electrical. The electrical energy is taken from the battery. Controlled by the engine, the ignition system periodically generates high voltage. This high voltage causes a spark discharge between the electrodes of the spark plug in the combustion chamber. The energy contained in the spark ignites the compressed air-fuel mixture. The energy taken from the battery is stored in the ignition coil for the periodic generation of high voltage.

This stored energy is used at the right moment in time to generate high voltage. This high voltage is generated inductively in the ignition coil according to the transformer principle. High voltage and ignition energy are sufficient to cover the increase in required ignition voltage resulting from wear in the system (Fig. 1).

Generation of the ignition spark

If there is sufficient high voltage, the ignition spark jumps across the electrodes of the spark plug. At the instant of ignition, i.e. when the energy-storage device discharges, the voltage across the spark-plug electrodes rises very quickly until the flashover voltage (ignition voltage) is reached. As soon as the spark is discharged, the voltage across the electrode drops to the spark

Fig. 1: Schematic of an electronic ignition system
1 Ignition coil with ignition driver stage, 2 High-voltage distributor, 3 Spark plug, 4 ECU,
5 Coolant-temperature sensor, 6 Throttle-valve switch, 7 Engine-speed sensor, 8 Sensor wheel, 9 Battery,
10 Ignition and starting switch.

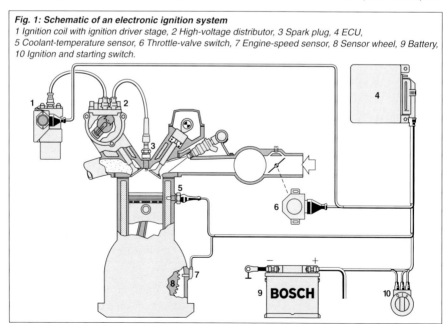

voltage. At the same time, a current flows in the now conductive spark gap. The air-fuel mixture is ignited during the burn time of the ignition spark (spark duration). As soon as the conditions required for discharge no longer obtain, the spark breaks off and the voltage decays to zero (Fig. 2). What has been described here applies only if the gas between the electrodes is quiescent. Higher flow velocities lead to a clear change in the spark characteristics.

The spark may be extinguished and reignited in the course of the so-called "spark duration". Phenomena of this kind are known as a follow-up spark.

Spark duration

Within the "spark duration", ignitable air-fuel mixture must be reached by the spark in order to obtain reliable ignition. The "spark duration" is the length of time for which the arc burns following the initial flashover between the electrodes until the residual stored energy decays. It must be maintained long enough to ensure contact between electrode and combustible mixture, despite any lack of homogeneity in the mixture (inconsistencies in mixture distribution).

Ignition voltage

The ignition voltage required by the spark plug is the maximum high voltage theoretically necessary for spark discharge.

The ignition voltage of the spark plug is the voltage at which the spark actually jumps across the electrodes. The high voltage causes a field strength between the electrodes, so that the spark gap is ionized and thus becomes conductive. The high voltage generated by the ignition system – the available ignition voltage – can exceed 30,000 V. The voltage reserve is the difference between this available ignition voltage and the minimum requirement at the spark plug. The minimum ignition voltage increases as a function of time due to the larger electrode gaps that accompany the aging

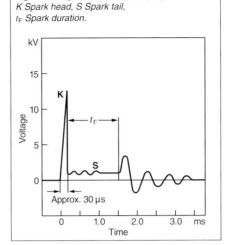

Fig. 2: Voltage between spark-plug electrodes
K Spark head, S Spark tail,
t_F Spark duration.

process. Ignition miss occurs when this process advances to the point where the requirement exceeds the available voltage.

Non-engine-related influences on the ignition-voltage requirement

The following factors determine the spark-plug voltage requirement:

Electrode gap: The minimum ignition voltage increases as a function of increasing spark plug gap.

Electrode configuration: Small electrode dimensions increase the intensity of the electrical field; this enhanced field strength can be employed to reduce the voltage requirement.

Electrode materials: Because the electrodes' electron work function varies according to conductor material, electrode materials influence the ignition voltage.

Insulator surface: If part or all of the electrical transfer between the electrodes is generated along the insulator, electrons from the insulator surface will reduce the ignition voltage.

Engine-related influences on the ignition-voltage requirement

Among the engine design factors that influence the minimum ignition-voltage requirement, compression (boost factor) is the most significant.

Spark-plug stress factors

Spark-plug function

The function of the spark plug is to introduce the ignition energy into the combustion chamber and to initiate the combustion of the air-fuel mixture by the electrical spark between its electrodes.

In conjunction with the other components of the engine, e.g., ignition and fuel-management systems, the spark plug has a decisive effect on the operation of the spark-ignition engine. It must permit reliable cold starting, it must guarantee that there is no misfiring during acceleration, and it must withstand the engine being operated for hours on end at maximum power. These requirements apply throughout the entire service life of the spark plug.

The spark plug is positioned in the combustion chamber at the point most suitable for igniting the compressed air-fuel mixture. It must, under all operating conditions, introduce the ignition energy into the combustion chamber without developing a leak and without overheating.

Design requirements

The spark plug must be designed to withstand extreme operating conditions: The plug is exposed to both the periodic, cyclical variations within the combustion chamber and to the external climatic conditions (Figures 1 and 2).

Electrical demands

When the spark plug is operated with electronic ignition systems, voltages of up to 30,000 V can occur. It is essential that the spark plug resists insulator arcing under these conditions. The deposits resulting from the combustion process, such as soot, carbon residues, ash from fuel and oil additives, will, under certain temperature conditions, conduct electrically. However, under such conditions there must be no arcing or breakdown across the insulator even at the high ignition voltages.

The electrical resistance of the insulator must be sufficient up to 1000°C, with only minimal deterioration in the course of the plug's service life.

Mechanical demands

The spark plug must withstand the pressures (up to approximately 100 bar) occurring periodically in the combustion chamber, whereby it must remain fully gas-tight. In addition, high mechanical strength is required, particularly of the ceramic, which is subjected to mechanical stress when being installed, as well as being stressed in operation by the spark-plug connector and the ignition cable. The spark-plug shell must absorb the tightening forces without suffering permanent deformation.

Resistance to chemical stress

The part of the spark plug projecting into the combustion chamber can become red-hot, as well as being exposed to the high-temperature chemical processes taking place inside the chamber. Components in the fuel can form chemically-aggressive deposits on the spark plug, affecting its operating characteristics.

Resistance to thermal stress

During operation, the spark plug, in rapid succession, absorbs heat from the hot combustion gases and is then exposed to the cold air-fuel mixture which is inducted for the next cycle. The insulator must therefore maintain a high level of resistance to thermal shock.

The spark plug must also dissipate the heat it absorbs in the combustion chamber as efficiently as possible to the engine's cylinder head, and the terminal side of the spark plug should heat up as little as possible.

Fig. 1: Pressure and temperature loading of the spark plug in a two-stroke engine

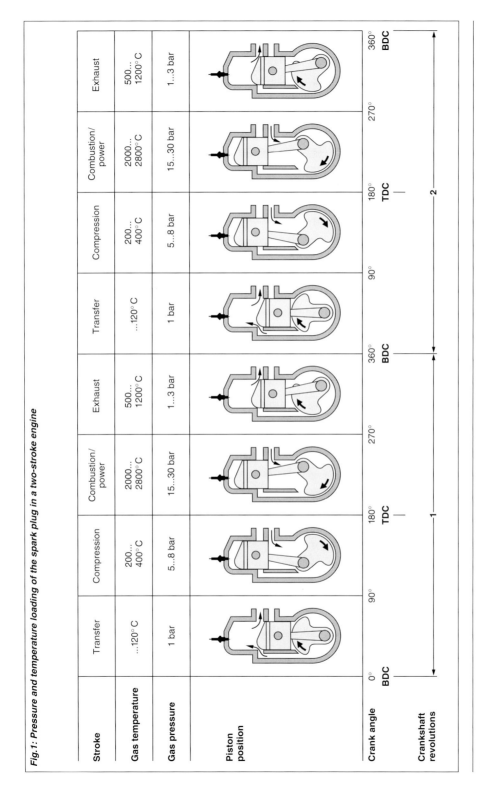

Stroke	Transfer	Compression	Combustion/ power	Exhaust	Transfer	Compression	Combustion/ power	Exhaust
Gas temperature	...120° C	200... 400° C	2000... 2800° C	500... 1200° C	...120° C	200... 400° C	2000... 2800° C	500... 1200° C
Gas pressure	1 bar	5...8 bar	15...30 bar	1...3 bar	1 bar	5...8 bar	15...30 bar	1...3 bar
Piston position								
Crank angle	0° BDC	90°	180° TDC	270°	360° BDC	90°	180° TDC	270°	360° BDC
Crankshaft revolutions	1				2			

183

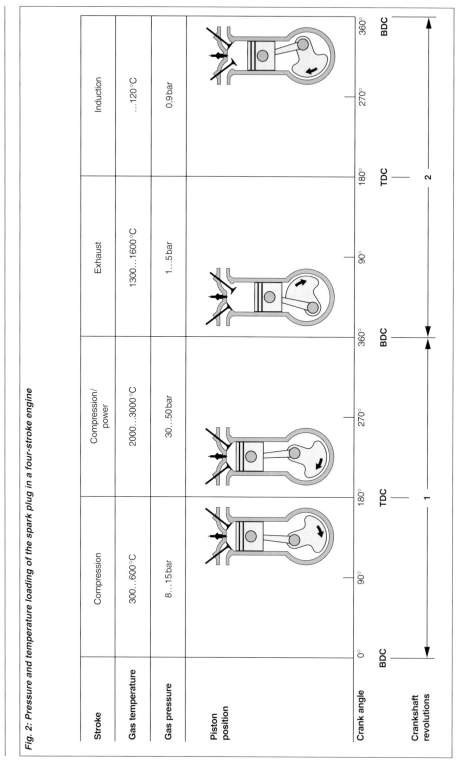

Fig. 2: Pressure and temperature loading of the spark plug in a four-stroke engine

Stroke	Compression	Compression/power	Exhaust	Induction
Gas temperature	300...600 °C	2000...3000 °C	1300...1600 °C	...120 °C
Gas pressure	8...15 bar	30...50 bar	1...5 bar	0,9 bar
Piston position				
Crank angle	0° BDC · · · 90° · · · 180° TDC	270° · · · 360° BDC	90° · · · 180° TDC	270° · · · 360° BDC
Crankshaft revolutions	1		2	

Spark-plug construction

Components

The spark plug consists of metal, ceramic and glass. These materials have different properties. Appropriate design of the spark plug makes full use of the positive properties of these materials. The terminal stud, insulator, shell and electrodes represent the most important parts of a spark plug. Center electrode and terminal stud are joined by a special conductive glass seal (Fig. 1).

Terminal stud

The steel terminal stud is melted, gastight, into the insulator with a special conductive glass seal which also serves as the electrical connection to the center electrode. On the end projecting out of the insulator, the terminal stud has a thread for attaching the spark-plug connector of the high-voltage ignition cable. In the case of connectors which conform to ISO/DIN Standards a so-called ISO/DIN terminal nut is screwed onto the thread of the terminal stud.

Insulator

The insulator is made of a special ceramic material and its function is to insulate center electrode and terminal stud from the shell. The dense microstructure of the special ceramic ensures high resistance to electrical breakdown (puncture). The surface of the connection side of the insulator is glazed. Moisture and dirt adhere less well to this smooth glazed surface, as a result of which leakage currents are largely prevented. The insulator houses both the center electrode and the terminal stud. The demands met in spark-plug applications for good thermal conductivity and high insulation resistance are in sharp contrast to the properties of most insulators. The material used by Bosch

for the spark-plug insulator consists of aluminum oxide to which small quantities of other materials have been added. After it has been stoved and glazed, this special ceramic satisfies the demands made of the spark-plug insulator for high insulation resistance, good thermal conductivity and both mechanical and chemical strength.

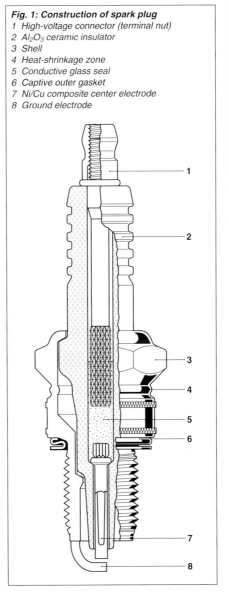

Fig. 1: Construction of spark plug
1 High-voltage connector (terminal nut)
2 Al_2O_3 ceramic insulator
3 Shell
4 Heat-shrinkage zone
5 Conductive glass seal
6 Captive outer gasket
7 Ni/Cu composite center electrode
8 Ground electrode

Shell

The shell is made of steel and its function is to secure the spark plug in the engine's cylinder head. The upper part of the shell has a hexagonal section to which the spark-plug wrench is applied, and the lower part is threaded. The surface of the spark-plug shell has an electroplated nickel coating to prevent corrosion, to keep the thread free and to prevent seizing, the latter point applying particularly in aluminum cylinder heads. Depending on the design of the shell, the spark plug can be provided with a seal ring (captive gasket). After the insulator has been inserted into the spark-plug shell, it is swaged and heat-shrunk in position in one operation by inductive heating under high pressure.

Electrodes

The wear on the electrodes is caused by erosion (burning away due to the ignition sparks) and by corrosion (chemical and thermal attack). These two factors cannot be treated separately as regards their effect on electrode wear. Wear increases the required ignition voltage. In addition, the electrodes must have good heat-dissipation properties. These requirements may call for different electrode shapes and electrode materials, depending on operating conditions and application (Fig. 2).

Ground electrode

The ground electrode is welded to the shell and usually has a rectangular cross-section. Depending upon the position of the ground electrode relative to the center electrode, a distinction is made between front and side electrodes (Fig. 3). The ground electrode's service life is highly dependent upon its heat dissipation, and on both ground and center electrodes suitable composite materials are employed to improve thermal dissipation and extend effective service life (Fig. 3a). Another factor affecting service life is the ratio of thermally exposed surface to thermally conductive cross-section.

Minimal dimensions, special designs and only partial coverage of the center electrode are all employed to obtain an optimal arc pattern at the ground electrode. The external surfaces and the contours of the areas facing the center electrode can also be designed to enhance performance.

Different spark plugs feature:
– different numbers of ground electrodes, and
– ground electrodes of varying dimensions.
Thicker ground electrodes and multiple electrodes, therefore, can both be used to extend spark-plug service life.

Center electrode

The center electrode of the conventional spark plugs (air gap between insulator nose bore and center electrode) is

---

Fig. 2: Electrode arrangement
a) Front electrode, b) Side electrodes, c) Surface-gap spark plug without ground electrode (for special applications).

a    b 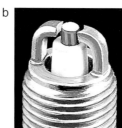   c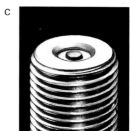

melted, gas-tight, into the insulator with a special conductive seal. The electrode has a slightly smaller diameter than the bore in the insulator nose. This is necessary in order to compensate for the different internal expansion which takes place between the electrode material and the insulator ceramic. The air gap thus produced is subject to very close tolerances and is of great importance with regard to the heat range.

The cylindrical center electrode projects from the insulator nose. Center electrodes made of precious metals are smaller in diameter than the compound electrodes which have a copper core and nickel-alloy jacket.

Electrode gap

The electrode gap is the shortest distance between the center electrode and the ground electrode (Fig. 5). The smaller the electrode gap, the lower the ignition-voltage requirement.

A narrow electrode gap will reduce the voltage required to produce an arc, but the short spark can transfer only minimal energy to the mixture, and ignition miss can result. Higher voltages are required to support an arc across a larger gap. This type of gap is thus effective in transferring energy to the mixture, but the attendant reduction in ignition-voltage reserves increases the risk of ignition miss.

The electrode gap is usually about 0.7...1.2 mm (Fig. 4). The precise optimized electrode gaps for the individual engines are specified by the engine manufacturer and are given either in the owner's manual or in the Bosch spark-plug sales literature.

Electrode shape

Electrode shape affects heat dissipation, resistance to wear, the ignition-voltage requirement and the way the arc is transferred to ignite the mixture.

The electrode shape is dependent on the type of spark gap and the spark position.

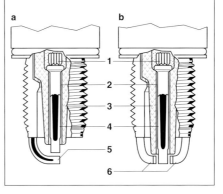

Fig. 3: Spark plugs with composite electrodes
a) With front electrode, b) With side electrodes.
1 Conductive glass seal, 2 Air gap, 3 Insulator nose, 4 Composite center electrode, 5 Composite ground electrode, 6 Ground electrodes.

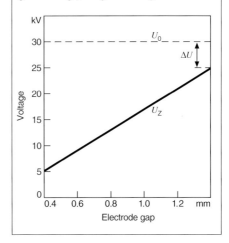

Fig. 4: Relationship between electrode gap and required ignition voltage
U_0 Secondary available voltage, U_Z required ignition voltage, ΔU Ignition voltage reserve.

Fig. 5: Electrode gap (EA)
a) Front electrode, b) Side electrode.

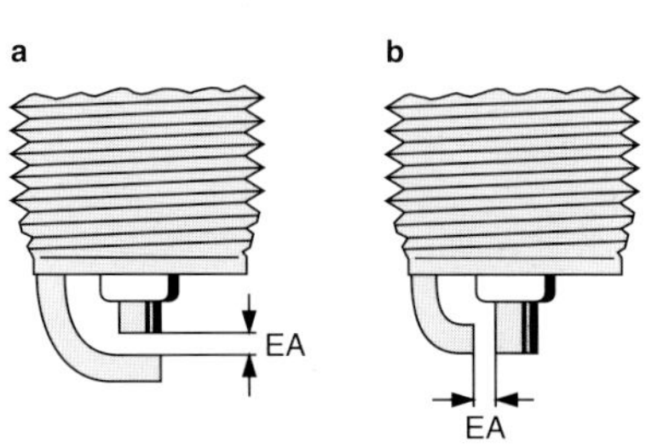

Spark gap

The arrangement of the electrodes determines the type of spark gap (Fig. 6).

Spark air gap
A linear spark is generated directly between the center and ground electrodes, igniting the air-fuel mixture located between them.

Semi-surface gap
The ignition spark forms between the center electrode and the surface of the insulator nose before arcing across a gas-filled gap to the ground electrode. Because a portion of the spark propagation takes place along this creepage-discharge path, a given ignition voltage

produces an arc across larger electrode gaps than with a conventional single-gap design.
These larger gaps can be employed to obtain better ignition patterns.

Spark position

The spark position is the position of the spark gap in the combustion chamber.
The electric sparks should jump across the point at which the air-fuel mixture flow conditions are particularly favorable. The arrangement of the electrodes and insulator determines from what position the air-fuel mixture is ignited by the electric spark.
The position of the spark f is referred to the front side of the shell (Fig. 7).
The standard spark projection is 3...5 mm, while spark plugs with extreme spark positions are available for special applications. Examples would be spark plugs featuring special spark positions for use in competition and special-purpose engines, in which the actual spark path is inside the spark-plug shell. This substantially reduces the amount of heat absorbed by the spark plug from the combustion chamber, helping to prevent the spark plug from overheating in competition use.

Fig. 6: Spark gap
a) Air spark gap directly to the ground electrode from the center electrode.
b) Surface/air spark gap from the center electrode to the ground electrodes via the insulator nose.

a

b

Fig. 7: Spark position (f).

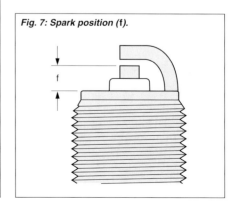

Electrode materials

Compound electrodes
The shunt sensitivity and the corrosion behavior of standard spark plugs with center electrodes made of a nickel-based alloy have been greatly improved by the development of a compound center electrode with a copper core (Fig. 8a).

Pure metals provide better thermal conductivity than alloys. At the same time though, pure metals such as nickel are more sensitive than alloys to aggressive chemical subtances in the combustion gases and to solid deposits.

For this reason, the jacket material of the compound electrode consists mainly of nickel, which is alloyed with chromium, mangangese and silicon. Each of the alloy additions has a special task to perform. Additions of manganese and silicon increase the chemical resistance, particularly against the very aggressive sulphur dioxide (the sulphur comes both from the fuel and from the lube oil).

Nickel-based alloys with silicon, aluminum and yttrium additives also improve resistance to oxidation and scaling.

The ground electrode, which must be flexible enough to allow gap adjustment, can be made of a nickel-based alloy or a composite material.

Such a structure (copper core with nickel jacket) satisfies stringent requirements for high levels of thermal conductivity and corrosion resistance in the ground electrode.

Silver center electrode
Silver displays the highest electrical and thermal conductivity of any substance. It also features extreme resistance to chemical deterioration when unleaded fuel is used. Resistance to thermal stresses can be substantially enhanced using composite particulate materials with silver as the basic substance. The characteristics described above are the reasons behind its use as an electrode material.

When solid silver is used for the center electrode, this can be reduced in diameter (Fig. 8b).

Despite the reduced diameter, the silver center electrode dissipates heat better than a comparable nickel-based electrode.

Platinum center electrode
Because platinum and platinum alloys display extreme resistance to corrosion, oxidation and melting, they are employed in the manufacture of electrodes for "Long-life" spark plugs.

Presuming the same stresses are applied, platinum electrodes used for any given application can be smaller than the equivalent nickel-based electrode (Fig. 8c).

Fig. 8: Center electrode materials
a) Composite material, b) Silver, c) Platinum.

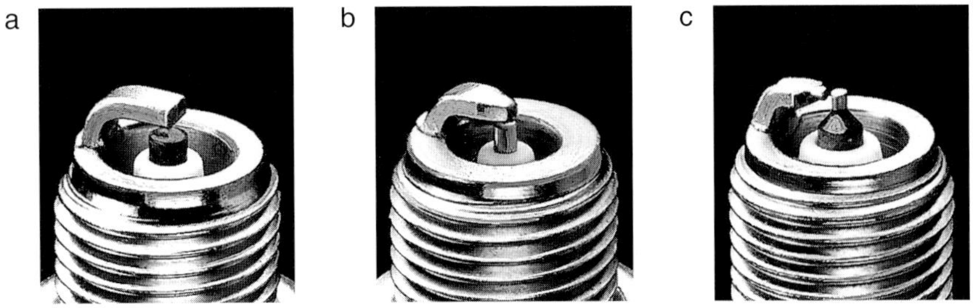

Spark-plug heat ranges

Spark-plug operating temperatures

Operating range

When unleaded fuel is used, the parts of the insulator tip which extend into the combustion chamber should not drop below 500°C – to ensure self-cleaning of the spark plug – and should not exceed approximately 850°C – to prevent auto-ignition (Fig. 1).

Particulate deposits (soot) are produced in the incomplete combustion processes that characterize cold starts. Most of these deposits leave the engine along with the exhaust gases, but some remain to form a coating on both the combustion chamber and the spark plug. As these deposits form on the insulator nose, they can produce a conductive path between the center electrode and the shell. This creepage path absorbs a portion of the ignition energy, thus forming a shunt path and reducing the current available for the ignition spark. Excessive contamination can therefore prevent a spark from being generated (Fig. 2).

The deposition of combustion residues on the insulator nose is greatly dependent on its temperature and takes place mainly below about 500°C. At higher temperatures, the carbon-containing residues on the insulator nose burn-off, as a result of which shunts cannot form, i.e. the plug "cleans" itself. The aim therefore, is to achieve an operating temperature at the insulator nose which is higher than the "self-cleaning limit" of about 500°C, whereby the self-cleaning temperature should be reached as quickly as possible after starting.

The upper temperature limit is about 900°C since above this temperature the air-fuel mixture can ignite prematurely on red-hot parts of the spark plug (auto-ignition). Uncontrolled ignition of this kind is highly detrimental to the engine and may cause irreparable damage within a short space of time.

For these reasons, the operating temperature of the spark plug must be kept within the above-mentioned limits.

Thermal loading capacity

The operating temperature is the equilibrium temperature which is reached be-

---

Fig. 1: Spark-plug working range
For different engine power outputs, the working range should be between 500 and 850 °C at the insulator.

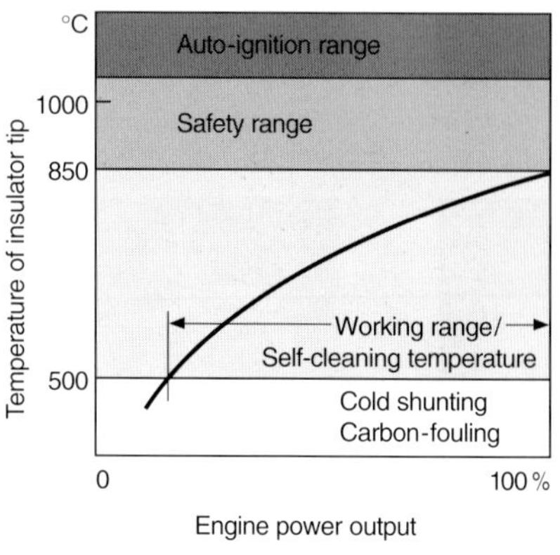

°C

Auto-ignition range

Safety range

1000

850

Temperature of insulator tip

500

Working range/ Self-cleaning temperature

Cold shunting
Carbon-fouling

0   100%

Engine power output

Fig. 2: Shunting due to fouled insulator nose leads to a reduced secondary available voltage
- - - - - Shunt current

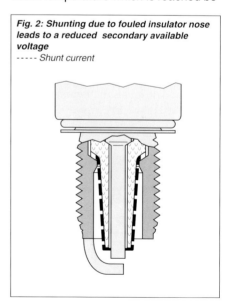

tween heat absorption and heat dissipation. The spark plug is heated by the heat generated during operation in the engine's combustion chamber. The spark-plug shell has more or less the same temperature as the cylinder head, while the temperatures reached by the insulator are considerably higher.

Some (approximately 20 %) of the heat absorbed by the spark plug is dissipated through the inflow of fresh mixture during the induction stroke. Most of the heat is transferred through the center electrode and insulator to the spark-plug shell and from there to the cylinder head (Fig. 3). The supply of heat to the spark plug is dependent on the engine. Engines with a high specific power output usually have higher combustion-chamber temperatures than engines with a low specific power output. The heat-absorbing properties of the spark plug must, therefore, be matched to the engine type in question.

The heat range is characteristic of the thermal loading capacity of the spark plug.

The heat range and the engine

The spark plug's heat range is an index of its capacity to withstand thermal loads. It must be adapted to the engine characteristic.

The different characteristics of automotive engines with respect to operating load, working principles, compression, engine speed, cooling, and fuel make it impossible to run all engines with a standard spark plug. The same spark plug would get very hot in one engine but would reach only a relatively low average temperature in another.

In the first case, the air-fuel mixture would ignite on the glowing parts of the spark plug projecting into the combustion chamber (auto-ignition) and, in the second case, the insulator tip would very soon be so badly fouled by combustion deposits that misfiring would occur due to shunts. In other words, one

and the same spark-plug type is not suitable for all engines. To ensure that the plug runs neither too "hot" nor too "cold" in a given engine, plugs with different load capacities were developed. The so-called "heat range", which is assigned to each spark plug, is used to characterise these loading capacities. The heat range is, therefore, a yardstick for selecting the correct spark plug.

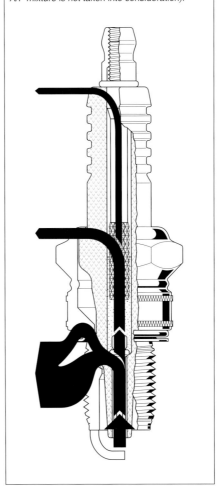

Fig. 3 Thermal conduction in the spark plug
A large proportion of the heat absorbed from the combustion chamber is dissipated by thermal conduction (small proportion of cooling of approximately 20 % due to flowpast of fresh A/F mixture is not taken into consideration).

The heat range and the spark plug

Heat range and design

As the above description indicates, each spark plug must be designed to remain within a specific temperature range during operation. Therefore, in order to remain within its operating range, the spark plug for a "hot-running" engine must efficiently dissipate heat acting upon it, while the plug for a "cold-running" engine must retain the heat. Various design factors - with special emphasis on the configuration of the insulator nose – can be applied to adjust the

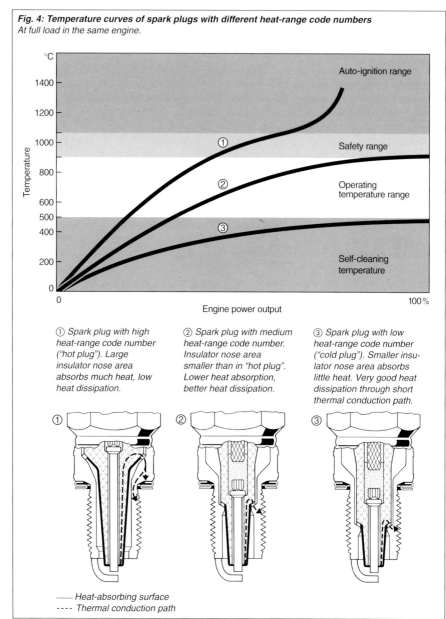

Fig. 4: Temperature curves of spark plugs with different heat-range code numbers
At full load in the same engine.

① *Spark plug with high heat-range code number ("hot plug"). Large insulator nose area absorbs much heat, low heat dissipation.*

② *Spark plug with medium heat-range code number. Insulator nose area smaller than in "hot plug". Lower heat absorption, better heat dissipation.*

③ *Spark plug with low heat-range code number ("cold plug"). Smaller insulator nose area absorbs little heat. Very good heat dissipation through short thermal conduction path.*

—— *Heat-absorbing surface*
---- *Thermal conduction path*

heat range for specific engines and applications.

Influence of insulator nose

Heat absorption is determined by the surface area of the insulator nose. If a large area is exposed to the combustion gases – this is achieved by having a long insulator nose – the insulator nose gets very hot. Conversely, with a short insulator nose, the area is small, and the nose remains cooler.

The heat is dissipated from the insulator nose through the center electrode and through the inner seal ring to the spark-plug shell. If the insulator nose is long, this heat transfer point formed by the seal ring is further away from the hottest point on the insulator nose than is the case with a short insulator nose. There-fore, it follows that spark plugs with a long insulator nose can absorb more heat and dissipate less heat (i.e. they are "hotter") than plugs with a short in-sulator nose ("cold" plug). Different lengths of insulator nose result, there-fore, in different characteristics, in diffe-rent heat ranges.

Heat-range code number

The heat range of a spark plug is identi-fied by a heat-range code number.
A low heat-range code number indica-tes a "cold plug" with low heat ab-sorption through its short insulator nose. A high heat-range code number applies to a "hot plug" with high heat absorption through its long insulator nose (Fig. 4). Heat-range code numbers have been specified to make it easier to differen-tiate between spark plugs of different heat ranges and to determine the right plug for the engine in question. The heat-range code number is a part of the spark-plug type designation. Low code numbers (e.g., 2...4) signify "cold" plugs. High code numbers (e.g., 7...10) signify "hot" plugs.

Spark-plug selection

Temperature-measuring spark plugs

Bosch works together with the engine manufacturers in determining the best spark-plug design for a given application. The temperature-measuring spark plug provides initial information on the cor-rect choice of spark plug. With a thermo-couple in the center electrode of a spark plug, it is possible to record the tempe-ratures in the individual cylinders as a function of engine speed and load.

This expedient represents a simple means of identifying the hottest cylinder and ensuring that the correct spark plug design is selected (Fig. 1).

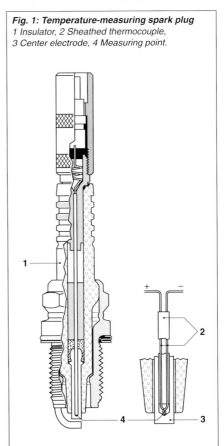

Fig. 1: Temperature-measuring spark plug
1 Insulator, 2 Sheathed thermocouple,
3 Center electrode, 4 Measuring point.

Ionic-current measuring method

With the ionic-current measuring method, the combustion process is used to specify the heat range. The ionization effect of flames makes it possible, by measuring the conductivity in the spark plug, to evaluate the time curve of the initiation combustion of the air-fuel mixture. This curve shows characteristic changes referred to the thermal loading of a spark plug (Fig. 2).

The advantage of this method over a single temperature measurement in the combustion chamber lies in establishing the probability of ignition, which depends not only on the temperature but also upon the individual engine and spark-plug design parameters.

In order to select the heat ranges of spark plugs, terms and definitions relating to the uncontrolled ignition of air-fuel mixtures have been laid down in accordance with an international agreement (ISO 2542–1972, Fig. 3):

Auto-ignition is taken to mean ignition which is independent of the ignition spark.

If ignition takes place prior to the electrical ignition point, this is pre-ignition. If it takes place after the ignition point, we speak of post-ignition. Post-ignition is non-critical as regards operation of the engine; conversely, pre-ignition may lead to serious damage. The spark plug must be selected in such a way that there is no pre-ignition.

The ionic-current measuring method makes it possible to select the heat range of a spark plug for any engine and also to measure the heat range in a test engine. In addition, the Bosch ionic-current measuring method makes it possible, by suppressing the ignition spark at certain intervals, to trace post-ignition and its percentage share in relation to the suppression rate as the combustion-chamber temperature rises (by advancing the ignition-timing Fig. 4).

A change in the ionic-current trace on the screen permits the precise determination, even without suppressing the electric ignition spark, of the transition from post-ignition to incipient pre-

---

Fig. 2: Diagram of ionic-current measurement
1 From ignition distributor, 2 Ionic-current adapter, 2a Break-over diode (BOD), 3 Spark plug, 4 Ionic-current device, 5 Oscilloscope.

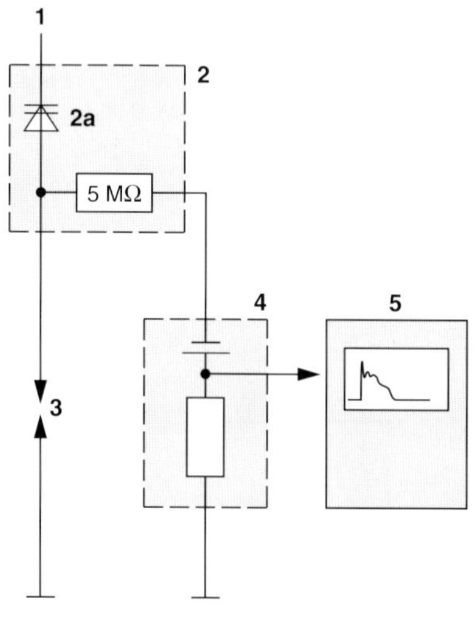

Fig.3: Definitions with regard to heat-range selection
Al Auto-ignition, TDC Top dead center
Pri Pre-ignition, Poi Post-ignition
HRR Heat-range reserve in °crankshaft
IP Ignition point in °crankshaft before TDC
α_z Ignition angle

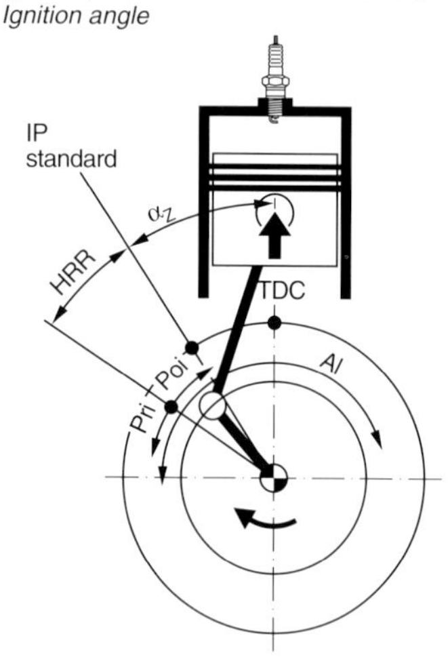

ignition. This makes the measuring method an additional aid in evaluating individual design parameters with regard to their tendency to produce auto-ignition under maximum loading.

The practical procedure is now explained with reference to an example: ionic-current measurement on three Bosch spark plugs with different heat ranges, under full-load operation, $n = 5000\,\text{min}^{-1}$, ignition timing factory-set .

Ionic current testing (example):

Spark plug series with heat range	% POST[1]	PRE[2]
WR9DC	100	ja
WR8DC	50	0
WR7DC	0	0

[1] POST = post-ignition
[2] PRE = pre-ignition

The spark plug with the highest heat-range code number shows 100 % post-ignition even with the factory-set ignition timing, i.e. each time the spark is suppressed, the compressed mixture is still ignited by the excessive heat at the insulator. Isolated cases of pre-ignition can also occur. Even the intermediate-range spark plug produces ignition every second time the current is suppressed - the safety reserves are still inadequate.

The spark plug with the lowest heat range promotes neither pre- nor post-ignition - the temperature of the insulator nose remains low enough to remove the danger of auto-ignition. This would be the recommended spark plug in this example.

Because the spark plug can be two heat ranges higher before pre-ignition occurs, the heat range safety margin is adequate.

The above remarks illustrate that spark plugs cannot simply be selected from a catalog and installed.

Spark plug specifications are generally determined in a process that includes close cooperation between engine and spark-plug manufacturers. The recom-

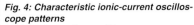

Fig. 4: Characteristic ionic-current oscilloscope patterns
a) Normal operating conditions,
b) Suppressed ignition without post-ignition,
c) Suppressed ignition with post-ignition,
d) Pre-ignition.

ZZP = Ignition point

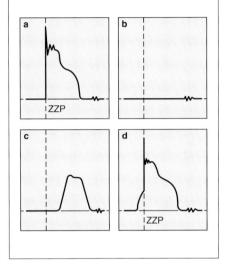

mendations of the vehicle manufacturer and the recommendations – including alternate heat ranges for different regions – contained in the Bosch sales catalogues should always be observed.

Application measurements on spark plugs are best performed on the engine test stand or chassis dynamometer.

Since the engine must be operated at full load over lengthy periods of time in order to establish the hottest operating point, it is not possible to conduct tests on public roads.

Operating behavior of spark plug

Changes during operation

During operation, the spark plug is subjected both to wear and to fouling and must, therefore, be replaced at regular intervals.

In the course of its service life, the spark plug undergoes changes which increase the required ignition voltage. When the required voltage reaches a value which can no longer be compensated for by the voltage reserve, the result is misfiring.

Furthermore, the operation of the spark plug can also be adversely affected by the aging of the engine.

Deposits can lead to heat tracking, with attendant negative effects on the ignition flame. The immediate results assume the form of ignition miss, leading to a substantial increase in exhaust emissions followed by damage to the catalytic converter.

Engine-related influences

As the engine ages, leakage may occur which leads to a higher content of oil in the combustion chamber. This results in heavy deposits of soot, ash and oil carbon on the spark plug and may lead to shunts. The result is misfiring.

Electrode wear

Characteristics
Electrode wear is the removal of material from the electrodes.

A visible sign of electrode wear is the increase in the electrode gap during the plug's service life. Electrode wear can be minimized through careful selection of shapes, materials and gap configuration (surface-air gap) for the electrode.

Two processes contribute to electrode wear:
– spark erosion, and
– corrosion in the combustion chamber.

Spark erosion and corrosion
The discharge of electrical sparks leads to an increase in the temperature of the electrodes. In conjunction with the aggressive combustion gases, there is clear wear at high temperatures. Melted-open, microscopically small sur-

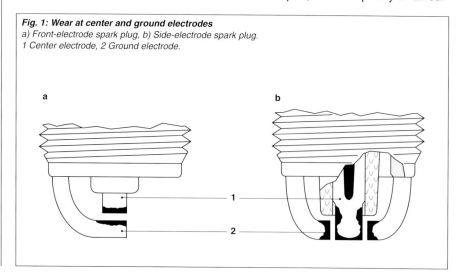

Fig. 1: Wear at center and ground electrodes
a) Front-electrode spark plug, b) Side-electrode spark plug.
1 Center electrode, 2 Ground electrode.

a

b

1

2

face areas are oxidized or react with other constituents in the combustion gases. The result is a removal of metal, which can be seen in the rounding of edges and also in the widening of the electrode gap (Fig. 1).

Heat-resistant materials – such as the noble metal platinum – can be used to minimize electrode wear.

Abnormal operating conditions

Abnormal operating conditions can irreparably damage the engine and the spark plug. These include:
– auto-ignition,
– knocking and
– high oil consumption (formation of ash and carbon residue).

Engine and spark plug may be damaged also by an incorrectly tuned ignition system, the use of spark plugs with the wrong heat range for the engine, or the use of unsuitable fuels.

Auto-ignition
Full-throttle operation can generate localized hot spots and cause auto-ignition at the following locations:
– at the tip of the spark plug's insulator nose,
– on the exhaust valve,
– on protruding sections of the head gasket, and
– on loose deposits.
Auto-ignition is an uncontrolled ignition process in which the temperatures in the combustion chamber can rise to such an extent as to cause serious damage to the engine and the spark plug.

Knocking
Knocking is uncontrolled combustion with a very steep rise in pressure. It is caused by the spontaneous ignition of portions of the mixture which have not yet been reached by the advancing flame front triggered by the ignition spark. Combustion takes place con-

siderably faster than normal (gentle) combustion. Pressure oscillations occur, with high peak pressures and high frequencies which are superimposed on the normal pressure curve (Fig. 2).
As the high-pressure waves hit the walls of the combustion chamber, their impact produces a metallic knocking sound.
The engine is subjected to severe mechanical stressing as a result of the high-pressure waves. The following engine components are endangered in particular:
– Cylinder head
– Spark plugs
– Pistons

Failure to recognize and deal with pre-ignition will inevitably lead to serious engine damage. The damage is similar to that associated with the cavitation damage that occurs when supersonic flow patterns are generated. On the spark plug, pitting on the ground electrode's surface is the first sign of pre-ignition.

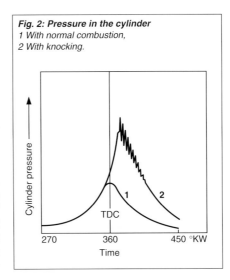

Fig. 2: Pressure in the cylinder
1 With normal combustion,
2 With knocking.

Types of spark plug

Seat

Depending on the type of engine, the seal between the spark plug and cylinder head is by means of a flat seat or a conical seat (Fig. 1).

The flat-seat version uses a captive gasket on the spark-plug shell as a sealing element. It is specially shaped and provides a permanently elastic seal if correctly mounted.

With the conical seat, without the use of a gasket, a conical surface of the spark-plug shell seals directly on a mating surface of the cylinder head.

Special spark plugs

Special-purpose spark plugs are available for unusual applications. These plugs are distinguished by the special design features used to adapt them to the operating and installation environment in a particular engine.

Spark plugs for motor racing

Due to their constant operation at full load, engines for racing vehicles are exposed to very high thermal loading. Spark plugs for these operating conditions usually have electrodes which are manufactured from precious metals (silver, platinum) and a short insulator nose. As a result of their short insulator nose, the heat absorption of these plugs is very low and heat dissipation through the precious-metal electrodes is high.

Spark plug with resistor

By means of a resistor fitted in the path to the spark gap of the spark plug, it is possible to reduce the transmission of the interference pulses to the high-tension ignition cables, with the result that the interference radiation is also reduced. Low current in the initial arcing phase also helps reduce electrode erosion. The resistor is formed by the special conductive seal between the center electrode and the terminal stud. The required resistance of the special seal is achieved by the selection of appropriate admixtures.

Fully-shielded spark plug

In cases where very high demands are placed on interference suppression (radios, car telephone), it may be necessary to shield the spark plug.

In fully-shielded spark plugs, the insulator is surrounded by a metal sleeve. The connection is inside the insulator. The shielded H.T. ignition cable is fastened onto the sleeve by means of a union nut. Fully-shielded spark plugs are watertight (Fig. 2).

Fig. 1: Flat seat with captive gasket (left), and conical seat without gasket (right)

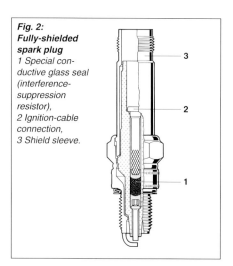

Fig. 2:
Fully-shielded spark plug
1 Special conductive glass seal (interference-suppression resistor),
2 Ignition-cable connection,
3 Shield sleeve.

Type designation

The identification of the types of spark plug is by means of a specific type designation (Fig. 3). This type designation contains all the important features of the spark plug with the exception of the electrode gap which is given additionally on the spark-plug packaging. The correct spark plug and electrode gap for the respective engine is specified by the engine manufacturer or is recommended by Bosch.

Fig. 3: Type designation code for Bosch spark plugs (Dimensions in mm)

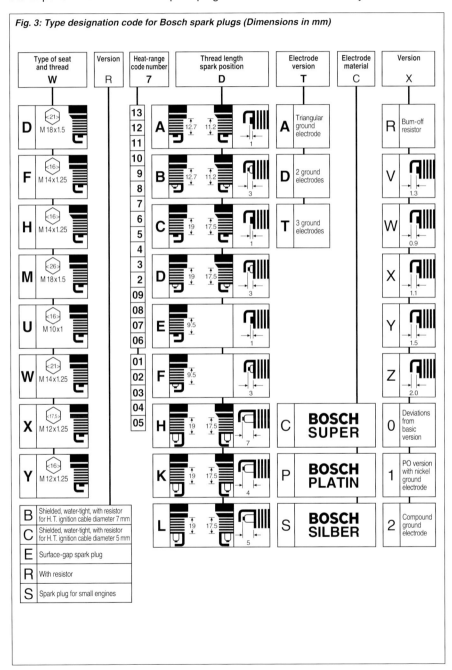

In practice

Fitting the spark plug

If the correct type is selected and correctly fitted, the spark plug is a reliable part of the ignition system.
Gap adjustments are recommended for front-electrode plugs only. The gap should not be adjusted on side-electrode spark plugs.

Removal

When removing the spark plug, first of all unscrew by a few turns. Then, using compressed air or a brush, clean the surrounding area in the cylinder head so that no dirt gets into the thread of the cylinder head or into the combustion chamber when the spark plug is removed. Only then screw out the spark plug completely.
If the spark plug is very tight, unscrew it only a little, so as not to damage the thread in the cylinder head. Then drip oil or penetrating oil onto the threads, screw the spark plug back in again and attempt after a few minutes to unscrew it completely.

Installation

When installing the spark plug in the engine, note the following:

– The contact faces on the spark plug and on the engine must be clean.
– Bosch spark plugs are treated with an anti-corrosion oil, so no supplementary lubricants are required. Seizing up is impossible because the threads are nickel-plated.
Spark plugs should, if possible, be tightened to the torque given in Table 1 using a torque wrench. When the spark plug is tightened, the tightening torque is transmitted from the hexagon section to the seat and the thread.
This means that the insulator may come loose if the spark-plug shell is warped due to excessive tightening torque or through tilting of the spark-plug wrench. This completely destroys the spark plug's thermal properties; such a plug can cause engine damage. Therefore, the tightening torque must not exceed a given value.
The tightening torques apply to spark plugs as new, i.e. to lightly oiled spark plugs.
In practice, spark plugs are often fitted without a torque wrench. Consequently, they are usually overtightened. Bosch therefore recommends the following rule-of-thumb procedure:

1. Screw the spark plug by hand into the clean thread as far as it will go. Then apply the spark-plug wrench. One of three procedures is now used:
– If you are installing new flat-seal spark plugs, turn an additional 90° after you first encounter resistance (Fig. 1),
– when re-installing used flat-seal spark plugs, the additional torquing angle corresponds to 5 minutes on the clock, or an angle of about 30°,
– when installing conical-seat plugs, turn the wrench by addiional angle corresponding to 2 to 3 minutes on the clock, or about 15° (Fig. 2).

Table 1. Tightening torques

Cylinder-heat material	Thread	Cast iron Tightening torque $N \cdot m$	Light alloy Tightening torque $N \cdot m$
Spark plug with flat seat	M 10x1	10...15	10...15
	M 12x1.25	15...25	15...25
	M 14x1.25	20...40	20...30
	M 18x1.5	30...45	20...35
Spark plug with conical seat	M 14x1.25	20...25	15...25
	M 18x1.5	20...30	15...23

2. When tightening or loosening the spark plug, the wrench should not be held at an angle; the insulator will otherwise be broken off or pushed to the side, and the spark plug destroyed.

3. In the case of box wrenches with a loose tommy bar, the hole for the tommy bar must be above the spark plug so that the tommy bar can be pushed through both holes in the box wrench. If the holes are lower and the tommy bar is inserted only through one hole, the spark plug will be damaged.

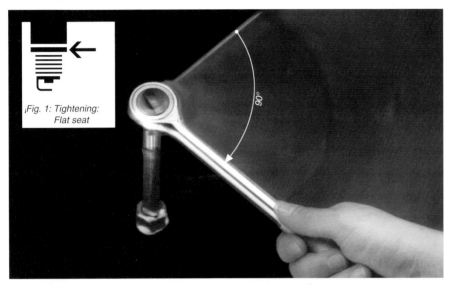

Fig. 1: Tightening:
Flat seat

90°

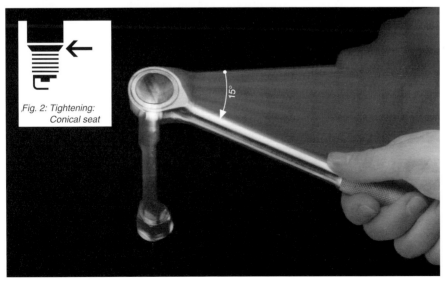

Fig. 2: Tightening:
Conical seat

15°

Mistakes and their consequences

Basically, a given engine type should be fitted only with the spark plugs specified by the engine manufacturer or with those recommended by Bosch. To rule out incorrect selection from the outset, the motorist should consult the Bosch Service specialist. The desired information is also provided in sales literature, such as catalogs, product stands with information boards or application summaries. The use of unsuitable types of spark plugs can lead to serious engine damage. The most frequently encountered mistakes are:

– incorrect heat range,
– incorrect thread length, and
– modifications/damage to seal face.

Incorrect heat-range code number

The heat-range code number must, under all circumstances, conform to the spark plug specifications of the motor-vehicle manufacturer or to the Bosch spark-plug recommendations.
Spark plugs with the wrong heat range for the engine can produce auto-ignition.

Incorrect thread length

The length of the thread on the spark plug must be the same as the length of the thread in the cylinder head.
If the spark-plug thread is too long, the spark plug projects too far into the combustion chamber.
Consequences:
– possible damage to the piston,
– coking-up of the spark-plug thread may make it impossible to remove the spark plug,
– spark plug overheating.
If the thread is too short, the spark plug does not project far enough into the combustion chamber.
Consequences:
– poor ignition of the mixture,
– spark plug does not reach its self-cleaning temperature,
– the lower threads in the cylinder head become coked up.

Modifications to the seat

On spark plugs with a conical seat, it is not permissible to use a washer or a seal ring. On flat-seat spark plugs, it is permissible to use only the captive gasket fitted to the spark plug. It must not be removed or replaced by a washer.
Without the gasket, the spark plug projects too far into the combustion chamber. This impairs efficient heat transfer between spark-plug shell and cylinder head, and the plug does not seal properly.
If an additional seal ring is used, the spark plug is not seated deep enough in the thread hole, and the transfer of heat from the spark-plug shell to the cylinder head is also impaired.

Spark-plug faces

Reading the spark plugs provides valuable information on spark-plug and engine operating conditions.
The appearance of the electrodes and insulator of the spark plug – the "spark-plug face" – provides information on spark-plug operation, mixture and the combustion process within the engine (Figures 3 to 5).

Reading the spark plugs is thus an important engine-diagnosis procedure. For an accurate reading, observe the following procedural guidelines: The vehicle must be operated under standard conditions before an attempt is made to read the spark plugs. If the reading is preceded by an extended period at idle, carbon deposits on the plug will render accurate analysis impossible; this problem is more serious immediately after a cold start. The vehicle should be driven about 10 km, at a variety of moderate loads and engine speeds. Extended idling prior to shutdown is to be avoided.

Fig. 3: Spark-plug faces. Part 1

① *Normal condition.*
Insulator nose grayish-white or grayish-yellow to brown. Engine is in order. Heat range of plug correct.
Mixture setting and ignition timing are correct, no misfiring, cold-starting device functioning.
No deposits from fuel additives containing lead or from alloying constituents in the engine oil.
No overheating.

② *Sooted – carbon-fouled.*
Insulator nose, electrodes and spark-plug shell covered with velvet-like, dull black soot deposits.
Cause: incorrect mixture setting (carburetor, fuel injection): mixture too rich, air filter very dirty, automatic choke not in order or manual choke pulled too long, mainly short-distance driving, spark plug too cold, heat-range code number too low.
Effects: Misfiring, difficult cold-starting.
Remedy: Adjust A/F mixture and choke device, check air filter.

③ *Oil-fouled.*
Insulator nose, electrodes and spark-plug shell covered with shiny soot or carbon residues.
Cause: too much oil in combustion chamber. Oil level too high, badly worn piston rings, cylinders and valve guides. In two-stroke engines, too much oil in mixture.
Effects: Misfiring, difficult starting.
Remedy: Overhaul engine, adjust oil/fuel ratio (2-stroke engines), fit new spark plugs.

④ *Lead fouling.*
Insulator nose covered in places with brown/yellow glazing which can have a greenish color.
Cause: Lead additives in fuel. Glazing results from high engine loading after extended part-load operation.
Effects: At high loads, the glazing becomes conductive and causes misfiring.
Remedy: Fit new spark plugs since cleaning the old ones is pointless.

Fig. 4: Spark-plug faces. Part 2

⑤ **Pronounced lead fouling**

Insulator nose covered in places with thick brown/yellow glazing which can have a greenish color.
Cause: *Lead additives in fuel. Glazing results from high engine loading after extended part-load operation.*
Effects: *At high loads, the glazing becomes conductive and causes misfiring.*
Remedy: *Fit new spark plugs since cleaning the old ones is pointless.*

⑥ **Formation of ash**

Heavy ash deposits on the insulator nose resulting from oil and fuel additives, in the scavening area, and on the ground electrode. The structure of the ash is loose- to cinder-like.
Cause: *Alloying constituents, particularly from engine oil can deposit this ash in the combustion chamber and on the spark-plug face.*
Effects: *Can lead to auto-ignition with loss of power and possible engine damage.*
Remedy: *Repair the engine. Fit new spark plugs. Possibly change engine-oil type.*

⑦ **Center electrode covered with melted deposits**

Melted deposits on center electrode. Insulator tip blistered, spongy, and soft.
Cause: *Overheating caused by auto-ignition. For instance due to ignition being too far advanced, combustion deposits in the combustion chamber, defective valves, defective ignition distributor, poor-quality fuel. Possibly spark-plug heat-range value too low.*
Effects: *Misfiring, loss of power (engine damage).*
Remedy: *Check the engine, ignition, and mixture-formation system. Fit new spark plugs with correct heat-range code number.*

⑧ **Partially melted center electrode**

Center electrode has melted and ground electrode is severely damaged.
Cause: *Overheating caused by auto-ignition. For instance due to ignition being too far advanced, combustion deposits in the combustion chamber, defective valves, defective ignition distributor, poor-quality fuel.*
Effects: *Misfiring, loss of power (engine damage). Insulator-nose fracture possible due to overheated center electrode.*
Remedy: *Check the engine, ignition, and mixture-formation system. Fit new sparkplugs.*

Fig. 5: Spark-plug faces. Part 3

⑨ **Partially melted electrodes**

Cauliflower-like appearance of the electrodes.
Possible deposit of materials not originating
from the spark plug.
Cause: Overheating caused by auto-ignition.
For instance due to ignition being too far
advanced, combustion deposits in the combustion chamber, defective valves, defective
ignition distributor, poor-quality fuel.
Effects: Power loss becomes noticeable before
total failure occurs (engine damage).
Remedy: Check engine and mixture-formation
system. Fit new spark plugs.

⑩ **Heavy wear on center electrode**
Cause: Spark-plug exchange interval has
been exceeded.

Effects: Misfiring, particularly during acceleration (ignition voltage no longer sufficient for the
large electrode gap). Poor starting.
Remedy: Fit new spark plugs.

⑪ **Heavy wear on ground electrode**
Cause: Aggressive fuel and oil additives.

Unfavorable flow conditions in combustion
chamber, possibly as a result of combustion
deposits. Engine knock. Overheating has
not taken place.
Effects: Misfiring, particularly during acceleration
(ignition voltage no longer sufficient for the large
electrode gap). Poor starting.
Remedy: Fit new spark plugs.

⑫ **Insulator-nose fracture**
Cause: Mechanical damage (spark plug has

been dropped, or bad handling has put pressure
on the center electrode). In exceptional cases,
deposits between the insulator nose and the
center electrode, as well as center-electrode
corrosion, can cause the insulator nose to
fracture (this applies particularly for excessively
long periods of use).
Effects: Misfiring, spark arcs-over at a point
which is inaccessible for the fresh charge of
A/F mixture.
Remedy: Fit new spark plugs.

Motronic engine management

The Motronic system

System overview

Motronic combines all the electronic systems for engine control in a single control unit (ECU) which, in turn, governs the actuating systems used to control the spark-ignition engine. Engine-mounted monitoring devices (sensors) gather the required operating data and relay the information to input circuits for:
– ignition (on/off),
– camshaft position,
– vehicle speed,
– gear selection,
– transmission control,
– air conditioner, etc.
Monitored analog data include:
– battery voltage,
– engine temperature,
– intake-air temperature,
– air quantity,
– throttle-valve angle,
– lambda oxygen sensor,
– knock sensor, etc.
as well as
– engine speed.

Input circuits located within the ECU convert these data for subsequent operations in the microprocessor. The microprocessor, in turn, uses these data to determine the engine's momentary operating conditions; this information serves as the basis for the ECU's command signals, which are amplified by power-output stages before being transmitted to the final-control elements used to control the engine. This system combines fuel injection, highest-quality mixture preparation and the correct ignition timing to provide mutual support over the entire range of operating conditions encountered in the spark-ignition engine.

Motronic versions

The descriptions and illustrations on the following pages refer to a typical Motronic configuration (Figure 1). Other Motronic systems are available to meet the special demands arising from specific national regulations as well as the requirements of the individual automobile manufacturers.

Basic functions

Control of the ignition and fuel-injection processes is (independent of version) at the core of the Motronic system.

Auxiliary functions

Additional open and closed-loop control functions – required in response to legislation aimed at reductions in exhaust emissions and fuel consumption – supplement the basic Motronic functions while making it possible to monitor all components exercising an influence on the composition of the exhaust gases. These include:
– idle-speed control,
– lambda oxygen control,
– control of the evaporative emissions control system,
– knock control,
– exhaust-gas recirculation (EGR) for reducing NO_X emissions, and
– control of the secondary air injection to reduce HC emissions.
The system can also be expanded to meet special demands from automobile manufacturers by including the following:
– open-loop turbocharger control as well as control of variable-tract intake manifolds for increased engine power output,

– camshaft control for achieving reductions in exhaust emissions and fuel consumption as well as enhanced output, and
– knock control along with engine and vehicle-speed governing functions, to protect engine and vehicle.

The acquisition and processing of the measured information is described in the chapters dealing with acquisition and processing of the operating data.

Vehicle management

Motronic supports the control units in other vehicle systems. It can, for instance, operate together with the automatic transmission's control unit to provide reductions in torque during shifting, thereby lessening transmission wear. Motronic can also work together with the ABS control unit to provide traction control (ASR) for enhanced vehicle safety.

The schematic system illustration below shows a maximal-configuration Motronic system. This type of system can be employed to satisfy
– the stringent emissions limits, and
– the requirement for an integral, on-board diagnosis (OBD) system for California vehicles from 1993 onward.

Fig. 1: System diagram of Motronic M5 with integrated diagnostics (OBD)

1 Carbon canister	10 Secondary-air valve
2 Shutoff valve	11 Air-mass meter
3 Canister-purge valve	12 Control unit (ECU)
4 Fuel-pressure regulator	13 Throttle-valve sensor
5 Injector	14 Idle actuator
6 Pressure actuator	15 Air-temperature sensor
7 Ignition coil	16 EGR valve
8 Phase sensor	17 Fuel filter
9 Secondary-air pump	18 Knock sensor

19 Engine-speed sensor
20 Engine-temperature sensor
21 Lambda oxygen sensor
22 Diagnosis interface
23 Diagnosis lamp
24 Pressure differential sensor
25 Electric fuel pump

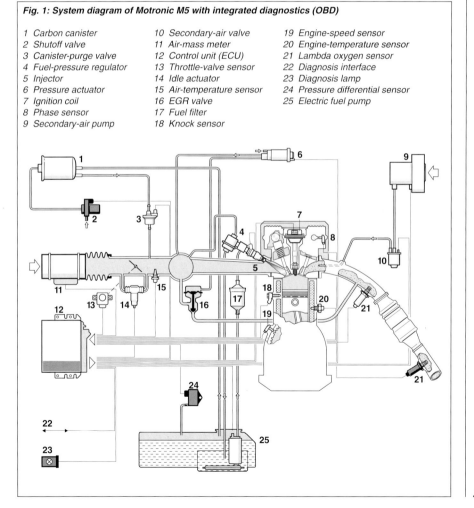

Fuel system

Fuel supply

Fuel-supply system

The fuel-supply system must be capable of providing the engine with the required quantity of fuel under all operating conditions. An electric pump draws the fuel through a filter while extracting it from the tank for delivery to the fuel-distribution rail with its electromagnetic injectors. The injectors spray the fuel into the engine's intake tract in precisely metered quantities. The excess fuel flows through the pressure regu-lator and back to the fuel tank (Figure 1).

The pressure regulator generally employs the pressure within the intake manifold as its reference. This characteristic pressure works in combination with the constant flow through the fuel rail (cool-ing effect) to prevent vapor bubbles from forming in the fuel. The resulting pressure differential at the injector usually remains constant in the 300 kPa range.

Where necessary, the fuel-supply system can also be designed to incorporate pressure attenuators to reduce pulsation in the fuel line.

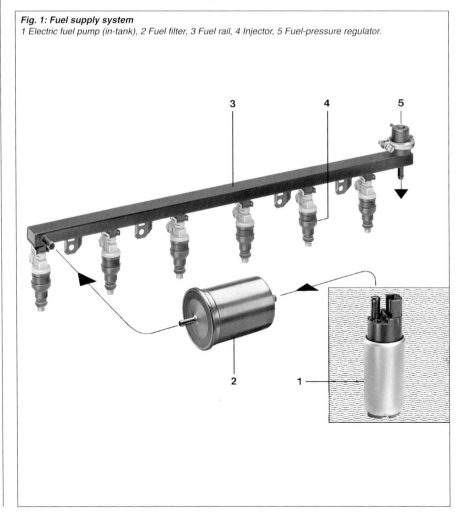

Fig. 1: Fuel supply system
1 Electric fuel pump (in-tank), 2 Fuel filter, 3 Fuel rail, 4 Injector, 5 Fuel-pressure regulator.

Electric fuel pump

Function

The electric fuel pump supplies a continuous flow of fuel from the tank. It can be installed either within the fuel tank itself ("in-tank") or at an external location in the fuel line ("in-line").

The in-tank pumps currently in general use (Figures 2 and 3) are integrated within the fuel tank's installation assembly along with the level sensor and a swirl plate to remove vapor bubbles from the fuel return line. When an in-line pump is used, hot delivery problems can be solved by using a supplementary in-tank booster pump to supply fuel from the tank at low pressure. To ensure that the delivery pressure in the system is maintained at the required level, the maximum supply capacity is always greater than the system's theoretical maximum requirement.

The fuel pump is activated by the engine-management ECU. A safety circuit interrupts fuel delivery when the engine is stationary with the ignition on.

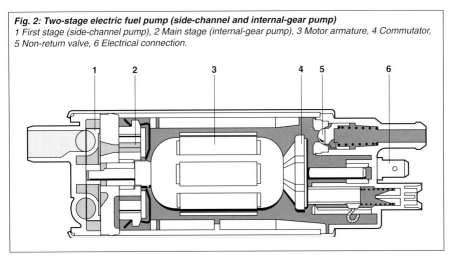

Fig. 2: Two-stage electric fuel pump (side-channel and internal-gear pump)
1 First stage (side-channel pump), 2 Main stage (internal-gear pump), 3 Motor armature, 4 Commutator, 5 Non-return valve, 6 Electrical connection.

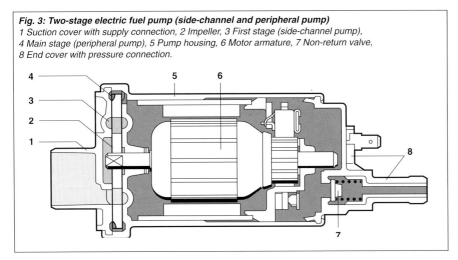

Fig. 3: Two-stage electric fuel pump (side-channel and peripheral pump)
1 Suction cover with supply connection, 2 Impeller, 3 First stage (side-channel pump), 4 Main stage (peripheral pump), 5 Pump housing, 6 Motor armature, 7 Non-return valve, 8 End cover with pressure connection.

Design

The electric fuel pump consists of the following elements:
– pump assembly,
– electric motor and end cover.

The electric motor and pump assembly are located in a common housing, where they are immersed in circulating fuel. This arrangement provides effective cooling for the electric motor. Because no oxygen is present, it is impossible for an ignitable mixture to form; there is no danger of an explosion. The end cover contains the electrical connections, the non-return valve and the hydraulic connection for the pressure side. The non-return valve maintains system pressure for a period of time after the unit is shut down to prevent vapor bubbles from forming. Interference-suppression devices can also be included in the end-cover assembly.

Design variations

Various design principles are employed to satisfy individual system demands (Figure 4).

Positive-displacement pumps

Roller-cell (RZP) and internal-gear pumps (IZP) are both classified as positive-displacement designs. Both types of pump operate by using variable-sized, circulating chambers to expose a supply orifice and draw in fuel as their volume expands. Once the maximum volume is reached, the supply orifice closes and the discharge orifice opens. The fuel is now forced out as the effective volume in the chamber decreases. The chambers on the roller-cell pump are formed by rollers circulating in a rotor plate. A combination of centrifugal force and fuel pressure forces them outward against the eccentric roller path. The eccentricity between rotor plate and roller path provides the constant increase and decrease in chamber volume.

Fig. 4: Principles of operation
a) Roller-cell pump
b) Peripheral pump
c) Internal-gear pump
d) Side-channel pump

a
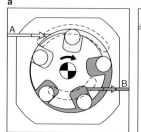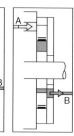

b
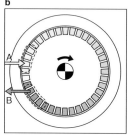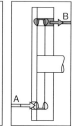

c
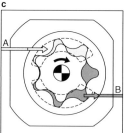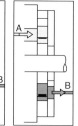

d
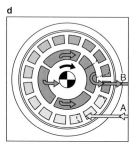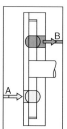

The internal-gear pump consists of an internal drive gear that moves against the surface of an eccentrically-mounted ring gear; the ring gear is equipped with one tooth more than the drive gear. As the mutually-sealed tooth flanks turn, variable chambers are formed between them. Roller-cell pumps can be used to obtain fuel pressures in excess of 600 kPa. Internal-gear pumps can supply up to 400 kPa, a figure adequate for virtually all Motronic applications.

Hydrokinetic flow pumps
The peripheral and side-channel pumps are both classified as hydrokinetic flow pumps. In these pumps an impeller accelerates the fuel particles before discharging them into the tract where they generate pressure via pulse exchange. The peripheral pump differs from its side-channel counterpart in its larger number of impeller blades and the shape of the impellers, as well as in the positions of the side channels, which – unlike those of the side-channel unit – are located on the circumference or periphery. Although peripheral pumps are only capable of generating maximum fuel pressures in the 300 kPa range, they do supply a continuous, virtually pulseless flow of fuel. This makes them particularly attractive for use in those vehicular applications where limiting noise is a major priority. Side-channel pumps can only produce pressures of up to 100 kPa. One important use for this type of unit is as a booster pump in systems with in-line main pumps; another major application is as the primary stage in a two-stage in-tank pump of the kind installed in vehicles susceptible to hot starting problems and/or with single-point fuel injection.

Fuel filter
Contaminants in the fuel can impair the operation of both pressure regulator and injectors. A filter is therefore installed downstream from the electric fuel pump. This fuel filter contains a paper element featuring a mean pore diameter of 10 μm. A backplate retains it in its housing. The replacement intervals are determined by the filter's volume and contamination levels in the fuel (Figure 5).

Fuel rail
The fuel flows through the fuel rail where it is evenly distributed to all injectors. The injectors are mounted on the fuel rail, which also usually includes a fuel-pressure regulator. A pressure attenuator may also be present. The dimensions of the fuel rail are selected to inhibit the local fluctuations in fuel pressure that could otherwise be triggered as the injectors run through their operating cycles. This prevents the injection quantities from reacting to changes in load and engine speed. Depending upon the particular vehicle type and its special requirements, the fuel rail can be made of steel, aluminum or plastic. It may also include an integral test valve, which can be used to bleed pressure for servicing as well as for test purposes.

Fuel-pressure regulator
Injection quantity should be determined exclusively by injection duration. Thus the difference between the fuel pressure in the distribution rail and the pressure in the intake tract must remain constant. A means is thus required for adjusting the fuel pressure to reflect variations in the load-sensitive manifold pressure. The fuel-presure regulator regulates the

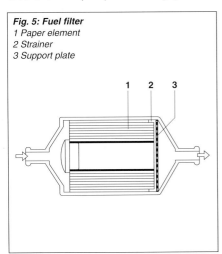

Fig. 5: Fuel filter
1 Paper element
2 Strainer
3 Support plate

amount of fuel returning to the tank to maintain a constant pressure drop across the injectors. The pressure regulator is generally positioned at the far end of the fuel rail to avoid impairing the flow within the rail. However, it can also be mounted in the fuel-return line.

The fuel-pressure regulator is designed as a diaphragm-controlled overflow pressure regulator (Figure 6). A rubber-fiber diaphragm divides the pressure regulator into two sections: fuel chamber and pressure chamber. The spring presses against a valve holder integrated within the diaphragm. This force causes a flexibly mounted valve plate to push against a valve seat. When the pressure exerted against the diaphragm by the fuel exceeds that of the spring, the valve opens and allows fuel to flow directly back to the tank until the diaphragm assembly returns to a state of equilibrium, with equal pressure exerted on both of its sides. A pneumatic line is provided between the spring chamber and the intake manifold downstream from the throttle valve, allowing the chamber to respond to changes in manifold vacuum. Thus the pressures at the diaphragm correspond to those at the injectors. As a result, the pressure drop at the injectors remains constant, as it is determined solely by the spring force and surface area of the diaphragm.

Fuel-pressure attenuator

The injectors' operating cycles and the periodic discharge of fuel that characterize the positive-displacement fuel pump both induce fluctuations in fuel pressure. Under unfavorable circumstances, the mountings for the electric fuel pump, fuel lines and fuel rail can transmit these vibrations to the vehicle's body. Noise from this source can be prevented using specially designed mounting elements and fuel-pressure attenuators. The layout of the fuel-pressure attenuator (Figure 7) is similar to that of the pressure regulator. In both cases a spring-loaded diaphragm separates the fuel from the air space. The spring force is calculated to lift the diaphragm from its

seat as soon as the fuel reaches operating pressure. This provides a variable fuel chamber which can accept fuel to ease pressure peaks and then release it again when pressure falls. The spring chamber can be fitted with a manifold-vacuum line to stay within the optimum operating range in the face of fluctuations in the fuel's absolute pressure. The pressure attenuator also shares the pressure regulator's installation flexibility, as it can also be mounted in the rail or in the fuel-return line.

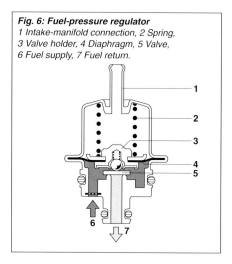

Fig. 6: Fuel-pressure regulator
1 Intake-manifold connection, 2 Spring,
3 Valve holder, 4 Diaphragm, 5 Valve,
6 Fuel supply, 7 Fuel return.

Fig. 7: Fuel-pressure attenuator
1 Spring, 2 Spring plate, 3 Diaphragm,
4 Fuel supply, 5 Fuel return.

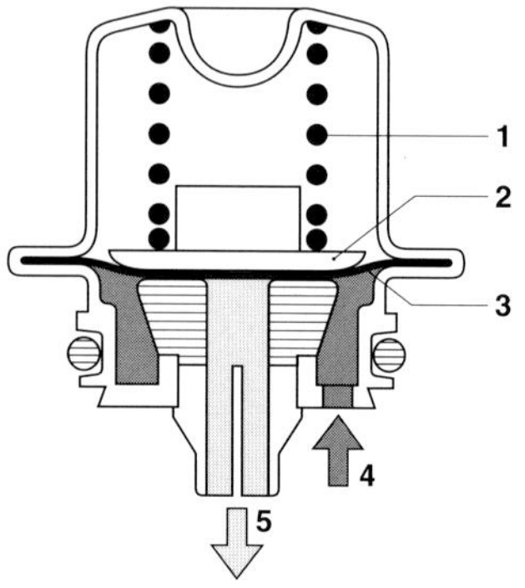

Fuel injection

Uncompromising demands for smooth running and low emissions in automobiles have made it necessary to provide thorough and precise mixture formation for every single work cycle. The fuel mass must be injected in quantities that are precisely metered to match the amount of intake air; in today's applications exact injection timing is acquiring increasing significance. For this reason, every cylinder is assigned an electromagnetic injector. The injector sprays the fuel – in precise quantities at a point in time determined by the ECU – directly toward the cylinder intake valve(s). Thus

condensation along the walls of the intake tract of the kind that leads to deviations from the desired Lambda value is largely avoided. Because the engine's intake manifold conducts only combustion air, its geometry can be optimized to meet the engine's dynamic gasflow requirements.

Electromagnetic injector

The electromagnetic injector contains a solenoid armature mounted on a valve needle (Figures 8 and 9), and travels through precise motions within the valve body. When the unit is at rest, a coil spring presses the valve needle against the seat to seal off the flow of fuel through

Fig. 8: Injector (top-feed)
1 Filter strainer in fuel supply, 2 Electrical connection, 3 Solenoid winding, 4 Valve housing, 5 Armature, 6 Valve body, 7 Valve needle.

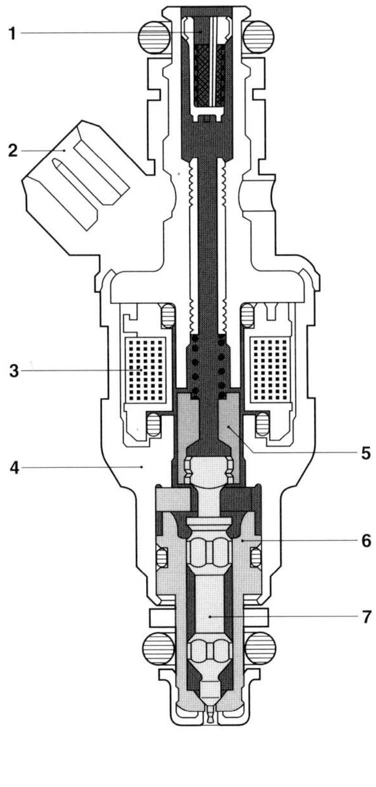

Fig. 9: Injector (bottom-feed)
1 Electrical connection, 2 Filter screen in fuel supply, 3 Solenoid winding, 4 Valve housing, 5 Armature, 6 Valve body, 7 Valve needle.

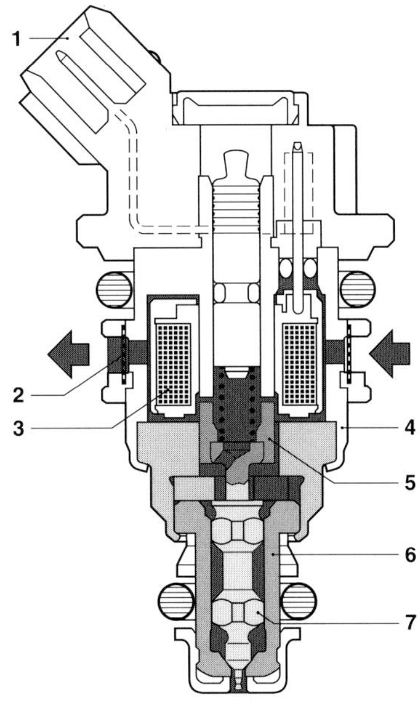

the outlet orifice and into the intake manifold. When the control transmits an activation current to the solenoid winding in the valve housing, the solenoid armature rises between 60 and 100 µm, lifting the valve needle in the process; the fuel can now flow through the calibrated orifice. The response times lie between 1.5 ... 1.8 ms at a control frequency of 3...125 Hz, depending upon the type of injection and the momentary engine speed and load conditions.

Different injector designs are employed to meet varying requirements:

Top-feed injector
Fuel enters the top-feed injector from above and flows through its vertical axis. This unit is installed in a specially-formed opening in the fuel rail. Sealing is provided by an upper seal ring, while a clip holds the unit in place. The lower end, which also has a seal ring, extends into the engine's intake manifold (Figure 8).

Bottom-feed injector
The "bottom-feed" injector is integrated within the fuel-rail assembly, where it is constantly immersed in flowing fuel. The fuel supply enters the unit from the side ("bottom-feed"). The fuel rail itself is mounted directly on the intake manifold.

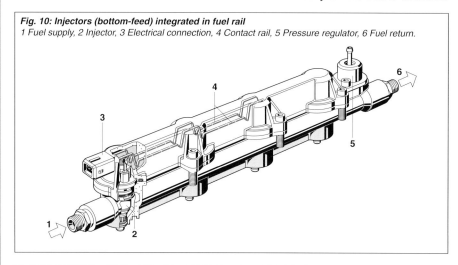

Fig. 10: Injectors (bottom-feed) integrated in fuel rail
1 Fuel supply, 2 Injector, 3 Electrical connection, 4 Contact rail, 5 Pressure regulator, 6 Fuel return.

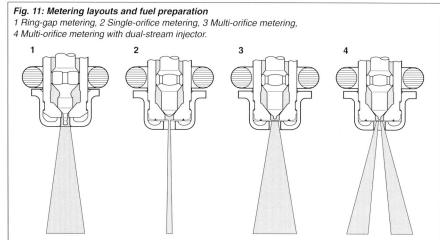

Fig. 11: Metering layouts and fuel preparation
1 Ring-gap metering, 2 Single-orifice metering, 3 Multi-orifice metering,
4 Multi-orifice metering with dual-stream injector.

The injector is retained in the fuel rail by either a clip, or a cover on the rail which can also house the electrical connections. Two seal rings prevent the fuel from escaping. This type of modular design provides several advantages; these include good starting and driving response with hot engines as well as low installation height (Figures 9 and 10).

Mixture formation

A variety of different fuel-metering arrangements are employed to satisfy the demand for the effective fuel atomization necessary for ensuring maximum homogeneity in the air-fuel mixture while simultaneously holding intake-tract condensation to a minimum. The injector's discharge orifice is specially calibrated to fulfill these requirements in the respective applications (Figure 11). On units with ring-gap metering, a section of the valve needle (pintle) extends through the valve body. The resulting ring gap forms the calibrated fuel-discharge orifice. The lower end of the pintle features a machined breakaway edge where the fuel atomizes before emerging in a tapered pattern.

On injectors with single-orifice metering, the pintle is replaced by a thin injection-orifice disk with a calibrated opening. Virtually none of the thin jet of fuel lands on the walls of the intake tract. However, fuel atomization is limited. Injectors featuring multi-orifice metering are fitted with an injection-orifice disk of the kind used in the single-orifice units, the difference being that the multi-orifice disk contains numerous calibrated openings. These are arranged to provide a tapered spray pattern similar to that achieved with annular-orifice metering devices, and provide comparable fuel atomization. The orifices can also be designed to provide two or more spray patterns. This makes it possible to achieve optimum fuel distribution via separate injection into the individual inlet runners on multi-valve engines. Meanwhile, air-shrouded injectors can provide even better mixture formation.

Combustion air traveling at the speed of sound is extracted from the intake manifold at a location upstream from the throttle valve; it then proceeds through a calibrated opening located directly on the injection-orifice disk. The interaction between fuel and air molecules provides thorough atomization. To allow air to be drawn in through the opening, a partial vacuum referred to atmospheric pressure is required in the intake manifold. The air-shrouded design is thus most effective during part-throttle operation (Figure 12).

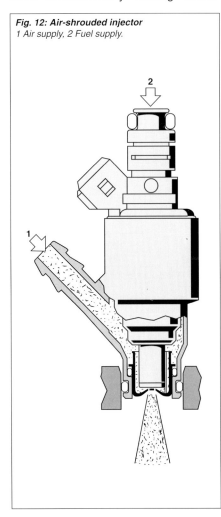

Fig. 12: Air-shrouded injector
1 Air supply, 2 Fuel supply.

High-voltage ignition circuit

The high-voltage ignition circuit generates the high-tension current required for ignition and then delivers it to the correct spark plug at precisely the right instant. The Motronic high-voltage circuit can be constructed according to any one of several design options:
– High-voltage circuit with one ignition coil, one power-output stage and a high-tension distributor (rotating voltage distribution).
– High-voltage circuit featuring one single-spark coil and one power-output stage per cylinder (stationary or electronic voltage distribution).
– High-voltage circuit with one dual-spark coil and one power-output stage for every two cylinders (stationary or electronic voltage distribution).

Ignition coil

Function
The ignition coil stores the ignition energy and produces the high voltages required to generate a spark when the ignition is triggered.

Design and operation
The ignition coil operates according to the laws of induction. The unit consists of two magnetically coupled copper coils (primary and secondary windings). The energy stored in the primary winding's magnetic field is transmitted to the secondary side. The transformation ratio for current and voltage is a function of the ratio of the numbers of coils contained in the respective windings of the primary and secondary circuits (Figure 1).

Modern ignition coils consist of single plates, combined to form a closed ferrous circuit, and a plastic housing. Within the housing the primary winding is wound on a bobbin mounted directly on the core. Further outward is the secondary wind-

ing; in the interests of enhanced arcing resistance, this assumes the shape of a disk or chamber winding. The housing, meanwhile, is filled with epoxy resin to provide effective insulation between the two windings, and between the windings and the core. The specific design configuration is tailored to match the individual application.

Ignition driver stage

Function and operation
Ignition driver stages featuring multi-stage power transistors control the flow of primary current through the coil, replacing the breaker points found on earlier ignition systems.
In addition, the ignition output stage is also charged with limiting both primary current and primary voltage. The primary voltage is restricted to prevent excessive increases in the supply of secondary voltage, which could damage components in the high-tension circuit. Restrictions on primary current hold the ignition system's energy output to a specified level. Power-output stages can be either internal (forming an integral part of Motronic) or external (located outside the Motronic unit).

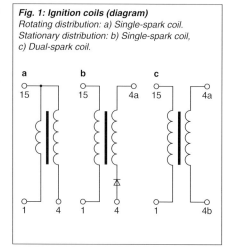

Fig. 1: Ignition coils (diagram)
Rotating distribution: a) Single-spark coil.
Stationary distribution: b) Single-spark coil,
c) Dual-spark coil.

High-voltage generation

The Motronic ECU activates the ignition driver stage during the calculated dwell period. It is within this period that the primary current within the coil rises to its specified intensity. The level of the primary current and the primary inductance in the ignition coil determine the level of energy stored in the ignition system. When the firing point arrives, the ignition driver stage interrrupts the flow of current. The flux in the magnetic field induces secondary voltage in the coil's secondary winding.

The potential secondary voltage (secondary voltage supply) depends upon a number of factors. These include the amount of energy stored in the ignition system, the capacity of the windings and the coil's transformation ratio, as well as the secondary load and the restrictions on primary voltage determined by the ignition system's driver stage. The supply of secondary voltage must always lie above the level of voltage required to generate a spark at the spark plug (ignition voltage requirement) The spark energy must be adequate for initiating combustion in the mixture, even if subsidiary sparking occurs.

When the primary current is switched, an undesired voltage of approx. 1...2 kV is induced in the secondary winding (switch-on voltage); its polarity is the opposite of that of the high-tension voltage. It is essential that arcing at the spark plug (switch-on spark) be avoided. Systems with rotating distribution use a distributor spark discharge gap for effective suppression of this phenomenon. On systems with stationary spark-distribution and single-spark coils a special diode is incorporated in the high-voltage circuit to perform the same function. With stationary spark-distribution and two-spark coils, the high arcing voltage encountered when two spark plugs are connected in series suppresses the switch-on spark, without supplementary measures being necessary.

Voltage distribution

Rotating voltage distribution

On conventional ignition systems, the high-tension voltage generated by the coil is transmitted to the correct cylinder by a mechanical distributor. Because Motronic uses electronics to regulate the distributor's auxiliary functions (formerly mechanical advance adjustment as a function of load and engine speed), the distributor can be simplified. The high-voltage distributor's individual components are:

– the insulated cover,
– the rotor with suppression resistor,
– the distributor cap with discharge terminals, and
– the interference-suppression shield.

The distributor's rotor is mounted directly on the camshaft.

Reliable high-voltage distribution can only be guaranteed within a certain dwell-angle range which is inversely proportional to the number of cylinders. Centrifugal rotor adjustment provides adequate range extension on 6-cylinder engines, but 8-cylinder systems usually need two 4-cylinder units.

Stationary voltage distribution

Distributorless, stationary or electronic voltage distribution is available in two alternative versions:

System with single-spark ignition coils
Each cylinder is equipped with a coil and an output stage, which the Motronic unit triggers in the appropriate firing order. Because distributor losses can no longer occur, it is possible to make the coils especially small. The preferred installation position is directly above the spark plug. Stationary distribution with single-spark ignition coils is universally suited for use with any number of cylinders. There are no restrictions on the adjustment range for ignition advance. It must be noted that the unit does require additional synchronization; this is provided by a camshaft sensor (Figure 2).

System with two-spark ignition coils

A single coil and one ignition output stage are assigned to two cylinders. Each end of the secondary winding is connected to one of the spark plugs. The cylinders are selected so that the compression stroke on one coincides with the exhaust stroke of the other. When the ignition fires, a spark arcs at both spark plugs. Because it is important to ensure that the spark produced during the exhaust stroke ignites neither residual gases nor fresh intake gas, there is a small restriction on the potential range of ignition advance angles.

This system does not require a synchronization sensor at the camshaft (Figure 3).

Connectors and interference suppressors

High-voltage cables

The high-voltage generated at the coil must be transmitted to the spark plug. This function is discharged by h.v. strength copper wires embedded in synthetic insulation material, with specially designed plug connectors for joining the high-tension components mounted on their ends. Every high-voltage lead represents a capacitive load for the ignition system, and reduces the supply of secondary voltage accordingly; thus the cables should be kept as short as possible.

Interference resistors, interference supression

The pulse-shaped high-tension discharge characteristic of every arc at the spark plug also represents a source of radio interference. The current peaks associated with discharge are limited by suppression resistors in the high-voltage circuit. To hold radiation of interference emanating from the high-voltage circuit to a minimum, the suppression resistors should be installed as close to the actual source as possible. Partial or complete encapsulation of the ignition system can

supply additional reductions in interference. The resistors for interference suppression are generally installed in the spark-plug connectors and the plug connections, while rotating distributors can also include a resistor at the rotor. Spark plugs with integral interference-suppression resistors are also available.

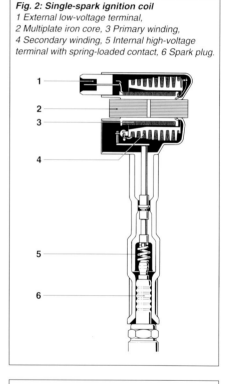

Fig. 2: Single-spark ignition coil
1 External low-voltage terminal,
2 Multiplate iron core, 3 Primary winding,
4 Secondary winding, 5 Internal high-voltage
terminal with spring-loaded contact, 6 Spark plug.

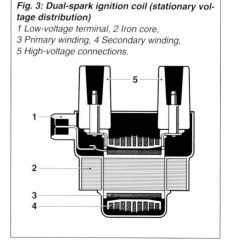

Fig. 3: Dual-spark ignition coil (stationary voltage distribution)
1 Low-voltage terminal, 2 Iron core,
3 Primary winding, 4 Secondary winding,
5 High-voltage connections.

It must, however, be remembered that increases in the resistance in the secondary circuit will be accompanied by additional losses within the ignition circuit, the ultimate result being a reduction in the ignition energy available at the spark plug.

Spark plug

The spark plug generates the spark for igniting the air-fuel mixture in the combustion chamber. It is a ceramic-insulated, gas-tight, high-voltage conductor leading into the combustion chamber. Once the sparking voltage is reached, the path between the center electrode and the ground electrode becomes conductive and converts the remaining energy from the coil into a spark.

The voltage level required for ignition depends upon the electrode gap, electrode geometry, combustion-chamber pressure and the A/F ratio at the firing point.
The spark plug's electrodes are subject to wear in normal engine operation. This wear results in higher voltage requirements. The ignition system must be capable of providing enough secondary voltage to ensure that adequate ignition voltage remains available under all operating conditions for the life of the spark plug.

Fig. 4: Spark plug
1 Terminal nut
2 Al₂O₃ ceramic insulator
3 Case
4 Heat-shrinkage zone
5 Conductive glass
6 Seal
7 Compound center electrode Ni/Cu
8 Ground electrode

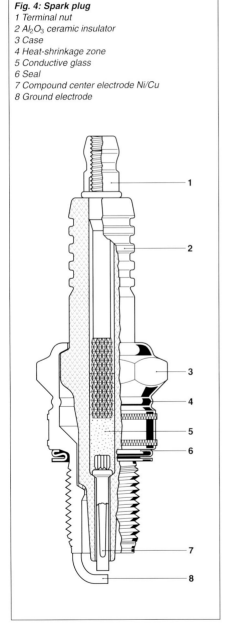

Operating-data acquisition

Engine load

One of the most important variables used for determining injection quantity and ignition advance angle is the engine's load state (load monitoring).

The various Motronic systems employ the following load sensors to monitor engine load:
– air-flow sensor,
– hot-wire air-mass meter,
– hot-film air-mass meter,
– intake manifold pressure sensor, and
– throttle-valve sensor.

In the Motronic system the throttle-valve sensor generally assumes the function of a secondary load sensor, supplementing one of the primary load sensors listed above. It is also employed as a primary load sensor in some isolated cases.

Air-flow sensor

The air-flow sensor is located between the air filter and the throttle valve, where it monitors the volumetric flow rate [m³/h] of the air being drawn into the engine. The force of the air stream acts against the constant return force of a spring, and the air flap's deflection angle is monitored via potentiometer. The potentiometer voltage is transmitted to the ECU

for comparison with the potentiometer's initial supply voltage. The resulting voltage ratio serves as an index of the induction air's volumetric flow rate. The ECU ensures accuracy by compensating for the effects of potentiometer aging and temperature when processing the resistance (Figure 1).

In order to prevent pulsation in the intake air stream from setting up oscillations in the air-flow sensor flap, the system also includes a counterflap and a "damping volume." The air-flow sensor is equipped with a temperature sensor. This transmits a temperature-sensitive resistance value to the control unit, allowing it to compensate for variations in air density arising from changes in the temperature of the intake air.

The air-flow sensor is still a component in many of the Motronic and L-Jetronic systems currently in production. The load sensors described in the following section are preferably installed, and will replace the flap-controlled air-flow sensor in future systems.

Air-mass meters

The hot-wire and hot-film air-mass meters are both "thermal" load sensors. They are installed between the air filter and the throttle valve, where they monitor the mass flow of the air being drawn into the engine. The two meters operate according to a common principle.

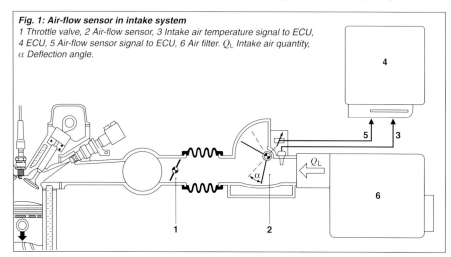

Fig. 1: Air-flow sensor in intake system
1 Throttle valve, 2 Air-flow sensor, 3 Intake air temperature signal to ECU, 4 ECU, 5 Air-flow sensor signal to ECU, 6 Air filter. Q_L Intake air quantity, α Deflection angle.

An electrically heated element is mounted in the intake-air stream, where it is cooled by the flow of incoming air. A control circuit modulates the flow of heating current to maintain the temperature differential between the heated wire (or film) and the intake air at a constant level. The amount of heating current required to maintain the temperature thus provides an index for the mass air flow. This concept automatically compensates for variations in air density, as this is one of the factors that determines the amount of warmth that the surrounding air absorbs from the heated element.

Hot-wire air-mass meter

The heated element on the hot-wire air-mass meter is a platinum wire only 70 μm in diameter. A temperature sensor is integrated within the hot-wire air-mass meter to provide compensation data for intake-air temperature. The main components in the control circuit are a bridge circuit and an amplifier. The heated wire and the intake-air temperature sensor both act as temperature-sensitive resistors within the bridge (Figures 2 through 4). The heating current generates a voltage signal, proportional to the mass air flow, at a precision resistor. This is the signal transmitted to the ECU.

Fig. 2: Components of the heated-wire air-mass meter
1 Temperature sensor, 2 Sensor ring with hot wire, 3 Precision resistor.
Q_M Mass flow.

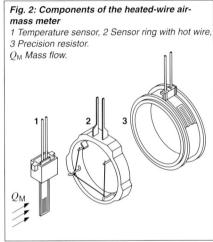

Fig. 3: Bridge circuit in heated-wire air-mass meter
R_H Hot wire, R_K Compensation resistor, R_M Measurement resistor, R_1, R_2 Adjustable resistors. U_M Measurement voltage, Q_M Incoming air mass per unit of time.

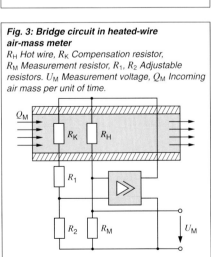

Fig. 4: Hot-wire air-mass meter
1 Hybrid circuit
2 Cover
3 Metal insert
4 Inner tube with hot wire
5 Housing
6 Screen
7 Retainer

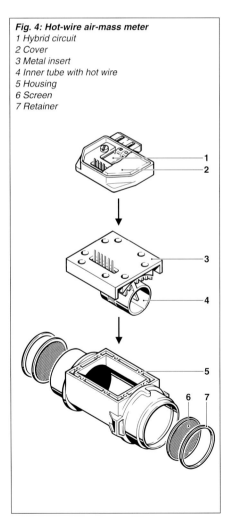

To prevent the "drift" that could result from contaminant deposits on the platinum wire, the wire is heated up to "burn-off" temperature for one second after the engine is switched off. This process vaporizes and/or splits off the deposits and cleans the wire.

Hot-film air-mass meter

The heated element on the hot-film air-mass meter is a platinum film resistor (heater). It is located on a ceramic plate together with the other elements in the bridge circuit. The temperature of the heater is monitored by a temperature-sensitive resistor (flow sensor) also included in the bridge.

The separation of heater and flow sensor facilitates design of the control circuitry. Saw cuts are employed to ensure thermal decoupling between the heating element and the intake-air temperature sensor.

The complete control circuitry is located on a single layer. The voltage at the heater provides the index for the mass air flow. The hot-film air-mass meter's electronic circuitry then converts the voltage to a level suitable for processing in the ECU (Figures 5 through 7).

This device does not need a burn-off process to maintain its measuring precision over an extended period. In recognition of the fact that most deposits collect on the sensor element's leading edge, the essential thermal-transfer elements are located downstream on the ceramic layer. The sensor element is also designed to ensure that deposits will not influence the flow pattern around the sensor.

Intake-manifold pressure sensor

A pneumatic passage connects the intake-manifold to this pressure sensor, which monitors the absolute pressure [kPa] within the intake manifold.

The unit can be constructed as an installation component for the ECU or as a remote sensor for mounting on or near the intake manifold. A hose connects the installation unit to the manifold.

Fig. 5: Hot-film air-mass meter
a) Housing, b) Hot-film sensor
(installed in center of housing).
1 Heat sink, 2 Intermediate component,
3 Power chip, 4 Hybrid circuit, 5 Sensor element.

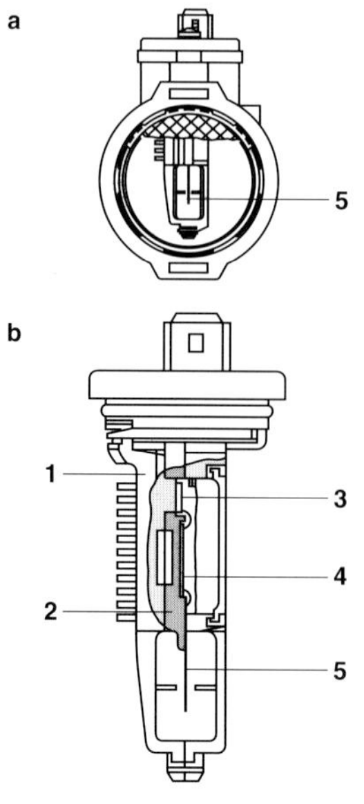

Fig. 6: Hot-film sensor element
1 Ceramic substrate, 2 Sawcut.
R_K Temperature-compensation sensor.
R_1 Bridge resistor, R_H Heater resistor,
R_S Sensor resistor.

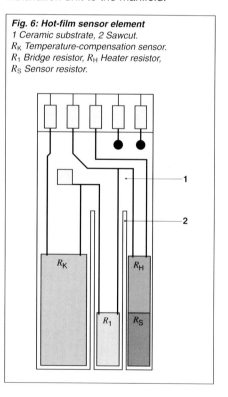

The sensor is divided into a pressure cell with two sensor elements and a chamber for the evaluation circuitry. Sensor elements and evaluation circuitry are located on a single ceramic layer (Figure 8).

The sensor element consists of a bell-shaped thick-layer diaphragm enclosing a reference volume with a specific internal pressure. The diaphragm's deflection is determined by the pressure in the intake manifold.

A series of piezo-resistive resistor elements is arranged on the diagram; the conductivity of these elements varies in response to changes in mechanical tension. These resistors are incorporated in a bridge circuit in such a manner that any deflection at the diaphragm will lead to a change in the bridge balance. The bridge voltage thus provides an indication of intake-manifold pressure (Figure 9).

The evaluation circuit amplifies the bridge voltage, compensates for temperature effects and linearizes the pressure response curve. The output signal from the evaluation circuit is transmitted to the ECU.

Throttle-valve sensor

This sensor provides a secondary load signal based on the angle of the throttle valve. The applications for this secondary load signal include providing information for dynamic functions, load-range recognition (idle, full or part-throttle), and serving as a backup signal in the event of main-sensor failure.

The throttle-valve sensor is attached to the throttle-valve assembly where it shares a common shaft with the throttle valve. A potentiometer evaluates the throttle valve's deflection angle and transmits a voltage ratio to the ECU via a resistance circuit (Figures 10 and 11).

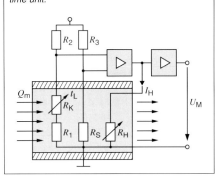

Fig. 7: Circuit of hot-film air-mass meter
R_K Temperature-compensation sensor, R_H Heater resistor, R_1, R_2, R_3 Bridge resistors, U_M Measurement voltage, I_H Heater current, t_L Air temperature, Q_M incoming air mass per time unit.

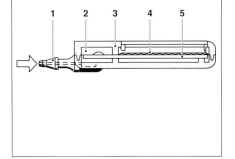

Fig. 8: Pressure sensor (for installation in ECU)
1 Pressure connection, 2 Pressure cell with sensor elements, 3 Sealing edge, 4 Evaluation circuitry, 5 Thick-film hybrid.

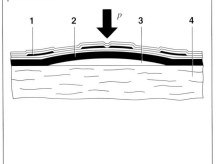

Fig. 9: Thick-film diaphragm in pressure sensor
1 Piezoresistive resistors, 2 Base diaphragm, 3 Reference pressure chamber, 4 Ceramic substrate.
p Pressure.

More exacting precision is required when the throttle-valve sensor is used as the primary load sensor. This higher level of precision is obtained by using a throttle-valve sensor incorporating two potentiometers (two angle ranges) as well as improved suspension.

The control unit determines the mass of the intake air by monitoring throttle-valve angle and engine speed. Data from temperature sensors allows the unit to respond to variations in the air mass due to temperature change.

Fig. 10: Throttle-valve sensor
1 Throttle-valve shaft, 2 Resistor track 1, 3 Resistor track 2, 4 Wiper arm with wiper, 5 Electrical connection.

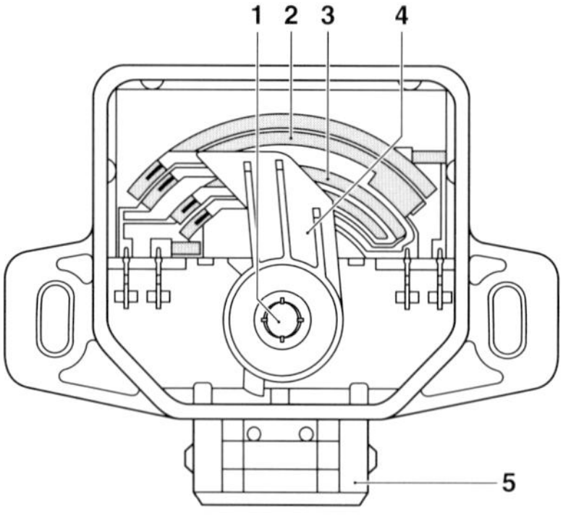

Fig. 11: Throttle-valve sensor circuitry
U_M Measurement voltage, R_1, R_2 Resistor tracks 1 and 2, R_3, R_4, R_5 adjustment resistors. 1 Throttle valve.

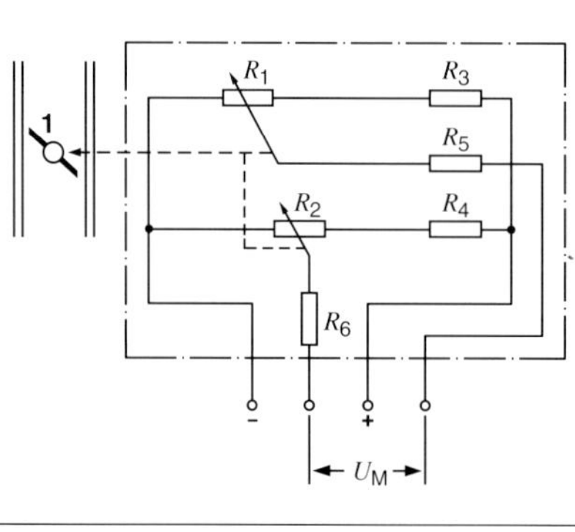

Engine speed, crankshaft and camshaft positions

Engine speed and crankshaft position

The degree of piston travel within the cylinder is employed as a measured variable for determining the firing point. The pistons in all cylinders are connected to the crankshaft via the connecting rods. A sensor at the crankshaft thus provides the information on the locations of the pistons in the cylinders.

The speed at which the crankshaft changes its position is the engine speed, defined in the number of crankshaft revolutions per minute (rpm). This also represents another important Motronic input variable for the Motronic unit, and is calculated from the crankshaft position signal. Although the signal from the crank-shaft sensor basically indicates crank-shaft position, which is then converted to an engine-speed signal in the ECU, the device has come to be known as the engine-speed, or rpm sensor.

Generating the crankshaft position signal

Installed on the crankshaft is a ferromagnetic ring gear with a theoretical capacity of 60 teeth, whereby two teeth are missing on the gear in question (tooth gap). An inductive speed sensor registers the 58-tooth sequence. This sensor consists of a permanent magnet and a soft-iron core with a copper winding (Figure 12).

The magnetic flux field at the sensor responds as the teeth on the sensor gear pass by, generating AC voltage (Figure 13). The amplitude of this AC voltage decreases as the interval between sensor and sensor gear increases, and rises in response to higher engine speeds. Sufficient amplitude is already available at a minimal engine speed (20 min^{-1}). Pole and tooth geometry must be matched. The evaluation circuit in the ECU converts the sinus voltage with its highly varying amplitudes into square-wave voltage with a constant amplitude.

Calculating the crankshaft position

The flanks of the square-wave voltage are transmitted to the computer via an interrupt input. A gap in the tooth pattern is registered at those points where the flank interval is twice as large as in the previous and subsequent periods. The tooth gap corresponds to a specific crankshaft position for cylinder no. 1. The computer synchronizes the crankshaft position according to this point in time. It then counts 3 degrees further for every subsequent positive or negative tooth flank. The ignition signals, however, must be transmitted in smaller stages. The duration between two tooth flanks is thus further divided by four. The time unit thus derived can be multiplied by two, three or four and added to a tooth flank for the ignition advance angle (allowing steps of 0.75 degrees).

Calculating segment duration and engine speed from the engine-speed sensor signal

The relatonship between the cylinders of the four-stroke engine is such that two crankshaft rotations (720 degrees) elapse between the start of each new cycle at cylinder no. 1.

This interval is the mean ignition interval, and is referred to as the segment time T_S. When the interval is distributed equally, the result is:

Fig. 12: Engine-speed sensor
1 Permanent magnet, 2 Housing, 3 Engine housing, 4 Soft-iron core, 5 Winding, 6 Ring gear with reference point.

Interval	Degrees	Teeth
2 cylinders	360	60
3 cylinders	240	40
4 cylinders	180	30
5 cylinders	144	24
6 cylinders	120	20
8 cylinders	90	15
12 cylinders	60	10

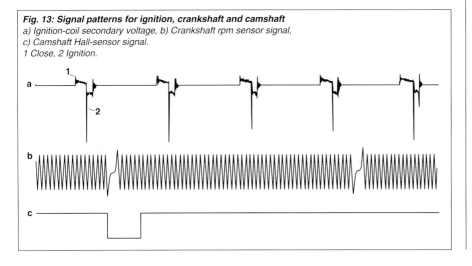

Fig. 13: Signal patterns for ignition, crankshaft and camshaft
a) Ignition-coil secondary voltage, b) Crankshaft rpm sensor signal, c) Camshaft Hall-sensor signal.
1 Close, 2 Ignition.

Ignition, injection and the engine speed derived from the segment time are recalculated for every new interval. The figure for rotational speed describes the mean crankshaft rpm within the segment time and is proportional to its reciprocal.

Camshaft position

The camshaft controls the engine's intake and exhaust valves while operating at half the rotating speed of the crankshaft. When a piston travels to top dead center, the camshaft uses the settings of the intake and exhaust valves to determine whether the cylinder is in the compression phase to be followed by ignition, or in the exhaust phase. This information cannot be derived from the crankshaft position.

If the ignition is equipped with a high-voltage distributor with a direct mechanical link to the camshaft, the rotor will point to the correct cylinder automatically: the ECU does not require supplementary information on the position of the camshaft. In contrast, Motronic systems featuring stationary voltage distribution and single-spark ignition coils require additional information, as the ECU must be able to decide which ignition coil and spark plug are due to be triggered. To do so, it must be informed as to the camshaft's position.

The position of the camshaft must also be monitored in those systems where separate injection timing is used for each individual cylinder, as is the case with sequential injection (SEFI).

Hall-sensor signal

Camshaft position is usually monitored with a Hall sensor. The monitoring device itself consists of a Hall element with a semiconductor wafer through which current flows. This element is controlled by a trigger wheel that turns together with the camshaft. It consists of a ferromagnetic material and generates voltage at right angles to the direction of the current as it passes the Hall element (Figure 13).

Calculating camshaft position

As the Hall voltage lies in the millivolt range, it is processed within the sensor before being transmitted to the ECU in the form of a switching signal. In the simplest case, the computer responds to trigger-wheel gaps by checking to see whether Hall voltage is present and whether or not cylinder no. 1 is on its power stroke.

Special trigger-wheel designs make it possible to use the camshaft signal as a backup for emergency operation in case of crankshaft (engine-speed) sensor failure. However, the resolution provided by the camshaft signal is too imprecise to allow it to be employed as a permanent replacement for the crankshaft speed sensor.

Mixture composition

Excess-air factor λ

The lambda oxygen sensor monitors the excess-air factor λ. Lambda defines the number for the mixture's A/F ratio. The catalytic converter functions best at $\lambda = 1$.

Lambda oxygen sensor

The Lambda oxygen sensor's outer electrode extends into the exhaust stream, while the inner electrode is exposed to the surrounding air (Figure 14).

The essential constituent of the oxygen sensor is a special-ceramic body featuring gas-permeable platinum electrodes on its surface. Sensor operation is based on the ceramic material's porosity, which allows oxygen in the air to diffuse (solid electrolyte). The ceramic material becomes conductive at higher temperatures. Voltage is generated at the electrodes when different oxygen levels are present on the respective sides. A stoichiometric air/fuel ratio of $\lambda = 1$ produces a characteristic jump (jump function) in the response curve (Figure 15).

The oxygen sensor's voltage and internal resistance are both sensitive to temperature. Reliable control operation is possible with exhaust-gas temperatures exceeding 350°C (unheated sensor), or 200°C (heated sensor).

Heated Lambda oxygen sensor

The design of the heated Lambda oxygen sensor is largely the same as that of the unheated version (Figure 16). A ceramic heater element warms the sensor's active ceramic layer from the inside, ensuring that its ceramic material remains hot enough for operation – even at low exhaust-gas temperatures. The heated sensor is protected by a tube with a restricted flow opening to prevent the sensor's ceramics from being cooled by low-temperature exhaust gases.

The heated sensor reduces the waiting period between engine start and effective closed-loop control. It also provides reliable control with lower-temperature exhaust gases (e.g., at idle). Heated sensors offer shorter reaction times for reduced closed-loop response intervals. This type of sensor also offers greater latitude in selecting the installation position.

Fig. 14: Lambda oxygen sensor location in exhaust pipe
1 Special ceramic coat, 2 Electrodes, 3 Contact, 4 Housing contact, 5 Exhaust pipe, 6 Ceramic shield (porous), 7 Exhaust gas, 8 Air.

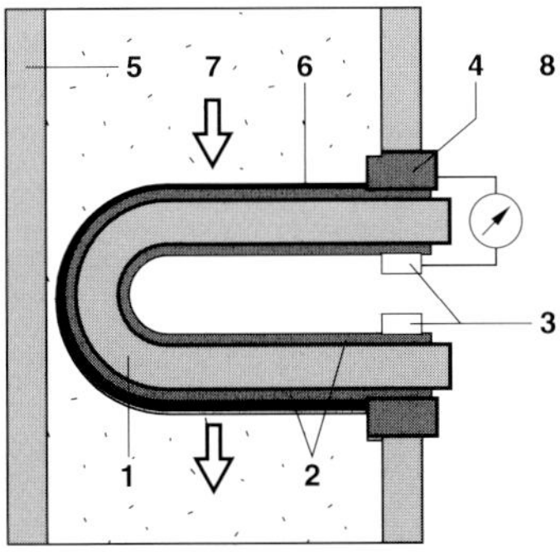

Fig. 15: Lambda oxygen sensor voltage curve at 600 °C operating temperature
a) Rich mixture (air deficiency)
b) Lean mixture (excess air)

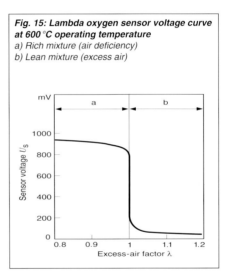

Fig. 16: Heated Lambda oxygen sensor
1 Probe housing, 2 Ceramic shield tube, 3 Electrical connections, 4 Shield tube with slits, 5 Active ceramic sensor layer, 6 Contact, 7 Shield, 8 Heating element, 9 Clamp connections for heater element.

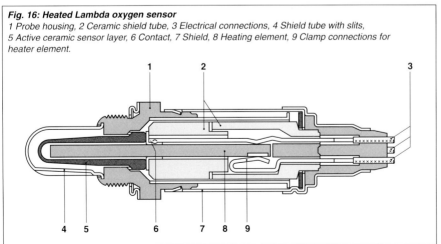

227

Combustion knock

Under certain conditions combustion in the spark-ignition engine can degenerate into an abnormal process characterized by a typical "knocking" or "pinging" sound. This phenomenon is an undesirable combustion process known as "knocking", which limits the engine's output and specific efficiency levels. It occurs when fresh mixture preignites in spontaneous combustion before being reached by the expanding flame front.

Normally initiated combustion and the piston's compressive force lead to the pressure and temperature peaks that produce self-ignition in the end gas (remaining unburned mixture). Flame velocities in excess of 2000 m/s can occur, as compared to speeds of roughly 30 m/s for normal combustion. This abrupt combustion process produces substantial local pressure increases in the end gas. The resulting pressure wave propagates until stopped by impact with the cylinder walls representing the outer extremity of the combustion chamber.

Chronic preignition is accompanied by pressure waves and increased thermal stresses at the cylinder-head gasket, piston and in the vicinity of the valves. All of these factors can lead to mechanical damage.

Fig. 17: Knock sensor
*1 Seismic mass, 2 Cast mass,
3 Piezoelectric ceramic, 4 Contacts,
5 Electrical connection.*

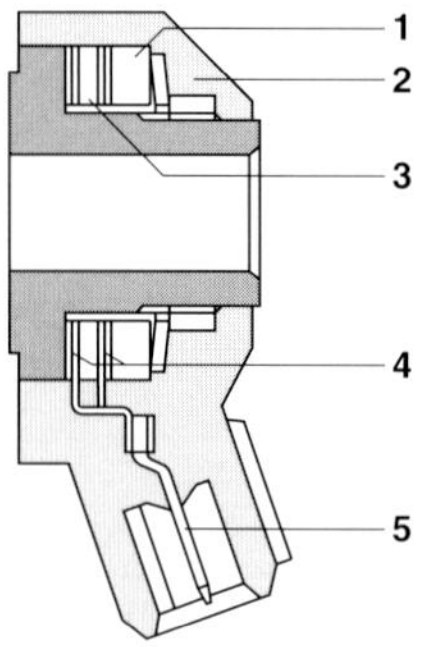

Fig. 19: "Listening" positions for the knock sensors
1 The knock sensor is located between the second and third cylinders. 2 If two knock sensors are fitted, these are located between the first and second, and the third and fourth cylinders.

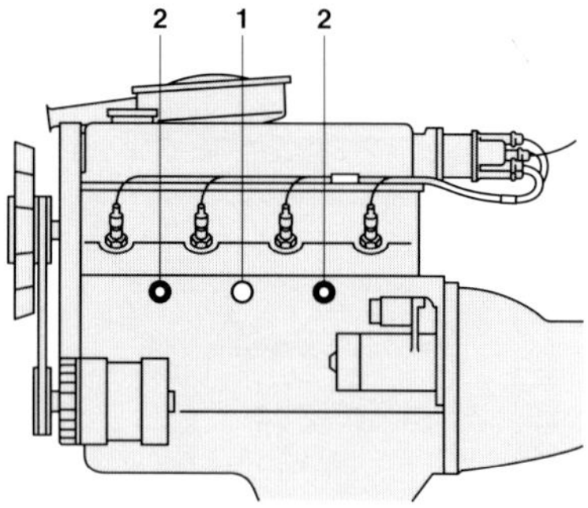

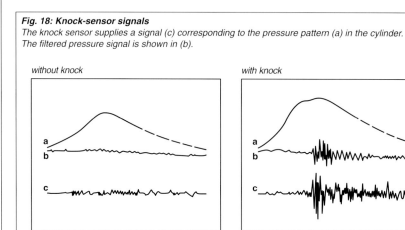

Fig. 18: Knock-sensor signals
The knock sensor supplies a signal (c) corresponding to the pressure pattern (a) in the cylinder. The filtered pressure signal is shown in (b).

without knock

with knock

The characteristic vibration patterns generated by combustion knock can be monitored by knock sensors for conversion into electrical signals, which are then transmitted to the Motronic ECU (Figures 17 and 18). Both the number and positions of the knock sensors must be carefully selected. Reliable knock recognition must be guaranteed for all cylinders and under all engine operating conditions, with special emphasis on high loads and engine speeds. As a general rule, 4-cylinder engines are equipped with one, 5 and 6-cylinder engines with two, 8 and 12-cylinder engines with two or more knock sensors (Figure 19).

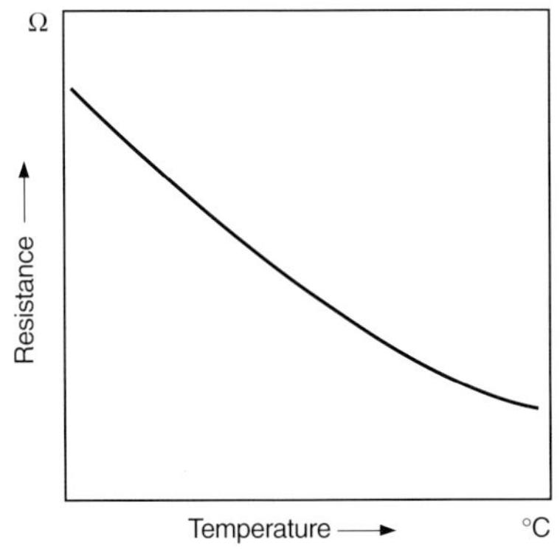

Engine and intake-air temperatures

The engine-temperature sensor incorporates a temperature-sensitive resistor which extends into the coolant circuit whose temperature it monitors. A sensor in the intake tract registers the intake-air temperature in the same fashion (Figure 20).

The resistor is of the negative temperature coefficient type (NTC, see Figure 21) and forms part of a voltage-divider circuit operating with a 5 V supply. An analog-digital converter monitors the resistor's voltage drop, which provides an index of the temperature. Compensation for the non-linear relationship between voltage and temperature is provided by a table stored in the computer's memory; the table matches each voltage reading with a corresponding temperature.

Battery voltage

The electromagnetic injector's opening and closing times are affected by the battery's voltage. Should voltage fluctuations occur in the vehicle's electrical system, the ECU will prevent response delays by adjusting the duration of the injection process. At low battery voltages the ignition circuit's dwell times must be extended to provide the coil with the opportunity to accumulate sufficient ignition energy.

Fig. 20: Engine-temperature sensor
1 Electrical connection, 2 Housing,
3 NTC resistor.

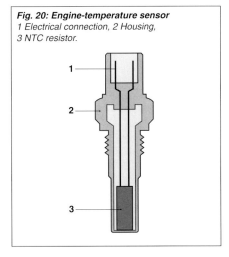

Fig. 21: Temperature-sensor response curve (NTC)

Processing operating data

Processing load signals

Monitored variables
The ECU uses the signals for load and engine speed to calculate a load signal corresponding to the air mass inducted into the engine during each stroke. This load signal serves as the basis for calculations of injection duration and for addressing the programmed response curves for ignition advance angle (Figure 1).

Monitoring air mass
Hot-wire or hot-film air-mass meters measure the air mass directly, producing a signal that is suitable for use as a para-meter in load-signal calculations. When an air-flow meter is used, density correction is also required before air mass and load signal can be determined.

In special cases monitoring errors due to heavy pulsation in the intake manifold also receive compensation in the form of a pulsation correction.

Monitoring pressure
Pressure-monitoring systems (using a pressure sensor to determine load) differ from air-mass monitoring systems in that no direct formulas are available for defining the relationship between intake pressure and the air-mass intake. The ECU therefore calculates the load signal with the aid of corrections stored in a program map.

Subsequent compensation is provided for changes in temperature and residual gas relative to the initial state.

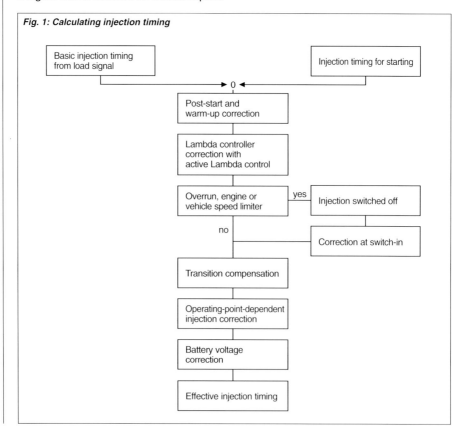

Fig. 1: Calculating injection timing

Basic injection timing from load signal → 0 ← Injection timing for starting

Post-start and warm-up correction

Lambda controller correction with active Lambda control

Overrun, engine or vehicle speed limiter — yes → Injection switched off

no

Correction at switch-in

Transition compensation

Operating-point-dependent injection correction

Battery voltage correction

Effective injection timing

Measuring throttle-valve angle

When a throttle-valve sensor is used, the ECU determines the load signal with reference to engine speed and throttle-valve angle. Compensation for variations in air density are based on readings for temperature and ambient pressure.

Calculating injection timing

Base injection timing

The base injection timing is calculated directly from the load signal and from the injector constants, and defines the relationship between the duration of the acti-vation signal and the flow quantity at the injector. This constant thus varies according to injector design. When the injection duration is multiplied by the injector constant the result will be a fuel mass corresponding to a particular air mass for each stroke.

The base setting is selected for an excess-air factor of $\lambda = 1$.

This remains valid for as long as the pressure differential between fuel and intake manifold stays constant. When it varies, a λ correction map compensates for this influence on injection times. Meanwhile, a battery-voltage corrector compensates for the effects that fluctuations in battery voltage have on the injectors' opening and closing times.

Effective injection time

The effective injection time results when the correction factors are included in the calculations. The correction factors are determined in corresponding special functions and provide adjustment data for varying engine operating ranges and conditions. The correction factors are used both individually and in combinations according to applicable parameters.

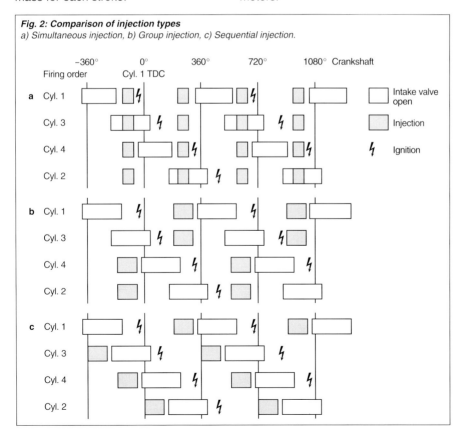

Fig. 2: Comparison of injection types
a) Simultaneous injection, b) Group injection, c) Sequential injection.

The process for calculating the injection time is illustrated in Figure 1. The individual operating ranges and conditions will be explained in more detail in the following chapters.

Once cylinder filling drops below a certain level, the mixture will cease to ignite. Restricting the injection time thus prevents the formation of unburned hydrocarbons in the exhaust gas.

For starting, the injection time is calculated separately using criteria independent of the calculated load signal.

Injection mode

In addition to the injection time, the injection mode is yet another important parameter for fuel economy and exhaust emissions. The range of options depends upon the type of injection system (Figure 2):
– simultaneous injection,
– group injection, or
– sequential injection.

Simultaneous injection

With simultaneous injection, the injection process is triggered twice per cycle at a specific point in time at all injectors, that is, once for each camshaft revolution, or once for every two crankshaft revolutions. The injection mode is static.

Group injection

Group injection combines the injectors in two groups, with each group being triggered once per cycle. The time interval between the two triggering points is equal to one crankshaft rotation period. This arrangement makes it possible to use the engine operating point as the essential criterion in selecting the injection mode while also preventing undesirable spray through the open intake valves throughout a wide range in the program map.

Sequential injection

This type of injection provides the highest degree of design latitude. Here, the injection processes from the individual injectors take place independently of each other at the same point in the cycle

referred to the respective cylinder. There are no restrictions on injection timing, which can be freely adapted to correspond with the optimization criteria.

Comparison

Group and sequential injection require a wider injector variation range (range extending from the minimum quantity at idle to the maximum under full throttle) than simultaneous injection.

Controlling dwell angle

The dwell angle varies the ignition coil's current-flow period according to engine speed and battery voltage. The dwell angle is selected to ensure availability of the required primary current at the end of the current flow time throughout the widest possible range of operating conditions.

The dwell angle is based on the ignition coil's charge time, which, in turn, depends upon battery voltage (Figure 3). A supplementary dynamic reserve makes it possible to supply the required current even during sudden shifts to high engine speeds.

The charge time is restricted in the upper rpm range to maintain an adequate arcing time at the spark plug.

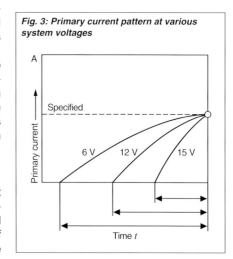

Fig. 3: Primary current pattern at various system voltages

Controlling ignition advance angle

A program map containing the basic ignition timing for various engine loads and speeds is stored in the memory of the Motronic ECU. This ignition advance angle is optimized for minimal fuel consumption and exhaust emissions.

Data for engine and intake-air temperature (monitored via sensors) provide the basis for corrections to compensate for temperature variations. The unit can supply additional corrections and/or revert to other program maps to adapt to all operating conditions. Thus the mutual effects of torque, emissions, fuel consumption, preignition tendency and drivability can all be taken into account. Special ignition-angle correction factors are active during operation with secondary air injection or exhaust-gas recirculation (EGR) as well as in dynamic vehicle operation (e.g., when accelerating).

The various operating ranges (idle, part throttle, full throttle, start and warm-up) continue to be taken into account. Figure 4 shows a flow chart describing ignition-angle processing.

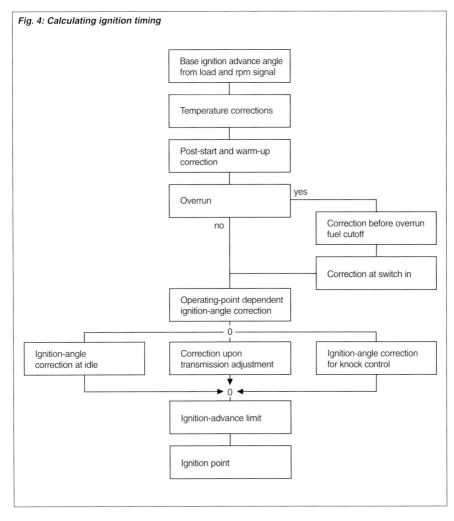

Fig. 4: Calculating ignition timing

- Base ignition advance angle from load and rpm signal
- Temperature corrections
- Post-start and warm-up correction
- Overrun — yes → Correction before overrun fuel cutoff → Correction at switch in
- no
- Operating-point dependent ignition-angle correction
- 0
- Ignition-angle correction at idle | Correction upon transmission adjustment | Ignition-angle correction for knock control
- 0
- Ignition-advance limit
- Ignition point

Operating conditions

Start

Special calculations are employed to determine the injection quantity for the duration of the starting procedure.

In addition, special injection timing is used for the initial injection pulses. The injection quantity is augmented in accordance with engine temperature to promote formation of a fuel film on the walls of the intake manifold, thereby compensating for the engine's higher fuel requirements as it runs up to speed. As soon as the engine starts to turn over, the quantity of supplementary fuel is reduced and then cancelled once the engine starts to run.

Ignition advance angle is also specially adjusted for starting. The adjustment occurs with reference to engine temperature and engine speed.

Post-start phase

The post-start phase is characterized by further reductions in the supplementary injection quantity. The reductions are based on engine temperature and the elapsed time since the end of the starting process. The ignition advance angle is also adjusted to correspond to the revised fuel quantities and the different operating conditions. The post-start phase terminates with a smooth transition to the warm-up phase.

Warm-up phase

Different strategies can be employed for the warm-up phase, depending upon engine and emissions-control design. The decisive criteria are drivability, emissions and improved fuel economy. A lean warm-up combined with retarded ignition timing raises the temperature of the exhaust gas. Another way to obtain high exhaust temperatures is to employ a rich warm-up mixture together with secondary air injection. Here air is injected into the exhaust system downstream from the exhaust valves for a brief period after the engine starts. A secondary air pump can provide this additional air. When the temperature is high enough, this excess air supports oxidation of HC and CO in the exhaust system while simultaneously generating the desired high exhaust temperatures (Figure 1).

Both of these measures help the catalytic converter to begin effective operation sooner.

The effects of the adjustments to ignition angle and injection timing can be supplemented by higher idle speeds. These are provided by a specially designed air injection unit, and also result in shorter warm-up times at the catalytic converter.

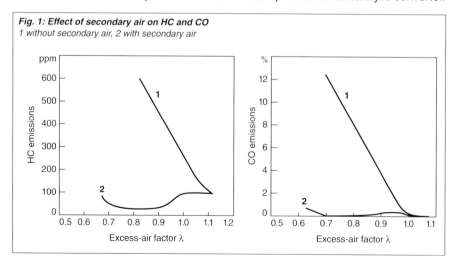

Fig. 1: Effect of secondary air on HC and CO
1 without secondary air, 2 with secondary air

Once the converter reaches operating temperature the injection is governed to $\lambda = 1$. This is accompanied by a corresponding adjustment in ignition angle.

Transition compensation

Acceleration/deceleration

A portion of the fuel sprayed into the intake manifold does not reach the cylinder in time for the next combustion process. Instead, it forms a condensation layer along the walls of the intake tract. The actual quantity of fuel stored in this film increases radically in response to higher loads and extended injection times.

A portion of the fuel injected when the throttle valve opens is used for this film. A corresponding amount of supplementary fuel must thus be injected to compensate and prevent the mixture from leaning out. Because the additional fuel retained in the wall film is released as the load factor drops, the injection time must be reduced by a corresponding amount during deceleration.

Figure 2 shows the resulting curve for injection times.

Overrun fuel cutoff/renewed fuel flow

When the throttle closes, the injection is switched off in the interests of reduced fuel consumption and lower exhaust emissions.

The injection stop is preceded by a reduction in the ignition advance to attenuate torque jump during the transition to trailing throttle.

The injection starts again once a specific reactivation speed – located above idle speed – is reached. Various activation speeds are stored in the ECU. These vary according to different parameters such as engine temperature and rpm dynamics, and are calculated to prevent excessive drops in engine speed, regardless of operating conditions.

When the injection resumes, it sprays in supplementary fuel to rebuild the fuel wall layer. The ignition advance angle is also adjusted to provide a smooth torque increase.

Closed-loop idle-speed control

Idle

The fuel consumption at idle is largely determined by the engine's efficiency and by the idle speed. A substantial proportion of the fuel consumed by vehicles in heavy urban traffic is actually burned at idle. The idle speed should thus be as low as possible. At the same time, the idle should never fall so far that rough running or stalling occur, even under additional loads such as electrical equipment, air conditioner, automatic transmission in gear, power steering, etc.

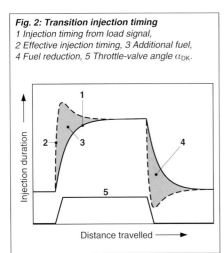

Fig. 2: Transition injection timing
1 Injection timing from load signal,
2 Effective injection timing, 3 Additional fuel,
4 Fuel reduction, 5 Throttle-valve angle α_{DK}.

Idle-speed control

The idle-speed control must maintain a balance between torque generation and engine load in order to ensure a constant idle speed. The load on the idling engine is a combination of numerous elements, including internal friction within the engine's crankshaft and valvetrain assemblies as well as the ancillary drives (for instance, for the water pump). The idle-speed control compensates for this internal friction, which, in turn, changes over the life of the engine. These loads are also extremely sensitive to temperature variations.

In addition to these internal sources of friction, there are also external factors such as the load from the air conditioner that was mentioned above. The load from these external factors is subject to substantial variations as ancillary devices are switched on and off. Modern engines with small flywheel weights and large-volume intake manifolds are especially sensitive to these load fluctuations.

Input variables

In addition to the signal from the engine-speed sensor, the idle-speed control circuit also requires information on throttle-valve angle in order to recognize the idle state (foot off accelerator pedal). Engine temperature is also monitored to allow advance compensation for the effects of temperature. An air mass is specified with reference to engine temperature and the target idle-speed; this idle speed is then corrected in closed-loop operation. Where present, the input signals from the air conditioner and automatic transmission also facilitate the correction process and provide supplementary support for closed-loop idle-speed control.

Fig. 3: Bypass actuator with hose connections

Fig. 4: Manifold-mounted bypass actuator

Actuator adjustments

Three options are available for adjusting the idle speed by means of adjustments at final-control elements:

Air control

The proven control procedure is to regulate air flow by means of a bypass to the throttle valve, or to adjust the throttle valve itself using either a variable throttle stop or a direct actuator unit of the kind found in "Electronic Throttle Control."

On bypass actuators designed for hose connection, the bypass to the throttle valve consists of air hoses and an actuator (Figure 3). More modern are bypass actuators for direct installation; this type of bypass-air regulation device is flange-mounted directly on the throttle-valve assembly.

Figure 4: Example of a single-winding rotary actuator for direct installation.

One disadvantage associated with bypass actuators is that they add to the throttle-valve's own leakage air. Once the engine is well run-in, the combined air flowing through the throttle valve and the bypass actuator could well exceed the air quantity that the engine needs at idle. At this point effective idle regulation is no longer possible. This liability disappears when adjustments to the throttle valve itself are employed to regulate the air flow. The idle throttle device uses an electric motor and gear drive to vary the position of the throttle valve's idle stop (Figure 5). Delays in idle repsonse are encountered when adjustments to air flow are used in systems with large-volume intake manifolds.

Adjustments to ignition advance angle

The second (and faster reacting) option is to adjust the ignition advance angle. Systems with an rpm-sensitive ignition advance angle react to sinking engine speeds by increasing the ignition advance to provide a boost in torque.

Mixture composition

Strict emissions-control regulations and a limited range of practical possibilities relegate the mixture-adjustment option to virtual insignificance.

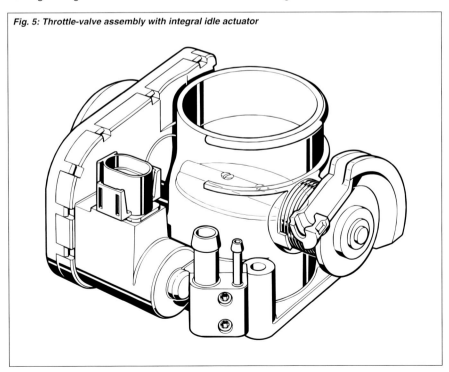

Fig. 5: Throttle-valve assembly with integral idle actuator

Lambda closed-loop control

Post-treatment of exhaust gases in a three-way catalytic converter is an effective means for reducing concentrations of harmful exhaust emissions. The converter transforms the three pollutants CO, HC and NO_X into H_2O, CO_2 and N_2.

Control range

The range available for simultaneous conversion of all three of the above components is extremely narrow: the "lambda window" ($\lambda = 0.99\ldots1$), which means that closed-loop Lambda control is essential.

A Lambda oxygen sensor is installed in the exhaust system upstream from the catalytic converter, where it monitors the exhaust-gas oxygen content.

Lean mixtures ($\lambda > 1$) produce a sensor voltage of approx. 100 mV, while a rich mixture ($\lambda < 1$) generates approx. 800 mV. At $\lambda = 1$ the sensor voltage jumps abruptly from one level to the other (Figure 6).

The ECU uses the signal from the air-mass meter and the monitored engine speed to generate an injection signal. At the same time, it also produces a supplementary Lambda-control factor from the Lambda-sensor signal for use in correcting the injection time.

Operation

The Lambda oxygen sensor must be operational before the Lambda closed-loop control circuit can function. An auxiliary evaluation circuit monitors this factor on a continuing basis. A cold oxygen sensor or damaged circuitry (short or open circuits) will generate implausible voltage signals which are rejected by the ECU. The heated Lambda sensors used in most systems are ready for operation after only 30 seconds.

Cold engines require a richer mixture ($\lambda < 1$) to idle smoothly. For this reason the Lambda closed-loop control circuit can only be activated once a set temperature threshold has been passed.

Once the lambda control is activated, the ECU uses a comparator to convert the signal from the sensor into a binary signal.

The controller reacts to the transmitted signal ($\lambda > 1$ = mixture too lean, or $\lambda < 1$ = mixture too rich), by modifying the control variables (with an initial jump followed by a ramp progression). The injection time is adjusted (lengthened or shortened), and the control factor reacts to the continuing data transfer by settling into a constant oscillation (Figure 7). The duration of the oscillation periods is determined by the flow times of the gas, while the "ramp climb" maintains largely constant amplitudes within the load

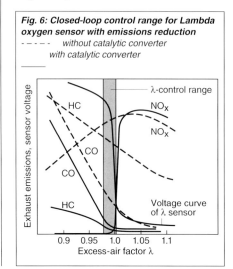

Fig. 6: Closed-loop control range for Lambda oxygen sensor with emissions reduction
----- without catalytic converter
⎯⎯ with catalytic converter

λ-control range
HC
NO_X
NO_X
CO
CO
HC
Voltage curve of λ sensor

Exhaust emissions, sensor voltage

0.9 0.95 1.0 1.05 1.1
Excess-air factor λ

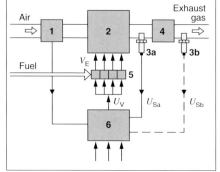

Fig. 7: Diagram of Lambda closed-loop control circuit
1 Air-mass meter, 2 Engine, 3a Lambda oxygen sensor 1, 3b Lambda oxygen sensor 2 (as required), 4 Catalytic converter, 5 Injectors, 6 ECU. U_S Oxygen-sensor voltage, U_v Injector control voltage, V_E Injection quantity

Air
Exhaust gas
Fuel
V_E
U_V U_{Sa} U_{Sb}
3a 3b

speed range despite variations in the travel time of the gas.

Lambda shift

The optimum conversion range and the voltage jump at the oxygen sensor do not coincide precisely. An asymmetrical control oscillation pattern can be used to shift the mixture into the optimal range ($\lambda = 1$). The asymmetry is obtained either by delaying the switch in the control factor after the voltage jump (from lean to rich) at the oxygen sensor or by providing an asymmetrical jump. This is the case when the voltage jump at the oxygen sensor during the transition from lean to rich is different from that produced at the change from rich to lean.

Adapting the pilot settings to the Lambda closed-loop control

Lambda closed-loop control corrects the subsequent injection process on the basis of the previous measurement at the oxygen sensor, whereby an unavoidable time lag results from the gas travel times. For this reason, the approach to a new operating point is accompanied by deviations from $\lambda = 1$ due to incorrect pilot control, a condition alleviated once the closed-loop control picks up the new cycle. Thus a special pilot control mechanism is needed to maintain compliance with emissions limits. The pilot-control is defined during adaptation to the engine and the Lambda response curve is stored in the ROM. However, revisions may become necessary due to the drift that can occur during the life of the vehicle. Among the drift factors are variations in the density and quality of the fuel. When the Lambda controller consistently repeats the same corrections in a certain load and engine-speed range, the pilot-control adaption mechanism recognizes this state. It corrects the pilot control for this range and records the correction in a RAM memory chip (with an uninterrupted current supply). The corrected pilot control is thus ready to respond immediately at the next start, assuming duty until the Lambda closed-loop control becomes operative.

Power interruptions in the current to the permanent memory are also recognized; the adaptation process then commences again with neutral default values providing the initial basis for operation.

Dual-sensor Lambda closed-loop control

Installing the Lambda oxygen sensor downstream of the catalytic converter provides better protection against contamination from the exhaust gas (here, "downstream" = on the tailpipe side). This type of backup sensor can provide a second control signal to augment the one from the main sensor upstream of the converter (here, "upstream" = on the engine side). The second signal is superimposed on the first to provide stable mixture composition over an extended period (Figure 7).

The superimposed control modifies the asymmetry in the constant oscillation pattern that is associated with control concepts based on the oxygen sensor mounted upstream from the converter; this compensates for the lambda shift. A Lambda closed-loop control strategy based solely on the downstream-mounted oxygen sensor would feature excessive response delays due to the gas travel times.

Evaporative-emissions control systems

Origins of fuel vapors
The fuel in the fuel tank is heated by:
- heat radiation from outside sources, and
- the excess fuel from the system return line which was heated during its passage through the engine compartment.

The result is the HC emissions that are usually emitted from the fuel tank in the form of vapor.

Limiting HC emissions
Evaporative emissions are subject to legal limits.
Evaporative-emissions control systems restrict these emissions. These systems are equipped with an activated charcoal filter (the so-called carbon canister) located at the end of the fuel tank's vent line. The activated charcoal in the canister binds the fuel vapors and allows only air to escape into the atmosphere, as well as serving as a pressure-release

device. In order to ensure that the charcoal can continually regenerate, an additional line leads from the carbon canister to the intake manifold. Vacuum is produced in this line when the engine runs, causing a stream of atmospheric air to flow through the charcoal on its way to the manifold. The fuel vapors stored in the activated charcoal are entrained by the air stream and conducted to the engine for combustion. A so-called canister-purge valve in the line to the intake manifold meters the flow of this regeneration or "cleansing" air (Figure 8).

Regeneration flow
The regeneration flow is an air-fuel mixture of necessarily indeterminate composition, since fresh air as well as air containing substantial concentrations of gasoline vapor can come from the carbon canister. The regeneration flow thus represents a major interference factor for the Lambda control system. A regeneration flow representing 1 % of the intake air and consisting solely of fresh air will

Fig. 8: Evaporative-emissions control system
1 Line from fuel tank to carbon canister, 2 Carbon canister, 3 Fresh air, 4 Canister-purge valve, 5 Line to intake manifold, 6 Throttle valve. Δp Difference between manifold pressure p_s and atmospheric pressure p_u.

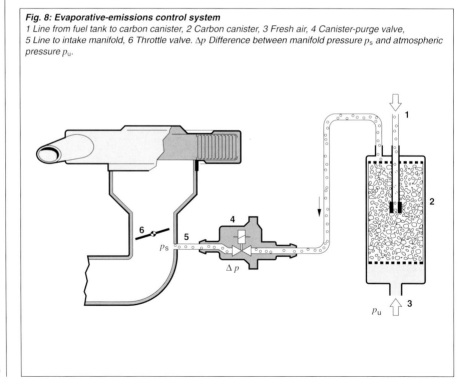

lean out the intake mixture by 1 %. A flow with a substantial gasoline component can enrichen the mixture by something in the order of 30 %, due to the effects on the A/F ratio λ of fuel vapor with a stoichiometric factor of 14.7. In addition, the specific density of fuel vapor is twice that of air.

Canister-purge valve

The canister-purge valve's control mechanism must ensure adequate air-purging of the carbon canister while holding Lambda deviations to a minimum (Figure 9).

ECU control operations

The canister-purge valve closes at regular intervals in order to allow the mixture adaptation process to function without being interfered with by tank ventilation. The canister-purge valve opens in a "ramp-shaped" pattern. The ECU "memorizes" the resulting Lambda control deviations as mixture corrections from the fuel-regeneration system. The

Fig. 9: Canister-purge valve
1 Hose connection, 2 Non-return valve,
3 Leaf spring, 4 Sealing element,
5 Solenoid armature, 6 Sealing seat,
7 Solenoid coil.

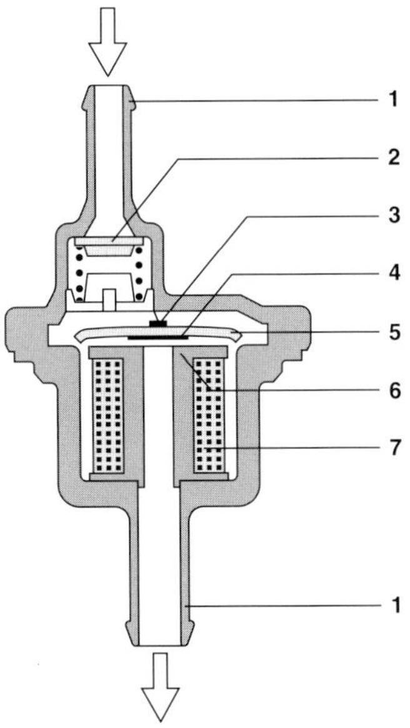

system is designed to operate with up to 40 % of the total fuel coming from the regeneration flow.

With the Lambda control system inactive, only small regeneration quantities are accepted, as there would be no control mechanism capable of compensating for the mixture deviations that would occur. The valve closes immediately in the overrun fuel cutoff mode to prevent unburned gasoline vapors from entering the catalytic converter.

Knock control

Electronic control of the ignition timing allows extremely precise adjustments of the ignition-advance angle based on engine rpm, temperature and load factor. Nevertheless, a substantial safety margin to the knock limit must be maintained. This margin is necessary in order to ensure that no cylinder will reach or go beyond its preignition limit, even when susceptibility is increased by risk factors such as engine tolerances, aging, environmental conditions and fuel quality. The resulting engine design, with its fixed safety margin, is characterized by lower compression and reduced ignition advance. The ultimate results are sacrifices in fuel economy and torque.

These liabilities can be avoided by using a knock sensor, whereby experience has shown that the compression ratio can be raised with accompanying improvements in both fuel economy and torque. With this device, it is no longer necessary to select the default ignition advance angle with the most knock-sensitive conditions in mind. Instead, a best-case scenario can be used (e.g., engine compression at lower tolerance limit, optimum fuel quality, cylinder with minimum preignition tendency). This makes it possible to operate each individual cylinder at the preignition limit for optimum efficiency in virtually all operating ranges for the life of the vehicle.

The essential prerequisite allowing this kind of ignition-angle program is reliable recognition of all preignition beyond a specified intensity, extending to every cylinder and throughout the engine's entire operating range. The knock sensors are solid-body sonic detectors installed at one or several suitable points on the engine. Here they detect the characteristic oscillation patterns that accompany knock and transform them into electrical signals before transmitting them to the Motronic ECU for processing. This ECU employs a special processing algorithm to detect incipient preignition in any of the combustion cycles in the respective cylinders. When this condition is recognized, the ignition advance angle is reduced by a programmed increment. When the knock danger subsides, the ignition for the affected cylinder is then slowly advanced back to the default setting. The knock recognition and knock-control algorithms are designed to prevent the kind of preignition that results in engine damage as well as audible knock (Fig. 10).

Adaptation

Real-world engine operation results in the individual cylinders having different knock limits, and therefore different ignition points. In order to adapt the default values to reflect the respective knock limits under varying operating conditions, individual ignition-retard increments are stored for each cylinder.

The data are stored in the non-volatile memory programs in the permanent RAM for engine speed and load factor. This allows the engine to be operated at optimum efficiency under all operating conditions without any danger of audible combustion knock, even during abrupt changes in load and rpm.

The engine can even be approved for operation with fuels having a low anti-knock quality. Generally, the engine is adjusted for use with premium-grade gasoline. Operation with regular-grade gasoline can also be approved.

Knock control on turbocharged engines

Systems combining boost pressure and knock control are especially effective on engines with exhaust-gas turbochargers.

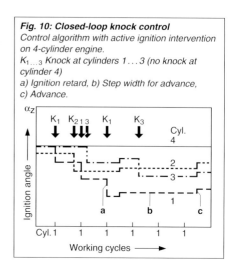

Fig. 10: Closed-loop knock control
Control algorithm with active ignition intervention on 4-cylinder engine.
$K_{1...3}$ Knock at cylinders 1...3 (no knock at cylinder 4)
a) Ignition retard, b) Step width for advance, c) Advance.

The initial response to ignition knock is to reduce the timing advance angle. Further action to reduce the pre-ignition tendency in the form of a reduction in boost pressure is initiated only once the ignition-retard limit – which varies according to the temperature of the exhaust gas – has been reached. This makes it possible to maintain exhaust-gas temperatures within acceptable limits while operating the turbocharged engine at the knock limit for optimum efficiency.

Boost-pressure control

Turbocharger boost

The exhaust-gas turbocharger has prevailed in the face of competition from other supercharging methods, such as pressure-wave and mechnical supercharging. Turbochargers make it possible to achieve high torque and output from small-displacement, high-efficiency powerplants. Because a turbocharged engine can be smaller than its naturally-aspirated counterpart producing the same amount of power, it boasts a higher power-to-weight ratio.

Automotive industry research has demonstrated that a small-displacement turbocharged engine with electronic boost control can provide improvements in fuel economy over a standard naturally aspirated engine equal to those achieved with a prechamber diesel. The main components of the exhaust-gas turbocharger are the compressor and the exhaust-gas impeller mounted on the other side of the same shaft. The exhaust-gas turbocharger transforms a portion of the energy in the exhaust gas into the rotation energy used to power the compressor. This, in turn, draws in fresh air and compresses it before blowing it through the intercooler, throttle valve, intake manifold and into the engine.

Actuators for exhaust-gas turbochargers

Passenger-car engines must be capable of generating substantial torque at low engine speeds. This is the reason why the turbocharger housing is dimensioned to operate most efficiently with lower mass exhaust-gas flow rates (for example, full load at $n = 2000$ min^{-1}). To prevent the turbocharger from overloading the engine at higher exhaust-gas mass flow rates, a bypass mechanism (waste gate) must be included in the housing to divert a portion of the flow around the turbine and into the downstream exhaust system. The bypass valve generally assumes the form of a flap in the turbine housing. Less common is a disk valve installed parallel to the turbine in a separate housing. Variable turbine geometry has still not been used for spark-ignition engines, but could also be combined with boost-pressure control (Figure 11).

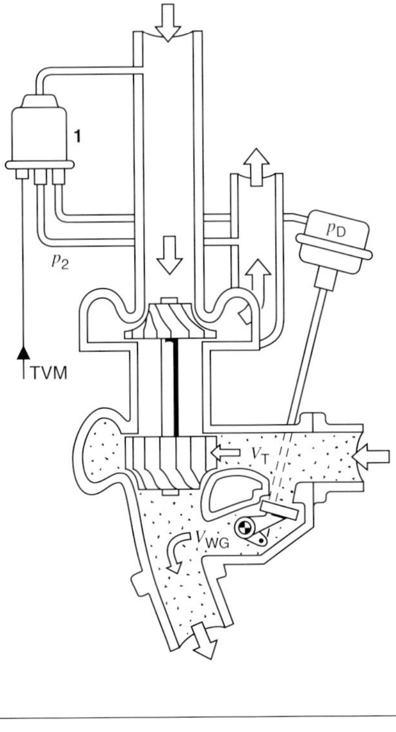

Boost-pressure (closed-loop) control

Pneumatic-mechanical closed-loop control systems use a turbocharger actuator directly exposed to the boost pressure at the turbocharger outlet. This layout provides only limited latitude for tailoring the progression of the torque curve through the engine speed range. There is only a full-load limit. It is not possible to provide control compensation for tolerances at full-load boost. At part load the closed bypass valve reduces efficiency. Acceleration from low engine speeds can be accompanied by delayed turbocharger reaction (turbo lag).

These disadvantages can be avoided with electronic boost-pressure control. The specific fuel consumption can be reduced in some part-throttle operating ranges. The system operates by opening the bypass valve, with the following results:
– residual work on the part of the engine and turbine output are reduced,
– pressure and temperature at the compressor outlet are lowered, and
– the pressure differential at the throttle valve is lowered.

Fig. 11: Actuator for electronic boost-pressure control

1	Pulse valve
p_2	Boost pressure
p_D	Pressure in diaphragm unit
TVM	Triggering signal from ECU to pulse valve
V_T	Flow volume through turbine
V_{WG}	Flow volume through waste gate

A linear relationship between torque curve and throttle-valve angle is also obtained, with improved sensitivity at the accelerator pedal. In order to provide the improvements listed above, the exhaust-gas turbocharger and the actuator must be perfectly adapted for use in the individual engine. The affected elements in the actuator are:
– the electropneumatic pulse valve,
– the effective diaphragm surface, stroke and spring in the diaphragm unit, and
– the diameter of the valve disk/flap at the waste gate.

Depending upon the load sensor, the setpoints stored in the Motronic ECU with electronic boost-pressure control are for pressure, air quantity or air mass. The setpoints for various engine speeds and throttle-valve angles are stored in a program map.

Actuators within the closed-loop control circuit adjust the monitored actual value to coincide with the value prescribed for the particular operating conditions. The calculated value is transmitted through the controller output in the form of a signal (pulse-width modulated) to the pulse valve. Within the actuator this signal modifies the control pressure and the stroke to change the effective opening at the bypass valve.

The temperature of the exhaust gases between the turbocharged engine and the turbine should never be allowed to exceed certain limits. This is why Bosch only uses boost-pressure control in conjunction with knock control. Knock control is the only means of allowing the engine to run with the maximum potential ignition advance throughout its service life. Running the engine at the optimal ignition advance angle for the specific operating conditions results in extremely low exhaust-gas temperatures.

Additional adjustments to boost pressure and/or mixture can be used to lower the temperature of the exhaust gas even further.

Limiting engine and vehicle speed

Extremely high engine speeds can lead to destruction of the engine (valve train, pistons). Engine-speed limiting prevents the maximum approved engine speed (redline) from being exceeded.
Motronic provides the option of restricting engine and vehicle speed by phasing out the injection.

When the maximum engine speed n_0 (or the maximum vehicle speed) is exceeded, the unit responds by suppressing the injection signals. This limits the speed of the engine (or vehicle).

The injection resumes normal operation once the speed falls below a narrow threshold.
This process is repeated at rapid intervals within an engine-speed tolerance range located around the prescribed maximum.

A reduction in operating response and smoothness calls the driver's attention to the engine speed and provides the motivation for an appropriate response.
Figure 12 illustrates the engine-speed curve's reaction to the engine-speed limitation.

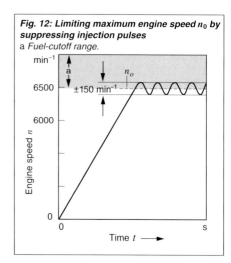

Fig. 12: Limiting maximum engine speed n_0 by suppressing injection pulses
a Fuel-cutoff range.

Exhaust-gas recirculation (EGR)

During valve overlap a certain amount of residual gas is returned from the combustion chamber to the intake manifold. This recirculated gas is then entrained along with the fresh air on the next intake stroke.

The actual amount of recirculated gas is determined by the valve overlap, and is thus a fixed variable relative to the various points on the operating curve.

The proportion of recirculated gas can be adjusted using either "external" exhaust-gas recirculation (EGR) with a Motronic-controlled exhaust-gas recirculation valve (Fig. 13), or with variable camshaft timing.

Up to a certain point, at least, larger amounts of recirculated gas can exercise a positive effect on energy conversion and thus on fuel consumption. An increase in recirculated gas also leads to lower combustion-chamber temperatures with corresponding reductions in the NO_x emission.

At the same time, once a certain point is passed a higher residual-gas component will lead to incomplete combustion. The results here are higher emissions of unburned hydrocarbons, increased fuel consumption and rough idling (Figure 14).

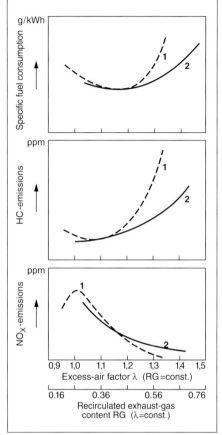

Fig. 14: Effect of residual exhaust-gas recirculation on fuel consumption and emissions
1 Excess-air factor λ (residual exhaust-gas component RG = constant),
2 Recirculated gas component RG (λ = constant).

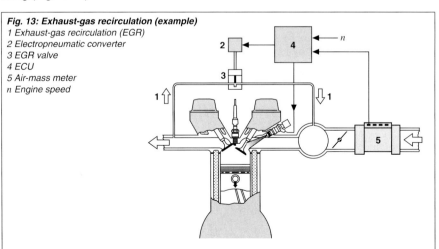

Fig. 13: Exhaust-gas recirculation (example)
1 Exhaust-gas recirculation (EGR)
2 Electropneumatic converter
3 EGR valve
4 ECU
5 Air-mass meter
n Engine speed

Camshaft timing

Camshaft timing can influence the spark-ignition engine in a variety of ways:
– higher torque and output, lower emissions and fuel consumption,
– control of the mixture composition, and,
– graduated or infinitely-variable intake and exhaust adjustment.

"Intake closes" timing plays a decisive role in determining the amount of cylinder filling for a given engine speed. When the intake valve closes early, maximum air will be inducted at low rpm, while longer intake durations shift the maximum toward higher engine speed ranges.

The phase in which the valves overlap (at "intake opens" and "exhaust closes") determines the amount of internal residual-gas recirculation.

Longer "valve open" durations due to advanced intake-valve timing will raise the proportion of recirculated gas, as they increase the mass of the gas returned to the intake manifold for reinduction. This reduces the mass of fresh air being drawn in at a given throttle-valve opening; at any given load point the throttle valve must open further to compensate. This "dethrottling" effect reduces the gas-exchange circuit to improve efficiency and lower fuel consumption.
The proportion of recirculated gas sinks when the intake cycle is shifted toward "retard." This provides improvements in fuel economy and operating smoothness.

Variable camshaft angle
Hydraulic or electric actuators turn the camshaft by increments corresponding to specified engine speeds or operating points (this system requires that at least one intake and one exhaust camshaft be located in the cylinder head). This varies the timing for "intake/exhaust opens" and/or "intake/exhaust closes" (Figure 15).
As an example, if the actuators turn the intake camshaft to delay "intake

opens/closes" at idle or at high rpm, the result will be a reduction in the proportion of recirculated gases at idle, or enhanced cylinder charging at higher engine speeds.
When the intake camshaft is turned toward earlier "intake opens/closes" at low or moderate engine speeds or in certain load ranges, the result is a higher maximum air charge to the cylinder.
This would also lead to a larger proportion of recirculated gas in the part-throttle range, with corresponding effects on fuel consumption and exhaust emissions (see page 53).

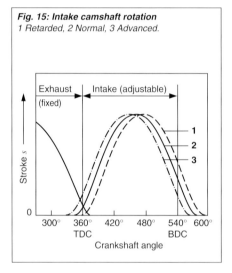

Fig. 15: Intake camshaft rotation
1 Retarded, 2 Normal, 3 Advanced.

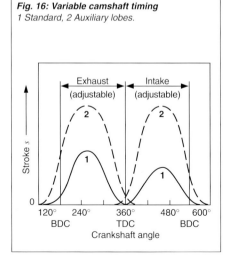

Fig. 16: Variable camshaft timing
1 Standard, 2 Auxiliary lobes.

Camshaft lobe control

Systems with camshaft lobe control modify the valve timing by alternately activating cam lobes with two different shapes. The first lobe supplies optimum valve timing and lift for intake and exhaust valves during lower and mid-range operation. A second cam lobe provides longer valve-opening times and lift, and becomes operational when the rocker arm to which it is connected is locked onto the standard rocker arm in response to engine speed (Figure 16).

An optimal but complicated process is infinitely-variable valve timing and lift adjustment. This concept employs cam lobes with 3-dimensional geometry and sliding camshafts to provide maximum latitude in engine design (Figure 17).

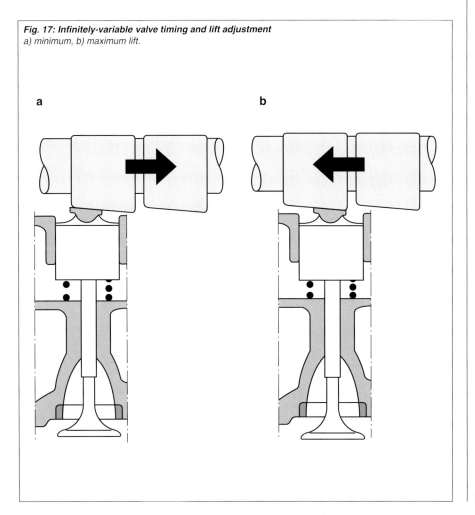

Fig. 17: Infinitely-variable valve timing and lift adjustment
a) minimum, b) maximum lift.

a

b

Variable-geometry intake manifold

The tandem objectives of engine design are maximum torque at low engine speeds and high output at the rated maximum. The engine's torque curve is proportional to the mass of the intake air as a function of engine speed.

One effective means of influencing torque is to provide the intake manifold with the appropriate geometrical configuration. The simplest method for providing intake boost is to exploit the dynamics of the incoming air. To ensure balanced distribution of the air-fuel mixture, intake manifolds for carburetor or single-point (Mono-Jetronic) injection systems need short intake runners with minimal variations in lengths.

The intake runners for multipoint systems transport only air; the injectors discharge the fuel. This arrangement offers a wider range of options in intake-manifold design. The standard manifold for a multipoint injection system consists of individual curved runners and a plenum chamber with throttle valve.

General principles:
– Short curved runners allow high maximum output accompanied by sacrifices in torque at lower engine speeds; whereby long runners provide an inverse response pattern.
– Large-volume plenum chambers can provide resonance effects in certain engine-speed ranges, leading to improved cylinder filling. They are also subject to potential faults in dynamic response; these assume the form of mixture variations under rapid load change.
Variable intake-manifold geometry can be used to obtain an almost ideal torque curve.

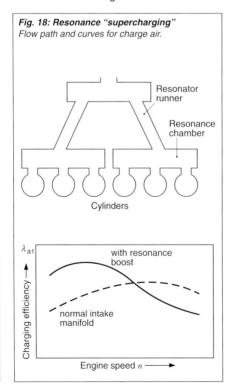

Fig. 18: Resonance "supercharging"
Flow path and curves for charge air.

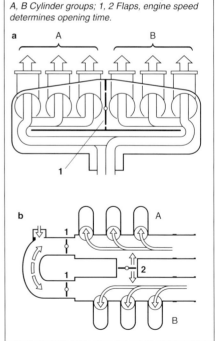

Fig. 19: Variable-geometry intake systems
Switchable: a) two-stage, b) three-stage.
A, B Cylinder groups; 1, 2 Flaps, engine speed determines opening time.

Intake oscillation boost

Each cylinder has an individual, fixed-length intake runner, usually connected to a plenum chamber. The energy balance is defined by a process in which the induction force from the piston is converted into kinetic energy in the gas column upstream from the intake valve. This kinetic energy then serves to compress the fresh charge.

Resonance boost

Resonance boost systems use short runners to connect groups of cylinders with equal ignition intervals to resonance chambers. These, in turn, are connected via resonance tubes to the atmosphere or a plenum chamber, allowing them to act as Helmholtz resonators.

Variable-geometry intake systems

Both types of dynamic supercharging augment the achievable cylinder charge, especially in the lower engine-speed range.

Variable-response intake systems use devices such as flaps to separate and connect system areas assigned to various groups of cylinders (Figure 19).
Variable-length intake runners operate with the first resonance chamber at low rpm. The length of the runner changes as engine speed increases, at which point a second resonance chamber opens (Figure 20).
Figure 21 shows the effects of variable intake-runner geometry on the brake mean effective pressure (bmep), which is used as an index for cylinder charging.

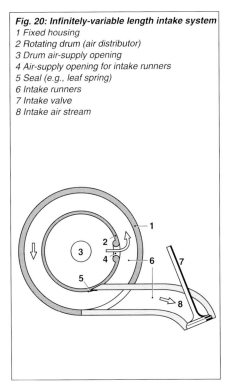

Fig. 20: Infinitely-variable length intake system
1 Fixed housing
2 Rotating drum (air distributor)
3 Drum air-supply opening
4 Air-supply opening for intake runners
5 Seal (e.g., leaf spring)
6 Intake runners
7 Intake valve
8 Intake air stream

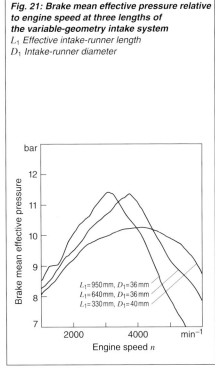

Fig. 21: Brake mean effective pressure relative to engine speed at three lengths of the variable-geometry intake system
L_1 Effective intake-runner length
D_1 Intake-runner diameter

L_1=950 mm, D_1=36 mm
L_1=640 mm, D_1=36 mm
L_1=330 mm, D_1=40 mm

Brake mean effective pressure (bar)

Engine speed n (min^{-1})

Integrated diagnosis

Diagnostic procedure

An "on-board diagnosis (OBD) system" is standard equipment with Motronic. This integral diagnostic unit monitors ECU commands and system responses. It also checks the individual sensor signals for plausibility. This test procedure is carried out constantly during normal vehicle operation.

The ECU stores recognized errors together with the operating conditions under which they occurred. When the vehicle is serviced, a tester can be used to read out and display the stored errors through a standardized interface. The information facilitates trouble-shooting for the service personnel.

In response to the demands of the California Air Resources Board, (CARB), diagnosis procedures extending far beyond those in earlier tests have been developed. All components whose failure could cause a substantial increase in harmful emissions must be monitored.

Diagnosis areas

Air-mass meter

The process for monitoring the air-mass meter provides an example of the Motronic system's self-diagnosis function. While the injection duration is being determined on the basis of intake-air mass, a supplementary comparison injection time is calculated from throttle-valve angle and engine speed. If the ECU discovers an excessive variance between the two, its initial response is to store a record of the error. As vehicle operation continues, plausibility checks determine which of the sensors is defective. The control unit does not store the corresponding error code until it has unequivocally determined which sensor is at fault.

Combustion miss

Combustion miss, as can result from factors such as worn spark plugs or faulty electrical contacts, allows unburned mixture to enter the catalytic converter. This mixture can destroy the converter, and represents an extra load on the environment. Because even isolated combustion failures result in higher emissions, the system must be able to recognize them. Figure 1 shows the effects of combustion miss on emissions of hydrocarbons (HC), carbon monoxide (CO) and oxides of nitrogen (NO_x).

Many potential methods of detecting combustion miss were tested, and monitoring the running response of the crankshaft proved to be the most suitable. Combustion miss is accompanied by a shortfall in torque equal to the increment which would normally have been generated in the cycle where the error occured. The result is a reduction in rotation speed. At high speeds and low loads the interval from ignition to ignition (period duration) is extended by only 0.2%. This means that the rotation must be monitored with extreme precision, while extensive computations are also required to distinguish combustion miss from other interference factors.

Catalytic converter

Yet another diagnostic function monitors the efficiency of the catalytic converter. For this purpose the Lambda oxygen sensor upstream of the catalytic converter is supplemented by a second downstream oxygen sensor. A correctly-operating converter will store oxygen, thus attenuating the Lambda control oscillations. As the catalytic converter ages, this response deteriorates until finally the signal pattern from the upstream sensor approaches that received from the downstream sensor. A comparison of the signals from the oxygen sensors thus provides the basis for determining the catalytic converter's condition. A warning lamp alerts the driver in the event of a defect.

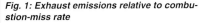

Fig. 1: Exhaust emissions relative to combustion-miss rate
Engine: 6-cylinder, 2.8 litre
US 94 emissions limits
HC = 0.25 g/mile
CO = 3.40 g/mile
NO_x = 0.40 g/mile

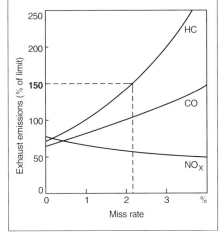

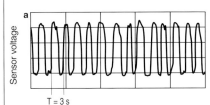

Fig. 2: Monitoring the Lambda oxygen sensor's dynamic response pattern
a) New sensor, b) Aged Type II sensor,
c) Aged Type III sensor.

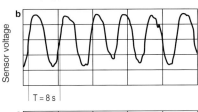

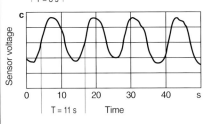

Lambda oxygen sensor

A stoichiometric air-fuel mixture must be maintained if the catalytic converter is to perform to its full potential. This is taken care of by the signals from the Lambda oxygen sensors. The fact that two oxygen sensors are fitted in each exhaust tract makes it possible to use the sensor downstream from the converter to check for control variations in the upstream unit. A Lambda oxygen sensor that has been exposed to excessive heat for a considerable period of time may react more slowly to changes in the air-fuel mixture. This increases the period duration for the Lambda control's two-state controller (Figure 2). A diagnosis function monitors this control frequency and informs the driver of excessive delays in sensor response via warning lamp.

The Lambda oxygen sensors' heating resistance is checked by measuring current and voltage. The Motronic ECU controls the heater resistance element directly, with no relay in between, to allow this test to be performed. The sensor signal is subjected continuously to plausibility checks, and the system responds to implausible signals by denying access to other functions depending upon the Lambda control. The appropriate error code is also stored in the fault memory.

Fuel supply

When the air-fuel mixture deviates from stoichiometric for extended periods of time, this condition is taken into account together with the mixture adaptation. If the deviations exceed specific predefined limits, this indicates that a fuel-system component or a fuel-metering device has moved outside specification tolerances. An example would be a faulty pressure regulator or load sensor, whereby the error could also stem from a leak in the intake manifold or exhaust system.

Secondary air injection

The secondary air injection activated after cold starts must also be monitored, as its failure would also influence emissions. This can be done using the signals from the Lambda oxygen sensors when the secondary air injecton is active, or it can be activated and observed at idle using a Lambda control test function.

Exhaust-gas recirculation (EGR)

Various options are available for diagnosing the exhaust-gas recirculation system, whereby two are in general use. With the first option, a sensor monitors the temperature increase at the location where the hot exhaust gases return to the intake manifold while the EGR is operating.

With the second procedure, the exhaust-gas recirculation valve is opened all the way with the vehicle on trailing throttle (overrun fuel cutoff). The exhaust gases flowing into the intake manifold cause its internal pressure to rise. A pressure sensor measures and evaluates the increase in manifold pressure.

Tank system

Emissions emanating from the exhaust system are not the only source of environmental concern; fuel vapors from the fuel tank are also a problem. In the near term the legal requirements will be limited to a relatively simple check of canister-purge valve operation. A means of recognizing leaks in the evaporative-emissions storage system will be required at a later date. Figure 3 illustrates the basic principle employed for this diagnosis. A cutoff valve closes off the storage system.

Then, preferably with the engine idling, the canister-purge valve is opened and the intake-manifold pressure spreads through the system. An in-tank pressure sensor monitors the pressure build-up to determine whether leaks are present.

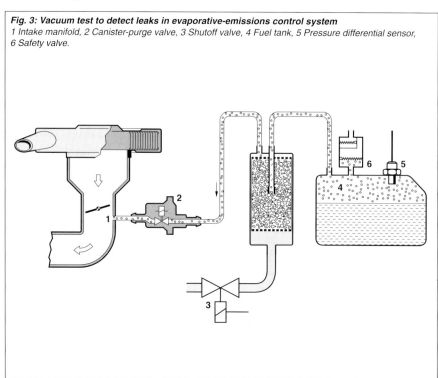

Fig. 3: Vacuum test to detect leaks in evaporative-emissions control system
1 Intake manifold, 2 Canister-purge valve, 3 Shutoff valve, 4 Fuel tank, 5 Pressure differential sensor, 6 Safety valve.

Other monitoring devices

The main emphasis of the new statutes applies to the engine-management system, but other systems (for instance, automatic transmission) are also monitored. These report any faults to the engine-management ECU, which then assumes responsibility for triggering the diagnosis lamp. Greater system complexity and ever more stringent environmental regulations are making diagnosis increasingly important.

Emergency running mode (limp-home)

In the interval between the initial occurrence of a fault and vehicle service, default settings and emergency-running functions assume responsibility for the ignition and air-fuel mixture. This allows the vehicle to continue operating, albeit with sacrifices in driving comfort. The ECU responds to recognized errors in an input circuit by replacing the missing information or reverting to a default value. When an output unit fails, specific backup measures corresponding to the individual problem are implemented. Thus the ECU reacts to a defect in the ignition circuit by switching off the fuel injection at the affected cylinder in order to prevent damage to the catalytic converter.

When the vehicle is serviced, the Bosch engine tester can be used to read out and display the faults and errors detected during operation (Figure 4).

Fig. 4: Bosch engine tester.

ECU

Function

The ECU is the "computer and control center" for the engine-management system. It employs stored functions and algorithms (processing programs) to process the input signals transmitted by the sensors. These signals serve as the basis for calculating the control signals to the actuators (e.g., ignition coil, injectors) which it manages directly via power output stages (Figure 1).

Physical design

The ECU is a metal housing containing a printed-circuit board with electronic componentry.

A multiple-terminal plug connector provides the link between ECU and sensors, actuators and power supply. Depending upon the specific ECU and the number of system functions, the plug can be of 35-, 55- or 88-pole design.

The amplifiers and power output components for direct actuator control are installed on heat sinks in the ECU. Efficient heat transfer to the bodywork is necessary due to the the the amount of heat that these components produce.

Environmental conditions

The ECU must withstand temperature extremes, moisture and mechanical loads with absolutely no impairment of operation. Resistance to electromagnetic interference, and the ability to suppress radiation of high-frequency static, must also be of a high order.

The ECU must be capable of errorless signal processing within an operating range extending from $-30°C$ to $+60°C$, at battery voltages that range from 6 V (during starting) to 15 V.

Power supply

A voltage regulator provides the ECU with the constant 5 V operating voltage needed for the digital circuitry.

Signal inputs

Various processes are employed to transmit the input signals to the ECU. The signals are conducted through protective circuits, while signal converters and amplifiers may also be present. The microprocessor can process these signals directly.

An analog/digital converter (A/D) within the microprocessor transforms analog signals (for instance, information on intake-air quantity, temperature of engine and intake air, battery voltage, Lambda oxygen sensor) into digital form.

The signal from the inductive sensor with information on engine speed and crankshaft reference point is processed in a special circuit to suppress interference pulses.

Signal processing

The input signals are processed by the microprocessor within the ECU. In order to function, this microprocessor must be equipped with a signal-processing program stored in non-volatile memory (ROM or EPROM). This memory also contains the specific individual performance curves and program maps used for engine control.

Due to the large number of engine and vehicle variations, some ECU's are equipped with a special version-code feature. This allows the manufacturer or service technician to feed supplementary program data into the program maps stored in the EPROM, making it possible to provide the operating characteristics desired for the particular version. Other types of ECU are designed to allow complete data banks to be programmed into the EPROM at the end of production (end-of-line programming). This reduces the number of individual ECU configurations required by the manufacturer.

A read/write memory component (RAM) is needed for storing calculated values and adaptation factors as well as any system errors that may be detected (diagnosis). This RAM requires an uninterrupted power supply to function properly. This memory chip will lose all data if the vehicle battery is disconnected. The ECU must then recalculate the adaptation factors after the battery is reconnected. To prevent this, some units therefore use an EEPROM instead of a RAM to store these required variables.

Transmitting the signal

The output stages triggered by the microprocessor supply sufficient power for direct control of the actuators. These output stages are protected against short circuits to ground, irregularities in battery voltage and the electrical overload that could destroy them.

At several output stages, the OBD diagnosis function recognizes errors and reacts by deactivating (where necessary) the defective output. The error entry is stored in the RAM. The service technician can then read out the error using a tester connected to the serial interface. Another protective circuit operates independently of the ECU to switch off the electric fuel pump when the engine-speed signal falls below a certain level. When some ECU's are switched off at the ignition/steering lock (Terminal 15, or "ignition off"), a holding circuit holds the main relay open until program processing can be completed.

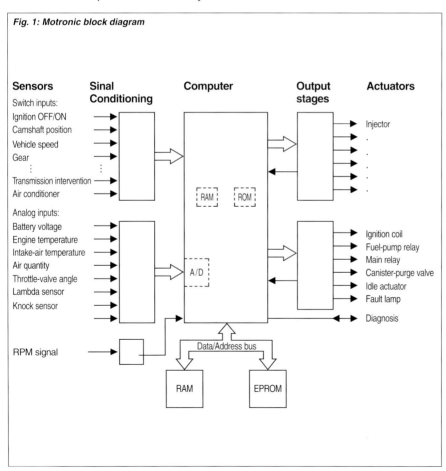

Fig. 1: Motronic block diagram

Interfaces to other systems

System overview

Increased application of electronic control systems in vehicles in areas such as
– transmission control,
– electronic throttle control (EMS, E-Gas, drive-by-wire),
– electronic engine management (Motronic),
– antilock braking system (ABS),
– traction control (ASR),
– on-board computer, etc.,
has made it necessary to combine the respective ECU's in networks. Data communications between control systems reduce the number of sensors and allow better exploitation of the individual system potentials.

The interfaces can be divided into two categories:
– conventional interfaces, with binary signals (switch inputs), pulse-duty factors (pulse-width-modulated signals),
– serial data transmission, e.g., Controller Area Network (CAN).

Conventional interfaces

In conventional automotive data-communications systems, each signal is assigned to a single line. Binary signals can only be transmitted as one of the two conditions "1" or "0" (binary code), for instance, air-conditioning compressor "ON" or "OFF".

Pulse-duty factors (potentiometer) can be employed to relay more detailed data, such as throttle-valve aperture.

The increasing levels of data exchange between the various electronic components in the vehicle means that conventional interfaces are no longer capable of providing satisfactory performance. The complexity of today's wiring harnesses is already difficult to manage, while the requirements for data communications between ECU's are on the rise (Figure 1). These problems can be solved by using

CAN (Controller Area Network), a bus system (bus bar) specially designed for automotive use.

Provided that the ECU's are equipped with a serial CAN interface, CAN can be used to relay the signals from the sources listed above.

Serial data transmission (CAN)

There are three basic applications for CAN in motor vehicles:
– to connect ECU's,
– bodywork and convenience electronics (Multiplex),
– mobile communications.
The following is limited to a description of communications between ECU's.

ECU networking

Here electronic systems such as Motronic, electronic transmission control, etc. are combined within a single network. Typical transmission times lie between approx. 125 kBits/s and 1kBit/s. These times must be high enough to maintain the required real-time response. One of the advantages that serial data transmission enjoys over conventional interfaces (e.g., pulse-duty factor, switching and analog signals) is the high speeds achieved without high loads on the central processing units (CPU's) in ECU's.

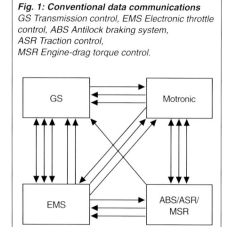

Fig. 1: Conventional data communications
GS Transmission control, EMS Electronic throttle control, ABS Antilock braking system,
ASR Traction control,
MSR Engine-drag torque control.

| GS | | Motronic |

| EMS | | ABS/ASR/ MSR |

Bus configuration

CAN works on the "multiple master" principle. This concept combines several equal-priority ECU's in a linear bus structure (Figure 2). The advantage of this structure is the fact that failure of one subscriber will not affect access for the others. The probability of total failure is thus much lower than with other logical arrangements (such as loop or star structures). With loop or star architecture, failure in one of the subscribers or the central ECU will result in total system failure.

Content-keyed addressing

The CAN bus system addresses the data according to content. Each message is assigned a permanent 11-bit identifier. This identifier indicates the contents of the message (e.g., engine speed). Each station processes only those data whose identifiers are stored in its acceptance list (acceptance check). This means that CAN does not need station addresses to transmit data, and the junctions do not need to administer system configuration.

Bus arbitration

Each station can begin transmitting its highest priority message as soon as the bus is free. If several stations start transmitting simultaneously, the resulting bus-access conflict is resolved using a "wired-and" arbitration arrangement. This arrangement assigns first access to the message with the highest priority, with no loss of either time or data bits. When a station loses the arbitration, it automatically reverts to standby status and repeats its transmission attempt as soon as the bus indicates that it is no longer occupied.

Message format

A data frame of less than 130 bits in length is created for transmissions to the bus. This ensures that the queue time until the next – possibly extremely urgent – data transmission is held to a minimum. The data frames consist of seven consecutive fields.

Standardization

The International Standards Organisation (ISO) has recognized CAN as a standard for use in automotive applications with data streams of over 125 kBit/s, along with two additional protocols for data rates up to 125 kBit/s.

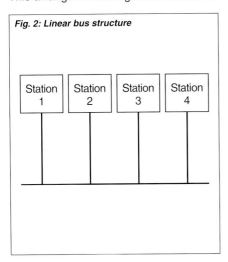

Fig. 2: Linear bus structure

| Station 1 | Station 2 | Station 3 | Station 4 |

Mono-Motronic engine management

System overview

The Mono-Motronic engine-management system is a low-pressure single-point injection system (fuel-injection subsystem) with integrated electronic map-controlled ignition (ignition subsystem). Combination of the two subsystems enables joint optimization of fuel-metering and ignition-control.

The heart of the Mono-Motronic system is an electronic control unit (ECU) which incorporates the high-performance microcomputer required for the processing not only of the fuel injection but also of the ignition control. Since, for instance, only one power supply and one case are needed, the outlay required for the single ECU is less than that which would be required for separate fuel-injection and ignition systems. This leads to increased reliability of the system as a whole and a more favorabe cost/benefit ratio.

The fact that the ECU utilises sensor signals for controlling the ignition and fuel-injection functions leads to the following Mono-Motronic advantages:
– Precise metering of the injected fuel quantity, and temperature-dependent adaptive ignition angle lead to warm-running adaptation with attendant fuel-consumption reduction,
– Minimization of fuel consumption together with favorable emissions figures as a result of precision ignition-angle adaptation covering the complete ignition map and under all operating conditions.
– Idle-speed stabilization due to dynamic ignition timing,
– Increase in driving comfort by ignition-timing intervention during acceleration and deceleration,
– With automatic transmissions, ignition-timing intervention for improved shifts.

Subsystem: Fuel injection

The intermittent electronically controlled single-point injection system is based on the familiar Mono-Jetronic. Functions have been added to improve driving comfort and to further improve the limp-home facilities in case of sensor failure.

The fuel is pumped by the electric fuel pump from the fuel tank, through the fuel filter, and to the central injection unit which is located directly on the intake manifold, The solenoid-operated injector, which injects a finely-atomized jet of fuel just above the throttle plate, and the fuel-pressure regulator, are situated in the injection unit's hydraulic stage.

The ECU calculates the basic injection quantity from the throttle-plate angle and the engine-speed signal. More or less fuel is injected to take into account such operating conditions as cold-start, post-start, warm-up, and overrun, as well as engine-speed limitation.

The vapors from the fuel tank are also returned to the running engine from the carbon canister (canister-purge).

Subsystem: Ignition

The ignition map stored in the ECU supersedes the centrifugal (mechanical) and vacuum advance mechanisms located in the ignition distributor. The ignition (advance) angle as a function of engine speed and load is stored in the ignition map. In addition, the ignition angle can be changed depending upon engine and intake-air temperature, throttle-valve setting, and throttle-valve angular velocity.

Rotating voltage distribution

If an ignition system with rotating high-voltage (HT) distribution is used, the distributor only retains the Hall triggering function for engine-speed measurement and the actual HT distributor. The ECU, which triggers the ignition's external driver stage, is responsible for the engine-speed and load-dependent ignition-timing adjustment and dwell-angle control. The HT distributor is responsible for assigning the ignition spark to the correct cylinder.

Distributorless (stationary) voltage distribution

If a distributorless ignition system (Fig. 1) is used, the mechanically driven HT distributor is dispensed with. The ECU distributes the primary voltage to the ignition coils which generate the HT and pass it directly to the spark plug of the respective cylinder. For example, a 4-cylinder engine is equipped with 2 dual-spark ignition coils which are triggered by the ECU through external power output stages. A speed sensor picks off the engine-speed information and the reference-mark signal for cylinder 1 (or 4) at a sensor wheel which is attached to the crankshaft.

Knock control

The Mono-Motronic can also be equipped with knock-control. This utilises the signal from the knock sensor on the engine block to adjust the ignition advance angle in order to take full advantage of the available fuel quality. The result is a reduction in fuel consumption while at the same time ensuring that the engine cannot be damaged by combustion knock.

Self-diagnosis

The ECU continually checks all the signals which are required for correct operation, and stores the fault type as soon as one of the parameters leaves its defined range. Using a diagnostic tester, faults can be read out from the fault store during servicing.

Supplementary functions

Exhaust-gas recirculation (EGR) and secondary-air injection are further possibilities for reducing toxic emissions.

Fig. 1: Schematic diagram of the Mono-Motronic
1 Injector, 2 Air-temperature sensor, 3 Fuel-pressure regulator, 4 Ignition coil, 5 Canister-purge valve, 6 Throttle actuator, 7 Carbon canister, 8 Pressure actuator, 9 Throttle-valve potentiometer, 10 ECU, 11 Fuel filter, 12 EGR valve, 13 Knock sensor, 14 Engine-speed sensor, 15 Engine-temperature sensor, 16 Lambda sensor, 17 Electric fuel pump.

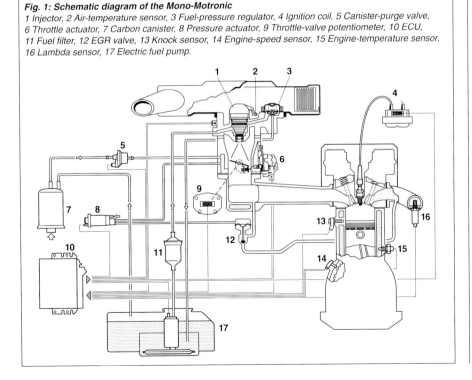

Vehicle electrical system

Power supply

Power supply
The on-board electrical system must be capable of ensuring that the vehicle can be started and operated at all times. Operation of electrical accessories for a reasonable period of time with the engine off, should not render subsequent starts impossible. Battery, starter, alternator and electrical system must be designed for mutually compatible operation. The main criteria are low weight, compact dimensions and low fuel consumption, whereby fuel economy is generally the predominating concern. The following factors must also receive special consideration:
– starting temperature,
– alternator current,
– engine speed in normal operation,
– electrical requirements, and
– charge voltage.

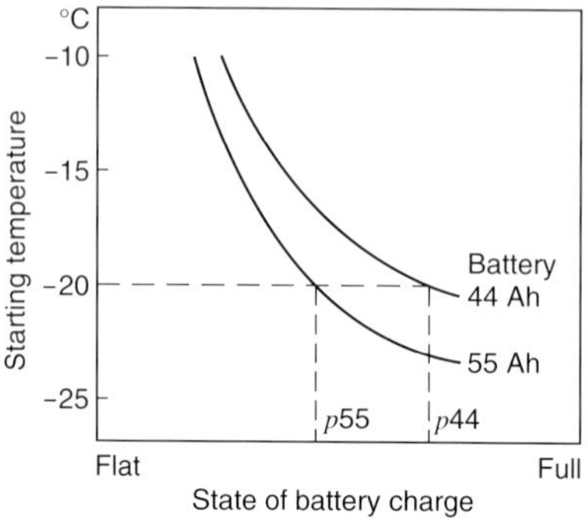

General specifications

Starting temperature
The temperature at which the engine can still be started is dependent, amongst other things, upon the battery (ampere-hour capacity, internal resistance and state of charge etc.) and starter (size, with or without reduction gear, excitation electrical/permanent etc.). If the engine is to be started at a temperature of $-20°C$ for instance, the battery must have a minimum state of charge p (Fig. 1).

Alternator current output
The amount of current generated by the alternator varies according to engine speed. At idle n_L, the alternator is only able to deliver a portion of its rated current. If the current drawn by the equipment I_V is greater than the alternator current I_G, e.g., when the engine is idling, the battery discharges and the voltage in the electrical system drops. If the equipment load draw I_V is less than alternator current I_G, a portion of the dif-

---

Fig. 1: Starting temperature
As a function of the state of battery charge.
p Minimum state of charge.

Starting temperature (°C) vs State of battery charge (Flat – Full). Curves for Battery 44 Ah and 55 Ah, with points p55 and p44 at −20°C.

Fig. 2: Current curve
Alternator current delivery I_G as a function of the alternator speed. I_V Load current,
n_L Alternator speed at engine idle.

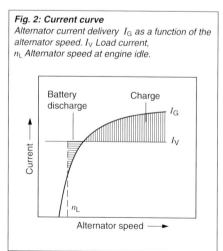

Current vs Alternator speed. Battery discharge, Charge, I_G, I_V, n_L.

ference flows into the battery as battery charge current I_B (Fig. 2).

Engine speed during vehicle operation

Engine speed – and thus alternator speed – vary according to the vehicle's operating patterns. The cumulative frequency curve for engine speed defines how frequently a specific engine speed is reached or exceeded during normal operation.

When congestion and traffic lights are encountered during rush-hour traffic, a substantial proportion of the engine's operation is at idle. When driving on the motorway, the idling rate is generally low (Fig. 3).

Regular-line bus engines also idle at bus stops. Electrical equipment or systems which are switched on with the engine switched off (e.g. at the terminus) have an unfavorable effect upon the state of battery charge. Tourist or long-haul buses generally have a low idling rate.

Electrical-load requirements

The time that the various electrical devices spend in active operation varies. We distinguish between continuous-draw devices (ignition, fuel injection etc.), extended-use devices (lights, heated rear window etc.) and intermittent-use devices (turn-signal lamps and stop lamps etc.). Use of many electrical devices varies according to season (air-conditioning in the summer, seat heating in the winter). The switch-on frequency of electrical radiator fans is dependent upon both temperature and vehicle operation. In winter, most drivers drive with their lights on in the rush hours (Table 3).

Charging voltage

The charging voltage of a storage battery must be higher under low-temperature conditions and lower under high-temperature conditions owing to the chemical processes which occur in the battery. The maximum permissible voltage at which the storage battery does not "gas" is shown on the curve of the voltage at commencement of gassing. Electrical equipment requires as constant a voltage as possible. The voltage must have a close tolerance for lamp bulbs in order to ensure that the service life and luminous intensity lie within the given limits. The voltage regulator restricts the upper voltage limit. It influences the under-voltage limit if the possible alternating current I_G is higher than the required equipment current I_V. Voltage regulators are generally fitted inside the alternator.

In the case of large deviations between regulator temperature and battery electrolyte temperature, it is advantageous if

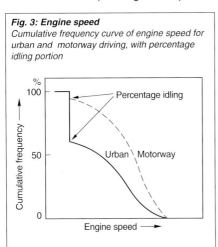

Fig. 3: Engine speed
Cumulative frequency curve of engine speed for urban and motorway driving, with percentage idling portion

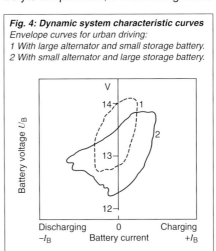

Fig. 4: Dynamic system characteristic curves
Envelope curves for urban driving:
1 With large alternator and small storage battery.
2 With small alternator and large storage battery.

the temperature for voltage regulation is sensed directly at the battery. A regulator designed to monitor actual voltage levels at the battery can be used to compensate for line losses between alternator and battery.

Dynamic system characteristic curve

The interaction of the:
− battery,
− alternator,
− electrical equipment,
− temperature,
− engine speed and
− transmission ratio engine/alternator
results in the system characteristic curve. It is specific to every combination and every operating condition and is thus a dynamic "statement". The dynamic system characteristic curve can be measured at the battery's terminals and recorded on an xy plotter (Fig. 4).

Charge-balance calculation

The charge-balance calculation must allow for the above influencing variables. The state of battery charge at the end of a typical driving cycle is determined with the aid of a computer program. A normal cycle for passenger cars is driving in rush hours (low engine speed) combined with winter operation (low charging current consumption by the battery). For vehicles with air-con-ditioning system (high current consumption), summer operation may be less favorable under certain circumstances. At the end of the cycle the battery's charge should be at least high enough to subsequently start the engine again at the prevailing temperature.

Lead storage battery

Principle of operation

The active materials of the lead storage battery are the lead peroxide (PbO_2) of the positive plate, the spongy, highly porous lead (Pb) of the negative plate and the electrolyte, dilute sulphuric acid (H_2SO_4). The electrolyte simultaneously acts as the ion conductor for charging and discharging. PbO_2 and Pb each assume typical electrical voltages (individual potentials) with respect to the electrolyte and, by subtracting these potentials, we obtain the externally measurable cell voltage. This is approximately 2 V in open-circuit condition. It rises during charging and drops during loading. When discharging, PbO_2 and Pb react with H_2SO_4 to form $PbSO_4$ (lead sulphate) and for this reason, the electrolyte loses SO_4 (sulphate) ions and the specific gravity of the electrolyte drops. During charging, the active materials PbO_2 and Pb are reconstituted from $PbSO_4$.

Table 1. Directions for mixing

Required specific gravity of electrolyte kg/l [1]	1.23	1.26	1.28	1.30	1.34
Volume ratio concentrated sulphuric acid (96%) to distilled water	1:3.8	1:3.2	1:2.8	1:2.6	1:2.3

Table 2. Electrolyte values of dilute sulphuric acid

State of charge	Battery version	Specific gravity of electrolyte kg/l [1]	Freezing threshold °C
Charged	Normal	1.28	−68
	For tropics	1.23	−40
Half-charged	Normal	1.16/1.20 [2]	−17...−27
	For tropics	1.13/1.16 [2]	−13...−17
Discharged	Normal	1.04/1.12 [2]	−3...−11
	For tropics	1.03/1.08 [2]	−2...−8

[1] At 20°C: the specific gravity of the electrolyte drops with increasing temperature and rises with decreasing temperature by approximately 0.01 kg/l per 14°C change in temperature.
[2] Low value: high electrolyte utilization, high value: low electrolyte utilization.

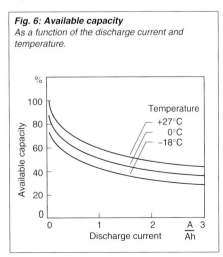

$$PbO_2 + 2H_2SO_4 + Pb \longleftrightarrow PbSO_4 + 2H_2O + PbSO_4$$

$\rightarrow$ Charging $\leftarrow$ Discharging

If charging is continued after a full state of charge has been reached, only electrolytic decomposition of water occurs, thus forming explosive gas (oxygen at the positive plate and hydrogen at the negative plate).

The specific gravity of the electrolyte can be taken as a measure of the state of charge.

This is subject to uncertainty owing to the design (see Table 2 with scatter band) and is the result of electrolyte stratification and battery wear with, in some cases, irreversible sulphation and/or intense sloughing off of sediment from the plates.

Cold behavior

The lower the state of charge, the lower is the specific gravity of the electrolyte. The result is an undesirable shift of the freezing point to higher temperatures. A storage battery with frozen electrolyte is only able to deliver low currents and cannot be used for starting.

Mixing fresh electrolyte

In order to avoid splashes, always pour concentrated sulphuric acid into distilled water and never vice versa. At the same time, stir the mixture with an acid-resistant rod (glass or plastic).

Tables 1 and 2 show how certain conventional electrolyte concentrations can be obtained by mixing. The figures can be interpolated in linear fashion for other values, i.e., intermediate values can be calculated accordingly.

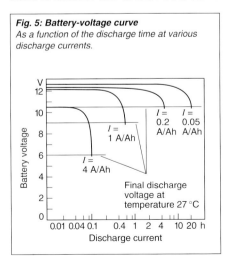

Battery characteristic values

Designation

In addition to mechanical features such as dimensions, mounting type and terminal-post design, it is chiefly the electrical values which are characteristic and these are measured in accordance with test standards (e.g. German Industrial Standard DIN 43539, Section 2). The starter batteries manufactured in the Federal Republic of Germany are identified in accordance with DIN 72310, 72311 by a 5-digit type number, the nominal voltage, the nominal capacity and the cold-discharge test current (only in the case of starter batteries). Example: 56618, 12 V 66 Ah 300 A.

Ampere-hour capacity

The ampere-hour (Ah) capacity is the amount of electricity which can be taken from a battery under specific conditions, expressed in Ah. It drops with increa-

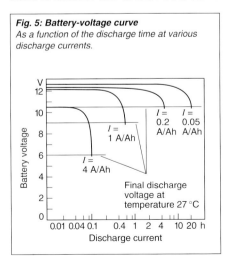

Fig. 5: Battery-voltage curve
As a function of the discharge time at various discharge currents.

Fig. 6: Available capacity
As a function of the discharge current and temperature.

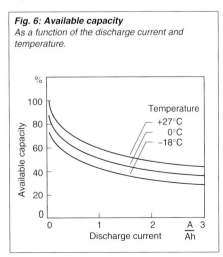

Fuel consumption

A small part of the fuel consumption is required to drive the alternator and move the weights of starter, storage battery and alternator (approx. 5% on a mid-size car).

Average fuel consumption for 100 km: for 10 kg weight approx. 0.1 l, for 100 W drive power approx. 0.1 l. Although slightly heavier, alternators with a higher part-load efficiency thus contribute to saving fuel.

Symbols and circuit diagrams

In modern vehicles, the electrical system consists of more than just the lights. Modern automotive systems include a large number of electric and electronic devices for open and closed-loop engine-management systems, and for comfort and convenience.

Circuit diagrams using standardized symbols are required to provide an overview of these complex vehicle circuits. Circuit diagrams in the form of schematic diagrams and terminal diagrams are an aid in trouble-shooting and diagnosis, as well as facilitating the installation of supplementary equipment, and the conversion or modification of the vehicle's electrical equipment.

Symbols

The electrical symbols on the following pages have been taken from the section "Circuit diagram for a passenger car with spark-ignition engine."

They are a representative selection of the standardized symbols used in vehicle wiring diagrams. With few exceptions these symbols correspond to the definitions of the International Electrotechnical Commission (IEC).

Some of the DIN standards have been modified for closer correspondence to the IEC recommendations, e.g., the symbols for inductance and electrical machinery. Since both rectangular and semicircular representations are valid options they have both been shown. However, the semicircular portrayals are recommended, as they facilitate comprehension on the part of an international audience and more accurately reflect the options provided by modern drawing and duplication technology.

Requirements

Symbols are the smallest components of a circuit diagram, and are the simplest way to represent an electrical device or part of a device. They illustrate how a device operates, and are used in circuit diagrams to illustrate how a sequence of events occurs. Symbols do not indicate the shapes and dimensions

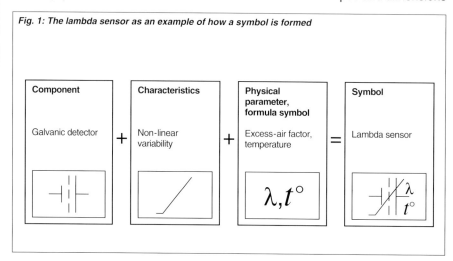

Fig. 1: The lambda sensor as an example of how a symbol is formed

Component		Characteristics		Physical parameter, formula symbol		Symbol
Galvanic detector	+	Non-linear variability	+	Excess-air factor, temperature	=	Lambda sensor
				λ, t°		

of the devices they represent, nor do they show the locations of the connections to the devices. Only by using this so-called detached method of representation, however, is it possible to illustrate how the devices are connected in the schematic diagram.

A symbol should satisfy the following requirements: it must be easy to identify, easy to understand, easy to draw and should clearly indicate the type of device which it represents. Symbols comprise symbol elements and symbol qualifiers.

The symbol qualifiers can take the form of letters, symbols, numbers, mathematical symbols, formula symbols, abbreviations of units or characteristics etc.

If a circuit diagram showing the internal circuitry of a device becomes too complex, or if the function of the device can be illustrated without showing all of the details, the circuit diagram for this specific device can be replaced by a single symbol (without internal circuitry, Fig. 1). Simplified representations are usually used for integrated circuits, with their typically high levels of spatial efficiency (a high degree of functional integration within individual components).

The symbols defined in DIN 40900, Sections 12 and 13, are prescribed for binary and digital circuits; these indicate both circuit and function. Symbols from DIN 40900, Part 13 are also used in computer and control technology.

Representation

Symbols are shown in their basic status, that is, they do not show the effect of physical parameters, i.e. the application of current, voltage and mechanical force. Other operating states, i.e., any condition that varies from the basic status defined above, is indicated by an adjacent double arrow.

Symbols and connecting lines (electrical lines and mechanical linkages), have the same width (to ensure microfilm legibility, at least 0.25 mm). In order to keep the connecting lines as straight as possible and to avoid crossed lines,

symbols can be turned in increments of 90° or shown as mirror images as long as their meaning remains the same. Connections can be made at any point on the symbols, with the exception of the symbols for resistors (terminals shown only at the ends) and connections for electromechanical actuators (terminals shown only at the sides).

A dot is used to represent a junction, whereas when crossed lines have no dot an electrical connection is not present. No special method is used to show connections to devices. Connecting points, plugs, sockets or bolted connections are identified by symbols only at points required for installation and removal. All other junctions are represented by dots.

Switching components which have a common actuator are drawn together such that the common actuating force is applied in one direction which is shown by the dashed line (– – –) which represents the mechanical linkage.

Selection of symbols

(see also Circuit Diagram)

Connections	Mechanical functions	
Conductor; conductor crossover (without or with connection) 	Switch positions (basic position: solid line) 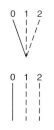	Variability and adjustability, not automatic (external), general
Shielded conductor 		Variability/adjustability, automatic, caused by applied physical variable, linear, non-linear
Mechanical linkage; crossover (without or with connection) 	Actuation by hand, by means of follower (cam), thermal (bimetal) 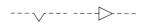	Variability/adjustability, general
Junction point, general; separable (if this has to be represented) ● ○	Detent, automatic return in direction shown by arrow (pushbutton)	**Switches**
		Momentary switch, make contact, break contact
Plug connection, plug, socket, 3-contact plug connection 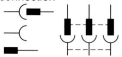	Actuation, general (mechanical, pneumatic, hydraulic); piston actuation 	Detent switch, make contact, break contact
Ground (equipment ground, vehicle ground) 	Actuation by rotational speed n, pressure p, quantity Q, time t, temperature $t°$ 	Changeover switch, break before make or make before break

	Relays	**Resistors**
Switch with two-way make contact and center position "Off" (e.g., turn-signal switch)	Actuation with one winding 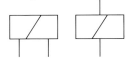	Resistor 
Switch with ganged make and break contacts	Actuation with two identical windings acting in the same direction 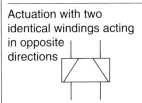	Potentiometer (with three connections) 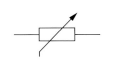
Double-make contact 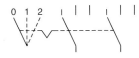	Actuation with two identical windings acting in opposite directions	Heating resistor, flame glow plug, glow plug, heated rear window 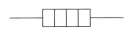

Multiple-position switch	Electrothermal actuator, thermal relay	**Various components**
		Antenna
Cam-operated switch, e.g. ignition contact breaker	Electromagnetic actuator, reciprocating solenoid	Fuse 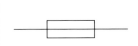
Thermostatic switch	Solenoid valve, closed	Permanent magnets
Release/triggering devices	Relay (actuator and switch) e.g.: n.c. contact operates without delay, n.o. contact with delay 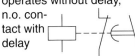	Horn; loudspeaker 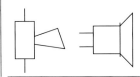

Device symbols	Automotive devices	
Dotted/dashed line for delineating or bordering related sections of the circuitry 	Battery	Pressure switch
	Socket (female contact)	Relay, general
Shielded device, border connected to ground	Light, headlamp	Solenoid valve, injection valve (injector), cold-start valve
Regulator	Horn, fanfare horn	Thermo-time switch
Electronic control unit (ECU)	Rear-window defroster	Throttle-valve switch
Indicating instrument; general, voltmeter, clock	Switch, general; without indicator lamp	Rotary actuator
Rotational-speed indicator, temperature indicator, linear-speed indicator	Switch, general; with indicator lamp	Auxiliary-air valve with electrothermal drive

Spark plug

Ignition coil

Ignition distributor, general

Voltage regulator, alternator with regulator

Starter motor with solenoid

Electric fuel pump, motor drive for hydraulic pump

Motor with fan, blower

Wiper motor

Car radio

Loudspeaker

Voltage stabilizer, stabilizer

Inductive sensor

Pulse generator, turn-signal flasher, intermittent control relay

Piezo-electric sensor

Lambda sensor

Air-flow meter

Air-mass meter

Flow-quantity indicator, fuel sender

Temperature switch, temperature sensor

Linear-speed sensor

ABS wheel-speed sensor

Circuit diagrams

The circuit diagram is a drawn representation of electrical devices by means of symbols, and can include illustrations or simplified design drawings as needed.

The circuit diagram illustrates the relationship between various devices, and shows how they are connected to one another. It may be supplemented by tables, graphs and descriptions. The type of wiring diagram depends upon the intended application (e.g., portraying circuit operation) and the type of representation.

To be intelligible, the circuit diagram must meet the following requirements:
– The representations must correspond with valid standards; explanations should be provided for any exceptions.
– The current flow should be portrayed moving from left to right and/or from top to bottom.

Block diagrams as used to portray automotive electrical systems feature unipolar illustrations. Internal component circuitry is not shown. These diagrams are designed as a rapid reference source, and provide an overview of the function of a circuit or a device.

Various types of schematic diagram (with different symbol arrangements) provide detailed representations of circuits. They illustrate operation, and can be employed as a reference for repair operations.

The terminal diagram (with terminal locations for the devices) is used by service facilities in replacing defective electrical equipment and in performing dealer installations.

Depending upon the type of representation, we distinguish between:
– unipolar and multipolar representation (according to symbol arrangement),
– assembled, semi-assembled, or detached representation, or representation with the devices shown in their actual locations. These possibilities can all be combined in one and the same circuit diagram.

Block diagram

The block diagram is a simplified representation of a circuit. Only the most important elements are included. This simplified diagram is designed to furnish a rapid overview of function, structure, layout and operation of an electrical system and/or its components. It also serves as a reference in selecting more detailed data (circuit diagram).

Squares, rectangles and circles together with attendant symbols are employed to illustrate the components. The basic reference is DIN 40 900, Section 2. Wiring is usually shown in the unipolar form.

Schematic diagram

The schematic diagram shows the elements of a circuit in detail. Individual current paths are clearly depicted, and indicate how an electrical circuit operates. In a schematic diagram, presentation of individual circuit components and their spatial relationship to each other must not interfere with the clear representation of the operation of the circuit which makes the diagram easy to read.

The schematic diagram must contain the following:
– Wiring,
– Device designations (DIN 40 719, Section 2) and
– Terminal designations (DIN 72 552, DIN 42 400).

It must be suitable for recording on microfiche (minimum line width 0.25 mm).

The schematic diagram may also include:
– Comprehensive representations including internal circuitry, to facilitate testing, trouble-shooting, maintenance and replacement (retrofit) procedures;
– Reference codes to assist in finding symbols and destinations, especially in detached-representation diagrams.

Circuit representation

The schematic diagram usually makes use of multi-line presentation. In accordance with DIN 40719, Section 1, symbols can be represented in the following ways, all of which may be combined within the same circuit diagram:

Assembled representation

All parts of a device are shown directly next to one another, and mechanical linkage of one part to another is indicated by a double line or broken connecting lines. As clarity would otherwise suffer, this type of illustration is suitable only for simple circuits.

Detached representation

Symbols for parts of electrical devices are shown separated and orientated such that each current path is as legible as possible. No attempt is made to place the symbols for individual devices or their component parts in the same relative positions to each other which they occupy in the actual equipment. Priority is assigned to a clear rectilinear portrayal, with minimal intersection of individual current paths.

Main purpose: To indicate function and operation of a circuit.

A system of symbols defined in DIN 40719, Section 2 indicates the relationships between the individual components. Each separately illustrated device symbol includes the code for the device.

Complete explanations of operation and circuit function should be provided for all devices illustrated outside the circuit whenever this is necessary to facilitate comprehension.

Topographical representation

With this type of representation, the position of the symbol either completely or partly corresponds to the position of the component within the device or part concerned.

Current paths and conductors

The current paths and conductors are to be illustrated in such a manner that they are clear and easy to follow. The individual current paths, which indicate signal flow from left to right and/or from top to bottom wherever possible, should be straight and free of intersections and changes in direction, and should generally run parallel to the border of the circuit diagram. When a number of conductors run parallel to each other, they must be represented in groups. The lines are portrayed in groups of three with intermediate spaces between the groups.

Lines of demarcation, borders

Dot/dash demarcation or border lines are used to separate parts within a circuit to indicate that such parts or devices belong together functionally or constructionally.

In illustrations of automotive electrical systems, these alternating dots and dashes represent a non-conductive border around a device or circuit component. The line will not always correspond with a device's housing, and is not related to the unit's dimensions. In high-voltage circuits this outer line is frequently combined with the protective conductor (PE), also represented as a broken dotted line.

Ground symbols

Due to its simplicity, a single conductor system, using metal vehicle components for ground, is generally employed. If conditions are not suitable for a perfect ground connection, or if voltages in excess of 42 V are being transmitted, then an insulated ground return line is installed.

All terminals represented by the ground symbol ($\perp$) are mutually connected, either through the vehicle's bodywork or via separate wiring.

All of the components containing a ground symbol must be mounted with a direct connecton to vehicle ground.

Connectors, identification, destination

For clarity, connecting lines (conductors and lines denoting mechanical linkage) can be broken if they would otherwise cover a long distance in the schematic diagram. Only beginning and end of the connecting line must be clearly evident. For this purpose, lines are identified and/or locations within the diagram where the lines terminate are indicated.

The codes for contiguous connectors match. Identification can be as follows:
– terminal designations (DIN 72552, DIN 42400),
– information concerning function,
– information in the form of alphanumeric symbols.

The line destination is given in parentheses so that it is not confused with the line identification; it consists of the section number of the destination.

Section identification

The section identification code given at the top border of the diagram is used for locating circuit sections (formerly referred to as current path). This identification can take 3 forms:
– consecutive numbers at equal intervals from left to right,
– indication of the content of the circuit sections,
– or a combination of the two.

Labelling

Devices, parts or symbols must be labelled in circuit diagrams by means of a letter and a cardinal number in accordance with DIN 40719, Part 2. This code is located to the left of, or underneath the symbol.
The prefix used to designate the type of device can be omitted if the device is clearly recognizable.

In nested devices, one device is a component part of another, e.g., starter M1 with built-in solenoid switch K6. The designation for the entire device is then:
– M1 – K6.

Identification of related symbols in detached representation: each individual symbol is shown separately and all symbols which pertain to a particular device are assigned a code corresponding to that used for the device itself.
Terminal designations (e.g., in accordance with DIN 72552) must be placed outside the symbol and, in the case of border lines, outside these lines if possible.

For horizontal current paths:
The data applying to the individual symbol are provided underneath it. The terminal code is above the connecting line, just outside the symbol proper.
For vertical current paths:
The data applying to the individual symbol are provided to its left. The terminal code is just outside the symbol. It the type is horizontal, the code is provided next to the connecting line on the symbol's right; if the type is vertical, it is on the left.

Terminal designations

The system of standard terminal designations prescribed for use in automotive applications has been designed to facilitate correct interconnection of devices and their wiring, with emphasis on repairs and installation.

The terminal designations are not at the same time wire designations, since devices with differing terminal designations could be connected to the ends of a single wire. It is therefore not essential that the terminal designations be provided on the wiring.

A complete listing of terminal designations is contained in DIN 72 552.

In addition, the designations defined in DIN-VDE standards may be used for electrical machinery.

Mutliple plug connections large enough to exhaust the range provided by DIN 72 552 receive consecutive numbers or letters, avoiding any characters which are already defined in the standards.

The terminal designations provided in Table 1 are only intended as examples; most of them are contained in the chapter on "Circuit diagram for a passenger car with spark-ignition engine."

Table 1. Examples of terminal designations

Terminal	Definition
	Ignition coil, ignition distributor
1	Low voltage
4	High tension
	Ignition distributor with two separate electrical circuits:
4a	from ignition coil I, Term. 4
4b	from ignition coil II, Term. 4
	Battery
15	Switched + downstream of battery (output of ignition and starting switch)
15a	Output at ballast resistor to ignition coil and starter
30	Input from positive battery terminal (direct)
31	Return line to negative battery terminal or ground (direct)
31b	Return line to negative battery terminal or ground, via switch or relay (switched negative)
	Electric motors
32	Return line
33	Main terminal connection
33a	Self-parking switch-off
33b	Shunt field

Terminal	Definition
33f	For 2nd lower-speed range
33g	For 3rd lower-speed range
33h	For 4th lower-speed range
33L	Counterclockwise rotation
33R	Clockwise rotation
	Turn-signal flasher (pulse generator)
49	Input
49a	Output
49b	Output, 2nd turn-signal circuit
49c	Output, 3rd turn-signal circuit
	Starter
50	Starter control (direct)
	Wiper motors
53	Wiper motor, input (+)
53a	Wiper (+), self-parking switch-off
53b	Wiper (shunt winding)
53c	Electric windshield-washer pump
53e	Wiper (brake winding)
53i	Wiper motor with permanent magnet and third brush (for higher speed)

Terminal	Definition		Terminal	Definition

Lighting technology

55	Fog lamp
56	Headlamp
56a	High beam, high-beam indicator lamp
56b	Low beam
56d	Headlamp-flasher contact
57a	Parking lamp
57L	Parking lamp, left
57R	Parking lamp, right
58	Side-marker lamps, tail lamps, license-plate lamps, and instrument-panel lamps
58L	Left, license-plate lamp
58R	Right, license-plate lamp

Alternator and voltage regulator

61	Alternator charge-indicator lamp
B+	Battery positive
B−	Battery negative
D+	Dynamo positive
D−	Dynamo negative
DF	Dynamo field
DF1	Dynamo field 1
DF2	Dynamo field 2
U,V,W	Alternator terminals

Audio

| 75 | Radio, cigarette lighter |
| 76 | Loudspeaker |

Switches

81	Break contact/change-over contact (input)
82	Make contact (input)
83	Multiple-position switch (input)

Current relay

84	Actuator/Relay contact (input)
84a	Actuator (output)
84b	Relay contact (output)

Switching relay

85	Actuator, end of winding to negative or ground (output) Actuator (input)
86	Start of winding
86a	Start of winding or 1st winding
86b	Winding tap or 2nd winding

Relay contact for break contacts and changeover contacts:

87	Input
87a	1st output (break-contact side)
87b	2nd output
87c	3rd output
87z	1st input
87y	2nd input
87x	3rd input

Relay contact for make contact:

| 88 | Input |

Relay contact for make contact and change-over contact (make-contact side):

88a	1st output
88b	2nd output
88c	3rd output

Relay contact for make contact:

88z	1st input
88y	2nd input
88x	3rd input

Directional signals (turn-signal flasher)

C	1st indicator lamp
C0	Main connection for indicator lamp separate from turn-signal flasher
C2	2nd indicator lamp
C3	3rd indicator lamp (e.g. when towing two trailers)
L	Turn-signal lamps, left
R	Turn-signal lamps, right

Section identity codes and device identifiers

Table 2 contains all the section codes contained in the section "Circuit diagram for a passenger car with spark-ignition engine." The sections are specific defined areas containing a specific system or device within the schematic diagrams.
Table 3 contains devices and their designations along with section numbers for passenger-car schematic diagrams.

Table 2. Sections

Section	System
1	Electrical power supply
2	Starting system
3	Ignition system with knock control El-K
4	Electronic fuel injection (EFI) KE-Jetronic
5	Lighting
6	Wash/wipe system
7	HVAC
8	Signalling system
9	Clock, radio
10	Displays and instruments
11	Antilock Braking System (ABS)

Table 3. Device identifiers

Identifier	Device	Section
A1	Trigger box El-K	3
A2	Radio	9
B1	Knock sensor	3
B2	Rotational-speed and reference-mark sensor	3
B3	Cylinder-identification sensor	3
B4	Lambda sensor	4
B5	Dual temperature sensor (engine)	4
B6	Vehicle-speed sensor	10
B7	Fuel-level sensing unit	10
B8	Temperature sensor (coolant)	10
B9	Loudspeaker	9
B10	Dimmer for instrument-panel lighting	5
B11	Supertone horn	8
B12	Horn	8
B13	Air-flow meter	4
B14	Electrodynamic pressure actuator	4
B15	Altitude sensor	4
B16	Wheel-speed sensor (ABS)	11
E1	High-voltage distributor	3
E2	Spark plugs	3
E3, 4	Fog-warning lamps	5
E5, 6	Upper-beam headlamps	5
E7, 8	Fog lamps	5
E9, 10	Lower-beam headlamps	5
E11, 12	Side-marker lamps	5
E13	License-plate lamp	5
E14, 15	Tail lamps	5
E16	Backup lamps	5
E17	Instrument lighting	5
E18	Instrument-panel lighting	5
E19	Rear-window defogger	7
F..	Fuses	
G1	Battery	1
G2	Alternator/Generator	1
H1	Charge-indicator lamp	10
H2	Low-oil-pressure lamp	10
H3	Hand-brake indicator lamp	10
H4	Upper-beam indicator lamp	10
H5	Turn-signal indicator lamp	10
H6...9	Turn-signal lamps	5
H10, 11	Stop lamps	5
H12	Rear-window defogger indicator lamp	7
H13	Diagnosis indicator lamp	4
H14	ABS fault/warning lamp	11

Circuit diagrams

Identifier	Device	Section	Identifier	Device	Section
K1	Fuel-pump relay	4	S11	Hazard-warning switch	5
K2	Side-marker-lamp		S12	Horn selector switch	8
	interrogate relay	5	S13	Horn button	8
K3	Supertone-horn relay	8	S14	Thermo-switch	7
K4	Engine-fan relay	7	S15	Rear-window-defogger	
K5	Rear-window defogger			switch	7
	relay	7	S16	Fan switch	7
K6	Intermittent-wiper relay	6	S17	Wiper switch	6
K7	Valve relay	11	S18	Washer switch	6
K8	Motor relay	11			
K9	Overvoltage protection		T1	Ignition coil	3
	relay	11			
			W1	Car antenna	9
M1	Starter motor	2			
M2	Cooling-fan motor	7	X1	ECU plug, EI-K	3
M3	Cabin-fan motor	7	X2	ECU plug, KE-Jetronic	4
M4	Wiper motor	6	X3	Coding plug	4
M5	Windshield-washer		X4	Plug, lamp-check	
	motor	6		module	5
M6	Return pump	11	X5	ECU plug, ABS	11
			X6	Plug, Check-Control	5
N1	Voltage stabilizer	10	X7	Socket, hazard-warning	
				relay	5
P1	Instrument cluster	10	X8	Plug, basic module	
P2	Electrical speedometer	10		for central vehicle	
P3	Tachometer	10		electronics	5
P4	Fuel gauge	10	X9	Diagnosis socket	9
P5	Engine-temperature		X10	Wheel-speed sensor,	
	indicator	10		ABS	11
P6	Clock	9			
			Y1	Idle actuator	4
R1	Fan resistor	7	Y2	Fuel-injection valves	
				(injectors)	4
S1	Ignition/starter switch	2	Y3	Electric fuel pump	4
S2	Throttle-valve switch	4	Y4	Canister-purge valve	4
S3	Oil-pressure switch	10	Y5	Hydraulic modulator	11
S4	Hand-brake switch	10	Y6	Solenoid valves	11
S5	Headlamp switch	5			
S6	Fog-lamp switch	5	L	Left	
S7	Dimmer switch	5	R	Right	
S8	Stop-lamp switch	5	V	Front	
S9	Turn-signal switch	5	H	Rear	
S10	Backup-lamp switch	5			

Circuit diagram for a passenger car with spark-ignition engine

Purpose

Circuit diagrams are the only way to provide an overview of complex automotive electrical systems and their numerous terminals and connections (Fig. 1). Modern systems include more than just the lights, and incorporate a large number of electric and electronic devices for open and closed-loop engine-management systems, as well as numerous accessories for convenience and comfort.

Design

The schematic diagrams in the following section (Figures 2 to 6) are examples of different vehicle circuits. They are intended to facilitate understanding of the text; they are not intended for use in manufacture or installation.

Coding examples

A1 Device designation (DIN 40 719)
15 Terminal designation (DIN 72 552)
1 Section code (DIN 40 719)

Fig. 1: Passenger-car wiring harness

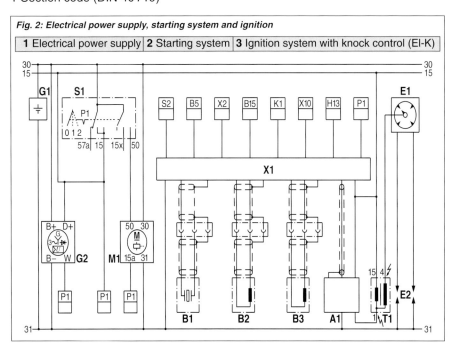

Fig. 2: Electrical power supply, starting system and ignition

1 Electrical power supply | **2** Starting system | **3** Ignition system with knock control (EI-K)

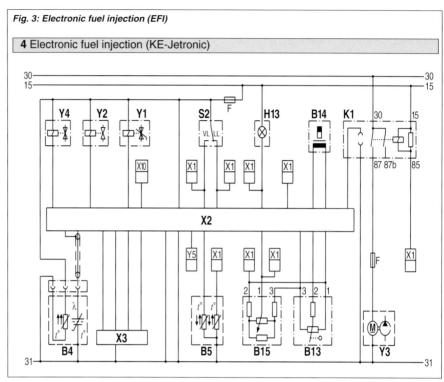

Fig. 3: Electronic fuel injection (EFI)

4 Electronic fuel injection (KE-Jetronic)

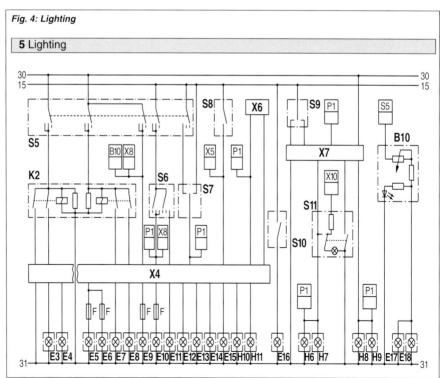

Fig. 4: Lighting

5 Lighting

Fig. 5: Electronic safety, comfort and convenience systems

6 Wash/wipe systems | **7** HVAC | **8** Signalling system | **9** Clock, radio

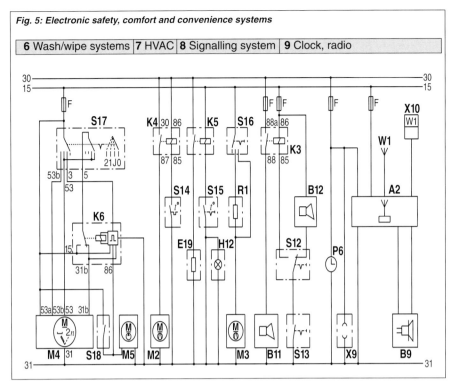

Fig. 6: Displays, instruments, and antilock braking system (ABS)

10 Displays and instruments | **11** Antilock braking system (ABS)

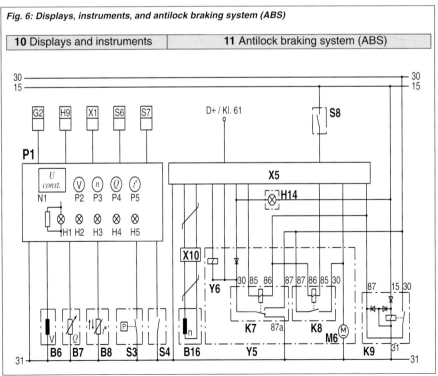

Terminal diagram

The terminal diagram shows the locations where electrical devices are connected. It also illustrates the external (and internal if required) conductive elements (wiring).

Representation

Individual electrical devices are illustrated using squares, rectangles, circles, symbols or illustrations, and their locations may correspond to their installed positions. The connections are represented by circles, dots, plug connectors, or simply by the connecting line.
The following forms of representation are conventionally used for automotive electrical systems:
– assembled representation, symbols defined in DIN 40 900 (Fig. 7a),
– assembled representation, device represented pictorially (Fig. 7b),
– detached, device indicated by symbol, connections with line destinations; color codes for wiring may be present (Fig. 8a),
– detached, device represented pictorially, connections with line destinations; color codes for wiring may be present (Fig. 8b).

Color code for electrical lines (as per DIN 47 002)

bl	blue	gn	green	ws	black
br	brown	or	orange	tk	turquoise
ge	yellow	rs	pink	vi	violet
gr	grey	rt	red	ws	white

Designation

Electrical devices are designated as defined in DIN 40 719, Section 2. Terminals and plug connections are designated using the terminal designations present on the device (Fig. 7).
Detached representations dispense with continuous connecting lines between devices. All conductors leaving a device are provided with a line destination code (DIN 40719, Section 2), consisting of the identifier for the element at the other end of the line and its terminal designation and – if necessary – the wiring color code as specified in DIN 47 002 (Fig. 9).

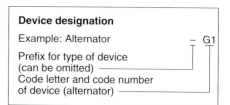

Device designation

Example: Alternator — G1
Prefix for type of device (can be omitted)
Code letter and code number of device (alternator)

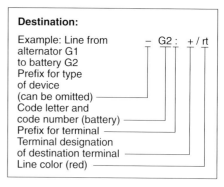

Destination:

Example: Line from alternator G1 — G2 : + / rt
to battery G2
Prefix for type of device (can be omitted)
Code letter and code number (battery)
Prefix for terminal
Terminal designation of destination terminal
Line color (red)

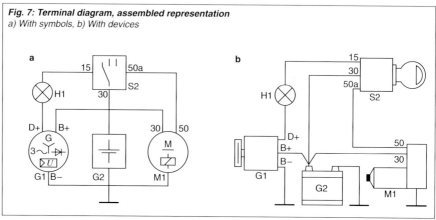

Fig. 7: Terminal diagram, assembled representation
a) With symbols, b) With devices

Fig. 8: Terminal diagram, detached representation
a) With symbols and destination, b) With devices and destination
G1 Alternator with voltage regulator
G2 Battery
H1 Charge-indicator lamp
M1 Starter motor
S2 Ignition and starting switch
XX Device ground to vehicle ground
YY Terminal for ground connection
:15 Conductor potential, e.g. Terminal 15

a   b

G1  D+ o— H1
                          B+ o— G2:+
                          B– o—|

G1  D+ o— H1
                          B+ o— G2:+
                          B– o—|

G2  + ⊂— G1:B+
                              S2:30
                              M1:30
                          – o—|

G2 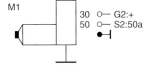 + ⊂— G1:B+
                              S2:30
                              M1:30
           – o—|

M1  30 o— G2:+
                          50 o— S2:50a
                          ●—|

M1 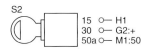 30 o— G2:+
                          50 o— S2:50a
                          ●—|

H1   ⊗   o— S2:15
          o— G1:D+

H1   ⊗   o— S2:15
          o— G1:D+

S2 |⟋ | 15 o— H1
          30 o— G2:+
          50a o— M1:50

S2   15 o— H1
          30 o— G2:+
          50a o— M1:50

Fig. 9: Device designation. Example: Alternator
a Device designation (code letter and code number)
b Terminal designation on device
c Device to ground
d Destination (code letter and code number/terminal designation and conductor color)

Device representation   Destination

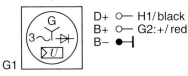

D+ o— H1/ black
B+ o— G2:+/ red
B– ●—|

G1

a   b   c   d

Calculation of conductor sizes

Quantities and units

Quantity	Designation	Unit
A	Conductor cross section	mm²
I	Current	A
l	Conductor length	m
P	Power required by load	W
R	Resistance (load)	Ω
S	Current density in conductor	A/mm²
U_N	Nominal voltage	V
U_{vl}	Permissible voltage drop in insulated conductor	V
U_{vg}	Permissible voltage drop in entire circuit	V
ϱ	Resistivity	Ω·mm²/m

Calculation

Always factor in voltage drop (line loss) and thermal losses when determining wiring diameters.

Calculation steps

1. Determine the current I for the electrical device: $I = P / U_N = U_N / R$
2. Use the U_{vl} figures in Table 2 to calculate conductor diameter A (for copper $\varrho = 0.0185$ Ω · mm²/m):
$A = I \cdot \varrho \cdot l / U_{vl}$
3. Round off A to the next higher figure as per Table 1.
Due to their physical weakness, separate wires of less than 1 mm² in diameter are not recommended.
4. Calculate actual voltage drop U_{vl}:
$U_{vl} = I \cdot \varrho \cdot l / A$
5. Check current density S to avoid excessive conductor temperatures ($S < 30$ A/mm² in sporadic use, consult Table 1 for diameter ratings and approved continuous currents).
$S = I/A$.

Table 1. Electrical copper conductors for automotive applications
Single-core, untinned, PVC-insulated. Permissible working temperature 70°C[2])

Nominal conductor cross-section mm²	Approx. number of individual wires[1])	Maximum resistance per meter[1]) at +20°C mΩ/m	Maximum conductor diameter mm	Nominal thickness of insulation[1]) mm	Maximum cable outer diameter[1]) mm	Permissible continuous current (standard value)[2]) at ambient temperature +30°C A	+50°C A
1	32	18.5	1.5	0.6	2.7	19	13.5
1.5	30	12.7	1.8	0.6	3.0	24	17.0
2.5	50	7.60	2.2	0.7	3.6	32	22.7
4	56	4.71	2.8	0.8	4.4	42	29.8
6	84	3.14	3.4	0.8	5.0	54	38.3
10	80	1.82	4.5	1.0	6.5	73	51.8
16	126	1.16	6.3	1.0	8.3	98	69.6
25	196	0.743	7.8	1.3	10.4	129	91.6
35	276	0.527	9.0	1.3	11.6	158	112
50	396	0.368	10.5	1.5	13.5	198	140
70	360	0.259	12.5	1.5	15.5	245	174
95	475	0.196	14.8	1.6	18.0	292	207
120	608	0.153	16.5	1.6	19.7	344	244

[1]) DIN ISO 6722, Part 3.   [2]) DIN VDE 0298, Part 4.

The figures for U_{vl} in Table 2 are used to calculate the dimensions of the positive conductor. Line losses in the ground (return) wire have not been factored in. For insulated wiring, the total length in both directions should generally be used.

The figures for U_{vg} are empirical values. They are not suited for wiring calculations, as they include extraneous factors such as contact resistance in switches, fuses, etc. and are not based exclusively on the conductor.

Table 2. Permissible voltage drop

Type of conductor	Permissible voltage drop in positive conductor U_{vl}		Permissible voltage drop in entire circuit U_{vg}		Comments
Nominal voltage U_N	12 V	24 V	12 V	24 V	
Lighting conductors					
from Terminal 30 of light switch	0.1 V	0.1 V	0.6 V	0.6 V	Current at
to lamps < 15 W					nominal voltage
to trailer socket					and
from trailer socket					nominal power
to lamps					
From Terminal 30 of light switch	0.5 V	0.5 V	0.9 V	0.9 V	
to lamps > 15 W					
to trailer socket					
From Terminal 30 of light switch	0.3 V	0.3 V	0.6 V	0.6 V	
to headlamps					
Charging cable					
From Terminal B+ of alternator	0.4 V	0.8 V	–	–	Current at
to battery					nominal voltage and nominal power
Control lines					
from alternator to voltage regulator	0.1 V	0.2 V	–	–	At maximum
(Terminals D+, D–, DF)					excitation current (Note 1)
Main starter cable	0.5 V	1.0 V	–	–	Starter short-circuit current at +20°C (Notes 2 and 3)
Starter control line					Maximum con-
From starter switch to Terminal 50					trol current
of starter					(Notes. 4 and 5)
Solenoid switch with single winding	1.4 V	2.0 V	1.7 V	2.5 V	
Solenoid switch with pull-in and hold-in	1.5 V	2.2 V	1.9 V	2.8 V	
windings					
Other control lines					Current at
From switch to relay, horn, etc.	0.5 V	1.0 V	1.5 V	2.0 V	nominal voltage

Notes
1. As far as possible all 3 control lines should have the same length and resistance.
2. In special cases in which a very long main starter cable is used, the U_{vl} value can be exceeded if the starting limit temperature is reduced.
3. If the main starter return cable is insulated, the voltage loss in the return line should not exceed that of the incoming line; voltage loss values of 4% of the nominal voltage in each line are permissible, for a total of 8%.
4. The U_{vl} values apply to solenoid-switch temperatures of between +50°C and +80°C.
5. If necessary, make allowance for the cable to the ignition/starter switch.

Electromagnetic compatibility (EMC) and interference suppression

Overview

The electromagnetic compatibility (EMC) defines an electrical system's ability to remain neutral in the vicinity of other systems. In other words, it is compatible, and besides not interfering with other systems it also remains impervious to such interference as might emanate from them. Referring to automotive applications, this means that the various electrical systems such as ignition, ABS, and radio etc., must function correctly in close proximity without interfering with each other. It also means though that the vehicle in its role as a complete system must remain neutral within its environment. In other words, it is not to interfere electrically with other vehicles, and it must not interfere with broadcast or communications transmissions of any kind. At the same time, the vehicle must remain fully operational when exposed to strong electromagnetic fields from the outside (e.g., when in the vicinity of radio transmitters). It is in view of these considerations that automotive electrical systems and the vehicle as a whole are designed to ensure electromagnetic compatibility.

Electromagnetic compatibility between systems in the vehicle

On-board electrical system

The power supply to the vehicle's electrical systems comes from an on-board electrical system which is used jointly by all equipment. This means that disturbances caused by a given system are received directly by the next system through the power supply. As shown in Fig. 1, disturbances from system I are passed on to the input of system II.
Such disturbances include, for instance, pulses (abrupt, very steep current or voltage-rise phenomena) which are generated during electrical switch-off and

Fig. 1: Mutual disturbance between two systems via the common power supply (A) and the common wiring harness (B and C)
System I: 1 ECU, 2 Actuator, 3 Sensor. System II: 4 ECU, 5 Actuator, 6 Sensor.

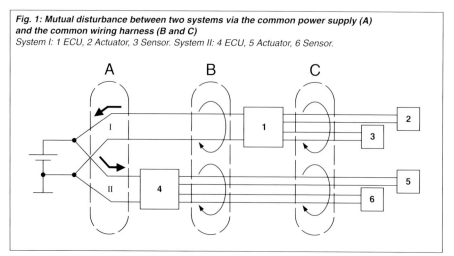

Table 1. Mutual influences in the voltage supply.

Test pulses as per DIN 40 389, Section 1			Classification of permissible pulse amplitudes			
Pulse shape	Internal resistance	Pulse duration	I	II	III	IV
1	10 Ω	2 ms	−25 V	−50 V	−75 V	−100 V
2	10 Ω	50 μs	+25 V	+50 V	+75 V	+100 V
3a	50 Ω	0.1 μs	−40 V	−75 V	−110 V	−150 V
3b			+25 V	+50 V	+75 V	+100 V
4	10 mΩ	to 20 s	12 V −3 V	12 V −5 V	12 V −6 V	12 V −7 V
5	1 Ω	to 400 ms	+35 V	+50 V	+80 V	+120 V

switch-on. They are grouped together and classified in DIN 40839, Section 1 (Table 1). Special test-pulse generators are needed to generate the pulses in accordance with these classifications.

Pulse shape 1. Source: Switch-off of an inductive load, e.g., of relays or valves.

Pulse shape 2. Source: Switch-off of motorized devices, e.g., fan motor which generates positive overvoltage on run-on.

Pulse shape 3a/3b: Simulates overvoltages which result from switching processes.

Pulse shape 4: Simulates the supply-voltage curve during starting.

Pulse shape 5. Source: "Load dump". Occurs when the alternator is supplying the battery with a high current and the connection between the two is suddenly interrupted.

The classification according to pulse amplitude permits optimum matching of interference sources (points at which interference originates) and potentially susceptible equipment for every vehicle.

The matching procedure can entail prescribing Class II for all the vehicle's interference sources, and Class III for all its susceptible devices (e.g., ECU's) taking a suitable safety margin into account. A shift to Classes I/II would be appropriate if suppression measures at sources of interference involve less outlay than measures at potentially susceptible equipment.
If, on the other hand, suppression at the potentially susceptible equipment is simpler and involves less outlay than measures at the interference sources, then a shift to Classes III/IV is advisable.

Apart from the disturbances due to pulses, high-frequency oscillations also have an unwanted effect on the vehicle electrical system. These are caused by rapid switching due for instance to the commutation in a DC motor or the operation of a microcomputer in an ECU. We are not dealing here with a single sinusoidal oscillation which can be defined using its frequency and amplitude, but with the superimposition of a number of harmonic components of various frequencies and amplitudes.

Instead of presenting the oscillation in the form of a characteristic as a function of time, it is customary to show the amplitudes of the individual harmonic components as a function of their frequencies, in other words to show the "spectrum" of the oscillation (Fig. 3). If the spectrum appears as a more or less smooth curve, one speaks of "broadband interference", on the other hand if the spectrum is composed of individual peaks one speaks of "narrow-band interference".

Above all, small electric motors and the alternator are the source of wide-band disturbance, the interference voltages that they transmit are covered by VDE 0879, Section 3 (see Table 2). Similar to pulse interference, the interference voltages are also sub-divided into various classes, thus permitting optimum matching to the particular application. Measurement of the transmitted disturbances takes place using a selective measuring receiver (similar to a radio) whose characteristics are defined in the above Standard. It is also important that the interference components originate from a vehicle electrical system with precisely defined electrical characteristics. Using an equivalent circuit of the vehicle electrical system (Fig. 2), it is possible to generate reproducible conditions.

Narrow-band interference (Fig. 3b) originates above all from ECU's with microcomputer.

Side-by-side in the wiring harness

Tight inductive and capacitive coupling exists between the vehicle's wires and cables due to them being combined in a wiring harness. The interference voltages on the power-supply lines as described in the previous section, are coupled into adjoining conductors in this wiring harness. If, for instance, a signal of several volts is coupled into a sensor line this can lead to malfunctions in the system which is dependent upon the sensor's signals. The lines to the actuators can also be regarded as potential sources of interference since automotive actuators are usually triggered by pulses which feature a steep voltage or current increase.

The following measures can be implemented to prevent this mutual interference:

– As far as possible, round off the flanks of the pulses (for instance, damping of pronounced voltage variations),
– Using diodes or resistors in the actuators to reduce pulse rise and pulse amplitude,
– Shield sensitive wires, and
– Route the wiring harness to keep coupling to a minimum.

Fig. 2: Basic circuit diagram of the equivalent circuit for the motor-vehicle electrical system In accordance with DIN 57 879, Section 3/VDE 0879, Section 3.
Connections: P-B test specimen, A-B power supply, M-B radio-interference measuring receiver. S Switch, B Reference ground (metal sheet, shielding of the equivalent circuit).

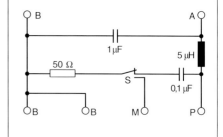

A check can be made during the system's development phase to determine whether the measures are adequate. This involves the coupling-in of disturbance into a branch of the wiring harness that leads to the ECU under test: Pulses are injected using a "capacitive clamp" and HF interference voltages using a "current clamp".

Car radio and car telephone

With regard to EMC, the same considerations apply for the car radio and car telephone as they do for every other electrical system in the vehicle. Complications arise from the fact that the car radio receives signals from the antenna of only a few microvolts. Furthermore,

the antenna not only picks-up the electromagnetic field from the (wanted signal) transmitters, but also from neighboring systems in the vehicle.
When car radio and car telephone are taken into account, this means that the interference emanating from the various sources in the vehicle must be suppressed to a level which is far below what would be necessary without these devices.
Interference with a narrow-band spectrum such as is generated by the microcomputers in ECU's is particularly troublesome. It cannot be distinguished from the wanted signals coming from the broadcast transmitters and makes it impossible to receive very weak stations.

Table 2: Permissible radio-interference voltage level for the interference-suppression levels in the individual frequency ranges as per DIN 57879, Section 3/VDE 0879, Section 3.

Interference-suppression level	Frequency range for:			
	LW 0.15...0.3 MHz	MW 0.5...1.65 MHz	SW 5.95...26.1 MHz	VHF 87.5...108 MHz
	Permissible radio-interference level in dB			
5	60	50	40	24
4	70	58	46	30
3	80	66	52	36
2	90	74	58	42
1	100	82	64	48
0	unlimited			

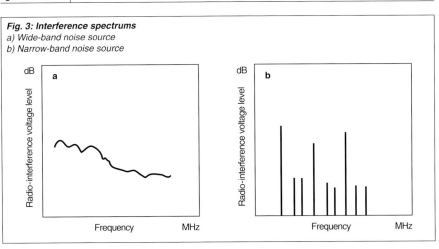

Fig. 3: Interference spectrums
a) Wide-band noise source
b) Narrow-band noise source

EMC between the vehicle and its environment

Radiation

In order that the vehicle does not interfere with radio, TV, and 2-way radio services, its radiation must not exceed the limits as detailed in Fig. 4.

The lawmakers stipulate that the electrical field strength is measured at a distance of 10 m from the vehicle. Details of measurement procedure, e.g. the receiver to be used and the evaluation of the measurements is given in VDE 0879, Section 1.

The ignition system is almost solely responsible for the vehicle's interference radiation. In a vehicle equipped for the operation of car radio and car telephone, electromagnetic compatibility exists between the vehicle's systems because steps have already been taken (for instance using shielding) to reduce the electromagnetic radiation and its effects. Such a vehicle not only complies with the legal limits in this respect, it is also well inside them.

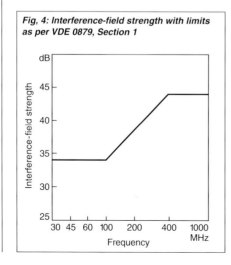

Fig, 4: Interference-field strength with limits as per VDE 0879, Section 1

Incident radiation

When a vehicle drives through a powerful transmitter's near field, this penetrates into the vehicle through gaps and openings in the bodywork and affects the vehicle's electrical system. The effects of this incident radiation depend essentially upon the bodywork and upon the wiring harness.

Formerly, in order to prove that the vehicle's electronic systems function perfectly even under such adverse conditions it was necessary to carry out tests in the vicinity of high-power transmitters. Nowadays, special test chambers are available which have been specifically equipped for the purpose, and which are surrounded by a metal screen to prevent the electromagnetic fields that are generated in the chamber from escaping into the environment. In addition, these chambers must be equipped with absorbers (non-reflecting elements) in order to prevent standing waves, i. e., nodes and antinodes, forming as a result of the screening and causing pronounced field-strength variations from point to point. Bosch uses an "absorber chamber" to investigate the performance of the vehicle's electrical systems as a whole under practical operating conditions. HF fields in the range from 10 kHz … 1 GHz can be generated, with provision for extending the range to 10 GHz, whereby 10 GHz = 10×10^9 Hz. Maximum field strength is at $E_{max.}$ = 200 V/m. Since such field strengths are hazardous to health, the test vehicle is operated remotely from a screened control room and monitored by video cameras. The chamber is screened by metal plates, and non-metallic materials (wood and plastic) are used for its interior so that measurements are not falsified. To prevent reflections, walls and ceiling are covered by pyramid-shaped absorber elements of graphite-filled poyurethane foam. The test vehicle is driven onto a roller-type test stand with which speeds of up to 200 km/h can be simulated. The test stand is suspended in a massive concrete ring so that vibrations are kept away from the building. A fan is provided with which up to 40,000 m³/h of air can be directed over the vehicle, a figure which corresponds to the headwind at approx. 80 km/h.

Compared to measurements in the open air, the absorber chamber has the advantage that both frequency and field strength can be varied considerably. This means the test of a vehicle's ability to resist incident radiation is not restricted to just a few frequencies and field strengths. By controlling the field strength up to the limit of the electronic equipment, information can also be obtained on safety dimensions. Although the incident radiation tests are informative, they have the disadvantage that they cannot be performed until the vehicle and its electronic equipment have reached an advanced stage of development. And if the measurements then prove that the resistance to incident radiation is inadequate, the chances if intervening in the design are very limited. It is therefore desirable to ascertain at an early stage of system design just how this system will perform when actually installed in the vehicle. Appropriate measures can then be taken. Three different test methods have been developed:

Test procedures
Line-conducted interference waves are coupled into the wiring harness of the system under test. They are generated using a "stripline" method, BCI (bulk current injection), or a TEM cell.

Stripline method Figs. 5 and 6
The designation "stripline" is derived from the 3.5 m long and 50 cm wide strip-shaped conductor which is located 15 cm above a conductive plate (counter-electrode).

A transverse electromagnetic wave is generated between the stripline and the counter-electrode which spreads out from the HF generator and extends as far as the "terminating resistor".

The system under test, comprising for instance ECU, wiring harness, and peripheral equipment (sensors and actuators), is located at about half height between the plate and the stripline. The wiring harness is aligned parallel to the stripline. The field strength between plate and stripline is then increased at a fixed frequency until the system either malfunctions or a specified maximum level is reached. If the process is now repeated with the frequency altered in sufficiently small steps, a diagram is generated showing the resistance to incident radiation.

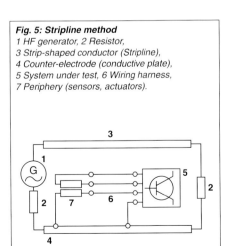

Fig. 5: Stripline method
1 HF generator, 2 Resistor,
3 Strip-shaped conductor (Stripline),
4 Counter-electrode (conductive plate),
5 System under test, 6 Wiring harness,
7 Periphery (sensors, actuators).

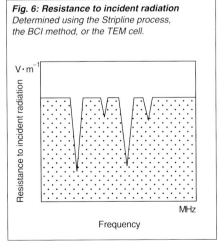

Fig. 6: Resistance to incident radiation
Determined using the Stripline process,
the BCI method, or the TEM cell.

Long-distance interference suppression

The aim of long-distance interference suppression is to reduce the interference-field strength to such a degree that radio and TV reception in the vicinity of the vehicle, for instance in nearby houses, is not interfered with. In the 30 ... 250 MHz frequency range, the interference-field strength following implementation of suppression measures is not to exceed the limits as defined by DIN 57879/VDE 0879, Section 1.

Short-distance (intensified) interference suppression

This form of interference suppression is applicable for vehicles which are equipped with their own transmitters and receivers or when such equipment is operated in the immediate vicinity.

Spark plugs

As with long-distance interference suppression, use is made of suppression connectors with built-in resistors. If necessary, these are shielded.

Ignition coil

The ignition coil is fitted with a 2.2µF suppression capacitor which must always be connected to the same ignition-coil terminal as the battery. It should never be connected to Terminal 1. If necessary, the HT ignition cable leading from the ignition coil (Terminal 4) is provided with a suppression connector.
Note: In vehicles with electronic ignition systems, a suppression capacitor with overvoltage limiting should be connected at Terminal 15 of the ignition coil.

Ignition distributor

In addition to the suppression distributor rotor used for long-distance interference suppression, each HT ignition cable leading from the ignition distributor is fitted with a distributor connector containing an interference-suppression resistor. On ignition distributors operating with breaker points, in order to reduce spark generation when the points open, a suppression filter must be connected at Terminal 1 of the distributor.

Fig. 9: Short-distance (intensified) interference suppression of an ignition system with non-shielded ignition coil
1 Shielded distributor connectors with suppression resistors, 2 Shielded HT ignition cables,
3 Metal-coated distributor cap, 4 Distributor rotor with suppression resistor (if not already fitted),
5 Suppression filter, 6 Shielded ignition-coil connector with suppression resistor,
7 Suppression capacitor, 8 Shielded spark-plug connectors with suppression resistors.

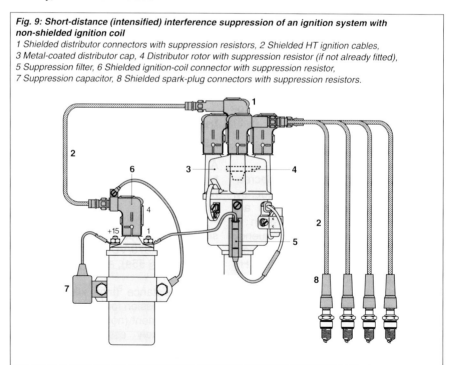

Shielded systems

Shielded systems permit short-distance interference suppression for satisfying the most exacting requirements. Such systems are used in vehicles with two-way radios or telephones, in radio location vehicles, and if particularly exacting requirements are made on reception quality.

Alternators

A suppression filter with adequate continuous current-carrying capacity (100 or 200 A) is to be connected in the alternator line to Battery B+ and if necessary in D+. The lines between alternator and suppression filter are to be completely shielded.

Ignition systems

It is advisable to use only ready-assembled HT ignition cables.
– The shielding leads right up to the ignition coil (for instance on police or emergency-service vehicles), or
– The ignition system, including ignition coil, is shielded completely. Frequently, instead of standard plugs with shielded connectors, fully shielded spark plugs are used, as well as completely shielded ignition distributors. The line to the ignition and starting switch is also provided with a suppression filter up to which the shielding must extend (applies particularly to military vehicles).

Electric motors

Shielding is not normally required for electric motors if they already have built-in suppression devices. In special cases, the motor is shielded (particularly the terminals), a suppression filter is fitted (size depending upon current loading), or the line between the suppression filter and the electric motor is shielded with suppression braiding.

Electrical instruments etc.

Usually, no shielding is required for such instruments. Standard suppression measures suffice.

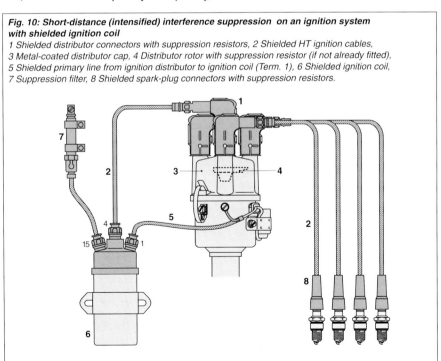

Fig. 10: Short-distance (intensified) interference suppression on an ignition system with shielded ignition coil
1 Shielded distributor connectors with suppression resistors, 2 Shielded HT ignition cables, 3 Metal-coated distributor cap, 4 Distributor rotor with suppression resistor (if not already fitted), 5 Shielded primary line from ignition distributor to ignition coil (Term. 1), 6 Shielded ignition coil, 7 Suppression filter, 8 Shielded spark-plug connectors with suppression resistors.

Tracking down the source of interference

1. Vehicle stationary, engine stopped, ignition OFF

Disturbed waveband	Type of interference (audible in receiver loudspeaker)	Interference occurs	Interference disappears	Source of interference
SW, MW, LW, partially also FM	Various types of noise	–	On selection of a different location	Source of interference outside the vehicle, e.g. high-tension lines, neon advertising signs etc., atmospherics, thunderstorms

2. Vehicle stationary, engine stopped, ignition ON

Disturbed waveband	Type of interference (audible in receiver loudspeaker)	Interference occurs	Interference disappears	Source of interference
SW, MW, LW, particularly FM	Humming noise (background noise, hissing) or howling in time with the wiper-blade movements	When the wiper is switched on	When the wiper is switched off	Wiper motor
	Hissing noise (crackling)	When one of the devices listed in the last column is switched on	After one of the devices listed in the last column is switched off	Electric fuel pump / Electric fan / Washer-pump assembly / Vehicle heater
	Clicking	When the brake pedal is pressed	After disconnecting the cable to the stop-lamp switch	Stop-lamp switch
	Rhythmic clicking	When the turn-signal indicators or the hazard-warning and turn-signal flashers are operated	When the turn-signal indicators or the hazard-warning and turn-signal flashers are switched off	Turn-signal flasher

3. Vehicle stationary, engine running

Disturbed waveband	Type of interference (audible in receiver loudspeaker)	Interference occurs	Interference disappears	Source of interference
SW, MW, LW, particulary FM	Crackling and clicking (ticking); depends on engine speed	At all engine speeds	After switching off the ignition	Ignition system
SW, MW, LW	Crackling or clicking	At various engine speeds, more pronounced with cold engine	When the V-belt is removed	V-belt (electrostatic charges)
SW, MW, LW, FM	High hissing or howl, pitch increases along with engine speed	At all engine speeds	When V-belt is removed	Alternator
	Crackling	At all engine speeds	When ignition is switched off	Voltage stabilizer for monitoring devices
	Crackling depends on engine speed	At all engine speeds	When ignition is switched off	Electric tachometer
FM	Clicking depends on engine speed	Especially when engine accelerates	When ignition is switched off at high speeds	Open-circuit suppression resistor in one of the HT ignition cables

4. Vehicle being driven

Disturbed waveband	Type of interference (audible in receiver loudspeaker)	Interference occurs	Interference disappears	Source of interference
Only SW, MW, LW	Crackling or clicking	Only at high road speeds and on dry roads (even if declutched or engine switched off)	Immediately the brakes are applied lightly	Tire interferences (electrostatic charges)
SW, MW, LW, FM	Crackling and occasional loss of reception	During vibration due to poor roads	When driving on good roads	Loose contacts, e.g., in the receiver (antenna)
	Crackling	When driving on cobblestones, or over potholes and bumps	Upon declutching when driving and braking lightly	Electrostatic charges on parts of the vehicle (e.g., running-gear joints and/or bearings)
			After establishing good ground connections between the individual parts of the vehicle body	Contact resistances between individual parts of the body (due to corrosion, oxidation, paint)
	Crackling with constant pitch	–	–	Electrostatic charges on the transmission due to bearings or toothed gears, possibly also between fan and radiator gills

Starter batteries

Summary

Purpose

Within the electrical system, the battery acts as the chemical storage device for the electrical energy generated by the alternator. It must be capable of briefly supplying high currents for cold starting (particularly at low temperatures). It must also supply some or all of the current required by other major system components for limited periods (idle, engine off). These functions are usually performed by a lead-sulphuric acid accumulator. Typical rated system voltages are 12V on passenger cars and 24V on trucks (using two 12-volt batteries in series).

Requirements

The system-defined battery requirements (starting current, capacity and charge-current absorption) must be satisfied throughout a temperature range of approximately $-30°C\ldots+70°C$; supplementary specifications apply for special applications (maintenance-free and vibration-resistant versions).

Battery design

A modern 12 V starter battery consists of six series-connected, individually partitioned cells in a polypropylene battery casing. Each cell contains one negative and one positive-plate stack, consisting of plates (lead grids and active material) and microporous insulating material (separators) between plates of polarity. The electrolyte is the sulphuric-acid

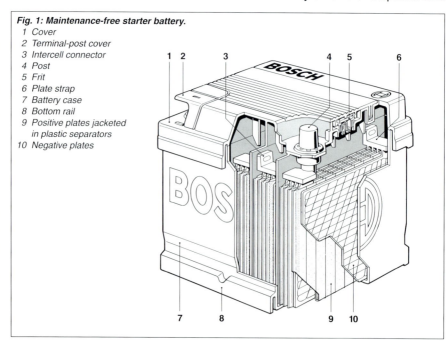

Fig. 1: Maintenance-free starter battery.
1 Cover
2 Terminal-post cover
3 Intercell connector
4 Post
5 Frit
6 Plate strap
7 Battery case
8 Bottom rail
9 Positive plates jacketed in plastic separators
10 Negative plates

solution which permeates the pores in the plates and separators and the voids in the cells. The terminals, cell connectors and plate straps are made of lead; the intercellular passages are tightly sealed. The battery's upper seal is the cover, bonded to the battery's lower casing in a hot-molding process during manufacture. On conventional batteries, each cell has a plug for initial filling, for maintenance and as a gaseous-discharge vent.

Although maintenance-free batteries (Fig. 1) usually appear to be tightly sealed, they are also provided with ventilation openings.

Battery versions

The maintenance-free battery

The maintenance-free battery defined in DIN standards features lead-alloy grids with a low antimony content to reduce gas generation and attendant electrolyte losses during charging.

This prolongs the electrolyte inspection intervals to:
– every 15 months or 25,000 km on low-maintenance batteries, and
– every 25 months or 40,000 km (DIN definition) on maintenance-free batteries.

There is never any need (and generally no means provided) to check the electrolyte level on completely maintenance-free (lead-calcium) batteries. With the exception of two minute vent orifices, this type of battery is completely sealed. As long as the electrical system continues to function normally (U = constant), electrolyte decomposition remains minimal, and the electrolyte reserves above the plates last for the life of the battery. This type of calcium battery affords the additional advantage of extremely limited self-discharge, providing it with a shelf life of up to several months (provided that it is fully charged at the outset). When a maintenance-free battery is recharged from an external source, the charge voltage should never exceed 2.3…2.4V per cell; overcharging at constant currents, and the use of chargers with a W charge curve (see charge curves, Fig. 2) will always lead to water consumption in a lead-acid battery.

Deep-cycle battery

Due to their special design characteristics (plate thickness, separator materials), standard automotive batteries are poorly suited for applications in which frequent and extreme discharge is encountered; standard batteries respond to these conditions with substantial wear at the positive plates (particularly through separation and sedimentation of the active material). In the deep-cycle battery, the separators include fiberglass mats to provide the positive mass with extra support and prevent premature sludge formation. Service life, as measured in charge-discharge cycles, is roughly twice as long as that provided by a standard battery. Deep-cycle batteries featuring pocket separators and felt layers have an even longer service life.

Vibration-proof battery

In the vibration-proof battery, an anchor of cast resin and/or plastic prevents the plate stacks from moving within the casing. To comply with DIN standards, this type of battery must survive 20 hours at 22 Hz sinusoidal vibration as well as a maximum acceleration of $6 \cdot g$, a requirement that is approximately ten times that placed on standard batteries. Vibration-proof batteries are used primarily in utility vehicles, construction equipment, tractors, etc. Designation code: Rf.

HD battery

The HD (Heavy Duty) battery is a combination of deep-cycle and vibration-proof battery. It is used in commercial vehicles subject to both high vibration stress and cyclic stress. This battery type is identified by the letters "HD".

"S" battery

The "S" battery shares its basic design with the deep-cycle version, compared to which it has thicker plates, but fewer of them. Although no low-temperature test current is specified for the S battery, its starting power is substantially less (approx. 35...40%) than that of comparable standard batteries. This battery is used in applications characterized by extreme cyclic variations, for instance, as a drive battery.

Battery states

Charging

Voltage limiting is used when charging the battery from the vehicle electrical system. The charging curve corresponds to the IU charging pattern, in which charge current drops automatically in response to increasing battery voltage. The IU method prevents harmful overcharging and ensures long service life.

Many service stations and home chargers still operate with a constant-current, or W-shaped charge curve (see "Charging curves"). In both cases, there is little or no reduction in charge current when the battery is fully charged. The results are substantial water consumption and corrosion at the positive grid.

Charging curves

The most common charging pattern is defined by the W curve (Fig. 2) of the kind usually provided by non-regulated chargers. Due to the charger's internal resistance, the charge current drops steadily as battery voltage increases (charging time 12...14 hours).

Because these battery chargers do not control the charging voltage, they are not optimal for use with maintenance-free batteries; here chargers operating on an IU or WU pattern should be used. With the IU curve (Fig. 3), the lead battery (2.4 V per cell) is supplied with a constant charge current (to protect the charger against overload) until gasing commences. The unit then reverts to a constant charge voltage (to protect the battery against overload) while sharply reducing the charge current. Provided that the initial current is high enough, recharging times of < 5 hours are possible with IU chargers.

Special variations on both the IU and W charging patterns are available (e.g., Wa, WOW, IUW). These can also be applied in combination to meet individual demands for charging time, terminal voltage and low maintenance.

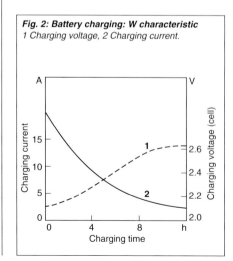

Fig. 2: Battery charging: W characteristic
1 Charging voltage, 2 Charging current.

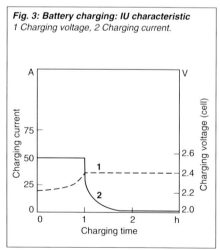

Fig. 3: Battery charging: IU characteristic
1 Charging voltage, 2 Charging current.

Discharge

Soon after discharging starts, the battery's voltage drops to a specific level which then falls relatively slowly when discharging continues. The ultimate voltage collapse occurs only just before complete discharge, upon exhaustion of one or more active components (positive mass, negative mass, electrolyte – Fig. 4).

Self-discharge

Batteries discharge themselves continually, even when no loads (electrical devices) are attached. At room temperature, a modern low-antimony battery will lose about 0.1 ... 0.2 % of its total charge each day. As the battery ages, antimony transfer to the negative plate, combined with other sources of contamination, can increase the rate to as much as 1 % per day. This ultimately leads to battery failure.

Rule of thumb for the influence of temperature:

The rate of discharge doubles with every 10°C increase in temperature.

The self-discharge rate of lead-calcium batteries is only one fifth as high, and it also remains constant throughout the battery's life (Fig. 5).

Battery maintenance

The electrolyte level in low-maintenance batteries should be checked in accordance with the manufacturer's instructions; when indicated, it should be topped-up to the MAX graduation using distilled or demineralized water. To minimize self-discharge, the battery should be kept clean and dry. A supplementary autumn examination of the electrolyte's specific gravity – or, should this be impossible, of the open-circuit voltage – is also advisable. The battery should be recharged when the specific gravity falls below 1.20 g/ml, or at an open-circuit voltage of under 12.2 V. Terminals, terminal clamps and installation clamps should be coated with acid-protection grease.

Batteries temporarily removed from service should be stored in a cool, dry place. The electrolyte's specific gravity and/or open-circuit voltage should be checked every 3 ... 4 months. The battery should be recharged whenever the figures drop below 1.20 g/ml or 12.2 V. Low-maintenance and maintenance-free batteries are best recharged using the IU method (see "Charging") and a maximum voltage of 14.4 V. This method allows adequate charging times – on the order of 24 hours – without any risk of overcharging.

Fig. 4: Battery discharge
1 Open-circuit voltage, 2 100 A discharge current, 3 50 A discharge current.

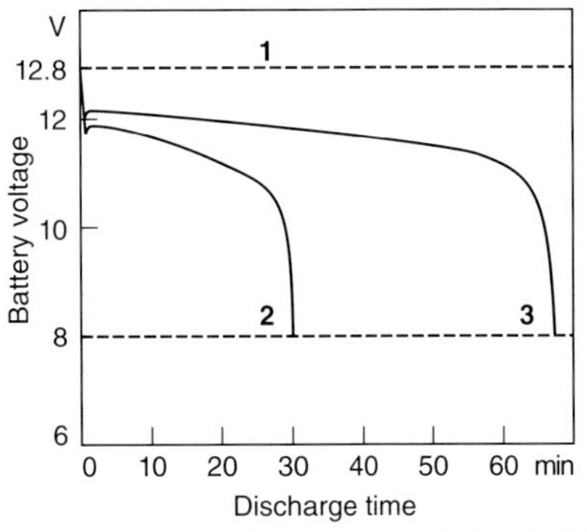

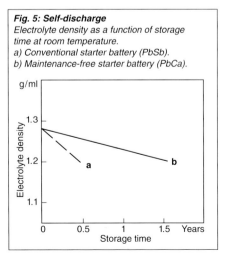

Fig. 5: Self-discharge
Electrolyte density as a function of storage time at room temperature.
a) Conventional starter battery (PbSb).
b) Maintenance-free starter battery (PbCa).

If a constant-current or W-curve battery charger is used, the current should be reduced to max. 1/10 of the rated capacity in A when visible gassing starts. As an example, this would be 6.6 A for a 66 Ah battery. The battery charger should be switched off about one hour later. Ventilate the charging area (explosive gases, explosion danger). Avoid sparks and open flames.

Battery malfunctions

Battery failures traceable to internal faults (such as short-circuits accompanying separator wear or loss of active mass, broken connections between cells and plates) can rarely be rectified through repair; the battery must be replaced. Internal shorts are indicated by major variations in the specific-gravity readings between cells (difference between max. and min. > 0.03 g/ml). It is frequently possible to charge and discharge a battery with defective cell connectors provided that the currents remain small, but attempts to start the engine will result in total voltage collapse, even if the battery is fully charged. If no defects can be found in a battery which consistently loses its charge (indication: low specific gravity in all cells, no starting power) or is overcharged (indication: high water loss), this suggests a malfunction in the vehicle's electrical system (defective alternator, constant current to electrical consumers with engine off – due to faulty relay, voltage regulator set too high or low, or completely inoperative). When a battery remains severely discharged for an extended period of time, the $PbSO_4$ crystals in the active mass become coarse, making the battery more difficult to recharge. Such a battery should be recharged by applying a minimal charge current (ca. 1/40 of rated amperage) for roughly 50 hours.

Safety precautions

Handling the battery
Prior to installation or removal of a new battery, to help avoid risks due to improper handling. the instruction manual accompanying the battery should always be studied. The chief sources of danger are the battery acid and the explosive gas (combination of oxygen and hydrogen) generated during charging. Tilting the battery for extended periods, or carelessness during electrolyte checks, can lead to sulphuric acid burns. Due to the danger of the oxyhydrogen gas exploding, extra caution should be applied during charging and when connecting and disconnecting jumper cables. The danger of gas explosions associated with sudden shorts or breaks in a circuit can be considerably reduced by avoiding sparks and open flames, but a residual risk always remains. For the reasons listed above, battery-charging areas should always be well ventilated, and eye protection and gloves should be worn during battery maintenance and installation.

In order to prevent sparks when the battery is connected or disconnected, all electrical equipment must be switched off, and the terminals must be connected in the proper sequence. The rules are:

– When installing the battery, always connect the positive cable first. The negative cable comes last. When removing the battery, first disconnect the negative, and only then the positive cable (assuming that negative is ground).

– When connecting a charger or external battery to jump a battery remaining connected in the vehicle, always start by connecting the positive terminal of the battery being charged to the positive terminal of the external booster. Then connect the negative cable from the external charger (battery) to an exposed metal surface on the vehicle, at least 0.5 m away from the battery.

– Always disconnect the cable from the negative terminal before commencing work in the vicinity of the battery or on the vehicle's electrical system. Shorts (with tools etc.) generate sparks and can cause burns.

Testing starter batteries
Specifications and test procedures for starter batteries are defined in DIN 43 539. Although these tests were conceived to evaluate the quality of new batteries, they are not necessarily suitable for defining all aspects of battery performance in the wide range of variegated conditions encountered in actual use.

The nominal capacity K_{20} defines the battery's electrical power output in ampere hours (A · h). The K_{20} specification stipulates that the battery must maintain a specified output current I_{20} (discharge current) for 20 hours at 27°C without dropping below the specified terminal discharge voltage of 10.5 V. The rated discharge current I_{20} is the current corresponding to the rated capacity supplied by the battery during the defined discharge period: $I_{20} = K_{20}/$ 20 h.

The low-temperature test current is a high-discharge current defined for each individual battery; it provides an index of low-temperature cold-start response under specific load conditions. Starting at an initial temperature of −18 ±1°C, the specified test current is maintained until the battery reaches a cutoff voltage (final discharge voltage) of 6 V.

Increased Ah capacity and low-temperature test current
Motor vehicles generally come from the factory equipped with batteries and alternators designed to satisfy starter and electrical system requirements under all standard operating conditions in a temperate climate. When additional electrical equipment is installed, or if the vehicle will be operated under severe conditions, it may be useful to investigate the option of installing a higher-capacity battery (which may be available in the same dimensions). When contemplating any modification of this kind, always observe the vehicle manufacturer's recommendations and/or consult your Bosch service representative.

Remember that batteries with higher starting capacities are characterized by lower internal resistance. The voltage drop is reduced, the voltage at the starter terminal U_S is higher. It is even possible that the starting current furnished by the battery will exceed the maximum specified for the starter. The starter is then subjected to excessively high currents during starting; the ultimate results can be melted windings in the starter motor or damage to the pinion and ring-gear assembly.

Battery chargers

Charge current and voltage settings
In chargers with programmed charging patterns (e.g., IU curve), a regulator continually monitors the instantaneous charge current and voltage. It compares the monitored data with stored setpoints, and employs a final controlling element to reduce the deviation to 0. This type of unit compensates for the fluctuations in mains voltage that could otherwise induce variations in charge current, with positive consequences for battery life and maintenance intervals.

Charge current
During normal charging, the battery is supplied with current corresponding to approx. 10% of its capacity (A · h). Several hours are required for a complete charge. Boost charging ($I_L = 5 · I_5$) can be employed to bring a fully discharged battery back up to approx. 80% of its rated capacity with no damage. Once the gassing voltage is reached, the charge current must be removed (e.g., Wa curve) or reduced (e.g., WOWa). These current-switching functions can be controlled by an adjustable charge-time limiter or an automatic switchoff device.

Alternators

Generation of electrical power in the motor vehicle

On-board electrical power

In order to supply the power required for the starter, for ignition and fuel-injection systems, for the ECU's to control the electronic equipment, for lighting, and for safety and convenience electronics, motor vehicles need their own efficient and highly reliable source of energy which must always be available at any time of day or night.

Whereas, with the engine stopped, the battery is the vehicle's energy store, the alternator becomes the on-board "electricity generating plant" when the engine is running. The alternator's task is to supply power to all the vehicle's current-consuming loads and systems (Fig. 1).

In order that the entire system is reliable and trouble-free in operation, it is necessary that the alternator output, battery capacity, and starter power requirements, together with the remaining electrical loads, are matched to each other as optimally as possible. For instance, following a normal driving cycle (e.g., town driving in winter) the battery must always be sufficiently charged so that the vehicle can be started again without any trouble no matter what the temperature. And the ECU's, sensors and actuators for the vehicle's electronic systems (e.g., for fuel management, ignition, Motronic, electronic engine-power control, antilock braking system (ABS), traction control (ASR) etc. must always be ready for operation.

Apart from this, the vehicle's safety and security systems as well as its signalling systems must function immediately, the same as the lighting system at night or in fog. Furthermore, the driver-information and convenience systems must always function, and with the vehicle parked, a number of electrical loads should continue to operate for a reasonable period without discharging the battery so far that the vehicle cannot be started again.

As a matter of course, millions of motorists expect their vehicle to always be fully functional, and demand a high level of operational reliability from the electrical system. For many thousands of miles – in both summer and winter.

Electrical loads

The electrical loads have differing duty cycles (Fig. 2). A differentiation is made between permanent loads (ignition, fuel injection etc.), long-time loads (lighting, car radio, vehicle heater etc.), and

Fig. 1: Alternator principle
The alternator rectifies the 3-phase alternating current to provide DC for supplying the electrical devices and for charging the battery.

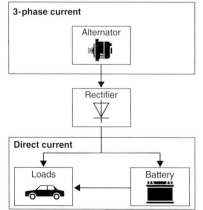

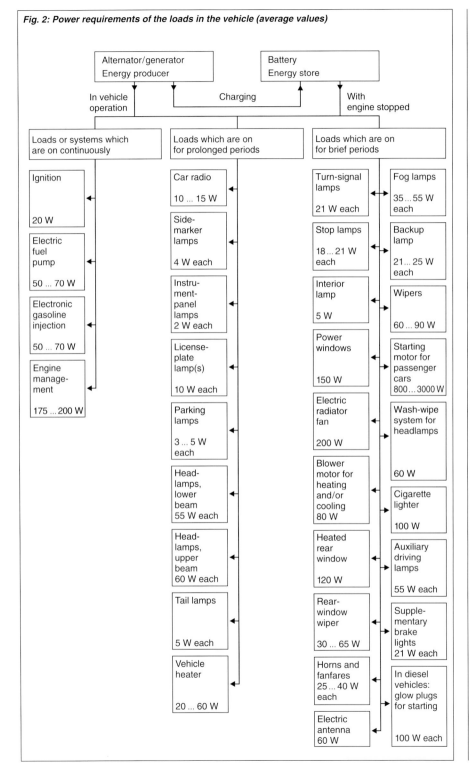

Fig. 2: Power requirements of the loads in the vehicle (average values)

Alternator/generator Energy producer	Battery Energy store

In vehicle operation — Charging — With engine stopped

Loads or systems which are on continuously	Loads which are on for prolonged periods	Loads which are on for brief periods

Loads or systems which are on continuously:

Ignition 20 W
Electric fuel pump 50 ... 70 W
Electronic gasoline injection 50 ... 70 W
Engine management 175 ... 200 W

Loads which are on for prolonged periods:

Car radio 10 ... 15 W
Side-marker lamps 4 W each
Instrument-panel lamps 2 W each
License-plate lamp(s) 10 W each
Parking lamps 3 ... 5 W each
Head-lamps, lower beam 55 W each
Head-lamps, upper beam 60 W each
Tail lamps 5 W each
Vehicle heater 20 ... 60 W

Loads which are on for brief periods:

Turn-signal lamps 21 W each	Fog lamps 35 ... 55 W each
Stop lamps 18 ... 21 W each	Backup lamp 21 ... 25 W each
Interior lamp 5 W	Wipers 60 ... 90 W
Power windows 150 W	Starting motor for passenger cars 800 ... 3000 W
Electric radiator fan 200 W	Wash-wipe system for headlamps 60 W
Blower motor for heating and/or cooling 80 W	Cigarette lighter 100 W
Heated rear window 120 W	Auxiliary driving lamps 55 W each
Rear-window wiper 30 ... 65 W	Supplementary brake lights 21 W each
Horns and fanfares 25 ... 40 W each	In diesel vehicles: glow plugs for starting 100 W each
Electric antenna 60 W	

short-time loads (turn signals, stop lamps etc.). Some electrical loads are only switched on according to season (air-conditioner in summer, seat heater in winter). And the operation of electrical radiator fans depends upon temperaure and driving conditions.

Charge-balance calculation

A computer program is used to determine the state of battery charge at the end of a typical driving cycle. Here, such influences as battery size, alternator size, and load input powers must be taken into account.

Rush-hour driving (low engine speeds) combined with winter operation (low charging-current input to the battery) is regarded as a normal passenger-car driving cycle. In the case of vehicles equipped with an air conditioner, summer operation can be even more unfavorable than winter.

Vehicle electrical system

The nature of the wiring between alternator, battery, and electrical equipment also influences the voltage level and, as a result, the state of battery charge.

If all electrical loads are connected at the battery, the total current (sum of battery charging current and load current) flows through the charging line, and the resulting high voltage drop causes a reduction in the charging voltage.

Conversely, if all electrical devices are connected at the alternator side, the voltage drop is less and the charging voltage is higher. This may have a negative effect upon devices which are sensitive to voltage peaks or high voltage ripple (electronic circuitry).

For this reason, it is advisable to connect voltage-insensitive equipment with high power inputs to the alternator, and voltage-sensitive equipment with low power inputs to the battery. Appropriate line cross-sections, and good connections whose contact resistances do not increase even after long periods of operation, contribute to keeping the voltage drop to a minimum.

Electrical power generation using alternators

The availability of reasonably priced power diodes as from around 1963, paved the way for Bosch to start with the series production of alternators. The alternator's design principle results in it having a far higher electromagnetic efficiency than the DC generator. This fact, together the alternator's much wider rotational-speed range, enables it to deliver power, and cover the vehicle's increased power requirements, even at engine idle. Since the alternator speed can be matched to that of the engine by means of a suitable transmission, this means that the battery remains at a high charge level even in winter during frequent town driving.

The increased power requirements mentioned above, result from the following factors: The increase in the amount of electrical equipment fitted in the vehicle, the number of ECU's required for the electronic systems (e.g., for engine management and for chassis control), and the safety, security and convenience electronics. The expected power requirements up to the year 2000 are shown in Fig. 3.

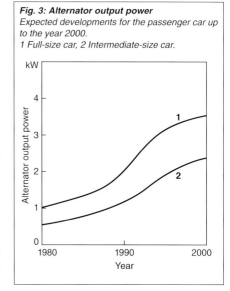

Fig. 3: Alternator output power
Expected developments for the passenger car up to the year 2000.
1 Full-size car, 2 Intermediate-size car.

Apart from these factors, typical driving cycles have also changed, whereby the proportion of town driving with extended stops at idle has increased (Fig. 4).

The rise in traffic density has led to frequent traffic jams, and together with long stops at traffic lights, this means that the alternator also operates for much of the time at low speeds corresponding to engine idle. Together with the fact that longer journeys at higher speeds have become less common, this has a negative effect on the battery's charge balance.

It is imperative that the battery continues to be charged even when the engine is idling.

At engine idle, an alternator already delivers at least a third of its rated power (Fig. 5).

Alternators are designed to generate charging voltages of 14V (28V for commercial verhicles). The three-phase winding is incorporated in the stator, and the excitation winding in the rotor.

The three-phase AC generated by the alternator must be rectified, the rectifiers also preventing battery discharge when the vehicle is stationary. The additional relay as required for the DC generator can be dispensed with.

Design factors

Rotational speed
An generator's efficiency (energy generated per kg mass) increases with rotational speed. This factor dictates as high a conversion ratio as possible between engine crankshaft and alternator. For passenger-cars, typical values are between 1 : 2 and 1 : 3, and for commercial vehicles up to 1 : 5.

Temperature
The losses in the alternator lead to increased alternator-component temperatures. The input of fresh air to the alternator is a suitable means of reducing component temperature and increasing alternator efficiency.

Vibration
Depending upon installation conditions and the engine's vibration patterns, vibration accelerations of between 500 ... 800 m/s^2 can occur. Critical resonances must be avoided.

Further influences
The alternator is also subjected to such detrimental influences as spray water, dirt, oil, fuel mist, and road salt.

Fig. 4: Vehicle standstill
Proportion of time at standstill. Developments for urban and city traffic (large towns) up to the year 2000.

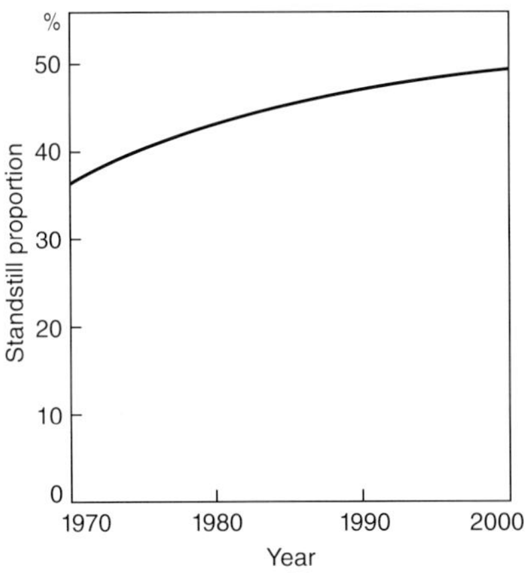

Fig. 5: Alternator current characteristic
At constant voltage.
n_L *Idle speed*, n_{max} *Maximum speed.*

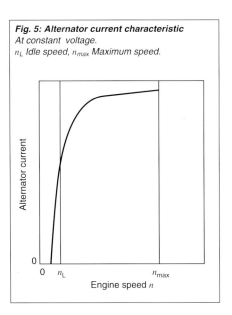

Electrical power generation using DC generators

Originally, the conventional lead-acid battery customarily fitted in motor vehicles led to the development of the DC generator, and for a long time this generator system was able to meet the majority of the demands made upon it. Consequently, until the middle of the seventies, most vehicles were equipped with DC generators. Today though, these have become virtually insignificant in the automotive sector and will not be dealt with in detail here.

With the DC generator, it proved to be more practical to rotate the winding system while locating the electrically excited magnet system in the stationary housing. The alternating current generated by the machine can be rectified relatively simply by mechanical means using a commutator, and the resulting direct current supplied to the vehicle electrical system or the battery.

Requirements to be met by automotive generators

The type and construction of an automotive electrical generator are determined by the necessity of providing electrical energy for powering the vehicle's electrical equipment, and for charging its battery.

Initially, the alternator generates alternating current (AC). The vehicle's electrical equipment though requires direct current (DC) for keeping the battery charged and for powering the electronic subassemblies. The electrical system must therefore be supplied with DC. The demands made upon an automotive generator are highly complex and varied:
– Supplying all connected loads with DC,
– Providing power reserves for rapidly charging the battery and keeping it charged, even when permanent loads are swiched on,
– Maintaining the voltage output as constant as possible across the complete engine speed range independent of the generator's loading,
– Rugged construction to withstand all the under-hood stresses (e.g., vibration, high ambient temperatures, temperature changes, dirt, dampness etc.),
– Low weight,
– Compact dimensions for ease of installation,
– Long service life,
– Low noise level.

Characteristics (summary)

The alternator's most important characteristics are:
– It generates power even at engine idle.
– Rectification of the AC uses power diodes in a three-phase bridge circuit.
– The diodes separate alternator and battery from the vehicle electrical system when the alternator voltage drops below the battery voltage.
– The alternator's far higher level of mechanical efficiency means that they are designed to be far lighter than DC generators.
– Alternators feature a long service life. The passenger-car alternator's service life corresponds roughly to that of the engine (up to 150,000 km), which means that no servicing is necessary during this period.

On vehicles designed for high mileages (trucks and commercial vehicles in general), brushless alternator versions are used which permit regreasing. Or bearings with grease-reserve chambers are fitted.
– Alternators are able to withstand such external influences as vibration, high temperatures, dirt, dampness.
– Normally, operation is possible in either direction of rotation without special measures being necessary. The magnetic-field system and the fan shape merely need adapting to the direction of rotation.

Basic principles

Electrodynamic principle

The basis for the generation of electricity is electromagnetic "induction" (from the Latin "inducere" to introduce [1]). The principle is as follows: When an electric conductor (wire or wire loop) cuts through the lines of force of a magnetic field, a voltage is induced in the conductor. It is immaterial whether the magnetic field remains stationary and the conductor rotates, or vice versa.

A wire loop is rotated between the North and South poles of a permanent magnet. The ends of this wire loop are connected through collector rings and carbon brushes to a volmeter. The continuously varying relationship of the wire loop to the poles is reflected in the varying voltage shown by the voltmeter. If the wire loop rotates uniformly, a sinusoidal voltage curve is generated whose maximum values occur at intervals of 180°. Alternating current (AC) flows as soon as the circuit is closed (Fig. 1).

[1] Introduction of a conductor into the magnetic field.

How is the magnetic field generated?

The magnetic field can be generated by permanent magnets. Due to their simplicity, these have the advantage of requiring a minimum of technical outlay, and are used for small generators (e.g., bicycle dynamos).

Electromagnets on the other hand permit considerably higher voltages and are controllable. This is why they are usually applied for generation of the (exciter) magnetic field.

Electromagetism is based on the fact that when an electric current flows through wires or windings these are surrounded by a magnetic field.

The number of turns in the winding and the magnitude of the current flowing through it determine the magnetic field's strength, which can be further increased by using a magnetisable iron core. In practical generator applications, in order to increase the effects of induction, a number of wire loops are used to form the "winding" which rotates in the magnetic field.

In electric machines, the complete rotating system comprising winding and iron core is referred to as the rotor.

When this principle is applied to the generator or alternator, a decisive advantage lies in the fact that the magne-

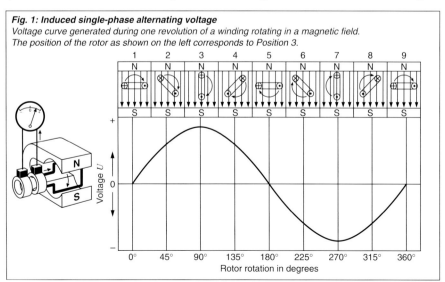

Fig. 1: Induced single-phase alternating voltage
Voltage curve generated during one revolution of a winding rotating in a magnetic field.
The position of the rotor as shown on the left corresponds to Position 3.

tic field, and with it the induced voltage, can be strengthened or weakened by increasing or decreasing the (excitation) current flowing in the (excitation) winding.

Except for a slight residual or remanence magnetism, the electromagnet in the form of the excitation winding loses its magnetism when the excitation current is switched off. If an external source of energy (e.g., battery) provides the exci-tation current, this is termed "external excitation". If the excitation current is taken from the machine's own electric circuit this is termed "self-excitation".

Principle of the alternator

3-phase current (3-phase AC) is also generated by rotating the rotor in a magnetic field, the same as with single-phase AC as described above. One of the advantages of 3-phase AC lies in the fact that it makes more efficient use of the electrical generator's potential. The generator for 3-phase AC is designated an "alternator" and its rotor comprises three identical windings (u, v, w) which are offset from each other by 120°. The start points of the three windings are usually designated u, v, w, and the end points x, y, z. In accordance with

the laws of induction, when the rotor rotates in the magnetic field, sinusoidal voltages are generated in each of its three windings. These voltages are of identical magnitude and frequency, the only difference being that their 120° offset results in the induced voltages also being 120° out-of-phase with each other, as well as being out-of-phase by 120° as regards time (Fig. 2).

Therefore, with the rotor turning, the alternator generates a constantly recurring 3-phase alternating voltage.

Normally, with the windings not connected, an alternator would require 6 wires to output the electrical energy that it has generated (Fig. 3a). However, by interconnecting the 3 circuits the number of wires can be reduced from 6 to 3. This joint use of the conductors is achieved by the "star" connection (Fig. 3b) or "delta" connection (Fig. 3c).

In the case of the "star" connection, which has a certain similarity with a series connection, the ends of the 3 winding phases are joined to form a "star" point. Since the sum of the 3 currents at any instant in time is always 0, the neutral conductor can be dispensed with.

The "delta" connection on the other hand is similar to a parallel connection.

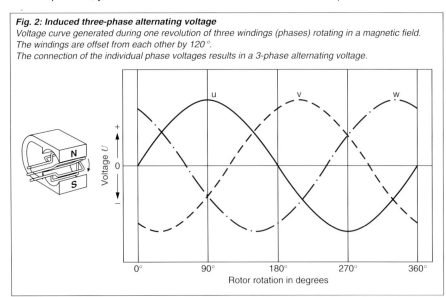

Fig. 2: Induced three-phase alternating voltage
Voltage curve generated during one revolution of three windings (phases) rotating in a magnetic field.
The windings are offset from each other by 120°.
The connection of the individual phase voltages results in a 3-phase alternating voltage.

Discussions up to this point have centered on the alternator version with stationary excitation field and rotating armature winding in which the load current is induced.

For automotive alternators though, the 3-phase (star or delta connected) winding system is in the stator (the stationary part of the alternator housing) so that the winding is often also referred to as the stator winding. The poles of the magnet together with the excitation winding are situated on the rotor.

The rotor's magnetic field builds up as soon as direct current ("excitation current") flows through the excitation wind-ing. When the rotor rotates, its magnetic field induces a 3-phase alternating voltage in the stator windings which provides the 3-phase current to power the connected loads.

Rectification of the AC voltage

The 3-phase AC generated by the alternator cannot be stored in the vehicle's battery nor can it be used to power the electronic components and ECU's. To do so, the three-phase AC must first of all be rectified. One of the essential prerequisites for this rectification is the availability of high-performance power diodes which can operate efficiently throughout a wide temperature range.

Rectifier diodes have a reverse and a forward direction, the latter being indicated by the arrow in the symbol. A diode can be compared to a non-return valve which permits passage of a fluid or a gas in only one direction and stops it in the other.

The rectifier diode suppresses the negative half waves and allows only positive half waves to pass. The result is a pulsating direct current. So-called full-wave rectification is applied in order to also make full use of all the half waves including those that have been suppressed.

Fig. 3: Connection of the three alternator windings
a) Windings not connected.
b) Star connection. Alternator voltage U and phase voltage U_p (component voltage)
differ by the factor $\sqrt{3} = 1.73$.
The alternator current I equals the phase current I_p
$U = U_p \cdot \sqrt{3}. \quad I = I_p$.
c) Delta connection. Alternator voltage U equals the phase voltage U_p.
The alternator current I and the phase current I_p differ by the factor $\sqrt{3} = 1.73$.
$U = U_p. \quad I = I_p \cdot \sqrt{3}$.

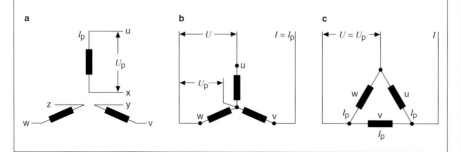

Bridge circuit for the rectification of the 3-phase AC

The operating principle of the diode in the rectification of an alternating current is shown in Fig. 4. Half-wave rectification is shown in Fig. 4a and full-wave rectification in Fig. 4b.

The AC generated in the 3 windings of the alternator is rectified in an AC bridge circuit using 6 diodes (Fig. 5).

Two power diodes are connected into each phase, one diode to the positive side (Term. B+) and one to the negative side (Term. B-). The positive half-waves pass through the positive-side diodes and the negative half waves through the negative-side diodes.

With full-wave rectification using a bridge circuit, the positive and negative half-wave envelopes are added to form a rectified alternator voltage with a slight ripple (Fig. 5c).

This means that the direct current (DC) which is taken from the alternator at Terminals B+ and B- to supply the vehicle electrical system is not ideally "smooth" but has a slight ripple. This ripple is further smoothed by the battery, which is connected in parallel to the alternator, and by any capacitors in the vehicle electrical system.

Fig. 4: Rectifier circuits
a) Half-wave rectification, b) Full-wave rectification.
$U_{G\sim}$ *AC voltage before the diodes,*
U_{G-} *Pulsating DC voltage after the diodes.*
1 Battery, 2 Excitation winding (G),
3 Stator winding, 4 Rectifier diodes.

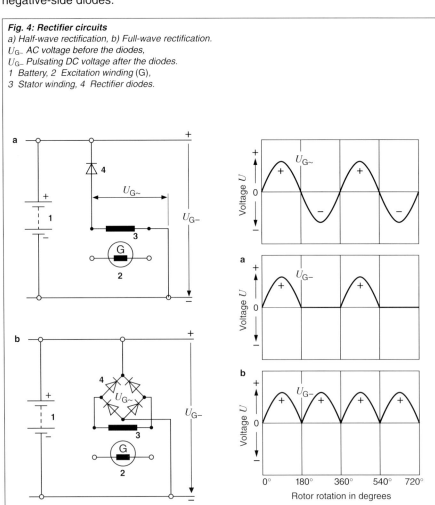

The excitation current which magnetizes the poles of the excitation field is tapped off from the stator winding and rectified by a full-wave bridge rectifier comprising the 3 "exciter diodes" at Term. D+, and the 3 power diodes at Term. B- (negative side).

With the aim of increasing power output at high speeds (above 3000 min^{-1}), so-called "auxiliary diodes" can be used to make full use of the alternator voltage's harmonic component.

Reverse-current block

The rectifier diodes in the alternator not only rectify the alternator and excitation voltage, but also prevent the battery discharging through the 3-phase winding in the stator. With the engine stopped, or with it turning too slowly for self-excitation to take place (e.g., during cranking), without the diodes battery current would flow through the stator winding.

With respect to the battery current, the diodes are polarized in the reverse direction so that it is impossible for battery-discharge current to flow. Current flow can only take place from the alternator to the battery.

Fig. 5: 3-phase bridge circuit
a) Three-phase AC voltage,
b) Formation of the alternator voltage by the envelope curves of the positive and negative half-waves,
c) Rectified alternator voltage.
U_P Phase voltage,
U_G Voltage at the rectifier (negative not to ground),
U_{G-} Alternator DC voltage output (negative to ground),
U_{Grms} r.m.s. value of the alternator DC voltage output.
1 Battery,
2 Excitation winding,
3 Stator winding,
4 Positive diodes,
5 Negative diodes.

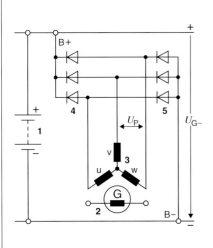

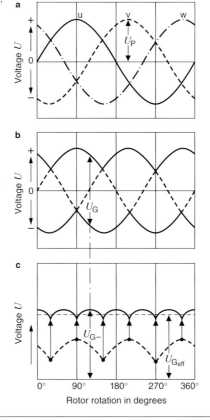

Rectifier diodes

Regarding their operation, the power diodes on the plus and negative sides are identical with each other. The difference between them lies merely in their special design for use as rectifiers in the alternator. They are termed positive and negative diodes, and in one case the diode's knurled metal casing acts as a cathode and in the other as an anode. The metal casing of the positive diode is pressed into the positive plate and functions as a cathode. It is connected to the battery's positive pole and conducts towards B+ (battery positive). The metal casing of the negative diode is pressed into the negative plate and functions as an anode. It is connected to ground (B–). The diode wire terminations are connected to the ends of the stator winding (Fig. 6). The positive and negative plates also function as heat sinks for cooling the diodes.

The power diodes can be in the form of Zener diodes which also serve to limit the voltage peaks which occur in the alternator due to extreme load changes (load-dump protection).

The circuits of the alternator

The following three circuits are standard for the alternator:

– Pre-excitation circuit (separate excitation using battery current)
– Excitation circuit (self-excitation)
– Generator or main circuit.

Pre-excitation circuit

When the ignition or driving switch (4) is operated, the battery current I_b first of all flows through the charge indicator lamp (3), through the excitation winding (1d) in the stator, and through the voltage regulator (2) to ground. In the rotor, this battery current serves to pre-excite the alternator.

Why is pre-excitation necessary ?

The reason is that in conventional alternators at the instant of starting, or at very low engine speeds, the residual magnetism (remanance) in the iron core of the excitation winding is so weak that it is insufficient to provide the self-

---

Fig. 6: Rectification of excitation current
1 Battery, 2 Excitation winding (G),
3 Stator winding, 4 Positive-plate diodes,
5 Negative-plate diodes, 6 Auxiliary diodes,
7 Exciter diodes.

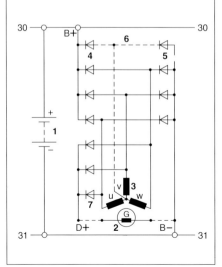

Fig. 7: Pre-excitation circuit
1 Alternator, 1a Exciter diodes, 1b Positive-plate diodes, 1c Negative-plate diodes,
1d Excitation winding, 2 Voltage regulator,
3 Charge indicator lamp, 4 Ignition switch,
5 Battery.

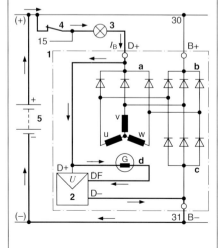

excitation required for building up the magnetic field and for generating the required voltage.

A power diode and an exciter diode are connected in series for each phase of the excitation circuit. Self-excitation can only take place when the alternator voltage exceeds the voltage drop across the two diodes (2 x 0.7 = 1.4 V).

This is precisely what the pre-excitation current does. It generates a magnetic field in the rotor which results in increasing generator voltage in the stator and, so to speak, helps the self-excitation to "get going".

When the engine runs up to speed following the start, the alternator must reach a certain speed in order to ensure that self-excitation is reliably initiated. This speed is higher than the idle speed, but once it has been reached the exciter field is strong enough for the alternator to deliver power even at idle.

Charge-indicator lamp

When the ignition or driving switch (4) is operated, the charge indicator lamp (3) in the pre-excitation circuit functions as a resistor and determines the magnitude of the pre-excitation current. A suitably dimensioned lamp provides a current which suffices to generate a sufficiently strong magnetic field to initiate self-excitation. If the lamp is too weak, as is the case for instance with electronic displays, a resistor must be connected in parallel to guarantee adequate alternator self-excitation. The lamp remains on as long as the alternator voltage is below battery voltage.

The lamp goes out the first time the speed is reached at which maximum alternator voltage is generated and the alternator starts to feed power into the vehicle electrical system.

Typical ratings for charge indicator lamps are:
2 W for 12 V systems,
3 W for 24 V systems.

Excitation circuit

During alternator operation, it is the task of the excitation current I_{exc} to generate a magnetic field in the rotor so that the required alternator voltage can be induced in the stator windings. Since alternators are "self-excited", the excitation current must be tapped off from the current flowing in the 3-phase winding.

Referring to Fig. 8, the excitation current I_{exc} takes the following route: Exciter diodes (1a), carbon brushes, collector rings, excitation winding, Term. DF of the voltage regulator (2), Term. D– of the voltage regulator, and back to the stator winding through the power diodes (1c). With the alternator operating, no external power source is required for self-excitation because the alternator excites itself. Separate excitation from an external source is only required upon alternator start-up.

The pre-excitation magnetic field induces a voltage in the stator winding which increases along with rising alternator speed until the alternator is fully excited and the alternator voltage is reached.

Fig. 8: Excitation circuit
1 Alternator, 1a Exciter diodes,
1b Positive-plate diodes,
1c Negative-plate diodes,
1d Excitation winding,
2 Voltage regulator, 3 Charge indicator lamp,
4 Ignition switch, 5 Battery.

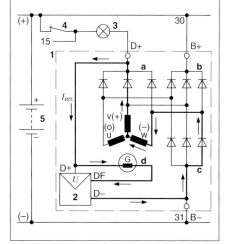

Generator circuit

The alternating voltage induced in the three phases of the alternator must be rectified by the power diodes in the bridge circuit before it is passed on to the battery and to the loads. The alternator current I_G flows from the three windings and through the respective power diodes to the battery and to the loads in the vehicle electrical system.

In other words the alternator current is divided into battery current and load current. In Fig. 10, the curves of the stator-winding voltages are shown as a function of the angle of rotation of the rotor. Taking a rotor with six pole pairs for instance, and an angle of rotation of 30°, the voltage referred to the star point at the end of winding v is positive, for winding w it is negative, and for winding u it is zero.

The resulting current path is shown in Fig. 9.

Current flows from the end of winding v and through the positive diodes (1b) to alternator terminal B+ from where it flows through the battery, or the load, to ground (battery terminal B–) and via the negative diodes (1c) to winding end w. Taking a 45° angle of rotation, current from the v and w winding ends takes the same path to winding end u. In this case, there is voltage present across all of the phases.

Both examples though are momentary values. In reality, the phase voltages and currents continually change their magnitude and direction, whereas the DC supplied for battery charging and for the electrical loads always maintains the same direction.

This is due to the fact that irrespective of the rotor's position, all the diodes are always involved in the rectification process.

For current to flow from the alternator to the battery, the alternator voltage must be slightly higher than that of the battery.

Fig. 9: Alternator circuit
1 Alternator, 1a Exciter diodes,
1b Positive-plate diodes,
1c Negative-plate diodes,
1d Excitation winding,
2 Voltage regulator, 3 Charge indicator lamp,
4 Ignition switch, 5 Battery.

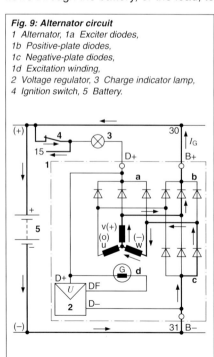

Fig. 10: Voltages in the stator windings
Voltage curves as a function of the angle of rotation of a rotor with 6 pole pairs.

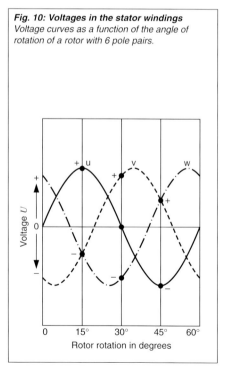

Voltage regulation

Why is it necessary to regulate the alternator voltage?

The voltage regulator is an essential alternator component whose task it is to maintain the alternator voltage practically constant across the whole of the engine speed range, irrespective of load and rotational speed.

The extensive variations in engine speed and the widely varying loads imposed on the alternator by the vehicle's electrical equipment are considerable, and make special measures necessary for automatically regulating the alternator voltage. Notwithstanding these continually changing operating conditions, steps must be taken to ensure that alternator voltage is limited to the specified level, even when driven at high speeds with low electrical loading. This voltage limitation protects the electrical equipment against overvoltage, and prevents battery overcharge.

In addition, the battery's electrochemical properties must be taken into account during charging. This means that normally the charging voltage must be slightly higher in cold weather in order to compensate for the fact that the battery is slightly more difficult to charge at low temperatures.

Principle of voltage regulation

The voltage generated by the alternator increases along with alternator speed and the excitation current. Considering a fully excited alternator which is not connected to the battery, and which is being driven without load, the voltage without regulation would increase linearly with alternator speed until it reaches about 140V at a speed of 10,000 min^{-1}. The voltage regulator controls the level of the alternator's excitation current, and along with it the strength of the rotor's magnetic field as a function of the voltage generated by the alternator (Fig. 11).

This enables the alternator terminal voltage U_{G-} (between terminals B+ and B−) to be maintained constant up to the maximum current.

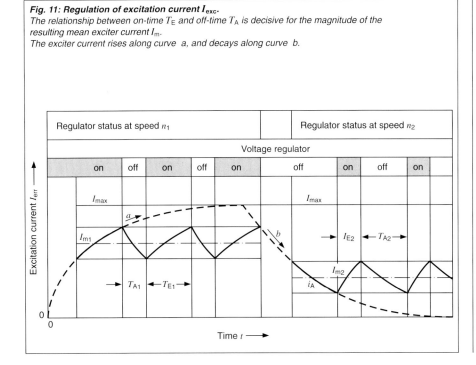

Fig. 11: Regulation of excitation current I_{exc}.
The relationship between on-time T_E and off-time T_A is decisive for the magnitude of the resulting mean exciter current I_m.
The exciter current rises along curve a, and decays along curve b.

The voltage-regulation tolerance zone for vehicle electrical systems with 12 V battery voltage is around 14 V, and for systems with 24 V battery voltage around 28 V. The regulator remains out of action as long as the alternator voltage remains below the regulator response voltage.

Within the tolerance range, if the voltage exceeds the specified upper value, the regulator interrupts the excitation current. Excitation becomes weaker and the alternator voltage drops as a result. As soon as the voltage then drops below the specified lower value, the regulator switches in the excitation current again, the excitation increases and along with it the alternator voltage. When the voltage exceeds the specified upper value again, the control cycle is repeated. Since these control cycles all take place within the milliseconds range, the alternator mean voltage is regulated in accordance with the stipulated characteristic.

The infinitely variable adaptation to the various rotational speeds is automatic, and the relationship between the excitation current "On" and "Off" times is decisive for the level of the mean exciting current (Fig. 11). At low rotational speeds, the "On" time is relatively long and the "Off" time short, the exciting current is interrupted only very briefly and has a high average value. On the other hand, at high rotational speeds the "On" time is short and the "Off" time long. Only a low excitation current flows.

Influence of ambient temperature

The regulator characteristic curves, that is the alternator voltage as a function of temperature, are matched to the battery's chemical characteristics. This means that at low temperatures, the alternator voltage is increased slightly in order to improve battery charging in the winter, whereby the input voltages to the electronic equipment and the voltage-dependent service life of the light bulbs is taken into account. At higher temperatures, alternator voltage is reduced slightly in order to prevent battery overcharge in summer.

Temperature compensation is achieved through suitable choice of components, e.g., of the Z-diodes. Fig. 12 shows the characteristic curves for 14 V alternator voltage. The voltage level is 14.5 V and has an incline of -10 mV/K.

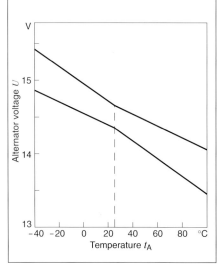

Fig. 12: Voltage-regulator characteristic
Permissible tolerance band for the alternator voltage (14 V) as a function of the intake-air temperature.

Alternator design

The theoretical principles and inter-relationships discussed so far are reflected in the technical construction of modern alternators. Individual versions can differ from each other in certain details according to their particular application. At present, the claw-pole alternator with compact diode assembly is still being installed in the majority of vehicles, but the compact alternator is coming more and more to the forefront. The major design differences between these two alternator types are the compact alternator's two internally-mounted fans, its smaller collector rings, and the location of the rectifier outside the collector-ring end shield.

The basic construction of a compact alternator is shown in Fig. 13:

– Stator (2) with 3-phase stator winding. The stator consists of mutually insulated, grooved laminations which are pressed together to form a solid laminated core. The turns of the stator winding are embedded in the grooves.

– Rotor (3), on the shaft of which are mounted the pole-wheel halves with magnet poles, the excitation winding, both fans, the ball bearings, and the two collector rings. The excitation winding consists of a single toroidal coil which is enclosed by the claw-pole halves. The relatively small excitation current is supplied via the carbon brushes which are pressed against the collector rings by springs.

– The pulley for the belt drive is also mounted on the rotor shaft.

Alternator rotors can be rotated in either direction. The fan design and the magnetic-field system must be changed in accordance with clockwise or counterclockwise rotation.

– The stator is clamped between the collector-ring end shield and the drive end shield. The rotor shaft runs in bearings in each end shield.

– Rectifiers with heat sinks (6). At least six power diodes and three exciter diodes for rectification of the 3-phase AC are pressed into the heat sinks.

– Collector rings (5). The excitation current flows to the rotating excitation winding through the carbon brushes and collector rings.

– Regulator (4) forms a unit with the brush holder for alternator mounting. This design is used almost exclusively.

– Regulator for mounting on the vehicle body (not shown). Used in rare cases on commercial vehicles as an alternative to the alternator-mounted version. Mounted at a protected location on the vehicle body, this regulator is electrically connected to the brush holder by plug-in connection.

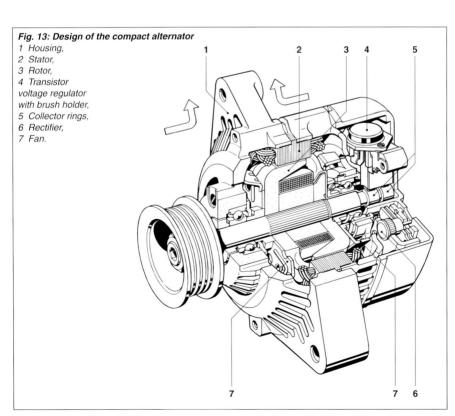

Fig. 13: Design of the compact alternator
1 Housing,
2 Stator,
3 Rotor,
4 Transistor voltage regulator with brush holder,
5 Collector rings,
6 Rectifier,
7 Fan.

Alternator versions

Design criteria

The following data are decisive for alternator design:
– Vehicle type and the associated operating conditions,
– Speed range of the engine with which the alternator is to be used,
– Battery voltage of the vehicle electrical system,
– Power requirements of the loads which can be connected,
– Environmental loading imposed on the alternator (heat, dirt, dampness, etc.),
– Specified service life,
– Available installation space, dimensions.

The requirements to be met by an automotive alternator differ very considerably depending upon application and the criteria as listed above. Regarding economic efficiency the criteria also vary along with the areas of application. It is therefore impossible to design an all-purpose alternator which meets all requirements.

The different areas of application, and the power ranges of the vehicle types and engines concerned, led to the development of a number of basic models which will be described in the following.

Electrical data and sizes

The vehicle size is not decisive for determining the required alternator output power. This is solely a function of the loads installed in the vehicle.

The selection of the correct alternator is governed primarily by:
– the alternator voltage (14 V/28V),
– the power output as a product of voltage and current throughout the rotational-speed range,
– the maximum current,
– the cutting-in speed.

With these electrical data, it is possible to define the electrical layout, and therefore the required alternator size.
The different alternator sizes are identified by a letter of the alphabet, and increase in alphabetical order. A further important feature is the alternator or rotor system (e.g., claw-pole alternator as a compact alternator or alternator with compact diode assembly, or with salient-pole rotor or windingless rotor). This characteristic is identified by numbers or letters. In addition, the various alternators are identified by an alphanumeric code e.g., GC, KC, NC, G1, K1, N1 for passenger cars, and K1, N1, T1 for commercial vehicles and buses.
Further variations are possible with regard to the type of mounting, the fan shape, the pulley, and the electrical connections.

Table 1. Alternator types.

Design	Application	Type	No. of poles
Compact	Passenger cars, motorcycles	GC, KC, NC	12
Compact diode assembly	Pass. cars, commercial vehs. tractors, motorcycles	G1	
	Pass. cars, commercial vehs., tractors,	K1, N1	
	Buses	T1	16
	Long-haul trucks, construction machinery	N3	12
Standard	Special vehicles	T3	14
	Special vehicles, ships/boats	U2	4, 6

Claw-pole alternators with collector rings

Claw-pole alternators with collector rings feature compact construction with favorable power characteristics and low weight. This leads to a correspondingly wide range of applications. These alternators are particularly suited for use in passenger cars, commercial vehicles, and tractors etc.

The T1 is a high-power version and is intended for vehicles with high power requirements (e.g., buses). The basic construction is shown in Fig. 1.

Features
The ratio of length to diameter is carefully selected to guarantee a maximum of power together with a low outlay on materials. This results in the compact shape with its large diameter and short length which is typical for this type of alternator. Furthermore, this shape also permits excellent heat dissipation.

The designation "claw-pole alternator" derives from the rotor's shape. Attached to the rotor shaft is the pole wheel, consisting of the two oppositely-poled pole halves whose claw-shaped pole fingers mesh in the form of north and south poles. These envelop the toroidal excitation winding which is situated between the two claw-pole halves on the pole body (Fig. 2).

The number of poles which can be realised in practice is limited. On the one hand, a low number of poles leads to a low machine efficiency, whereas on the other the more poles there are, the higher is the magnetic leakage. For this reason, such alternators are designed as 12-pole or 16-pole machines depending upon the power range.

Compact alternators
Types GC, KC, and NC

Application
The conversion to compact alternators for newly registered passenger cars (new vehicles) has been practically completed.

The advantages of this generator type are:
– Power increase of 25% as a result of increasing the alternator's maximum speed,
– Low-noise (increasingly important in commercial-vehicles),
– Increased service life of the carbon brushes and collector rings.

Operating principle
Fig. 3 shows a compact alternator with a 12-pole pole wheel (6 North poles and

---

Fig. 1: Basic construction of the claw-pole alternator with collector rings

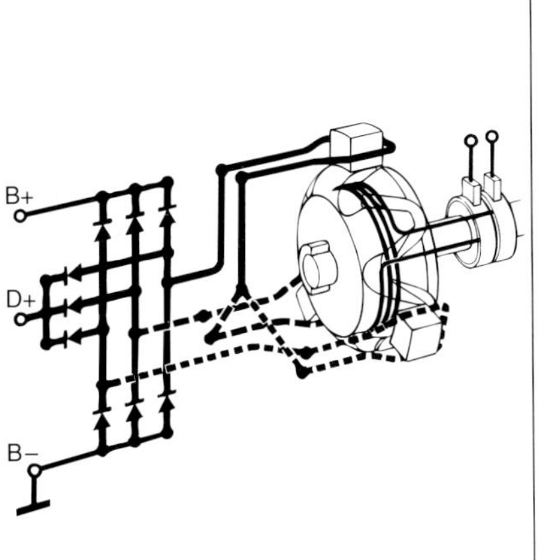

B+

D+

B−

Fig. 2: The components of a 12-pole claw-pole rotor

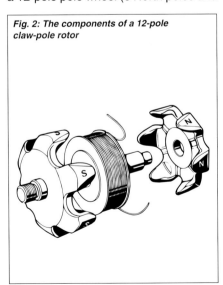

6 South poles = 6 pole pairs). The magnetic flux flows through the pole body and the left-hand pole half and its pole fingers, across the air gap to the stationary laminated stator core with stator winding, from where it flows back to the pole body through the right-hand pole half and completes the magnetic circuit. When the rotor turns, this field of force (field for short), cuts through the three phases of the stationary stator winding. There are therefore 12 pole passes for one rotor revolution (360°). Each pole pass induces a voltage half-wave which is alternatively positive and negative. Consequently for one revolution of the rotor $12 \times 3 = 36$ voltage half-waves are induced in the three windings of the stator, in other words six complete sinusoidal waves are generated in each phase for each revolution of the rotor.

The generated current is divided into primary current and excitation current. After rectification, the primary current flows as operating current via terminal B+ to the battery and to the loads.

Construction

Compact alternators are dual-flow-ventilated, self-excited 12-pole alternators with claw-pole rotor, small-dimensioned collector rings, and Zener-type power diodes. The 3-phase AC winding is located in the stator and the excitation system in the rotor (Fig. 3). Special winding techniques are used to increase the coil/space factor in the stator core, thereby at the same time improving the power/space ratio.

The stator core is fastened at its center lamination in the casing and centered using the end shields. These measures lead to a high degree of precision in the assembly of the alternator, and a low level of "magnetic" noise.

It was possible to even further reduce the noise level by chamfering the claw poles at their trailing edges in addition to clamping the stator core at its center lamination.

Two interior-mounted fans ventilate the alternator by drawing air through it.

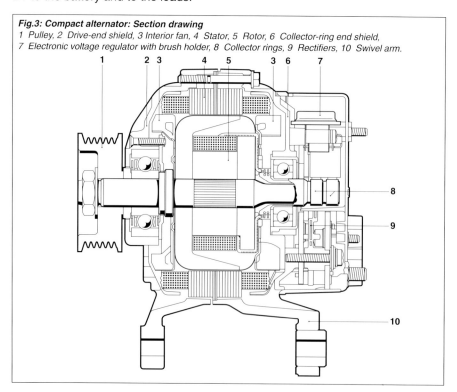

Fig.3: Compact alternator: Section drawing
1 Pulley, 2 Drive-end shield, 3 Interior fan, 4 Stator, 5 Rotor, 6 Collector-ring end shield,
7 Electronic voltage regulator with brush holder, 8 Collector rings, 9 Rectifiers, 10 Swivel arm.

This ventilation system results in a lower fan noise due to the reduction of the noise-emission level. It also means that the designer has a higher degree of freedom regarding the alternator installation point on the engine.

The considerably reduced collector-ring diameter leads to a drop in their peripheral speed. This in turn means that there is less wear at the collector-ring surface as well as at the carbon brushes so that carbon-brush wear is no longer a limiting factor for the alternator's service life. The transistor voltage regulator is integrated in the carbon-brush holder. The Z-diode rectifiers are designed in "sandwich" form and are protected against corrosion by a plastic coating. Z-diodes provide additional protection against overvoltages and voltage peaks.

With Z-diodes, in case of increasing voltage in the reverse direction, the current increases rapidly above a given voltage due to avalanche or Zener breakdown.

Alternators with compact diode assembly Type G1, K1, and N1

Application
The compact generator is increasingly superseding the compact-diode-assembly alternator as the preferred alternator for passenger cars and commercial vehicles. For special applications (in particular for special-purpose commercial vehicles) which for instance necessitate a specific form of corrosion protection, or a version with hose-connection adapter for fresh-air input, a compact-diode-asembly alternator is still installed.

Operating principle
The compact-diode-assembly alternator and the compact alternator have practically the same operating principle. Fig. 4 shows a Type K1 alternator the pole wheel of which comprises 12 poles (6 North and 6 South poles = 12 pole pairs). Here too, the magnetic working flux flows through the pole core,

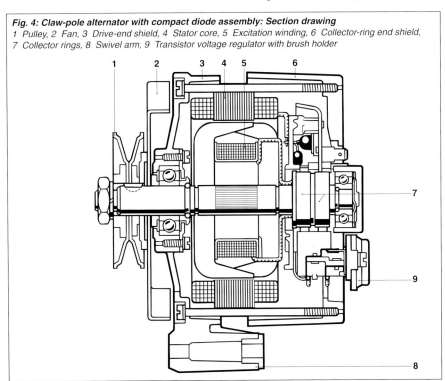

Fig. 4: Claw-pole alternator with compact diode assembly: Section drawing
1 Pulley, 2 Fan, 3 Drive-end shield, 4 Stator core, 5 Excitation winding, 6 Collector-ring end shield,
7 Collector rings, 8 Swivel arm, 9 Transistor voltage regulator with brush holder

the left-hand pole half and its fingers, across the air gap to the stationary stator core and stator winding, finally completing the magnetic circuit by returning to the pole core through the right-hand pole half. When the rotor turns, this field of force (field for short), cuts through through the three phases of the stationary stator winding. There are therefore 12 pole passes for one rotor revolution (360°). Each pole pass induces a voltage half-wave which is alternatively positive and negative. Consequently for one revolution of the rotor $12 \times 3 = 36$ voltage half-waves are induced in the three windings of the stator, in other words six complete sinusoidal waves are generated in each phase for each revolution of the rotor.

Construction
Compact-diode-assembly alternators have 12 poles, they are single-flow internally ventilated and feature self-excitation. Instead of being inserted into a cylindrical housing, the stator core is clamped between the drive end shield and the collector-ring end shield. The rotor runs in bearings in each of these end shields. The fan and the pulley are attached to the drive-end-shield side of the rotor shaft.

The excitation winding is supplied with excitation current through the carbon brushes. These are mounted in the collector-ting end shield and pressed against the collector rings by springs.

The six power diodes for rectification of the generator voltage are press-fitted in the heat sinks of the collector-ring end shield. The excitation diodes are integrated in the rectifier printed-circuit board. In the majority of versions, the voltage regulator forms a unit together with the brush holder and is attached to the outside face of the collector-ring end shield.

The K1 and N1 alternators are equipped as follows for special applications:
– In case of very high outside temperatures, cool air is drawn in through a hose and connection adapter.
– The maximum rotor speed can be increased to 18,000 min-1 by precision-balancing and by special measures taken on the excitation winding, collector rings, and fan.
– A special corrosion protection is available for particularly adverse installation conditions.
– Zener power diodes can be used for rectification in order to protect sensitive components against the effects of voltage peaks resulting from load dump and operation without battery.

Commercial-vehicle alternators
The T1 and double-T1 alternators for commercial vehicles have the following special features:
The collector-ring chamber is encapsulated to prevent wear on rings and brushes due to water and dust.
A possibility is provided for regreasing, or grease-supply chambers are provided. Additional rectifier diodes are necessary for the increased alternator power.
As a rule, the following alternator types are not used for spark-ignition engines, and are therefore not dealt with in detail here.

Salient-pole alternators with collector rings
These alternators are used mainly on large engines with a high electrical-power demand.
The shape of the salient-pole rotor is characteristic for this alternator type. It has only 4 or 6 oblong salient poles each of which are wound with an excitation winding.

Alternators with windingless rotor (without collector rings)
These alternators are used on engines which feature a particularly long service life. One of their typical features is that the inner pole with excitation winding also remains stationary. The alternator's only rotating component is the windingless rotor with pole wheel (without excitation winding or collector rings).

Voltage-regulator versions

The mechanical electromagnetic contact (or vibrating-type) regulators and the electronic (transistor) versions are the two basic versions of voltage regulator.

Whereas the electromagnetic regulator is today practically only used for replacement purposes, the (monolithic or hybrid) transistor regulator is standard equipment on all alternator models.

Electromagnetic contact-type regulators

The excitation current is varied by opening and closing a movable contact in the excitation-current circuit which is pressed against a fixed contact by a spring. When the rated voltage is exceeded, the movable contact is lifted off by an electromagnet.

The contact regulators which are suitable for alternator applications are of the single-element type. That is, regulators with a voltage-regulator element comprising an electromagnet, an armature, and a regulating contact.

In the single-element, single-contact regulator (Fig. 1), the contact opens and closes as follows: The magnetic force and the spring force of a suspension and adjusting spring are both applied to the regulating armature.

As soon as the alternator voltage exceeds the set value, the electromagnet pulls in the armature and opens the contact (position "b"). This switches a resistor into the excitation circuit which reduces the excitation current and with it the alternator voltage. When the alternator voltage drops below the set voltage the magnetic force is also reduced, the spring force predominates and closes the contact again (position "a"). This opening and closing cycle is repeated continually.

The single-element double-contact regulator (Fig. 2) operates with a second pair of contacts which permit 3 switching positions.

The regulating resistor is short-circuited in position "a" and a high excitation current flows. In position "b" the resistor and the excitation winding are connected in series and the excitation current is reduced. In position "c", the excitation winding is short-circuited and the excitation current drops to practically zero.

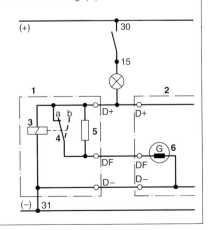

Fig. 1; Diagram of a single-element single-contact regulator
1 Regulator, 2 Alternator, 3 Electromagnet,
4 Regulating contact, 5 Regulating resistor,
6 Excitation winding (G).

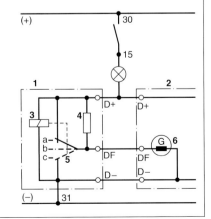

Fig. 2: Diagram of a single-element double-contact regulator
1 Regulator, 2 Alternator, 3 Electromagnet,
4 Regulating resistor, 5 Regulating contact,
6 Excitation winding (G).

Transistor regulators

Transistor regulators are used solely with alternators. Thanks to its compact dimensions, its low weight, and the fact that it is insensitive to vibration and shock, this regulator can be integrated directly in the alternator.

Whereas the first transistor regulators were built from discrete components, modern-day versions all use hybrid and monolithic circuitry.

The transistor regulator's essential advantages are:
– Shorter switching times which permit closer control tolerances,
– No wear (= no servicing),
– High switching currents permit a reduction in the number of types,
– Spark-free switching means no radio interference,
– Insensitive to shock and vibration, and climatic effects,
– Electronic temperature compensation also permits closer control tolerances,
– Compact construction allows direct mounting on the alternator, irrespective of alternator size.

Principle of operation

Basically speaking, the operating principle is the same for all transistor types. The Type EE transistor regulator is used here as an example, and Fig. 3 shows its operation between the "On" and "Off" states.

The principle of operation is easier to understand when one considers what happens when the alternator's terminal voltage rises and falls.

The actual value of the alternator voltage between terminals D+ and D– is registered by a voltage divider (R1, R2, and R3). A Zener diode in parallel with R3 functions as the alternator's setpoint generator. A partial voltage proportional to the alternator voltage is permanently applied to this diode.

The regulator remains in the "On" state as long as the actual alternator voltage is below the set value (Fig. 3a).

The Z-diode's breakdown voltage has not yet been reached at this point. That is, no current flows to the base of transistor T1 through the branch with the Z-diode. T1 is in the blocking state.

With T1 blocked, a current flows from the exciter diodes via terminal D+ and resistor R6 to the base of transistor T2 and switches T2 on. Terminal DF is now connected to the base of T3 by the switched transistor T2. This means that T3 always conducts when T2 is conductive. T2 and T3 are connected as a Darlington circuit and form the regulator's driver stage. The excitation current I_{exc}. flows through T3 and the excitation winding and increases during the "On" period, causing a rise in the alternator voltage U_G. At the same time, the voltage at the setpoint generator also rises. The regulator assumes the "Off" state as soon as the actual alternator voltage exceeds the setpoint value (Fig. 3b).

The Z-diode becomes conductive when the breakdown voltage is reached, and a current flows from D+ through resistors R1, R2 in the branch with the Z-diode, and from there to the base of transistor T1 which also becomes conductive.

As a result, the voltage at the base of T2 is practically 0 referred to the emitter, and transistors T2 and T3 (driver stage) block. The excitation circuit is open-circuited, the excitation decays, and the alternator voltage falls as a result.

As soon as the alternator voltage drops under the set value again, and the Z diode switches to the blocked state, the driver stage switches the excitation current on again.

When the excitation current is open-circuited a voltage peak would be induced due to the excitation winding's self-induction (stored electrical energy) which could destroy transistors T2 and T3. A "free-running diode" D3 is connected parallel to the excitation winding, and at the instant of open-circuiting absorbs the excitation current thereby preventing the formation of a dangerous voltage peak.

The control cycle in which the current is switched on and off by connecting the excitation winding alternately to the alternator voltage or short-circuiting it with the free-wheeling diode is repeated periodically. Essentially, the on/off ratio depends on the alternator speed and the applied load. The ripple on the alternator DC is smoothed by capacitor C. Resistor R7 ensures the rapid, precise switch-over of transistors T2 and T3, as well as reducing the switching losses.

Hybrid regulators

The transistor regulator using hybrid technology comprises a hermetically encapsulated case, in which are enclosed a ceramic substrate, protective thick-film resistors, and a bonded integrated circuit (IC) incorporating all the control functions. The power components of the drive stage (Darlington transistors and the free-wheeling diode) are soldered directly onto the metal socket in order to ensure good heat dissipation. The electrical connections are via glass-insulated metal pins.

The regulator is mounted on a special brush holder and directly fastened to the alternator without wiring.

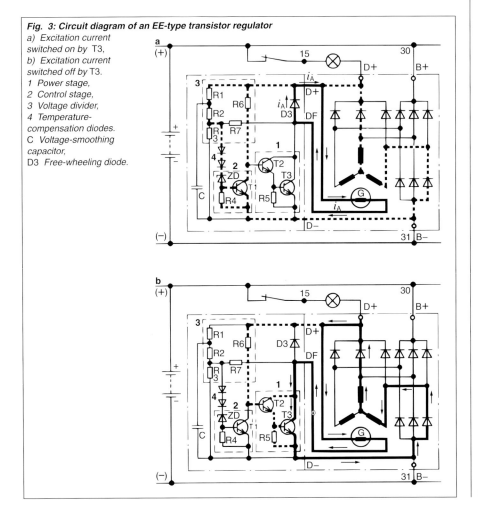

Fig. 3: Circuit diagram of an EE-type transistor regulator
a) Excitation current switched on by T3,
b) Excitation current switched off by T3.
1 Power stage,
2 Control stage,
3 Voltage divider,
4 Temperature-compensation diodes.
C Voltage-smoothing capacitor,
D3 Free-wheeling diode.

Due to the Darlington circuit in the power stage (two transistors), there is a voltage drop of about 1.5 V in the current-flow direction.

The circuit diagram (Fig. 4) shows an alternator fitted with an EL-type hybrid regulator.

The hybrid regulator's advantages can be summed up as follows:
– Compact construction, low weight, few components and connections,
– High reliability in the extreme under-hood operating conditions met in automotive applications.

Normally, hybrid regulators using conventional diodes are used with compact-diode-assembly regulators.

Monolithic regulators

The monolithic regulator has been developed from the hybrid regulator. The functions of the hybrid regulator's IC, power stage, and free-wheeling diode have been incorporated on a single chip. The monolithic regulator uses bipolar techniques.

The compact construction with fewer components and connections enabled reliability to be even further improved.

Since the output stage is in the form of a simple power stage, the voltage drop in the current-flow direction is only 0.5 V.

Monolithic regulators in combination with Z-diode rectifiers are used in compact alternators.

Multifunction voltage regulator

In addition to voltage regulation, the multifunction regulator can also trigger an LED/LCD display instead of the charge-indicator lamp, as well as a fault display to indicate under-voltage, V-belt breakage, or excitation interruption.

The alternator no longer needs excitation diodes. The signal for "engine running" can be taken from Terminal L. Terminal W provides a signal which is proportional to engine speed. The actual voltage value is taken from Terminal B+ on the alternator.

The power loss associated with the charge indicator lamp in the instrument cluster is often excessive. It can be reduced by using an LED/LCD display instead. Multifunction regulators permit the triggering of lamp bulbs as well as of LED/LCD display elements in the instrument cluster.

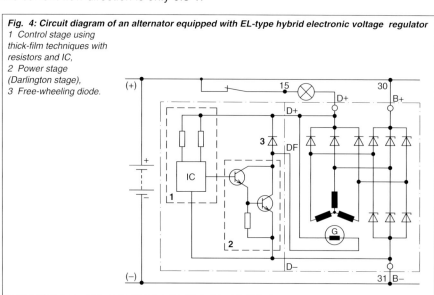

Fig. 4: Circuit diagram of an alternator equipped with EL-type hybrid electronic voltage regulator
1 Control stage using thick-film techniques with resistors and IC,
2 Power stage (Darlington stage),
3 Free-wheeling diode.

Overvoltage-protection devices

Usually, with the battery correctly connected and under normal driving conditions, it is unnecessary to provide additional protection for the vehicle's electronic components. The battery's low internal resistance suppresses all the voltage peaks occurring in the vehicle electrical system.

Nevertheless, it is often advisable to install overvoltage protection as a precautionary measure in case of abnormal operating conditions. For instance, on vehicles for transporting hazardous materials, and in case of faults in the vehicle electrical system.

Reasons for overvoltage

Overvoltage may occur in the vehicle electrical system as the result of regulator failure, influences originating from the ignition, switching off of devices with a predominantly inductive load, loose contacts, or cable breaks. Such overvoltages take the form of very brief voltage peaks lasting only a few milliseconds which reach a maximum of 350 V and originate from the coil ignition. Overvoltages are also generated when the line between battery and alternator is open-circuited with the engine running (this happens when an outside battery is used as a starting aid), or when high-power loads are switched off. For this reason, under normal driving conditions, the alternator is not to be run without the battery connected. Under certain circumstances though, short-term or emergency operation without battery is permissible.

This applies to the following situations:
– Driving of new vehicles from the final assembly line to the parking lot,
– Loading onto train or ship (the battery is installed shortly before the vehicle is taken over by the customer),
– Service work etc.

With towing vehicles and agricultural tractors it is also not always possible to avoid operation without the battery connected. The overvoltage protection device guarantees that overvoltages have no adverse effects on operation, although it does require extra circuitry.

Types of protection

There are three alternatives for implementing overvoltage protection:

Z-diode protection
Power Z-diodes can be used in place of the rectifier power diodes. Z-diodes limit high-energy voltage peaks to such an extent that they are harmless to the alternator and regulator. Furthermore, Z-diodes function as a central overvoltage protection for the remaining voltage-sensitive loads in the vehicle electrical system.

The response voltage of a rectifier equipped with Z-diodes is 25...30 V for an alternator voltage of 14 V, and 50...55 V for an alternator voltage of 28 V.

Compact alternators are always equipped with Z-diodes.

Surge-proof alternators and regulators
The semiconductor components in surge-proof alternators have a higher electric-strength rating. For 14 V alternator voltage the electric strength of the semiconductors is at least 200 V, and for 28 V alternator voltage 350 V.

In addition, a capacitor is fitted between the alternator's B+ terminal and ground, which serves for short-range interference suppression.

The surge-proof characteristics of such alternators and regulators only protect these units, they provide no protection for other electrical equipment in the vehicle.

Overvoltage protection devices

Normally, overvoltage protection devices are only fitted in the 24 V electrical systems of commercial vehicles and busses, and are therefore only discussed here briefly.

The semiconductor circuits of the overvoltage protection devices are connected to alternator terminals D+ and D– (ground) (Fig. 1).

The protection device responds to voltage peaks by short-circuiting the alternator excitation winding. Alternator and regulator are the main beneficiaries of such devices, and to a lesser degree the other voltage-sensitive equipment in the vehicle electrical system.

Generally, alternators are not provided with polarity-reversal protection. If battery polarity is reversed (e.g., when starting with an external battery), this will destroy the alternator diodes as well as endangering the semiconductor components in other equipment.

Free-wheeling diode

The free-wheeling diode (also known as a suppressor diode or anti-surge diode) has already been mentioned in the description of the transistor regulator.

When the regulator switches to the "Off" status, upon interruption of the excitation current a voltage peak is induced in the excitation winding due to self-induction. Sensitive semiconductor components can be destroyed if precautionary measures are not taken. The free-wheeling diode is connected in the regulator parallel to the alternator's excitation winding. Upon the excitation winding being interrupted, the free-wheeling diode "takes over" the excitation current and permits it to decay, thus preventing the generation of dangerous voltage peaks.

A similar effect can occur on vehicles which are equipped with inductive loads remote from the alternator regulator. Thus, when electromagnetic door valves, solenoid switches, magnetic clutches, motor drives, and relays etc. are switched off, voltage peaks can be generated in the windings of such equipment due to self-induction, and can endanger the diodes and other semiconductor components.

These induced voltages can be rendered harmless by means of a free-wheeling diode.

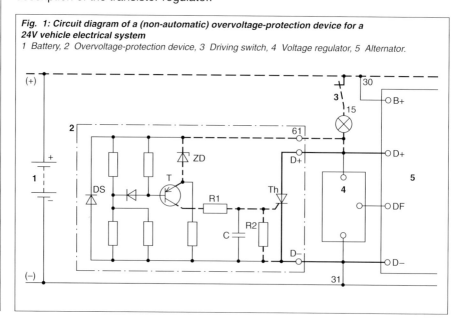

Fig. 1: Circuit diagram of a (non-automatic) overvoltage-protection device for a 24V vehicle electrical system
1 Battery, 2 Overvoltage-protection device, 3 Driving switch, 4 Voltage regulator, 5 Alternator.

Power losses

Efficiency

Losses are an unavoidable by-product when converting mechanical energy into electrical energy. Efficiency is defined as the ratio between power input to the conversion unit and power taken from it.

The maximum efficiency of an air-cooled alternator is approximately 65%, a figure which drops rapidly when speed is increased.

Under normal driving conditions, an alternator usually operates in the part-load range. Mean efficiency is around 55%.

Presuming the same loading, using a larger, heavier alternator means that operation can take place in a more favorable portion of the efficiency curve (Fig. 1).

On the other hand, the increased efficiency of the larger alternator can be offset by an accompanying increase in fuel consumption. What must be taken into account though is the increased moment of inertia which results in a higher energy input for accelerating the rotor.

The alternator is typical for a permanently operating vehicle assembly, and regarding fuel-consumption must first of all be optimized with respect to efficiency and then with respect to weight.

Sources of power loss

The power losses are shown in Fig. 2 below. The major losses are either "iron losses", "copper losses" or "mechanical losses". Iron losses result from the hysteresis and eddy currents produced by the alternating magnetic fields in the rotor and the stator. They increase superproportionally along with frequency. That is, along with the rotational speed and with the magnetic induction. The copper losses represent the resistive losses in the rotor and the stator. Their extent is proportional to the power-to-weight ratio, i.e., the ratio of generated electrical power to the mass of the effective components. The mechanical losses include friction losses at the rolling bearings and at the sliding contacts as well as the windage losses of the rotor and the fan. At higher speeds, the fan losses increase considerably.

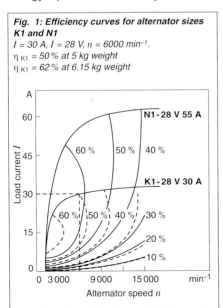

Fig. 1: Efficiency curves for alternator sizes
K1 and N1
$I = 30\ A$, $I = 28\ V$, $n = 6000\ min^{-1}$.
$\eta_{K1} = 50\%$ at 5 kg weight
$\eta_{K1} = 62\%$ at 6.15 kg weight

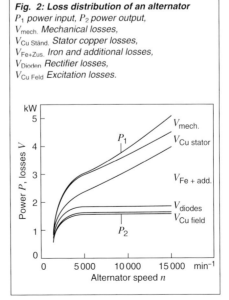

Fig. 2: Loss distribution of an alternator
P_1 power input, P_2 power output,
$V_{mech.}$ Mechanical losses,
$V_{Cu\ Ständ.}$ Stator copper losses,
$V_{Fe+Zus.}$ Iron and additional losses,
V_{Dioden} Rectifier losses,
$V_{Cu\ Feld}$ Excitation losses.

Characteristic curves

Alternator performance

The characteristic performance of the alternator at a variety of different speeds is shown by the characteristic curves. Due to the constant transmission ratio between alternator and engine, the alternator must be able to operate at greatly differing speeds.

As the engine takes the alternator from standstill up to maximum speed, the alternator passes through certain speeds. Each of these rotational speeds is of particular importance for understanding the alternator's operation and each has therefore been allocated a specific name.

Normally, the curves for alternator current and drive power are shown as a function of the rotational speed (Fig. 1). The characteristic curves of an alternator are always referred to a constant voltage and precisely defined temperature conditions. For instance, an ambient temperature of 80°C (or a room temperature of 23°C) is specified for the limit-temperature test.

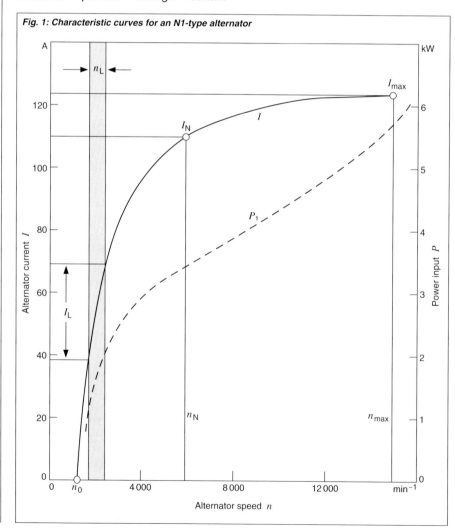

Fig. 1: Characteristic curves for an N1-type alternator

Current characteristic curve (I)

n_0 0-Ampere speed
The 0-Ampere speed is the speed (approx. 1000min^{-1}) at which the alternator reaches its rated voltage without delivering power. This is the speed at which the curve crosses the min^{-1} abscissa. The alternator can only deliver power at higher speeds.

n_L Speed with engine idling
I_L Current with engine idling
With the speed increasing, alternator speed n_L is reached with the engine at idle. This point is shown as an area in Fig. 1 since the precise value depends upon the transmission ratio between engine and alternator. At this speed, the alternator must deliver at least the current required for the long-term consumers. This value is given in the alternator's type designation. In the case of compact-diode-assembly alternators, $n_L = 1500$ min^{-1}, for compact alternators $n_L = 1800$ min^{-1} due to the usually higher transmission ratio.

n_N Speed at rated current
I_N Rated current
The speed at which the alternator generates its rated current is stipulated as $n_N = 6000$ min^{-1} The rated current should always be higher than the total current required by all loads together. It is also given in the type designation.

n_{max} Maximum speed
I_{max} Maximum current
I_{max} is the maximum achievable current at the alternator's maximum speed. Maximum speed is limited by the rolling bearings and the carbon brushes as well as by the fan. With compact alternators it is 18,000 ... 20,000 min^{-1}, and for compact-diode-assembly alternators 15,000 ... 18,000 min^{-1}. In the case of commercial vehicles, it is 8,000 ... 15,000 min^{-1} depending upon alternator size.

n_A Cutting-in speed
The cutting-in speed is defined as that speed at which the alternator starts to deliver current when the speed is increased for the first time. It is above the idle speed, and depends upon the pre-excitation power, the rotor's remanence, the battery voltage, and the rate of rotational-speed change.

Characteristic curve of power input (P_1)

The characteristic curve of power input is decisive for drive-belt calculations. Information can be taken from this curve concerning the maximum power which must be taken from the engine to drive the alternator at a given speed. In addition, the power input and power output can be used to calculate the alternator's efficiency. The example in Fig. 1 shows that after a gradual rise in the medium-speed range, the characteristic curve for power input rises again sharply at higher speeds. This is due to the increased power required to drive the fan at higher speeds.

Explanation of the type designation

Every Bosch alternator carries a rating plate containing type designation and 10-digit Part Number which in the case of alternators always starts with 0 12 ....
The type designation gives information on the alternator's most important technical data such as current at engine idle and rated voltage etc.

Example of a type designation
K C ($\rightarrow$) 14 V   40−70 A

K   Alternator size (stator OD),
C   Compact-Alternator,
($\rightarrow$) Direction of rotation, clockwise,
14 V Alternator voltage,
40 A Current at $n = 1800$ min^{-1},
70 A Current at $n = 6000$ min^{-1}.

Cooling and noise

The alternator is considerably effected by the heat from the engine and exhaust system, and by its own heat losses. And when the engine compartment is encapsulated for sound-proofing reasons, this leads to even higher temperatures. In the interests of functional reliability, all heat must be removed, otherwise not only the soldered joints and insulation can be damaged but above all the heat-sensitive semiconductor components. In particular, there is a limit to the permissible heat-up of the semiconductor diodes, which means that the heat they develop must be dissipated completely. For this reason they are pressed into large-area heat sinks which feature a high level of thermal conductivity so that they are able to dissipate the diode heat into the flow of cooling air. Depending upon alternator version, maximum permissible ambient temperature is limited to 80...100°C. There are a variety of different measures which can be applied to guarantee adequate alternator cooling. Whichever method is chosen, it must guarantee that even under the hostile under-hood conditions encountered in everyday operation, component temperatures remain within the specified limits ("worst-case" consideration).

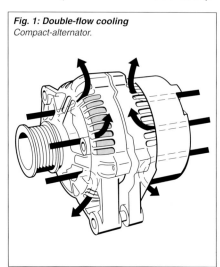

Fig. 1: Double-flow cooling
Compact-alternator.

Cooling without fresh-air intake

Through-flow cooling is the most common cooling method applied for automotive alternators. Radial fans for one or both directions of rotation are used.
Since both the fan and the alternator shaft must be driven, the cooling-air throughput increases along with the speed. This ensures adequate cooling irrespective of alternator loading.
In order to avoid the whistling noise (siren effect) which can occur at specific speeds, the fan blades on some alternator types are arranged asymmetrically.

Single-flow cooling
Compact-diode-assembly alternators use single-flow cooling. The external fan is attached to the drive end of the alternator shaft. Air is drawn in by the fan at the collector-ring or rectifier end, passes through the alternator, and leaves through openings in the drive end shield.

Double-flow cooling
Due to their higher specific power, compact alternators are equipped with double-flow cooling. The compact alternator's two fans are mounted inside the alternator on the drive shaft to the left and right of the rotor's active section. The two air streams enter the alternator axially through openings in the drive and collector-ring end shields, and leave through openings around the alternator's circumference (Fig. 1).
One essential advantage lies in the use of smaller fans, with the attendant reduction of fan-generated aerodynamic noise.

Cooling with fresh-air intake

When fresh air is used for cooling purposes, a special air-intake fitting is provided on the intake side in place of the
air-intake openings. A hose is used to
draw in cool, dust-free air from outside
the engine compartment.

For instance, with the T1 alternator the
cooling air enters through the air-intake
fitting, flows through the alternator and
leaves again through openings in the
drive end shield. With this type of generator also, the cooling air is drawn
through the alternator by the fan.

It is particularly advisable to use the
fresh-air intake method when engine-
compartment temperatures exceed
80°C and when a high-power generator
is used. With the compact alternator,
the fresh-air method can be applied for
cooling the rectifiers and the regulator.

Noise

The more emphasis that is placed on
quiet-running vehicles, the more important it is to reduce alternator noise.

Alternator noise is comprised of two
main components: Aerodynamic noise
and magnetically induced noise.

Aerodynamic noise can be generated
by the passage of the cooling air
through narrow openings, and at the
fan when speeds exceed 3000 min-1. It
can be limited by careful routing of the
cooling air and by using smaller fans
with asymmetrically arranged blades.

In individual cases, mechanical noise
can be caused by ball bearings in which
hardened grease together with the
effects of moisture ingress lead to "stick-
slip" oscillations at very low temperatures. The remedy here is to use well-
sealed ball bearings together with
greases which retain their lubricity even
at low temperatures.

Magnetically induced noises are attributable to strong local magnetic fields
and the dynamic effects which result
between stator and rotor under load.
There are a number of measures which

can be taken to limit magnetic noise.
These include air-gap increases and
tighter manufacturing tolerances etc.

One of the most effective measures for
reducing radially radiated noise is the
"claw-pole chamfer". Here, the claw-
pole's trailing edge is chamfered
(Fig. 2). This measure reduces the
effects of armature reaction caused by
the stator currents. When the alternator
is electrically loaded, the armature reaction causes a pronounced field displacement in the air gap which in turn
leads to the generation of noise. Optimization of this measure can result in a
noise reduction of 10 dB(A). This appro-
ximates to a reduction of about 50% in
individual noise perception.

Account must also be taken of the effect
of the alternator's position on the engine. Structure-borne noise excites the
alternator mounting bracket and affects
the alternator's oscillatory characteristics and its noise generation. A resilient
alternator mounting can prevent this
coupling completely.

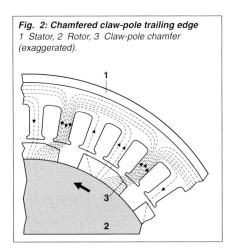

Fig. 2: Chamfered claw-pole trailing edge
1 Stator, 2 Rotor, 3 Claw-pole chamfer
(exaggerated).

Alternator circuitry

Sometimes, the alternator or the vehicle electrical system is confronted with requirements which cannot always be fully complied with by the standard series-production versions.

For such cases, there are special circuitry variants available which can be implemented individually or in combination.

Parallel-connected power diodes

As already dealt with in the section on semiconductor devices, diodes can only be loaded up to a certain current level without damage. At high currents, excessive heat-up would destroy the diodes. This is particularly important when considering the heavily loaded power diodes in the 3-phase AC bridge circuit. through which the entire alternator current flows.

However, the alternator's maximum achievable power output is limited by the maximum possible generator cur-

rent. And high-power alternators feature a generator current which is so high that the six power diodes in the normal 3-phase AC bridge circuit are unable to handle it.

For this reason, such alternators are equipped with two or more parallel-connected power diodes for each phase. As a result, the alternator current is divided between the parallel-connected diodes so that the individual diodes are no longer overloaded.

The circuit diagram of an alternator using this principle is shown in Fig. 1. Two power diodes are connected in parallel for each phase, which means that the 3-phase AC rectifier comprises 12 power diodes instead of six.

Auxiliary diodes at the star (neutral) point

On alternators with star-connected stator windings, the ends of the windings are joined at a single point, the star or neutral point.

Since, at least theoretically, the addition of the three phase currents or phase voltages is always zero at any instant in time, this means that the neutral conductor can be dispensed with.

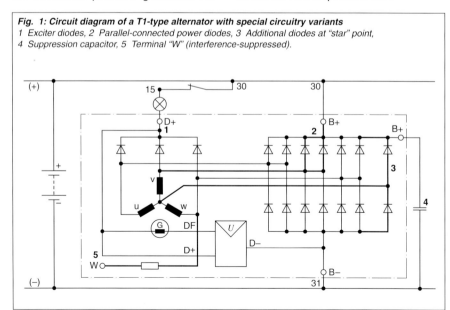

Fig. 1: Circuit diagram of a T1-type alternator with special circuitry variants
1 Exciter diodes, 2 Parallel-connected power diodes, 3 Additional diodes at "star" point,
4 Suppression capacitor, 5 Terminal "W" (interference-suppressed).

Due to harmonics and slight differences in the claw-system geometry, it is possible for the neutral point to assume a varying potential which changes periodically from positive to negative. This potential is mainly caused by the "third harmonic" which is superimposed on the fundamental wave and which has three times its frequency (Fig. 2). The energy it contains would normally be lost, but instead it is rectified by two diodes connected as power diodes between the neutral point and the positive and negative terminals (Fig. 1). As from around 3000 min-1, this leads to an alternator power increase of max. 10 %. These auxiliary diodes slightly increase the ripple of the alternator voltage.

Operation of alternators in parallel

If demanded by power requirements, alternators with the same power rating can be connected in parallel. Special balancing is not necessary, although the voltage regulators concerned must have the same characteristics, and their characteristic curves must be identical.

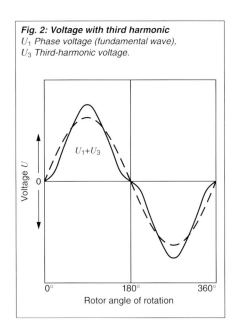

Fig. 2: Voltage with third harmonic
U_1 Phase voltage (fundamental wave),
U_3 Third-harmonic voltage.

Voltage U

U_1+U_3

0

0°　　　　180°　　　360°

Rotor angle of rotation

Terminal "W"

For specific applications, Terminal "W" can be connected to one of the three phases as an additional terminal (Fig. 1). It provides a pulsating DC (half-wave-rectified AC) which can be used for measuring engine speed (for instance on diesel engines).

According to the following equation, the frequency (number of pulses per second) depends on the number of pole pairs and upon alternator speed.

$$f = p \cdot n/60$$
f Frequency (pulses per second),
p Number of pole pairs (6 on Size G, K and N; 8 on Size T),
n Alternator speed (min^{-1}).

Interference-suppression measures

The main source of electrical interference in the SI engine is the ignition system, although some interference is also generated by alternator and regulator, as well as by other electrical loads. If a 2-way radio, car radio, or car telephone etc. is operated in the vehicle itself or in the vicinity, it is necessary to install intensified interference suppression of alternator and regulator. For this purpose, alternators can be equipped with a suppression capacitor (if not already connected as standard) which is attached to the outside of the collector-ring shield. On compact alternators it is already integrated in the rectifier.

Older versions of the contact regulator are combined with an interference-suppression filter or are replaced by an interference-suppressed version. Transistor regulators do not require additional suppression measures. If Terminal "W" is connected, this can be suppressed with a resistor which is installed in the "W" line (Fig. 1).

Operation of alternators in the vehicle

In the vehicle, engine, alternator, battery, and electrical loads, must be considered as an interrelated system.

Energy balance in the vehicle

When specifying or checking alternator size, account must be taken of the battery capacity, the power consumption of the connected loads, and the driving conditions.

Alternator size and battery capacity are specified by the automaker in accordance with the electrical loads installed in the vehicle and the normal driving conditions. Individual circumstances can deviate from the above conditions though. On the one hand because the operator installs extra electrical equipment in the vehicle, and on the other because driving conditions differ considerably from those taken as normal.

These considerations are intended to underline the fact that the total input-power requirements, together with the individual driving conditions, are of decisive importance with regard to the loading of the alternator and battery.

An adequate state of battery charge is the prime consideration. It is decisive for sufficient energy being available to start the engine again after it has been switched off. The battery functions as an energy store which supplies the various loads, and which in turn must continually be charged by the alternator in its function as the energy supplier. On the other hand, if the energy drawn from the battery exeeds that supplied to it, even a high-capacity battery will gradually discharge until it is "empty" (or "flat"). The ideal situation is a balance between input and output of energy to and from the battery (Fig. 1).

Thus, a correctly dimensioned alternator is decisive for an adequate supply of on-board energy. An under-rated (i.e. overloaded) alternator is not able to keep the battery sufficiently charged, which means that battery capacity cannot be fully utilized.

Consequently, if power demand is increased, for instance as a result of fitting extra equipment, it is advisable to replace the standard fitted alternator by a more powerful version. One of the most important steps to be taken when ascertaining the electrical system's charge balance is the registration of all the installed electrical loads (including retrofitted equipment), together with their power inputs and the average length of time they are switched on (short-term, long-term, or permanent loads). Similarly, the driving cycles as dictated by the traffic situation must also be considered. These include, for instance, low alternator speeds typical for town traffic coupled with repeated standstills, expressway traffic with congestion, and high alternator speeds on clear first-class roads. The time of day (journeys mainly by daylight or during the dark), and the season (winter or summer driving with the related temperatures and weather), also have an affect.

We can sum up as follows:

Even under the most unfavorable operating conditions, in addition to powering all the electrical loads, the alternator power must suffice to keep the battery sufficiently charged so that the vehicle is always ready for operation.

An expert should be consulted before the final selection of alternator size and its matching to the appropriate battery. The following example illustrates the loading of the vehicle's energy household by the electrical loads under a variety of different conditions:

Fig. 1: Charge balance
Current flow between alternator, battery, and electrical devices, with constant power demands from the loads, and varying alternator operating conditions.

In general, the following applies:

$$I_G = I_W + I_B$$

Where:
I_G Alternator current
I_W Equipment current
I_B Battery current

The battery current may be positive or negative, depending on whether the battery is being charged or is discharging.

Unfavorable situation: Low alternator speed

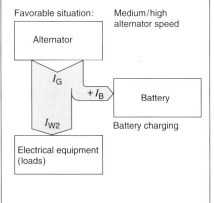

Favorable situation: Medium/high alternator speed

Operation of high-beam headlamps

These are used mainly for overland trips at high engine speeds (i.e., high alternator speeds), and with low traffic density. They are switched to low-beam in the event of oncoming traffic. High-beam headlamps are not required in town traffic with its low engine speeds and short distances. These types of load are no problem for the vehicle's energy household. The alternator is operated at a speed which ensures that all loads are supplied with enough electrical energy and that the battery is charged. Here, the operating conditions are favorable.

Operation of fog lamps

On the other hand, the situation is not so favorable regarding fog lamps. Since fog forces the driver to drive slowly, this means that fog lamps are usually switched on in the lower engine-speed range at which the alternator does not yet generate full power. And even when traffic approaches, the fog lamps are not switched off, so that their overall switched-on time is relatively long. Here, the operating conditions are unfavorable. In many cases, the loading placed on the vehicle's energy household also depends upon the driver's skill and common sense.

Operation of rear-window heating

Although the rear-window heater is a relatively high current consumer, it only remains on briefly until the backlite has cleared. However, if the driver then forgets to switch the heater off, this results in a considerable drain on the vehicle's energy household as provided by the alternator and battery

Operation of other loads

Compared to the examples dealt with above, electronic equipment, turn-signal indicators, horn, and instrument cluster, are insignificant as regards the loading they impose on the system.

Determining the correct alternator

(Example refers to the Table below)
The following method enables a check to be made whether the installed alternator version suffices for supplying the vehicle electrical system:

1. Determine the power input for all the loads that are switched on permanently or for prolonged periods at 14 V. The sum results in a power input of $P_{W1} = 350$ W.

2. Determine the power input of all short-term loads at 14 V.

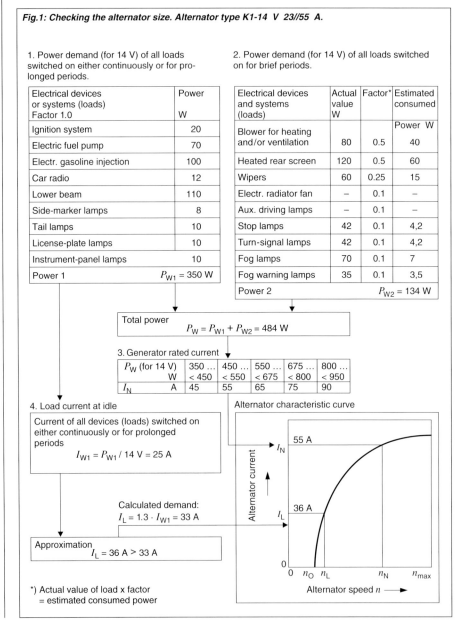

Fig.1: Checking the alternator size. Alternator type K1-14 V 23//55 A.

1. Power demand (for 14 V) of all loads switched on either continuously or for prolonged periods.

Electrical devices or systems (loads) Factor 1.0	Power W
Ignition system	20
Electric fuel pump	70
Electr. gasoline injection	100
Car radio	12
Lower beam	110
Side-marker lamps	8
Tail lamps	10
License-plate lamps	10
Instrument-panel lamps	10
Power 1	$P_{W1} = 350$ W

2. Power demand (for 14 V) of all loads switched on for brief periods.

Electrical devices and systems (loads)	Actual value W	Factor*	Estimated consumed Power W
Blower for heating and/or ventilation	80	0.5	40
Heated rear screen	120	0.5	60
Wipers	60	0.25	15
Electr. radiator fan	–	0.1	–
Aux. driving lamps	–	0.1	–
Stop lamps	42	0.1	4,2
Turn-signal lamps	42	0.1	4,2
Fog lamps	70	0.1	7
Fog warning lamps	35	0.1	3,5
Power 2			$P_{W2} = 134$ W

Total power
$$P_W = P_{W1} + P_{W2} = 484 \text{ W}$$

3. Generator rated current

P_W (for 14 V) W	350 ... < 450	450 ... < 550	550 ... < 675	675 ... < 800	800 ... < 950
I_N A	45	55	65	75	90

4. Load current at idle

Current of all devices (loads) switched on either continuously or for prolonged periods
$$I_{W1} = P_{W1} / 14 \text{ V} = 25 \text{ A}$$

Calculated demand:
$$I_L = 1.3 \cdot I_{W1} = 33 \text{ A}$$

Approximation
$$I_L = 36 \text{ A} > 33 \text{ A}$$

*) Actual value of load x factor = estimated consumed power

Alternator characteristic curve

55 A

36 A

The sum results in a power input of:
$P_{W2} = 134$ W (rounded off).
The system's total power input P_W results from the addition of P_{W1} und P_{W2}:
$P_W = 484$ W.

3. Using the reference table, it is now possible to determine the minimum rated current necessary: $I_N = 55$ A. Provided the correct size of alternator has been fitted, this rated current, or a higher figure, appears in the type designation - in our example 55 A.

4. A further check can be made using the alternator current I_L at engine idle. I_L can be taken from the alternator's characteristic curve, provided that the alternator speed n_L at engine idle is known. In our example, the alternator speed is:
$n_L = 2000$ min^{-1}.
Practical experience has shown that for passenger cars, at engine idle I_L should exceed the current I_{W1} by a factor of 1.3. I_{W1} results from the input power P_{W1} for all permanent and long-term loads. This ensures efficient battery charging even at engine idle and when only short distances are travelled.

In the example:
At idle, the alternator delivers a current of $I_L = 36$ A. The current I_{W1} is calculated from the power P_{W1} ($I_{W1} = P_{W1}/14$ V). This results in $I_{W1} = 25$ A from which a required current of 33 A is calculated. Since $I_L = 36$ A, this means that the power demand is safely covered.

Alternator installation and drive

Installation
The motor-vehicle operator usually has little say concerning the alternator or regulator fitted in his vehicle. And in every vehicle, the alternator's installation position is dependent upon the conditions prevailing in the engine compartment due to construction and design.

However, certain basic factors must always be borne in mind concerning installation:
– Good accessibility for readjusting the V-belt tension and for any maintenance work which may be required,
– Adequate cooling for alternator waste heat as well as for heat conducted and radiated from the engine.
– Protection against dirt, moisture, shock, impact, fuel and lubricants (ingress of gasoline leads to the danger of fire and explosion, and diesel fuel damages the carbon brushes and collector rings).

Almost without exception, alternators which are driven by the engine through normal V-belts are attached by means of a swivel-arm mounting. In addition to the mounting using a swivel bearing, an adjustment facility (to pivot the alternator around a swivel arm) is provided for adjusting the V-belt tension.
If the alternator is driven through a ribbed V-belt (poly-V belt), the alternator is usually rigidly mounted. The belt is adjusted using a belt tensioner (Fig. 2).

Fig. 2: V-belt and ribbed V-belt alternator drive

Fig.:VW

In special cases, large alternators are cradle-mounted in a recess directly on the engine.

Irrespective of the type of mounting, all alternators must have good electrical connection to the engine block. Furthermore, since current return from the electrical system is in the most cases via ground, there must be a highly conductive ground connection of adequate cross-section between engine and chassis.

Buses and special-purpose vehicles are often equipped with extra return lines in order to reduce voltage losses and thereby increase safety.

Electric cables and lines only provide efficient connection if they are provided with properly attached terminals or plug connectors.

Alternator drive

Alternators are driven directly from the vehicle engine. As a rule, drive is via V-belts. Less frequently, flexible couplings are used.

The belt drive (using V-belts, ribbed-V belts etc.) is the most important element in the transmission of power, and as such it is subject to exacting requirements:
– The belt material must have very high flexural strength,
– Belt slip leads to heat-up and wear, and in order to prevent it, longitudinal stretch should remain at a minimum as the belt gets older.

Investigations conducted by ADAC (Germany's largest automobile club) have revealed that V-belt damage is a frequent cause of breakdown. It is therefore important to use V-belts which comply with the above requirements and which are capable of a long service life. Typical for automotive applications are the "open-flank" belt and the ribbed-V belt.

The "open-flank" design (Fig. 3) features high flexibility, coupled with extreme lateral rigidity and resistance to wear. Particularly with small-diameter pulleys, this leads to improved power transmission and a longer service life compared to conventional rubber-jacketed V-belts.

The high flexibility of the ribbed-V belt (Poly-V belt, Fig. 4) permits very small bending radiuses. This in turn means

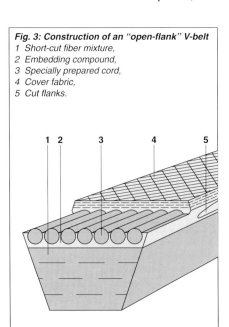

Fig. 3: Construction of an "open-flank" V-belt
1 Short-cut fiber mixture,
2 Embedding compound,
3 Specially prepared cord,
4 Cover fabric,
5 Cut flanks.

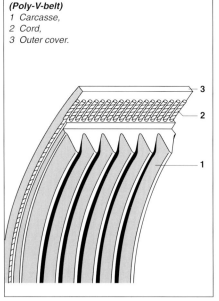

Fig. 4: Construction of a ribbed V-belt (Poly-V-belt)
1 Carcasse,
2 Cord,
3 Outer cover.

that small-diameter pulleys (minimum dia.: 45 mm) can be fitted to the alternators thus permitting higher transmission ratios. The back of the belt may also be used to transmit power, thus enabling a number of aggregates (alternator, radiator fan, water pump, power-steering pump etc.) to all be driven from a single belt with an adequate wrap angle around each pulley wheel.

Usually, a single V-belt suffices to drive small-power alternators. With large-power alternators on the other hand, two V-belts are more common in order to overcome the alternator's resistance to turning which is inherent in its higher power.

Depending upon application, pulley wheels and fan wheels are available which have either been turned or stamped from sheet metal, and which can be combined with each other as required (Fig. 5).

The pulley wheel's correct diameter depends upon the required transmission ratio between engine and alternator.

Being as the speed ranges covered by the multitude of engines concerned differ considerably from each other,

there is a wide variety of different pulley-wheel diameters available.

The transmission ratio must take into account the fact that the alternator's permitted maximum speed must not be exceeded at the engine's maximum speed.

Notes on operation

Battery and regulator must be connected when the alternator is operated. This is the normal operating setup and the installed electronic equipment and semiconductor devices perform efficiently and safely.

Emergency operation without the battery connected results in high voltage peaks which can damage equipment and components. Here, efficient emergency operation is only possible if precautionary measures are taken.

There are three alternatives:
– Protection using Z-diodes
– Surge-proof alternator and regulator
– Overvoltage protection devices.

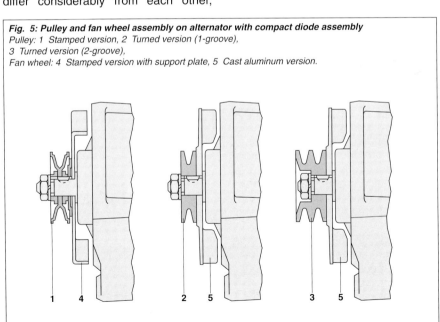

Fig. 5: Pulley and fan wheel assembly on alternator with compact diode assembly
Pulley: 1 Stamped version, 2 Turned version (1-groove),
3 Turned version (2-groove),
Fan wheel: 4 Stamped version with support plate, 5 Cast aluminum version.

Connecting the battery into the vehicle's electrical system with the wrong polarity, immediately destroys the alternator diodes, and can damage the regulator, no matter whether the engine is switched off or running. The same damage can occur if an external voltage source is used as a starting aid and the terminals are reversed.

Special circuitry is available to safeguard against reverse-polarity damage. When the battery is falsely connected, engine start is blocked in order to protect alternator and regulator.

The charge-indicator lamp acts as a resistor in the alternator circuit. If a correctly rated lamp is fitted which draws enough current, the resulting pre-excitation current provides a magnetic field which is strong enough to initiate alternator self-excitation.

When the charge-indicator lamp lights up, this merely indicates to the driver that the ignition or driving switch is switched on and that the alternator is not yet feeding power into the electrical system. The lamp goes out as soon as the alternator's self-excitation speed is reached and the alternator supplies energy to the electrical system. The lamp therefore provides an indication that alternator and regulator are functioning correctly, that they are correctly connected, and that the alternator is supplying current.

The charge-indicator lamp gives no indication as to whether, and as of what speed, the battery is being charged. When the alternator is heavily loaded, it can happen that even though the lamp has gone out, the battery is not being charged but discharged. The lamp gives no information concerning the state of battery charge even though it is erroneously referred to as the "charge-indicator lamp".

If the lamp is defective (broken filament), this means that pre-excitation current cannot flow and self-excitation first sets in at very high speeds. This error is noticeable when the lamp fails to light up with the engine at standstill and the ignition switched on.

If there is an open-circuit in the excitation circuit, in the pre-excitation line, or in the alternator ground line, and the alternator breaks down completely as a result, the driver is not warned of this fact even though the charge-indicator lamp is intact.

Here, it is necessary to connect in an additional resistor (Fig. 6) so that the charge-indicator lamp lights up to inform the driver of the open-circuited excitation circuits.

If the charge-indicator lamp fails to go out even at high speeds, this indicates a fault in the alternator itself, at the regulator, in the wiring, or at the V-belt.

Service life, mileage, maintenance intervals

Using a variety of statistical methods, and taking typical operating conditions into account, it is possible to calculate specific average service lives, mileages, and driving cycles for different categories of vehicle (passenger car, commercial vehicle, long-haul truck, town and long-distance buses, and construction machinery).

Fig. 6: Circuit for fault indication in the event of an open circuit in the exciter circuit.
1 Alternator, 2 Charge indicator lamp, 3 Resistor, 4 Ignition switch, 5 Battery.

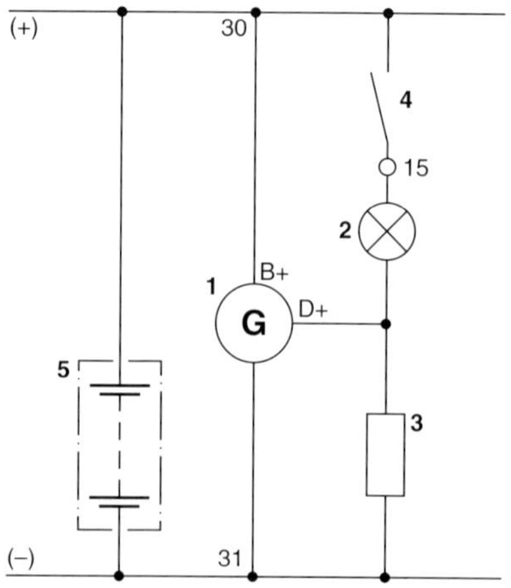

Considering the different fields of application of these vehicle categories, the requirements and criteria for the economic efficiency of their alternators also differ. This leads to there being a range of alternators available for different service lives and maintenance intervals.

Depending upon version and application, passenger-car alternators with encapsulated ball bearings have service lives of 100,000 ... 200,000 km.

Presuming that the engine's service life until it is replaced or has a major overhaul corresponds to that of its alternator, this makes specific maintenance work on the alternator unnecessary. The grease in the bearings suffices for this period.

Due to the use of particularly wear-resistant components, the alternators installed in trucks and buses for instance achieve mileages of 200,000 ... 300,000 km. One prerequisite is that they are equipped with suitable ball bearings, featuring enlarged grease chambers for instance.

Engines which are designed to cover mileages exceeding 300,000 km before their first major overhaul are equipped with alternators featuring windingless rotors and high-rating rolling bearings.

Provided the alternator is installed in a location which is relatively free from dirt, oils, and grease, the carbon-brush wear is negligible due to the low excitation currents involved. Basically speaking, carbon-brush wear has no effect on alternator mileage.

Testers and test equipment

Alternators can only be tested efficiently using the correct testers and test equipment.

Fig. 7 shows an example of a Bosch workshop tester which must be available in every good workshop in order that effective customer service can be carried out.

This equipment incorporates measuring instruments with which it is possible to properly check and identify faults in windings, diodes, and regulators.

Bosch is one of the leading manufacturers of automotive equipment, and as such also manufactures the appropriate workshop equipment, especially for the automotive service organisation. Production of this equipment started as far back as 1928, and today the Bosch program ranges from the pocket-sized motor tester up to the largest-size chassis dynamometer.

The reasons behind Bosch's commitment in this field are obvious: Bosch is, itself, the manufacturer of a large proportion of the equipment to be tested. Consequently, Bosch has more than ample knowledge regarding what must be tested and how it must be tested. And this know-how is incorporated in the development of the Bosch workshop equipment. The result is that apart from being extremely reliable, these testers and test equipment are designed and constructed so that each and every important component and assembly in the vehicle can be quickly and reliably tested.

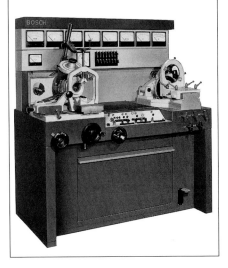

Fig. 7: Combination test bench for alternators, diodes, starters, ignition distributors, and ignition coils

Starting systems

Basics

Starting

Internal-combustion engines must be started by a separate system because they cannot self-start like electric motors or steam engines. When starting these engines, considerable resistance resulting from compression, piston friction and bearing friction (static friction) must be overcome. These forces depend greatly on engine type and number of cylinders, as well as on lubricant characteristics and engine temperature. Frictional resistance is highest at low temperatures.

Even under severe conditions, the starter (also known as the "starting motor") must crank the SI engine fast enough so that it can form the combustible air-fuel mixture required for starting, and diesel engines fast enough to reach their self-ignition temperature.

To satisfy these requirements, the starter must rotate the flywheel at a minimum starting speed. It must also con-

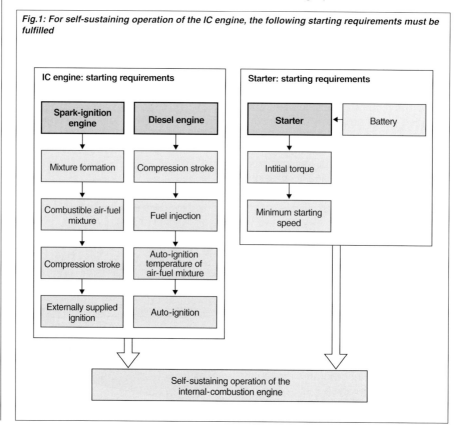

Fig.1: For self-sustaining operation of the IC engine, the following starting requirements must be fulfilled

tinue to support rotation during initial combustion to maintain momentum until the engine can sustain operation.

Electric motors (DC, AC and three-phase), as well as hydraulic and pneumatic motors are used as starting motors for internal-combustion engines.

The DC series-wound electric motor is particularly well-suited for use as a starting motor, because it generates the high initial torque required to overcome cranking resistance and to accelerate the engine's internal masses. In the majority of cases, starting-motor torque is transmitted to the engine via a starter pinion and a ring gear on the crankshaft-mounted flywheel. However, V-belts, toothed belts and chains are also used, as is direct transmission to the crankshaft.

As a result of the high gear ratio between the starter pinion and the ring gear on the engine flywheel, the "pinion-type starter" can be designed for low torque and high speed, thus allowing small, lightweight starters to be used.

An additional advantage is that the energy required to start the engine can be supplied by the same battery normally used to operate the other electrical devices in the vehicle electrical system (Fig. 1).

For this reason, the starter cannot be viewed as an independent component, but, rather, must be discussed as an integral part of the electrical system.

Both starter and battery are sized such that even under adverse operating conditions cranking power is available long enough to start the engine. Because the starter draws more current than any other vehicle electrical system, it is often decisive in determining the battery specifications.

The starter itself (Fig. 2) must meet the following requirements:

– continuous readiness for starting
– sufficient starting power at different temperatures
– long service life for a high number of starts (particularly if the vehicle is used primarily for in-city driving)

– robust design to withstand meshing, cranking, vibration, corrosion due to dampness and road salt, dirt, temperature cycles within the engine compartment etc.
– low weight and small size, and
– longest possible maintenance-free service life.

The starter must be designed for the other components of the starting system and the engine with which it is used, because starting requirements vary widely and the effect of temperature is highly significant.

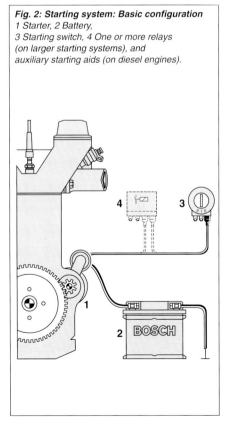

Fig. 2: Starting system: Basic configuration
1 Starter, 2 Battery,
3 Starting switch, 4 One or more relays
(on larger starting systems), and
auxiliary starting aids (on diesel engines).

Starting requirements

In designing a starting system, both engine specifications and starting requirements must be considered. These requirements include:
– Mininum starting temperature. This is the lowest engine and battery temperature at which the system must ensure that the engine starts (Fig. 3),
– The engine's resistance to rotation. This equals the resistance to rotation, as measured at the crankshaft at the minimum starting temperature (thus including permanently-connected ancillaries, Fig. 4)
– Minimum required engine speed at the minimum starting temperature,
– Starter pinion/ring gear ratio,
– Rated voltage of the starting system,
– Specifications/capacity of the starter battery,
– Length and resistance of the cable from the battery to the starter (voltage drop),
– Torque, speed and capacity of the starter (starter characteristic curve, starting process), etc.

Of particular importance in this respect is the minimum starting temperature, i.e. the lowest temperature at which an engine with a given electrical system, a defined state of battery charge, and given oil viscosity can be brought to self-sustaining speed.

An engine's minimum starting temperature is defined by the climatic conditions at the place of use, the conditions under which the engine must operate and economic considerations (the power required of a starting system, as well as its costs, increase rapidly in response to downward definitions of the minimum starting temperature).

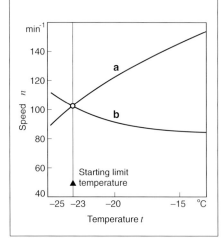

Fig. 3: Starting limit temperature (example)
a) Starter speed; decreases as the temperature drops due to increased internal resistance of the battery.
b) Minimum required initial engine speed; increases as temperature drops due to increased cranking resistance. The intersection of both curves yields the starting limit temperature (here –23 °C).

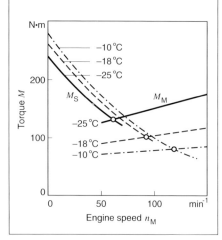

Fig. 4: Engine torques (cranking resistances) and starter torques
M_S Starter torque for various temperatures (referred to the engine crankshaft)
M_M Torque required for starting a 3-liter SI engine at the different temperatures shown. The intersection point of the relevant curves determines the speed at which the engine is cranked at –25 °C, –18 °C, and –10 °C.
The torque curve is is referred to a 20% discharged 55 Ah battery.

In the example below, a 2.2 kW starter and a 12 V, 90 Ah, 450 A battery are required for a minimum starting temperature of −23°C. The battery in the example is discharged to 80% of its rated capacity (Fig. 3). The colder the engine, the higher the rotating speed needed to get it started. Ideally, the starter should compensate for the engine's cold response pattern with higher output speeds.

Unfortunately, since it depends upon the battery for its energy supply, and the battery responds to colder temperatures with a disproportionate increase in internal resistance, the starter turns more slowly. Bosch frequently examines these patterns in starting and cranking tests in the cold-climate chamber at its Technical Center for Automotive Electrical Systems.

Starter systems intended for application within Europe are usually designed with reference to the minimum starting temperatures listed in Table 1.

The starting resistance – the torque required to overcome friction and inertia and turn the crankshaft – is largely a function of engine displacement and oil viscosity (index of the engine's internal friction).

As a general rule, the mean rotational resistance in spark-ignition engines continues to increase as a function of crankshaft speed (on diesels, in contrast, resistance peaks at 80 to 100 min⁻¹ before again falling as the relatively high levels of compression energy are fed back into the system). The intersection of the engine and starter torque curves (Fig. 4) indicates the engine's rotational speed at any given temperature.

Additional factors include: Engine design and number of cylinders, bore/stroke ratio, compression ratio, engine speed, mass of engine's moving parts, crankshaft assembly, etc., along with bearings, additional loads from clutch assembly, transmission, etc.

The minimum starting speed will vary substantially according to the design of the engine and its induction system. Auxiliary starting devices are another important factor on diesel engines. Table 2 provides some interesting empirical data.

Table 1.	
Starting limit temperatures	
Engines for	Starting limit temperatures
Passenger cars	−18...−25 °C
Trucks and buses	−15...−20 °C
Tractors	−12...−15 °C
Drive and equipment engines on ships	−5 °C
Diesel locomotives	+5 °C

Tabelle 2.	
Empirical values for minimum cranking speeds	
Required cranking speeds at −20 °C	Cranking speed min⁻¹
Reciprocating-piston SI engine	60...90
Rotary-piston SI engine	150...180
Direct-injection diesel engine	
without starting aid	80...200
with starting aid (e.g. glow plug)	60...140
Pre-chamber and whirl-chamber diesel engines without starting aid	100...200
with glow-plug starting aid	60...100

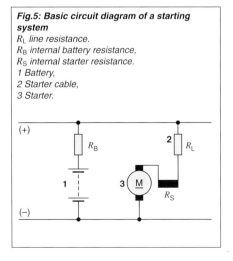

Fig.5: Basic circuit diagram of a starting system
R_L line resistance.
R_B internal battery resistance,
R_S internal starter resistance.
1 Battery,
2 Starter cable,
3 Starter.

Figure 6 illustrates an actual starting process. The engine's combustion mixture starts to ignite at the minimum starting speed. The torque curve then rises during the transition to self-sustaining operation (Curve 1, simplified illustration showing constant progression).

The engine's torque has been superimposed on the downward curve (Curve 2) for starter torque. In this transitional phase, the engine's speed rises to the levels required for self-sustaining operation. The starter reverts to a supporting function which continues until it is overtaken by the engine.

The sum of the two torque curves provides a theoretical composite curve (Curve 3, broken line). In actual practice, initial fluctuations in the combustion process that started at Point A mean that this theoretical curve is achieved only sporadically. This condition continues until engine operation becomes consistent at Point B. At Point C the starter is deactivated and the engine continues to operate without external assistance.

Starting-system voltage ratings
Starting systems are available with various rated voltages:
– Passenger cars today generally have 12 V systems.
– Tractors, small auxiliary power units and marine engines also usually have 12 V systems.
– Systems designed for 24 V are used in some engines of this type as well as in special-purpose vehicles.
– Trucks and buses use 12 V and 24 V systems.
– The starters on large commercial vehicles are generally rated at 24 V, as the higher voltage makes it possible to obtain higher specific output from more compact starters.

Capacity rating
Along with its voltage rating, the starter's rated capacity is also an essential index of performance.

The capacity rating is a precisely defined parameter determined on the test bench. It is referred to the largest permissible battery for the starter in question, with a 20 % discharge at a temperature of −20°C. It is connected to the starter via a cable with a resistance of 1 mΩ. These criteria guarantee that the starter will operate even under adverse conditions. The torque transmitted through the starter pinion represents its generated torque minus iron, copper and friction losses.

Starter output is therefore highly dependent upon line resistance and internal battery resistance. The lower the internal resistance of the battery, the higher the starter output.

Some of the testing employed to determine starter performance under severe conditions is carried out in the cold-climate chamber (Fig. 7).

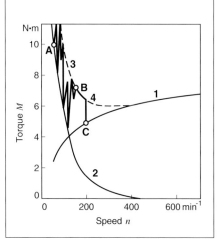

Fig. 6: Internal-combustion engine: Starting procedure
1 Theoretical engine torque assuming smooth combustion,
2 Starter torque,
3 Theoretical total torque (sum of curves 1 and 2),
4 Actual total torque as a result of irregular combustion.
A Irregular combustion begins
B Uniform engine speed
C Self-sustaining engine operation

Starting systems for passenger cars

A passenger car is defined as a motor vehicle designed to transport a maximum of 9 persons.

Passenger-car starting systems generally have pre-engaged-drive starters with a rated output of approximately 2 kW. The standard rated voltage is 12 V. These systems can start spark-ignition engines up to a displacement of approx. 7 liters and diesels up to approx. 3 liters. The required cranking power greatly depends on the type of combustion: a diesel engine requires a more powerful starter than a spark-ignition engine of equal size.

Passenger-car starter circuits are usually very simple. The engine is located in the vicinity of the driver, who is usually easily able to hear when the engine starts. The driver is therefore not likely to attempt to restart an engine which is already running, thereby possibly damaging the starter pinion as it attempts to engage the ring gear on the rotating flywheel. For this reason, passenger cars usually do not have special start protection and monitoring devices. Many passenger-car models, though, have ignition/starter switches which incorporate additional start repeating blocks to avoid any possibility of accidental starter operation.

Fig. 7: Arctic conditions can be simulated in cold chambers for testing automotive equipment.

Starting systems for passenger cars with spark-ignition engines

The basic circuit for this starting system is shown in Figure 8. The starting system is usually activated by a multiple-position ignition/starter switch. The ignition system is switched on before the key reaches the "start" position, because the ignition system must be switched on for the spark-ignition engine to start, and must remain on for the engine to run.

Ignition continues after the starter is switched off, and allows the spark-ignition engine to continue running.

In systems with breaker-triggered ignition coils with dropping resistors, starting can be facilitated by increasing the available voltage. This is done by bridging the ignition coil dropping resistor, and requires starters with an additional terminal (15a).

Starting systems for commercial vehicles

Commercial vehicles are vehicles which are designed to carry more than 9 persons, goods and/or for pulling trailers. This category of motor vehicles comprises the following main vehicle groups:

– Buses (e.g. minibuses, public-transport buses, articulated buses)
– Trucks of various sizes
– Special-purpose vehicles (e.g., tankers, fire-department vehicles, tow trucks, sanitation-department vehicles)
– Towing vehicles (e.g., road-construction vehicles or tractors and tractor trailers).

Because there are so many different types of commercial vehicles, starting systems must be designed for each specific type of vehicle and engine. Tractors and light-duty commercial ve-

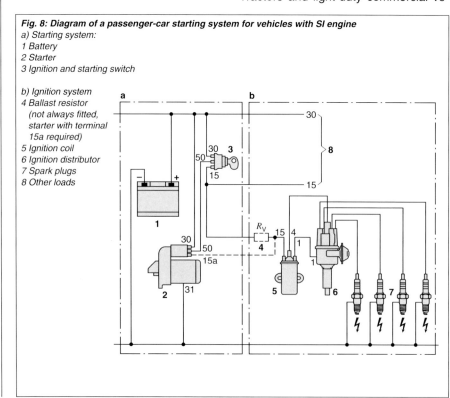

Fig. 8: Diagram of a passenger-car starting system for vehicles with SI engine
a) Starting system:
1 Battery
2 Starter
3 Ignition and starting switch

b) Ignition system
4 Ballast resistor
  (not always fitted,
  starter with terminal
  15a required)
5 Ignition coil
6 Ignition distributor
7 Spark plugs
8 Other loads

hicles such as delivery trucks and mini-buses, are usually equipped with simple 12 V starting systems which – apart from higher starter output – are very similar to common passenger-car starting systems. Switching relays and protective relays of the kind found in heavier commercial vehicles are not necessary for trouble-free starting.

Medium-duty commercial vehicles with spark-ignition engines with displacements of up to approximately 20 l normally have 12 V starting systems, whereas comparable vehicles with diesel engines up to approximately 12 l have 12 V or 24 V starting systems.

Heavy-duty commercial vehicles have only 24 V starting systems fed by two series-connected 12 V batteries.

Starting systems which have a rated voltage of 24 V are advantageous, particularly if the battery and the starter are far apart from each other. Line losses are reduced, so that a given battery provides better starting. Available voltage also determines the amount of power which can be delivered by the starter. For this reason, "hybrid" 12/24 V systems are used in some vehicles. These systems provide 12 V for vehicle accessories, but provide a starter voltage of 24 V.

Systems with start-locking

In some applications, the operator will not necessarily be able to hear the starter or determine if the engine has started (e.g., rear-engined buses). More complex circuitry is then required for effective protection of starter and ring gear.

Figure 9 illustrates a starting system for a heavy-duty vehicle. The circuit incorporates an electronic start-locking relay designed to provide multiple protection for the starting system:

– starter deactivates after successful engine start,
– lockout prevents starter from engaging with engine running,

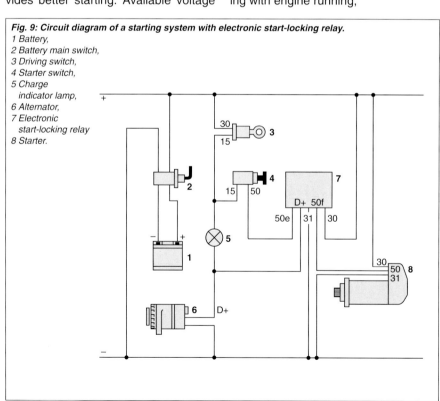

Fig. 9: Circuit diagram of a starting system with electronic start-locking relay.
1 Battery,
2 Battery main switch,
3 Driving switch,
4 Starter switch,
5 Charge
   indicator lamp,
6 Alternator,
7 Electronic
   start-locking relay
8 Starter.

– lockout prevents starter from engaging for as long as the crankshaft continues to turn,
– lockout when starter fails to start the engine.

In the last two cases, a programmed time must elapse before the relay will release the circuit; this prevents premature attempts to re-engage the starter.

Systems with 12/24 V battery changeover

A number of heavy-duty vehicles – primarily trucks – have a 12/24 V hybrid system (Fig. 10). In these systems, all electrical devices (except the starter), including the alternator, are designed for a rated voltage of 12 V. The starter, however, is operated at a rated voltage of 24 V. This higher voltage allows the starter to generate the power necessary to start large engines.
For this purpose, the 12/24 V systems incorporate a battery change-over relay. The two 12 V batteries in the vehicle are connected in parallel to supply a voltage of 12 V for the electrical system during normal vehicle operation or with the engine off. When the starter switch is pressed, the battery change-over relay automatically connects both batteries in series temporarily to provide the starter with a voltage of 24 V. The electrical system continues to supply 12 V to all other electrical devices.
After the starter switch is released, the starter is switched off and the batteries are again connected in parallel. The batteries are recharged by the 12 V alternator (Terminal B+) while the engine is running.

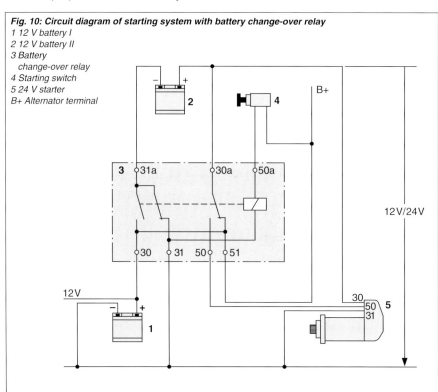

Fig. 10: Circuit diagram of starting system with battery change-over relay
1 12 V battery I
2 12 V battery II
3 Battery
  change-over relay
4 Starting switch
5 24 V starter
B+ Alternator terminal

Basic starter design

Most starters incorporate the following subassemblies:
- electric starter motor,
- solenoid switch, and
- pinion-engaging drive

Electric starter motor

Operating principle
The electric motor converts electric current into rotary motion. In doing so, it converts electrical energy to mechanical energy.

When current flows through a conductor in a magnetic field, a force is generated which is proportional to the amount of current and the strength of the magnetic field, and is greatest when the current and the magnetic field are perpendicular to each other.

A loop which can freely rotate within a magnetic field is the most efficient design. When current flows through the loop, it normally assumes a position which is perpendicular to the magnetic field, and is held in this position by magnetic force. If the direction in which the current flows is reversed at this static neutral point, the loop continues to rotate. The torque of the loop then continues in the same direction of rotation, and allows the loop to rotate continuously. The commutator is responsible for this current reversal, and, in this example, consists of two semicircular segments which are connected to the two ends of the loop and which are insulated from one another. Two carbon brushes transfer the current to the individual loops (Fig. 2a).

In order to achieve uniform torque, the number of loops must be increased. Their additive individual torques produce a much higher, uniform total

Fig. 1: Starter subassemblies
1 Electric starter motor, in some cases with reduction gear,
2 Solenoid switch with electrical connections, in some cases with additional control relay,
3 Pinion-engaging drive.

Combined series/shunt-wound motors (Compound motors)

Large starters use compound-wound motors which have a shunt winding and a series winding which act in two stages. In the first stage, the armature current is limited because the shunt winding is connected in series with the armature and acts as a dropping resistance. This keeps the meshing torque of the armature low. In the second stage, the full current is applied to the starter motor which then develops its full torque. The shunt winding is now connected in parallel with the armature and the series winding is additionally connected in series with the armature (Fig. 2, bottom left). When the pinion returns to its initial position, the shunt winding stops the armature quickly.

Fig. 4: Starter assemblies "Solenoid switch and pinion-engaging drive"
(on a pre-engaged-drive starter).

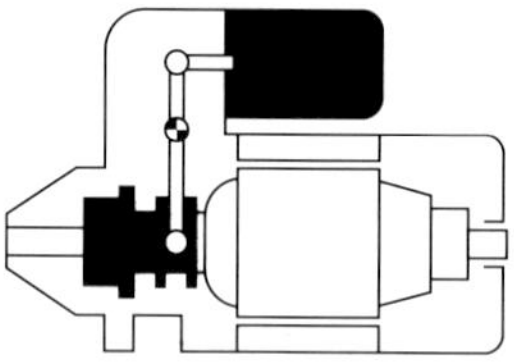

Fig. 5: Sectional diagram of a solenoid switch
1 Armature, 2 Pull-in winding, 3 Hold-in winding, 4 Solenoid armature, 5 Contact spring, 6 Contacts, 7 Terminal, 8 Moving contact, 9 Switching pin (2-part), 10 Return spring.

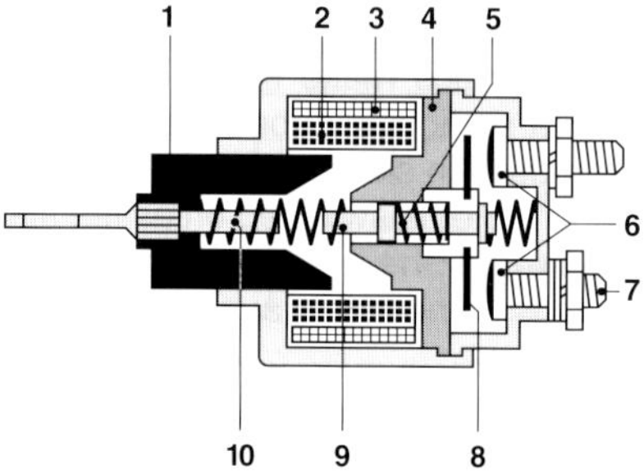

Solenoid switch

Relays are used to switch high currents with relatively low control currents. The starter current in passenger cars, for example, is up to approximately 1000 A, and up to approximately 2600 A in commercial vehicles. The low control current, on the other hand, can be switched using a mechanical switch (starter switch, ignition/starter switch, driving switch).

The solenoid assembly is an integral part of the starter (Fig. 4), and is actually a combined relay and engagement solenoid. It has two functions:

– Pushing the the pinion forward so that it engages in the ring gear of the engine and
– closing the moving contact for the main starter current.

The structure of the solenoid switch is shown in Figure 5. The solenoid armature, which is an integral part of the switch housing, enters the solenoid coil from one end and the movable relay armature enters from the other. The distance between the solenoid armature and the relay armature represents the total armature stroke. The solenoid housing, solenoid armature and relay armature together form the magnetic circuit.

In many switch designs, the relay winding comprises a pull-in winding and a hold-in winding. This configuration is very favourable in terms of thermal loadability and the magnetic forces which can be produced. At the beginning of the pull-in phase, increased magnetic force overcomes meshing resistance. When the starter circuit is closed, only the hold-in winding acts; the pull-in winding is shorted. The somewhat lower magnetic force of the hold-in winding is now sufficient to hold the relay armature until the starter switch is again opened.

After the starter is switched on, the magnetic force pulls the relay armature into the winding. This armature movement moves the pinion axially and also closes the main current contact. Return springs between the individual components open this main current circuit again when the starter is switched off and return the relay armature to its initial position. The solenoid switch design allows the electrical contacts to be grouped together.

Larger starters do not include a solenoid switch. Instead, the starter solenoid and the control relay for the electrical switching are two separate units.

Pinion-engaging drive

The starter's end-shield assembly consists of the pinion-engaging drive with pinion, overrunning clutch, engagement element (lever or linkage to control engagement travel) and pinion spring. This starter subassembly is responsible for coordinating the thrust motion of the solenoid switch and the rotary motion of the electric starter motor and transferring them to the pinion (Figures 4 and 6).

Pinion

The starter engages the ring gear on the engine flywheel by means of a small sliding gear called the pinion (Fig. 7). A high conversion ratio (normally between 10:1 and 15:1) makes it possible to overcome the high cranking resistance of the internal-combustion engine using a relatively small but high-speed starter motor. Thus, the starter dimensions and weight can be kept small. To ensure perfect meshing between starter pinion and

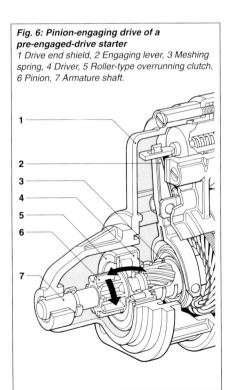

Fig. 6: Pinion-engaging drive of a pre-engaged-drive starter
1 Drive end shield, 2 Engaging lever, 3 Meshing spring, 4 Driver, 5 Roller-type overrunning clutch, 6 Pinion, 7 Armature shaft.

1
2
3
4
5
6
7

Fig. 7: Starter pinion
To facilitate engagement with the ring gear, the pinion teeth are chamfered slightly.

flywheel ring gear, capable of transmitting the starting torque and then disengaging at the desired moment, special pinion tooth patterns are necessary:

– The pinion gear teeth have an involute shape to promote meshing (engagement-pattern tooth design derived from a special mathematical progression),
– The faces of the pinion gear teeth, and those of the ring gear depending upon starter design, are chamfered
– By contrast with gears which remain meshed all the time, the center distance between the pinion and ring gear is increased in order to ensure great enough backlash at the tooth flanks
– The outer face of the pinion in its rest position must be a certain minimum distance away from the face of the ring gear and
– In order to achieve long service life, pinion and ring gear materials and hardening methods are matched to each other.

As soon as the engine starts and accelerates past the cranking speed, the pinion must automatically demesh in order to protect the starter, i.e. the connection between the starter shaft and the engine flywheel must automatically be broken. For this reason, starters also incorporate an overrunning clutch and a mechanism to mesh and demesh the pinion.

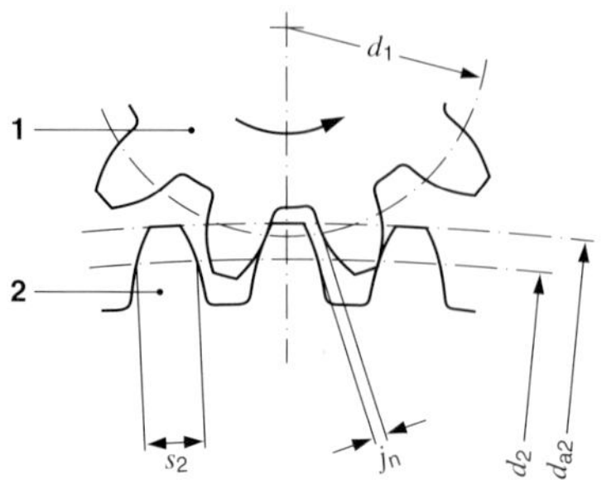

Pinion-engaging drive
The pinion-engaging drive must, in all cases, be designed such that the thrust movement of the solenoid switch and the rotary motion of the electrical starter motor can occur at the same time – but independently – under all meshing conditions. At the same time, individual engagement mechanism designs vary according to starter size. These differences are reflected in the designations applied to the starter type.

Pre-engaged drive
In pre-engaged-drive starters, the thrust movement of the solenoid switch is transferred to the driver (with pinion) which rides in a helical spline in the armature shaft. This design results in combined axial and rotary motion which greatly facilitates the meshing of the pinion.

Sliding-gear starter, electromotive pinion drive
In this type of sliding-gear starter, the engagement solenoid switch is mounted along the armature's axis. The pinion is actuated by an engagement rod extending through the hollow armature shaft. The armature simultaneously starts to slowly turn in order to facilitate engagement. Once the gears engage, the motor reverts to full-power in order to turn the engine flywheel.

Sliding-gear drive, mechanical pinion rotation
Sliding-gear starters with external solenoid switch engage the pinion by moving the entire gear assembly forward along its axis. If the gears do not mesh immediately, a second mechanical unit rotates the pinion in a second stage.

Fig. 8: Starter pinion engaged with the ring gear
1 Starter pinion
d_1 Reference diameter
2 Ring gear
d_2 Reference diameter, d_{a2} Tip diameter,
s_2 Tooth face width,
j_n Backlash.

Overrunning clutch

In all starter designs, the rotary motion is transmitted via an overrunning clutch. The overrunning clutch allows the pinion to be driven by the armature shaft, however it breaks the connection between the pinion and the armature shaft as soon as the accelerating engine spins the pinion faster than the starter.

The overrunning clutch is located between the starter motor and the starter pinion and prevents the armature of the starter motor from being accelerated to excessive speed when the engine starts.

Roller-type overrunning clutch
Pre-engaged drive starters are equipped with a roller-type overrunning clutch as a protective device (Fig. 9). The most important component of the clutch is the clutch shell with roller race which forms part of the driver and thus communicates with the armature shaft via a spiral spline. Rollers which are free to move within the roller race lock the pinion shaft to the clutch shell.

At rest, coil springs press the rollers into the narrow areas between the clutch shell race and the cylindrical part of the pinion shaft to lock the pinion to the armature shaft when the starter is operated. When the starter armature shaft rotates, the rollers become wedged in the narrow areas.

When the engine starts and spins the starter pinion faster than the no-load speed of the starter armature, the rollers become loose and are pushed – against the force of the coil springs – into the wide areas. This unlocks the pinion from the armature shaft.

The advantage of this type of overrunning clutch is that only small masses need be accelerated and the engine's effective overrunning torque is relatively low.

Armature braking

Sometimes, a second attempt must be made to start the engine. The starter armature, however, must first be quickly stopped.

In the case of pre-engaged drive starters, this is accomplished simply by the return spring which presses the pinion-engaging drive or armature against a friction washer or brake disc after the starter is switched off. The resulting friction stops the armature. In the case of permanent-magnet excitation, magnetic force additionally acts to brake the armature as it runs down.

On inertial-drive starters, the shunt field limits the no-load speed and ensures that the armature stops quickly.

Other types include a special braking circuit with a reverse winding. This unit is activated in parallel to the regular motor armature when the starter disengages.

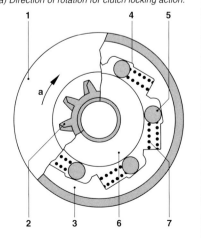

Fig. 9: Roller-type overrunning clutch
1 Clutch cover, 2 Pinion, 3 Driver with clutch shell, 4 Roller race, 5 Roller, 6 Pinion shaft, 7 Coil spring, a) Direction of rotation for clutch locking action.

Starter types

Summary

There are many different kinds of internal-combustion engines and vehicle electrical systems, and there are therefore just as many different operating conditions which determine the design of electrical starting systems and compatible starters. A broad range of starter types must therefore be available. The most important starter characteristics are:

- Rated voltage
- Rated output
- Direction of rotation
- Starter size (diameter of starter-motor field frame)
- Type
- Design.

Rated voltage is determined by the type of starter used. Small starters are designed for 12 V, medium-sized starters for 12 and 24 V and large starters for various rated voltages between 24 and 110 V, depending upon application. The starter's performance specifications are defined according to whether the unit will be used on a diesel or spark-ignition engine (starters for diesel engines must be more powerful) and the engine's displacement. The starter pinion's rotating direction is determined by the unit's installation position and the engine's normal operating direction. The starter's size is a function of the required power rating.

The basic design is determined by the pinion-engagement concept being used which, in turn, is largely determined by the starter's power rating and the resulting dimensions. The unit's mechanical construction features will depend upon space requirements, mounting type and operating conditions (Figures 2 and 3).

Type designation
The type designation provides pertinent initial information and is given together with the part number in the technical starter documents (Fig. 1).

Starter labelling
Starter labels (stamped into the housing) are a combination of part number, direction of rotation and rated voltage.
Example: 0 001 314 002 → 12 V.

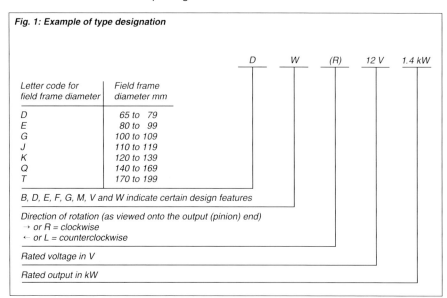

Fig. 1: Example of type designation

| | | D | W | (R) | 12 V | 1.4 kW |

Letter code for field frame diameter	Field frame diameter mm
D	65 to 79
E	80 to 99
G	100 to 109
J	110 to 119
K	120 to 139
Q	140 to 169
T	170 to 199

B, D, E, F, G, M, V and W indicate certain design features

Direction of rotation (as viewed onto the output (pinion) end)
→ or R = clockwise
← or L = counterclockwise

Rated voltage in V

Rated output in kW

Fig. 2: Chart of starter types

Pinion-engaging drive, function	Reduction-gear	Design E Pinion-engaging drive M Motor, R Relay	Based on design	Similar types	Starter-motors
Pre-engaged drive Pinion moves forward with screw action until it meets ring gear, and is meshed by solenoid switch. Meshing is facilitated by spiral spline. Full starter current is switched on at the end of solenoid travel.	without	 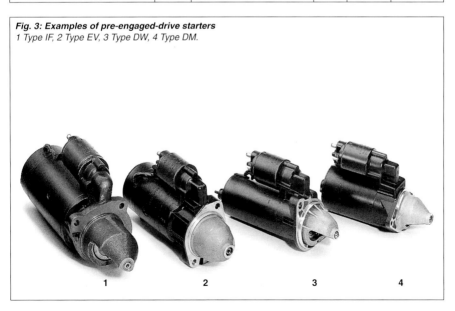	IF	ID	Series-wound motor
	with		EV	–	Motor with permanent-magnet excitation
			DW	–	
	without		DM	–	
Sliding-gear drive with mechanical pinion rotation Pinion moves straight forward until it meets the ring gear, and is meshed by solenoid switch. Two-stage mechanical pinion-engaging drive facilitates meshing. Full starter current is switched on after complete meshing.	without		KE	–	Series-wound motor
Sliding-gear drive with electromotive pinion rotation Pinion moves straight forward until it meets ring gear, and is meshed by engagement solenoid. Simultaneous slow motor start-up to facilitate meshing (electrical first stage). Full starter current is switched on just before end of pinion travel (second stage).	without		KB	QB	Compound-wound motor
			TB	–	
	with		TF	auf TB-Basis	

Fig. 3: Examples of pre-engaged-drive starters
1 Type IF, 2 Type EV, 3 Type DW, 4 Type DM.

1   2   3   4

Pre-engaged-drive starters without reduction gear

The main features of pre-engaged starters without reduction gear are the electric motor with direct drive, the attached solenoid switch, the pinion-engaging drive for axial and rotary pinion movement and the roller-type overrunning clutch.

Type IF with series-wound motor

Design
The design and internal circuitry of a pre-engaged drive starter without reduction gear are illustrated in Figures 4 and 5.

Starter motor:
These starters have DC series-wound motors in which the excitation and armature windings are connected in series. The motor drives the pinion-engaging drive directly in a ratio of 1:1. The extension of the armature shaft has a helical spline which holds the driver of the pinion-engaging drive (Fig. 6).

Solenoid switch:
Pre-engaged-drive starters without reduction gear are actuated by an integral solenoid switch with pull-in and hold-in windings. The solenoid armature has a slot in its protruding end in which the end of the engaging lever fits with a certain amount of free play. This free play allows the return spring to pull the solenoid armature back to its initial position to switch off the starter, and quickly pull the moving contact away from the fixed contacts. This is necessary so that the starter can be switched off quickly in the event of the engine not being started.

Pinion-engaging drive:
The driver which rides in the helical spline of the armature shaft is coupled to the pinion via a roller-type overrunning clutch. The direction of the helical spline is selected so that the pinion, which cannot turn, is pushed into the

Fig. 4: Section through an IF-type pre-engaged-drive starter
1 Hold-in winding, 2 Pull-in winding, 3 Return spring, 4 Engaging lever, 5 Meshing spring, 6 Roller-type overrunning clutch, 7 Pinion, 8 Armature shaft, 9 Stop ring, 10 Terminal, 12 Bridging contact, 13 Solenoid switch, 14 Commutator end shield, 15 Commutator, 16 Brush holder, 17 Pole shoe, 18 Armature, 19 Stator frame, 20 Excitation winding.

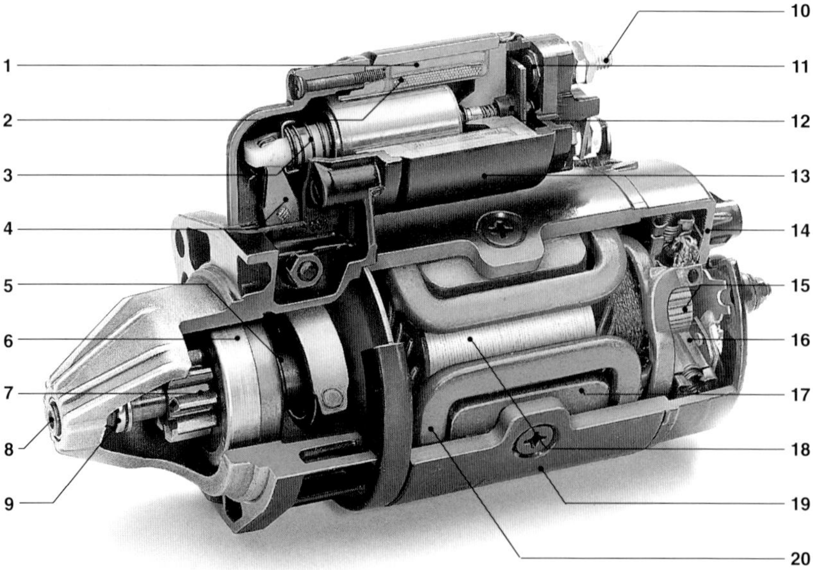

ring gear when the armature shaft rotates. The driver has two guide rings or discs which are engaged by the forked end of the engaging lever which moves the driver axially. The meshing spring sits between the guide ring and driver to allow the engaging lever to move against its stop so that the starter current is always switched, even if the pinion meets but does not engage the ring gear (the contacts close shortly before the engaging lever reaches its end position).

The driver and pinion are moved axially by the engaging lever while they are simultaneously augered forward by the helical spline until the pinion reaches its stop. The helical spline thus prevents torque from being imparted to the engine until the pinion is fully meshed. The overrunning clutch transmits the force of the starter armature to the engine flywheel after the pinion is fully meshed, and breaks this connection as soon as the engine speed exceeds the speed of the starter.

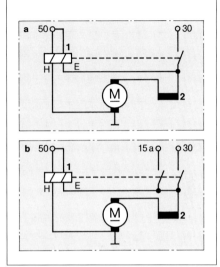

Fig. 5: Internal connections of pre-engaged-drive starters
a) Basic circuit
b) With terminal 15a as connection for ignition-coil ballast resistor.
E Pull-in winding, H Hold-in winding.
1 Solenoid switch, 2 Excitation winding.

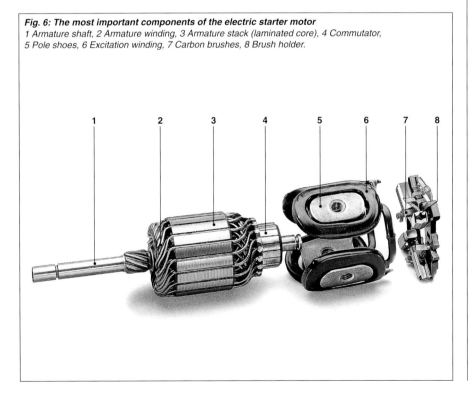

Fig. 6: The most important components of the electric starter motor
1 Armature shaft, 2 Armature winding, 3 Armature stack (laminated core), 4 Commutator, 5 Pole shoes, 6 Excitation winding, 7 Carbon brushes, 8 Brush holder.

Operation

In pre-engaged-drive starters, the total meshing travel is the sum of the axial travel and the helical travel.

Axial travel:
When the starter switch or the ignition/starter switch is operated, the pull-in and hold-in windings of the solenoid switch are also energized. The solenoid armature pulls in the engaging lever against the force of a return spring. The engaging lever, via guide rings and a meshing spring, pushes the driver with pinion against the ring gear on the engine flywheel; the driver and pinion simultaneously rotate due to the action of the helical spline. The starter motor armature does not yet turn in this phase, because the main current for the excitation and armature windings has not yet been switched on.

If the pinion can immediately engage the ring gear, the pinion moves forward until it reaches the end of its travel and the moving contact in the solenoid switch meets the solenoid contacts (Fig. 7, Pos. 2). The starter motor is now switched on.

If a pinion tooth meets a ring-gear tooth, the pinion cannot immediately mesh with the ring gear. As a result, the meshing spring is compressed via the engaging lever and the guide rings until the moving contact in the solenoid switch meets the solenoid contacts (Fig. 7, Pos. 3).

The starter motor is now switched on and begins to turn. Initially, the pinion turns along the ring gear surface. At the first opening, the pinion gears respond to the pressure exerted by the engagement spring and, especially, the helical motion along the engagement axis, by meshing with the teeth in the ring gear.

Helical travel:
At the end of the solenoid travel, the solenoid switch contacts close – independent of the pinion position – and switch on the starter current. The starter armature now begins to rotate, and the helical spline forces the pinion, which is prevented from turning by the ring gear with which it has meshed, even further into the ring gear until it contacts the stop ring of the armature shaft.

When the starter circuit is closed, the pull-in winding is simultaneously shorted. Now only the hold-in winding acts. However, its magnetic force is sufficient to hold the solenoid armature in its pulled-in position until the engine is started (Fig. 7, Pos. 4).

Demeshing:
After the engine starts and the speed of the starter pinion exceeds the no-load speed of the starter motor, the roller-type overrunning clutch described earlier breaks the connection between the pinion and the armature shaft. This keeps the armature from being rotated too fast and damaged. The pinion remains meshed as long as the engaging lever is held in the engaged position. The engaging lever, driver and pinion are returned to their initial positions by the return spring only when the starter is switched off. The return spring also ensures that the pinion remains in its rest position in spite of engine vibration until the starter is again operated.

Type DM with permanent-magnet motor

Starter Type DM with a permanent-magnet field is designed for use in passenger vehicles powered by spark-ignition engines with swept volumes of up to 1.9 liters. It is up to 15 % lighter, and is smaller than customary starter types designed for the same operating conditions.

The weight reduction helps to improve fuel economy. The compact dimensions are important because the increasing number of ancillaries on the internal-combustion engine combine with lower front-end designs to place underhood space at a premium.

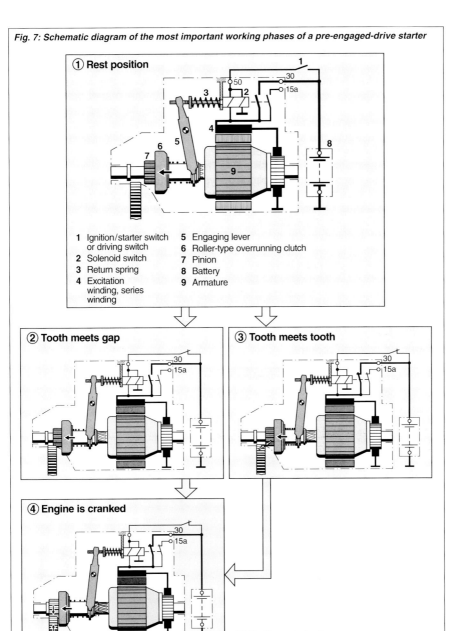

Fig. 7: Schematic diagram of the most important working phases of a pre-engaged-drive starter

① **Rest position**

1 Ignition/starter switch
  or driving switch
2 Solenoid switch
3 Return spring
4 Excitation
  winding, series
  winding
5 Engaging lever
6 Roller-type overrunning clutch
7 Pinion
8 Battery
9 Armature

② **Tooth meets gap**

③ **Tooth meets tooth**

④ **Engine is cranked**

③ *Tooth meets tooth*
Unfavorable meshing position. Pinion tooth meets ring-gear tooth. Engaging lever in end position, meshing spring compressed, pull-in winding not energized. Main current flows, armature rotates. Pinion attempts to mesh with ring gear.

① *Rest position*
No current supplied to starter, pinion demeshed.

② *Tooth meets gap*
Favorable meshing position. Pull-in and hold-in windings are energized. A pinion tooth meets a gap in the ring gear, and the pinion meshes immediately. The starter position just before the main current is switched on is shown.

④ *Engine is cranked*
End position. Engaging lever in end position, pull-in winding not energized. Main current flows, pinion is fully meshed. Engine is cranked.

367

Design

The design and internal circuitry of pre-engaged-drive starter Type DW are shown in Figures 11 to 14.

Starter motor with reduction gear:
A DC motor with permanent-magnet excitation is used as the starter motor. Permanent magnets are used in place of electromagnets (pole shoes with excitation winding) in the excitation circuit. The lengths of the armature and permanent magnets are graded depending upon the rated output of the starter.
This starter design allows the size of the electric starter motor and, therefore, the size of the starter as a whole to be drastically reduced, thus significantly reducing weight.

The reduction gear converts the motor's high output speed to a lower speed appropriate for starting, boosting torque to the required levels in the process.

Solenoid switch:
As in all other pre-engaged-drive starters, the solenoid switch which actuates the driver and closes the starter circuit is mounted on the starter and transfers movement to the components on the armature shaft via the engaging lever. All versions of starter Type DW are fitted with the same solenoid switch.

Pinion-engaging drive:
The pinion-engaging drive with roller-type overrunning clutch is of the same design and operates in the same way as the drive described above for other pre-engaged-drive starters, and is used for all starter versions.

Operation

The reduction-gear starter Type DW operates no differently from the other pre-engaged-drive starters. The only difference is in the electrical circuitry which does not include the excitation winding normally connected in series. When the starter circuit is closed, current flows directly to the carbon brushes and the armature.

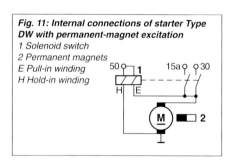

Fig. 11: Internal connections of starter Type DW with permanent-magnet excitation
1 Solenoid switch
2 Permanent magnets
E Pull-in winding
H Hold-in winding

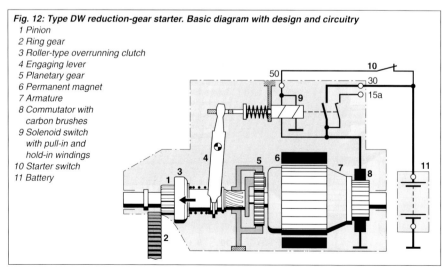

Fig. 12: Type DW reduction-gear starter. Basic diagram with design and circuitry
1 Pinion
2 Ring gear
3 Roller-type overrunning clutch
4 Engaging lever
5 Planetary gear
6 Permanent magnet
7 Armature
8 Commutator with carbon brushes
9 Solenoid switch with pull-in and hold-in windings
10 Starter switch
11 Battery

Fig. 13: Armature and planetary gear (reduction gear) of a Type DW reduction-gear starter
1 Planetary gear carrier shaft with helical spline, 2 Internal gear (ring gear), also serves as intermediate bearing, 3 Planet gears, 4 Sun gear on armature shaft, 5 Armature, 6 Commutator.

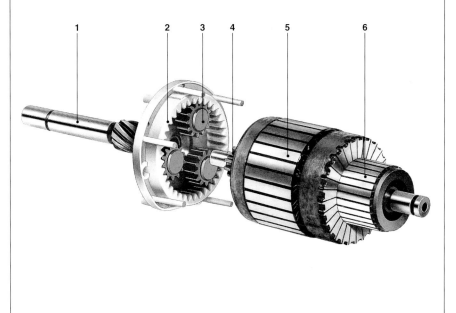

Fig. 14: Type DW reduction-gear starter with permanent-magnet motor. Cutaway view
1 Drive end shield, 2 Pinion, 3 Solenoid switch, 4 Terminal, 5 Commutator end shield, 6 Brush plate with carbon brushes, 7 Commutator, 8 Armature, 9 Permanent magnet, 10 Field frame, 11 Planetary gear (reduction gear), 12 Engaging lever, 13 Pinion-engaging drive.

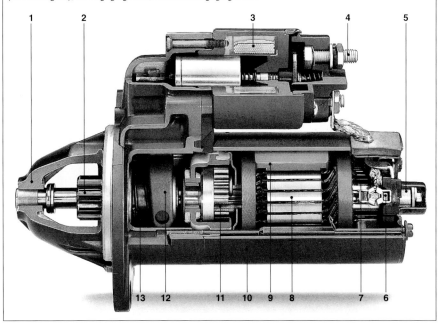

Starting-system installation

Installing the starter

Starters are mounted either ahead of the flywheel next to the crankcase or behind the flywheel next to the transmission. Depending upon design, starters are either flange-mounted or are mounted in a cradle such that they make good electrical contact with the engine.

Small and medium-sized flange-mounted starters usually use a two-hole flange (Fig. 1), whereas larger starters use an SAE flange (named after the Society of Automotive Engineers). In various models an additional support is provided in order to reduce the effect of vibration on the starter (Fig. 2).

Cradle-mounted starters are held in place by strong hold-down clamps (Fig. 3).

Starters are generally mounted horizontally with the terminals and the solenoid switch on top. Starters whose bearings must be lubricated at frequent intervals due to adverse operating conditions (dust, dirt) must have freely accessible lubrication points.

A pilot on the starter allows the starter to be centered and the proper gear backlash to be maintained.

Main starter cable

A look under the hood of a passenger car will reveal that the cable from the battery to the starter has an unusually large cross section. The distance between the battery and the starter, and thus the cable length, are also kept short. This indicates how important the starter cable is. The cross section of an electrical conductor always depends upon the electrical devices connected to it. The largest load in the vehicle – if only briefly for starting the engine – is always the starter. For this reason, the size of the battery and the routing and cross section of the starter cable are determined by the starter itself.

When starting the engine, extremely high current flows between the battery and the starter. When the starter pinion is engaged and the starter is stalled, a short-circuit current of 335 A flows briefly, for instance on the DM-type starter. The starter cable must therefore have as low a resistance as possible in order to keep the voltage drop to a minimum. The resistance of the supply and return line together should not exceed

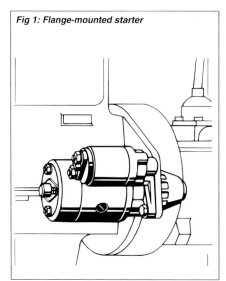

Fig 1: Flange-mounted starter

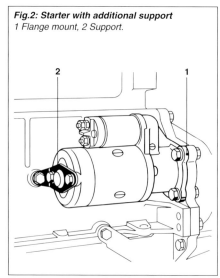

Fig.2: Starter with additional support
1 Flange mount, 2 Support.

1 mΩ, and the maximum permissible voltage drop for a rated voltage of 12 V and 24 V is limited to 0.5 V and 1.0 V respectively. The starter cable must therefore be as short as possible and have an adequate minimum cross section.

Example:
Starter Type DW 12 V 1.4 kW for spark-ignition engines with swept volumes of up to 3 liters draws a short-circuit current of 427 A when connected to a battery with a nominal capacity of 66 Ah. Taking into consideration the increase in the cable temperature and the voltage drop, a 1.9 m long starter cable should have a minimum cross section of approximately 30 mm^2 (rounded up to the next larger standard cross section of 35 mm^2).

In most cases, the starter is grounded to the engine by its housing. A ground cable then returns from the engine to the battery. If the starter has an insulated ground cable, the starter need not be physically grounded to the engine. The starter terminals are protected by rubber sleeves or caps.

The following parameters determine the cross section of a starter cable:
– Current consumption of the starter under short-circuit conditions (zero speed) and the brief permissible cable loading in terms of temperature
– Starter-cable material and its specific resistance (copper cables are usually used due to their favourable material characteristics)
– Cable length
– Rated voltage of the starting system and permissible voltage drop under short-circuit conditions.

Starter switch

Switches which are normally used in starting systems are, in most cases, manual mechanical switches. They are used for either directly switching small starters or indirectly switching large starters via additional relays.

Single-purpose starter switch
The simplest type of starter switch is the pushbutton which is a standard single-purpose switch with "on" and "off" positions. The pushbutton returns automatically to its initial position.

Ignition/starter switches
Ignition/starter switches with built-in locks are multi-purpose switches for battery ignition systems. They are used to switch current from a central point to most of the vehicle loads including the ignition system and the starter. The various types of switches are distinguished by the number of switch positions or by whether or not they have built-in restart locks. The customary switch positions "off-on-start" can be extended to include the positions "parking lights" and/or "radio". The switch returns automatically to the basic "on" position from the final "start position".

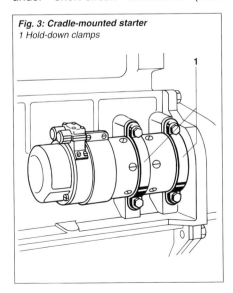

Fig. 3: Cradle-mounted starter
1 Hold-down clamps

Relays

Relays are normally installed to control large starters. These relays perform different functions, depending upon the specific application:

– Switching the high starter currents,
– Preventing damage to the starter or ring gear,
– Controlling the start-repeating relay in case the engine fails to start.

Battery change-over relay

Various heavy-duty commercial vehicles feature a combined 12/24V electrical system. This type of 12/24 system (12V standard system voltage, 24V for starting) must include a battery relay (Fig. 4). It switches the contacts in such a way that the two 12 V batteries previously connected in parallel are temporarily connected in series to supply the starter with a voltage of 24 V.

Start-locking relay

The start-locking relay is used in cases where it is difficult to monitor the starting procedure. It protects the starter, the pinion and the engine ring gear in commercial vehicles with underfloor or rear engines, remotely controlled starting systems and fully automatic starting systems (e.g., standby power units).

The following functions must be fulfilled in all cases:

– Shut-off after successful start
– Blocked restart with engine running
– Blocked restart with engine running down
– Blocked restart after failed start.
In the last two cases, a restart is only possible after the integrated blocking time has elapsed.

The electronic start-locking relay combines the advantages of low weight and minimum number of moving parts. In addition, very long starter cables (as would otherwise be needed with rear-engined vehicles for instance) are no longer necessary since Terminal 50 at the starter receives current directly from Terminal 30 of the start-locking relay, instead of from the remote starter switch.

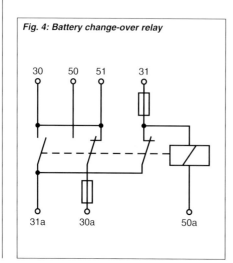

Fig. 4: Battery change-over relay

30   50   51   31

31a   30a   50a

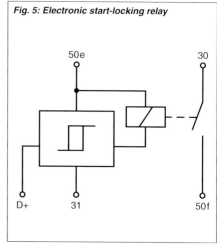

Fig. 5: Electronic start-locking relay

50e   30

D+   31   50f

Operation and maintenance

Operation

The starting procedure is normally very short at moderate temperatures with a starting system which is operating properly. But even at low temperatures, at which the engine is harder to start, the starter should not be continuously operated for more than 10 s due to its high current consumption. If the engine fails to start, wait for 30 to 60 s so that the starter can cool down and the battery can recover.

Maintenance, customer service

Experience has shown that passenger-car starters do not require special maintenance in the course of vehicle inspec-tion as long as they are not used more often than normal and are not subjected to unusually severe operating conditions. The average starter has a service life which is roughly the same as the engine to which it is mounted. However, the starting system should be checked at appropriate intervals if it is subjected to severe loading such as in commercial vehicle use with frequent starts. This is because the engines in vehicles driven primarily in city traffic are started roughly 2000 times per year, assuming an annual mileage of 15,000 km. Such frequent use leads to increased system wear which eventually begins to affect starter performance. Because commercial vehicles usually are required to last much longer than passenger cars, the starters in these vehicles must always be checked at prescribed maintenance intervals.

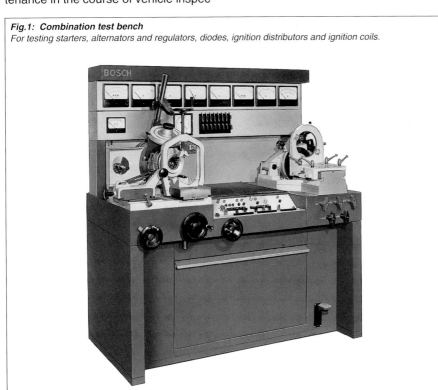

Fig.1: Combination test bench
For testing starters, alternators and regulators, diodes, ignition distributors and ignition coils.

Index of headings

D

E

F

G

H

I